The Attraction of Opposites

The Attraction of Opposites
Thought and Society in the Dualistic Mode

Edited by
David Maybury-Lewis and Uri Almagor

Ann Arbor
The University of Michigan Press

Library of Congress Cataloging-in-Publication Data

The Attraction of opposites : thought and society in the dualistic
mode / edited by David Maybury-Lewis and Uri Almagor.
    p.   cm.
Includes bibliographies and index.
ISBN 0-472-10094-7   — ISBN 0-472-08086-5 (pbk.)
    1. Dualism—Cross-cultural studies.   2. Ethnophilosophy.
3. Social structure—Cross-cultural studies.   4. Structural
anthropology.   I. Maybury-Lewis, David.   II. Almagor, Uri.
GN468.2.A87   1989   89-4771
305—dc19   CIP

to
Claude Lévi-Strauss
and the memory of
W. H. R. Rivers
(1864–1922)

Preface

There are societies all over the world that organize their social theories
or their social institutions in rigorously binary form. This cannot simply
be attributed to binary tendencies in human thought, since the phenomenon is widespread but not universal. Nor can it be explained as a primitive
form of social organization, where societies are divided into two halves
or moieties. Such societies still exist and have been well studied, but the
analyses gathered in this volume show that they are manifestations of
dualism, not its essence.

In this book we try to understand the human predilection for such
binary systems by examining the different modalities of them found in five
continents. The issue is not esoteric. Dual organization, in the broad sense,
is a kind of social theory very different from the ones that underlie the
social thought and social action of modern societies, especially in the
West. Yet it has been prominent in the past and continues to be found in
contemporary societies the world over. The study of it therefore tells us
something important about human beings, for it elucidates a mode of
thought and social organization that has represented an attractive option
throughout human history.

Such a widespread human tendency can only be studied in a broadly
comparative fashion, yet this is easier said than done. The social theories
and social practices of dualistic societies involve their cosmologies, their
ideas about time and aesthetics, their ways of dealing with age and gender,
their structures for coping with power, hierarchy, competition and exchange, and a host of other factors. The organization of such ideas and
institutions in the dualistic mode has been the subject of detailed studies
carried out in various parts of the world, but the comparison of such
analyses has not been carried very far, perhaps because it posed such a
daunting scholarly challenge.

In the academic year of 1980–81 the editors of this volume were together at Harvard, where they had the opportunity to compare the dual-

istic societies of East Africa with those of central Brazil. These discussions invariably alluded to different kinds of dualism found in other parts of the world. We decided therefore to bring together scholars who had done recent fieldwork in markedly dualistic societies, so that the results of our research could be placed in a properly comparative context. We planned a conference that would gather specialists from different areas of the world and enable them to spend enough time together, so that their discussions would advance the general understanding of a problem at once so broad and so fundamental that it risked being abandoned before it was solved.

We invited colleagues who had worked in all corners of the world to come to Jerusalem in June 1983 for a conference. We managed to assemble scholars who had research experience in Australia, Melanesia, Indonesia, East Africa, Brazil, the Andes, and North America. It needs to be stressed that it was not possible, nor was it our intention to bring in people to represent every part of the world where something resembling dual organization could be said to exist. Nevertheless, we much regret that among those who were unable to accept our invitation to the conference were the three specialists on India, so we were left at the last minute with the Indian subcontinent unrepresented. We regret their absence, not as a gap in our coverage, for the volume is not intended to be a survey of dualism around the world, but for the loss of their particular perspective on our common theme. We did not solicit essays from specialists on India (or from anywhere else) who could not attend the conference, for we feel that the essays in this volume should reflect the discussion that took place in Jerusalem as well as their authors' research interests.

All of the participants in our conference had already published on various aspects of dual organization. The meeting in Jerusalem gave them the opportunity to present their ideas to others who were struggling with similar analytical problems in other parts of the world. The conference was planned to facilitate and allow plenty of time for discussions, which were both intense and continuous throughout the four days of the meeting. The five-day tour of Israel that followed, in which most of the participants joined, gave us further opportunity to continue our discussions informally. We believe that this prolonged opportunity to explore each other's ideas and materials helped all the contributors (and not least the editors) to clarify the central issues in the study of dualism. Certain common themes emerged from the welter of ethnographic detail, and it is these that we emphasize in this volume.

Dual organization is, above all else, a system for discerning an order in the scheme of things and imposing it on the unruly complexity of events. It is therefore appropriate that a volume devoted to the topic should be organized by two editors who have sought to complement each other's efforts. We knew from our own research that such complementarity is not achieved without strain, but it has proved invaluable in dealing with the complexities of organizing the conference that gave rise to this volume and for producing the volume itself.

Neither task has been easy. It was difficult to raise the funds necessary to bring such a far-flung group of scholars together to discuss a topic that some granting agencies thought was highly esoteric. We are therefore especially grateful to the people who helped us to raise the money for the meeting: K. C. Chang, at that time chairman of the Department of Anthropology at Harvard, Pia Maybury-Lewis, Abraham Rosman, and Paula Rubel. We gratefully acknowledge grants from the Baer Foundation and from the Faculty of Arts and Sciences at Harvard University, which paid for the travel of the participants to Jerusalem and for much of the cost of preparing the volume. We would also like to thank Joseph Yahav, dean of the Faculty of Social Sciences; Zwi Schiffrin, director of the Harry S. Truman Institute; and Erik Cohen, then chairman of the Department of Sociology and Anthropology; all at the Hebrew University in Jerusalem, for their support in making the local arrangements for the conference. We gratefully acknowledge the financial support of the Harry S. Truman Institute and the Authority for Research and Development of the Hebrew University, which covered the costs of local accommodation and conference facilities for our participants in Jerusalem.

The preparation of this volume has involved difficulties of another kind. We have concluded that the widespread incidence of dualism in human societies is due to its offering a solution to problems of conceptual and social order that are a perennial human preoccupation. In order to demonstrate this, we have to present ethnographic evidence from various parts of the world. These data would normally be offered in detail to be read largely by area specialists. Here we have tried to include enough information to convince readers of the richness and flexibility of the binary option, while at the same time making the volume as a whole accessible to readers who are not necessarily specialists in any of the areas covered. This entailed a long process of editing and reediting that was as painful for the editors as it was for some of our contributors.

Once the volume was offered for publication, there were further delays, for readers found it a time-consuming task to report comprehensively on a collection of essays that was so broadly comparative and so firmly rooted in the ethnographic details of societies in different parts of the world. The present volume has been improved by the helpful comments of certain careful readers, whom we wish to thank even while they remain anonymous. We wish, however, to acknowledge our especial gratitude to Robert McKinley whose careful reading of the manuscript in its early stages was unusually helpful. It has thus taken nearly five years for this volume to go to press, although the essays of our contributors have been in final form since 1987 and, in some cases, since 1986. It is only the editors who have had the license to make changes in the volume since then.

Some people participated in the discussions in Jerusalem but have not contributed to the volume. We would like to thank Ray Abrahams, Harvey Goldberg, Zwi Werbloski, Richard Werbner, and Ifrah Zilberman for their penetrating and helpful comments. We also want to thank Nili Almagor for the work she did, both during the conference and during the preparation of the volume, to enable us to bring the whole venture to a successful conclusion.

The contributors to this volume are unanimous in wishing to dedicate it to two great scholars whose writings on dual organization were milestones in our understanding of this bewildering and complex phenomenon. The book is therefore dedicated to Claude Lévi-Strauss, whose provocative and inspiring writing has led us all to reexamine and revise our understanding of binary theory and dualistic practice in human societies; and to the memory of W. H. R. Rivers, of whose pioneering work on dual organization Lévi-Strauss once wrote, "No one has said anything not already anticipated by that great theoretician."

Contents

Introduction

The Quest for Harmony

David Maybury-Lewis

This book considers a puzzling phenomenon: why do societies all over the world organize their social thought and their social institutions in patterns of opposites? This is reported from so many different parts of the world that it is clearly a kind of system that human beings keep inventing and living by, independently of each other. Yet it has been difficult to explain why this should be so. The difficulty is compounded by the fact that it is not even clear exactly what the essence of such a system is.

For a long time anthropologists focused on a strikingly exotic aspect of it, namely on moieties (or halves). Many societies divide themselves into halves and require their members to belong to one moiety or the other. Some societies divide themselves into exogamous moieties or intermarrying halves. Such systems were usually found among remote tribal peoples, so that they came to be regarded as primitive forms of society, much as bivalves are regarded as primitive forms of life.

The evidence presented in this book makes clear that the theoretical preoccupation with moieties was a mistake, and that binary systems are not particularly primitive. Moiety systems are only one of the possible institutional expressions of dualistic social thinking. If, however, it is dualistic systems of social thought that provide the basis for the binary institutional patterns (including moiety systems) that are commonly referred to as "dual organization," then we face another potential problem: how do we identify such systems in the absence of moieties? As Rodney Needham (1980) has most recently shown, every human society recognizes and attaches some importance to polarities of logic or experience. How then are we to distinguish societies that make binary distinctions that are secondary or even trivial from those that lay sufficient stress on the procedure to qualify as dual organizations?

Part of the problem lies in the use of the term "dual organization."

The phrase is misleading for it is so often taken to refer specifically to social organization. Indeed it was this focus on social organization, and a rather exotic form of social organization at that, that led anthropological thinking into its blind alley. The problem was seen as one of explaining moieties and marriage systems that would, it was thought, offer a key to the understanding of primitive societies. Our problem, however, is not to explain the social institutions of primitive societies but rather to explain the attraction of dualistic philosophies and thus to understand a fundamental feature of all human experience.

The apparent difficulty of defining "dual organization" is thus a false problem. The object of our investigation is not a class of societies that has to be defined. It is a procedure, namely the use of polarity in social thought and social action. Our purpose is to understand the significance of this procedure by studying the different ways in which it functions in different kinds of society. In doing so, it becomes immediately clear that we are dealing with a continuum. At one end of it are societies that believe the cosmos to be structured by the interaction of opposing principles and whose social thought and social institutions reflect this. Such societies include some of the empires of antiquity, certain recent kingdoms in Indonesia, and various tribal societies in the present day. Then there are those societies who believe in the interaction of complementary principles in a binary cosmos, but whose social institutions do not reflect this belief, and then there are societies where such a belief is an integral part of their folk tradition but is no longer significant at the systemic level of social thought. Examples of this are present-day Chinese who believe that the world is governed by the interaction of yin and yang, or contemporary Latin Americans who feel that it is ordered by the mutual interaction of hot and cold principles. Finally, at the other end of the continuum, are those societies that attach some importance to binary distinctions, such as the opposition of male and female, but do not link these distinctions to other oppositions at the systemic level in a dualistic ideology. Most modern, industrial societies lie at this end of the continuum, where some polarities are believed to be fundamental, but where they are considered relatively insignificant in terms of social thought or social institutions.

Our problem, then, is to understand the panhuman interest in polarity that led to the development of dualistic philosophies and of binary social systems independently of each other all over the world. It is also to understand why such systems tend to disappear in the course of modernization.

The antiquity and wide distribution of this kind of thinking is well established. In ancient Egypt, for example, the pharaoh's titles stressed his dominion over Upper Egypt and Lower Egypt. This was not done merely for geographical or historical reasons, but for philosophical and cosmological ones. Similarly the pharaohs were not only styled as rulers of Upper and Lower Egypt; they were also thought to be the embodiments of Horus and Seth, the gods whose implacable hostility to each other was the very symbol of conflict. Frankfort discusses these ideas in *Kingship and the Gods* (1948:19–22) and sums them up as follows: "The dualistic forms of Egyptian kingship did not result from historical incidents. They embody the peculiarly Egyptian thought that a totality comprises opposites." This is not, however, a peculiarly Egyptian thought. It is in fact a way of thinking that is extraordinarily widespread and lies at the heart of what is commonly known as dual organization.

A similar premise was the foundation of ancient Chinese thinking, which postulated two opposing and complementary principles, the yin and yang, whose interaction provided the basis for all things in the universe. This idea is a very old one in China. It is mentioned in the *Book of the Master Mo* in the fourth century B.C. and discussions of the interactions between yin and yang occur frequently in the *Book of the Master Chuang* in the third century B.C. The precept was of special significance to the Taoists in the fourth century B.C., whose philosophy of the Tao or Way stressed the importance of understanding the cosmos and putting oneself in harmony with it. In fact many scholars feel that yin and yang were first used as philosophical terms in the fifth chapter of the fifth appendix of that important Taoist text the *I Ching,* where it is stated: "One Yin and one Yang; that is the Tao" (Joseph Needham 1956:274).

Later thinkers, whom Joseph Needham (1956) referred to as "phenomenalists" and whom Schwartz (1985) called the philosophers of "correlative cosmology," elaborated a philosophical approach based on yin-yang theorizing that coexisted and in some sense competed with both Confucianism and Taoism.[1] This philosophy was systematized by Tsou Yen at the beginning of the third century B.C. (Joseph Needham 1956:274) and is of special interest for students of dualism. These thinkers held that the universe was composed of five elements, but that these depended in turn on the interaction between yin and yang. Yin is associated with shade, cold, dark, the inside, and femaleness, whereas yang is associated with sun, heat, light, the outside, and maleness. The theorists of the "school of *yin* and *yang*" (Schwartz 1985:350–82) insisted that human affairs were part of the cosmic scheme of things, thus there was a resonance between human actions and natural events. They affected each other in one vast organismic system. Wise men therefore should seek to under-

---

1. This discussion of the philosophers of correlative cosmology is based on Joseph Needham 1956 and Schwartz 1985. See also Granet [1929], especially for discussions of peasant custom and belief in ancient China.

stand the system and to harmonize the workings of society and the desires of individuals with it. In that way the system could be used to the advantage of humankind. Alternatively, when people (especially rulers) struck discordant notes by acting against the cosmic scheme of things, this inevitably resulted in natural calamities. The important thing therefore was to understand the harmony of the universe and to align oneself, both socially and individually, with it. That is why kings had to perform appropriate sacrifices, at the appropriate times of year, wearing appropriate robes, and facing in appropriate directions in the hall of light (*ming-t'ang*), which was clearly understood to be a microcosmic representation of the cosmic order. Furthermore it was not only the ruler or other powerful men who should act in accordance with the cosmic scheme of things. The common people were also expected to orient their actions and their ceremonies in such a way as to harmonize with it.

Schwartz emphasized the contrast between the Taoists and the correlative cosmologists. Taoists urged individuals to harmonize themselves with an ultimately mysterious universe by following the Way. They sought a wholeness in the One that would ultimately transcend and encompass the Two. Correlative cosmologists believed, on the other hand, that society itself could be harmonized with the cosmic scheme of things, once this was properly understood and manipulated (Schwartz 1985:385). Both schools of thought believed in the possibility of attaining harmony with a scheme of things generated by the interaction of two fundamental principles. It is this that links them to the dualistic systems we are considering. Taoism sought harmony outside of society by transcending the dualism of immediate experience. Correlative cosmology sought it through society by conforming to the dualism of the world. While correlative cosmology is more obviously related to the dualistic systems described in this book, the ideas of Taoism also find their parallels among them. Wholeness as the conjunction of opposites is, as we have seen, an idea not restricted to Taoists. It is the next step of transcendence that distinguishes the Tao from the more comprehensively dualistic philosophies. Yet the Indonesian societies discussed in this volume that consider their own dualism to be the result of a shattered wholeness which they are constantly seeking to recreate share the fundamental preoccupation of the Taoists.

The Taoists and the correlative cosmologists of ancient China are particularly interesting for our purposes because their views of the world, while based on the fundamental interaction of yin and yang, were not comprehensively dualistic. Dualism was the dominant organizing principle in their cosmologies, but it coexisted with monism, with a quintipartite division of the universe and so on. This is worth stressing because some scholars, notably Lévi-Strauss in his famous paper "Do dual organizations exist?" (1956), have assumed that proper dual organizations should be dualistic in every aspect of their conceptual and social organization. Such "proper" dual organizations may not exist, but societies committed to dualism in social thought and social action certainly do.

Moreover the theories of the yin-yang school of correlative cosmologists were not primitive in the sense that they antedated and were superceded by subsequent movements in Chinese thought. On the contrary, they were fully developed later than Taoism and Confucianism and held their own with these other philosophies throughout the early Han period (in the second and first centuries B.C.) and, although under increasing challenge, in the later Han period of the first and second centuries A.D. (Schwartz 1985:381).

Joseph Needham considered the arguments of scholars who believed that the yin-yang theory originated in the dualism of Zoroastrianism in ancient Persia, which then influenced China. He did not accept this view, suggesting instead that "ideas of such simplicity . . . might easily have arisen independently in several civilizations" (1956:277). The philosophy did have immense success in China, however, which Needham attributed to the "Chinese tendency to find in all things an underlying harmony and unity rather than struggle and chaos" (1956:277).

This Chinese tendency may account for the success of correlative cosmology in China, but Needham is right to stress that the ideas behind it are not particularly Chinese. We have already noted the ancient Egyptian belief that a totality must consist of the union of opposites and have pointed out that such an idea was not peculiar to Egypt. It was certainly found in ancient Greece, where Heraclitus argued that the unity present in the scheme of things derived from the combination of opposites. The Zoroastrian philosophy that was thought by some to have inspired the Chinese does indeed place great stress on dualism, yet from these dualistic premises it derived a system that is sharply distinct from the thinking of the societies we discuss in this volume.

Zoroaster held that the principles of light and darkness were engaged in a constant struggle, with all the things of this world made up of the blending of these opposing forces. The emphasis was more on the struggle than the blending. Indeed Zoroastrians did not search for the perfect synthesis of the principles that constituted the scheme of things. Instead they looked for the ultimate victory of light over darkness and good over evil (Zaehner 1967). Mani gave a new twist to Zoroastrian ideas by insisting that the forces of light and of darkness were separate creations. In Manichaean theory the evil forces of darkness had invaded and contaminated the world of light. The world and all of humanity within it was a mixture of light and darkness. Eventually the forces of darkness would be expelled and all the light in the world and in humankind would be restored to the realm of light. At that time the universe would be consumed in a great fire that would last 1,468 years and the powers of darkness would thereafter be confined to their own separate realm. Meanwhile, the only salvation for human beings lay in repudiating the dark and material side of themselves, in transcending themselves in effect as they aspired to pure light (Lieu 1985:149–52; Runciman 1947:13–15).

Zoroastrianism and Manichaeism were therefore doctrines of separation, rather than theories of the synthesis of opposites. This is also true of the later Gnostic sects. What is generally referred to as religious dualism is thus a radical variation on and a departure from the ideas that inform the dualistic societies we are considering (see Whaling 1986). Religious dualism emphasizes the constant struggle between the principles of Good and Evil, which are sometimes regarded as independent creations, and looks forward to a time when the world will be transformed by the victory of Good over Evil. In constrast, the dualistic theories we are considering emphasize the necessary complementarity of opposites that make up the scheme of things. They hope for the most harmonious balance between them and believe that human societies and human individuals should do their best to attune themselves to this cosmic harmony.

This is clearly what lies at the heart of Australian aboriginal philosophy. So, in this volume, Maddock deepens our understanding of Australian moiety systems, while Yengoyan insists on the conceptual dualism (without moieties) that permeates Pitjantjatjara culture. Both authors conclude that aboriginal societies all show an overriding commitment to dualism at the systemic level that is expressed in their cosmologies, their classifications, or their institutions.

Tuzin makes a similar point in discussing the peoples of Papua New Guinea. When he distinguishes between the elementary and complex dual organizations of the region (by which he means the societies having exogamous moieties as opposed to those with moieties that do not regulate marriage) he argues that these societies constantly have recourse to binary thinking and binary patterns of institutions.

The essays on Indonesia likewise discuss societies that show a major preoccupation with polarity, irrespective of moiety systems. Fox, Traube, and Valeri focus on processes of social classification and show how (as Fox puts it) "dualism is a prevalent conceptual resource in eastern Indonesia." Valeri shows how ideas that are not linked to social groups elsewhere in Indonesia can be expressed through moiety systems. The moiety system he describes in the Moluccas, however, is very different from the Australian and Melanesian ones. The Siwa and Lima moieties are endogamous and they have an asymmetric and antagonistic relationship to each other. They also encompass a much larger population—or rather populations, for they cross-cut different political units—than the tribal moiety systems in Australia and elsewhere.

It is clear that different areas of the world evince different styles of dualism, which like fugues are demonstrably of the same family of compositions but whose themes and variations are intriguingly diverse. It might be objected that some societies that rely on binary institutions do not subscribe to such explicit cosmological and social theories as the ones we have so far been discussing. Tuzin, for example, mentions in his essay that the dualistic principles of the complex binary systems in Papua New Guinea may not be fully recognized by the people who live by them. But he goes on to make a compelling argument that dualism is a principle used, by the Ilahita Arapesh at least, with extraordinary semiotic and social productivity to "transfigure nearly everything it touches in sociocultural life." Not only does it transform, it also stabilizes, for the village of Ilahita has developed a peculiarly baroque form of dualism in order to maintain a much larger population than in other Arapesh communities. Tuzin stresses the importance in Arapesh metaphysics of the successful conjunction of complementary opposites. It seems clear, then, that the Arapesh unite metaphysical speculation on this issue with considerable virtuosity in creating equilibrium through dualism. They cannot therefore serve as an example of a society whose binary institutions are somehow independent of its philosophical commitment to dualism.

If the Arapesh confirm my argument, might not the Maasai, discussed in Spencer's essay, offer an exception to it? East African dualism revolves around theories of age and seniority and their expression in age-set systems, although there is much more to it than just that. The special interest for our purposes of Spencer's essay on the Maasai is the contrast that it presents with the essays of Hinnant on the Guji and Almagor on the Dassanetch. Hinnant discusses the rich cosmological theory that is the rationale for Guji dualism and Almagor shows that the Dassanetch are similarly explicit about the philosophical underpinnings of their system. The Maasai, by contrast, emerge from Spencer's presentation as more pragmatic. They are certainly most sophisticated in their appreciation of the theory of different kinds of age-set systems and subtle in their calculations of how to use them to their own advantage; but their dualism seems at first sight to be more the cumulative result of political calculation by individuals and groups than the enactment of cosmological or philosophical principles.

This impression is strengthened by Spencer's comparison of his analysis of Maasai dilemmas and the cumulative effects of their solutions with Barth's (1981) analysis of segmentary opposition among the Pathans in terms of game theory. Barth's argument is that the objective constraints on political actors in Pathan culture lead to a situation where leaders (as rational players of the Pathan game) will regularly create situations where two major factions are ranged against each other. The system is not binary because it is set up with dualistic philosophical preoccupations, but simply because it regularly turns out that way. In fact the regularity is so predictable that it can be institutionalized, and the factions named like political parties. Barth mentions the Gar and Samil factions among the southern Pathans and the Hinawi and Ghafari in southern Arabia (1981:80) and compares them to the Labour and Conservative parties in Great Britain (1981:71).

This brings us right back to Lowie's famous remark that Republicans and Democrats in the United States could be considered a form of dual organization, but this would seem far removed from the kind of commitment to binary ideas and social institutions that is characteristic of the majority of the societies we have been discussing. Yet there is a connection that is worth exploring.

The Maasai show us the way. From one point of view they resemble the Pathans; but Spencer makes it clear that he does not believe that either the Pathans or the Maasai keep recreating their systems solely out of self-interested action. There are cultural rules in each case that precede the action and define the way the game is played. If we consider the norms, both explicit and implicit, that govern Maasai behavior and indeed give them their sense of being Maasai, and the outcomes that are consciously produced as a result of following these norms, then the Maasai begin to resemble the Ilahita Arapesh. They may not have an explicit philosophical commitment to binary forms of thought and society, but they do consciously manipulate their own dualistic system in a series of oscillations that constitutes their own version of equilibrium. Almagor has emphasized the central importance of groups known to East African specialists as "alternations" (after Gulliver 1958:902–4) within the age-set systems of the region. A man automatically belongs to the opposite alternation of his father, the same thing happens to his son, and so on. The Maasai do not have alternations in this technical sense but Spencer's analysis of their age organization shows that it is itself a set of variations on the theme of alternation.

Alternation, whether as idea or procedure, is one of the classic means of creating equilibrium. That is why it is so frequently found in dualistic societies. The Maasai case supports my argument that such societies are preoccupied with the struggle to maintain equilibrium. The Pathans and the Arabs discussed by Barth also believe strongly in the virtue of equilibrium. So individual leaders will try to maximize their advantage and the power of their faction, playing the game as if they hoped to eliminate the opposition altogether. But they know that this can never happen, precisely because the membership of the factions changes if one of them becomes too strong and the balance between them is reconstituted.

It is hard to say whether such a system is dualistic by accident or design. It may have arisen by accident — that can be determined by historical investigation — but it is certainly kept in place by design. Maasai and Pathans consciously maintain the kind of stability through equilibrium that they value. In this they resemble other binary systems that are instituted as part of a philosophical preoccupation with dualism. Among the Xavante of central Brazil, for example, every community was formally divided between a dominant faction and the opposition. My analysis of this contrast (Maybury-Lewis 1967) showed how it functioned like the government and the opposition in parliamentary systems.

The comparison of such dualistic systems with the opposition between Conservative and Labour in Britain[2] or between Republicans and Democrats in the United States is thus more than simply a piquant analogy. These modern systems of government obviously have different histories from the dualistic societies we are discussing and they are not kept in place because of any philosophical commitment on the part of their electorates to the complementarity of opposites. But these two-party systems share a critically important characteristic of dual organization. They are maintained because the societies that instituted them believe that the kind of alternation and equilibrium they provide is a guarantee of stability. This is quite clear in both Britain and the United States. Each society has striven to maintain itself as essentially a two-party system. The considerable literature extolling the virtues of the two-party systems stresses that they are, on one hand, more open and democratic than one-party systems, but, on the other, that they are *more stable* than multiparty systems. Duverger's discussions of the special characteristics of two-party systems illustrate this point very well. He analyzed the bipolar tendencies in political life that are formalized in two-party systems under particular circumstances (1963:215–16). He showed that the prototype of such systems, the British one, grew out of factional antipathies that were later organized into a two-party system (1972:78). This system has been deliberately maintained by the simple-majority single-ballot system of voting favored by Britain and the United States (1963:217). The point is that the

2. Barth was of course writing before the emergence of the Liberal-Social Democratic Alliance, at a time when Britain was firmly committed to a two-party system.

strong sentiments in both countries for maintaining political systems based on only two parties with any hope of taking power derive from a belief in the stability that such systems are thought to offer.

This digression into modern political systems shows that the preoccupation with equilibrium is not peculiar to committedly dualistic societies, nor does the maintenance of equilibrium through a balance of opposing forces guarantee social order. Human societies are everywhere conscious of change and almost everywhere preoccupied with stability. Two-part systems, like the dualistic societies discussed in this volume, have elected to maintain that stability by means of institutionalized equilibrium.

The point is worth stressing, because the concern with equilibrium was once thought to be a primitive characteristic of dualistic societies. Such societies were equated with moiety systems, which in turn were thought to be finely calibrated reciprocity systems that could only function if they maintained their internal symmetry and egalitarianism. Once the flux of events brought hierarchical or asymmetrical tendencies into such systems, it was thought that they would cease to be properly dualistic. Hence proper "dual organizations" were considered highly vulnerable to history.

The most influential exponent of such views was Lévi-Strauss, who tried to account for the emergence and disappearance of moiety systems in terms of a general theory of kinship (1949). According to this theory, dual organization was the most elementary way of institutionalizing reciprocity through marriage. The theory could not, however, account for the many societies whose moiety systems have nothing to do with marriage. Meanwhile it became clear that moiety systems themselves were not a class of phenomena that it is useful to isolate for analysis. Their character and meaning are everywhere determined by the wider social systems of which they form a part. These social systems are, in turn, often intimately related to others that dispense with moieties. Moieties are, in short, an aspect of dualistic societies, not the essence of them.[3]

Similarly, the equilibrium sought by dualistic societies is a matter of cosmology and social theory as much as of social practice. Accordingly, it can not only accommodate hierarchy and asymmetry but, as the essays in this volume show, it often presupposes it. Dualistic societies do not

---

3. This had been recognized by earlier writers, but they did not develop the insight. Rivers, for example, pointed out in 1924 that bilateral cross-cousin marriage could produce the same effect as exogamous moieties, with the result that there was not only a fit between the two institutions but that they could often be found independently of each other. Yet he continued to focus his attention on moiety systems. Hocart recognized the complexity of dual organizations, but his characteristically perceptive discussion of them was, equally typically, inconclusive ([1936]:262–90). Meanwhile, when Lévi-Strauss (1956) tried to take the discussion of dual organization beyond moiety systems, he neither modified his original theory nor developed a new one.

substitute their binary classifications for a sense of history, while living in the fool's paradise of a precarious equilibrium guaranteed by moiety systems or other social arrangements. On the contrary, they may feel there is a grand order in the scheme of things, but it is a cosmic equilibrium that offers no immediate guarantees. People in such societies are keenly aware that the conflicting principles that maintain the harmony of the universe in the long run can unbalance their individual and social lives in the short run. They therefore see their binary systems as involving them in a constant effort to harmonize with these forces and to hold them in dynamic tension. So the villages of the Indians of central Brazil (described in this volume by Seeger and Maybury-Lewis) are themselves microcosms of the universe, and the rituals performed by their inhabitants seek to maintain their societies in harmony with the cosmic scheme of things, just as did the rituals of the Han emperors in their Halls of Light.

Meanwhile the apparently timeless classifications used by so many of these societies are in fact preoccupied with time and with process — whether it be violent and disruptive change or the more insidious threat of social entropy. Their dualism is therefore not a disinterest in nor a negation of history. It is a way of controlling history.

Indeed some of the dualistic systems described in this volume have shown themselves to be marvelously impervious to the ravages of time. The society of the Incas, as described by Zuidema, is especially interesting in this respect, for it contained all of the elements that I have been discussing. Inca society was organized socially and spatially in conformity with a fundamentally dualistic cosmology. It was linked to the cosmos through the Inca himself, who mediated in his own person the oppositions that made up the universe. Moreover the Incas organized a large and populous empire, located in a mountainous region that is difficult to travel in even today, in terms of a fundamental opposition between Hanan (Upper) and Hurin (Lower) moieties.

The Spanish conquest destroyed the Inca empire in the sixteenth century and imposed an alien rule on the subjects of the Inca. Yet their descendents still maintain a recognizable version of the original Incaic dual organization in their own cosmology and in the organization of their own communities (see, for example, Flores 1971; Isbell 1978; and Skar 1981). Here then is a dualistic system of thought and social organization that imposed moiety systems on an empire and that has survived through four centuries of subsequent repression.

The remarkable history of dualism among the Andean Indians takes us back to our original question. What is it that makes dualism such an attractive and resilient principle in symbolic and social organization?

The idea that a major opposition or a set of interconnected oppositions is inherent in the scheme of things cannot be derived from the mechanisms of human thought itself, for although such an idea is, as we have seen, found in many parts of the world, it is not universal. Even if it could be shown that human thought processes are inherently binary, and that human minds are therefore in some sense programmed to select binary options, that still would not answer our question. We would still be left facing the issue posed at the beginning of this essay: why do some societies pay little attention to these binary systems of thought and action while others insist on them as the framework of their existence?

It is clear that polarities loom large in human thought. All cultures note and deal with such oppositions as night-day (or darkness-light), male-female, sky-earth, life-death, and a host of others.[4] Hertz made this point in his famous essay on the preeminence of the right hand ([1909]: 95–96), and Lloyd (1966) and Hallpike (1979) took his contention as their point of departure in writing respectively about early Greek thought and about primitive thought. All of them argued that binary classifications reflect — or at least accommodate — oppositions in the real world, what Hallpike referred to as "the twoness of reality" (1979:234). But these arguments still leave our basic question unanswered. If reality imposes its "twoness" on human thinking, then why do only some societies organize themselves around this dualism and how do others transcend it?

Rodney Needham considered these issues (1987:200–235) and suggested that the world did not unambiguously generate oppositions; instead, he argued that these oppositions were constructions put upon natural phenomena by the human mind. Nevertheless he acknowledged "a universal tendency to think in twos" (1987:229). But this formulation returns us to the fundamental questions: why should this be so and why do only some societies then institutionalize this form of thinking?

Lloyd, in his fascinating analysis of early Greek thought, suggested possible answers to these questions. He argued that certain aspects of nature do indeed impress the mind with their duality. These oppositions then become culturally salient when they are imbued with religious significance. Finally, he argued that antithesis was the simplest form of classification, suggesting that its very simplicity might account for its widespread use in human systems of thought (1966:80).

There are difficulties with the argument from logical simplicity, as Rodney Needham has pointed out (1987:219–21). In this essay I have been developing an argument that incorporates Lloyd's other two suggestions —

---

4. For a discussion of other oppositions that are frequently given formal recognition in societies around the world, see Rodney Needham 1973.

the natural impact on human thought of certain oppositions and the cultural elaboration of them. Whatever the ambiguities and uncertainties of oppositions in nature, human cultures universally regard certain distinctions as polar oppositions and, furthermore, as oppositions that merit theoretical speculation. There is no society that does not recognize a fundamental opposition between male and female or between life and death, however these oppositions may be elaborated or mediated in different cultures. Similarly, the alternation between light and dark, usually (but not always) thought of in its most immediate form as the opposition between day and night, is accepted universally as a basic condition of existence in this world. These oppositions are not fundamental in the logical sense that they derive from an elementary principle that compels the human mind by virtue of its irreducible simplicity. They are fundamental because they are universally recognized as being the essential conditions of human existence.

It is possible to conceive of a world without sexual dimorphism — indeed it is a commonplace of modern biology that there are species in this world that reproduce without needing two sexes to do so. It is possible to conceive of a world where darkness or light does not exist. This is logically difficult, for without one pole of the antithesis, the other pole would be meaningless, but it is cosmologically much easier. In fact many religious systems — and not only the Manichaeans who made the separation of light and darkness into separate worlds the centerpiece of their creed — are preoccupied with light and darkness and the prospects for abolishing the latter altogether. It is also possible to conceive of a world without death (and therefore without life as we know it) and this too is a major preoccupation of much religious thinking. The point is that none of these conceptions apply to the world as we know it. They are all born out of speculation concerning the facts of this world, which are that an ordered relationship between male and female, light and dark, life and death are essential conditions of human existence. Formally these oppositions are simply antitheses, but culturally they are much more than that. They are highly charged antitheses over which people have brooded since time immemorial.

The attractiveness of dualistic thinking lies, then, in the solution it offers to the problem of ensuring an ordered relationship between antitheses that cannot be allowed to become antipathies. It is not so much that it offers order, for all systems of thought do that, but that it offers equilibrium. Dualistic theories create order by postulating a harmonious interaction of contradictory principles. The existence of fundamental antithesis is everywhere perceived as being part of human existence in this world. Dualistic theories insist that these antitheses do not tear the world apart, and humankind with it, because they are part of a cosmic scheme in which they are harmonized.

Similarly, the experience of conflict and the necessity of resolving it is also an unavoidable part of human experience. Dualistic theories likewise offer a solution to the problem of social order by holding out the promise of balancing contending forces in perpetual equilibrium.

If dualistic thinking offers the reassurance of cosmic harmony and dual organization offers the parallel advantage of peace on earth, then it is understandable that societies have had such widespread recourse to them. We now know that the accumulation of polarities (or "recurrent antitheses" as Lloyd [1966:41] called them) in dualistic societies is not characteristic of the thought or the social organization found only in small-scale, tribal societies. On the contrary, the systematic use of polarities is widespread in human cosmology and philosophy and it has been used socially to organize empires. Why, then, did these dualistic elaborations recede?

The answer as usual appears to be part social and part conceptual. Dualistic theory postulated harmony through equilibrium. Dualistic practice seeks to institutionalize the balance of contending forces in order to maintain that harmony in society. Relatively small-scale societies had (and still have) little difficulty in living within such a social and conceptual framework. The ancient empires organized along dualistic lines were ruled by divine kings, who linked the social with the cosmic order while mediating in their persons the contending forces that might otherwise create havoc in the scheme of things. But this solution was no longer acceptable as the political realm became progressively detached from the cosmological. Some of our best evidence for this process comes from ancient China, where, through the works of scholars such as Schwartz and Joseph Needham, we can follow the fortunes of the yin-yang school of correlative cosmologists and see how their ideas gradually ceased to define the ideology of the empire.

Divine kingship is not of course the only way to institutionalize dualism in a complex polarity. Diarchic systems, stressing the necessary interaction of sacred and secular rulers, offered another way of maintaining the balance between cosmic oppositions. Dumezil's (1948) classic analysis of the relationship between Mitra and Varuna offers a good example of this. But diarchy introduces a significant change in the nature of a dualistic system. As soon as the polar principles that counterbalance each other are represented by sacred and secular authorities, the exercise of power eventually leads to a struggle between them. It is characteristic of the long process of "modernization" since antiquity that secular authorities have everywhere established their supremacy over sacred ones. Modern states may occasionally claim to have the blessing of God for their actions, but they do not usually expect their political organization to be in harmony with cosmic principles. So, when modern theorists or politicians praise the stability guaranteed by a two-party system, they are focusing on the social order and not concerning themselves with the cosmic one. Yet their preoccupation is not far removed from that of a tribal society that relies on its dual organization to guarantee its equilibrium. The difference lies only in the degree to which either group believes that its social arrangements keep it aligned with some sort of cosmic harmony. It is precisely this conviction that has eroded over time.

That erosion is a result of the spread of scientific thinking. Scientific thought is skeptical of cosmic harmony, though individual scientists may well believe in it. In fact, Joseph Needham argued that the scholars of the I Ching in ancient China were engaged in "field thinking" of the kind found in modern genetics, embryology, or chemistry. He suggested that "some elements of the structure of the world as modern science knows it was prefigured in their speculations" (Needham 1956:276–77). But modern science is less interested in the maintenance of equilibrium than it is in understanding the flux of events. Heraclitus combined these preoccupations in his view that the world was in a constant state of flux, generated by the interaction of contradictory principles, and since his time such ideas have been taken up by a number of philosophers, most notably by Hegel. It is, however, the reassurance of equilibrium that is missing from the later dialectical theories, and it was precisely that reassurance that gave the theories their philosophical and religious power in earlier times. Lévi-Strauss was right, then, to stress, as he did in *The Savage Mind* (1962), the connection between the spread of scientific thought and the rise of historical consciousness. It was these twin forces that undermined the rationale for dualistic societies by exalting process and change over state and stability.

Yet the dualistic theories that once guided ancient civilizations have not simply evaporated. In modern societies they have become, in intellectualized form, the special province of religion or philosophy. Alternatively they are still to be found in the folk beliefs of people for whom the interaction of fundamental principles such as yin and yang or hot and cold remain important ideas by which they organize their lives.

It is from the systemic level in modern nations, from the national ideology or social organization, that such theories and institutions have disappeared. Nowadays they are found at the systemic level only in societies like those described in this book—societies that have been left in comparative isolation by nation states, or in areas that have succeeded in maintaining their traditional cultures in the face of modernization.

Dualism as social theory and social practice has shown itself to be varied, sophisticated, versatile, and enduring. Its appeal and worldwide distribution derive from the elegant solution it offers by combining human experience with human preoccupations in a harmonious equilibrium theory. Yet ultimately it gives way before a process of modernization that produces intellectual and social fragmentation of a kind that even a dualistic system is unable to synthesize.

REFERENCES

Barth, F. 1959. Segmentary opposition and the theory of games: A study of Pathan organization. *Journal of the Royal Anthropological Institute* 89:5–22.
———. 1981. *Features of person and society in Swat.* London: Routledge and Kegan Paul.
Dumézil, G. 1948. *Mitra Varuna: Essai sur deux représentations Indo-Européennes de la souveraineté.* Paris: Gallimard.
Duverger, M. 1963. *Political parties: Their organization and activity in the modern state.* New York: Science Editions.
———. 1972. *Party politics and pressure groups.* New York: Thomas Y. Crowell.
Flores, Salvador. 1971. Duality in the socio-cultural organization of several Andean populations. *Folk* 13:65–88.
Frankfort, H. 1948. *Kingship and the gods: A study of ancient Near Eastern religion as the integration of society and nature.* Chicago: University of Chicago Press.
Granet, Marcel. [1929] 1960. *Chinese civilization: A political, social and religious history of ancient China.* New York: Meridian Books.
Gulliver, P. H. 1958. The Turkana age organization. *American Anthropologist* 60:900–922.
Hallpike, C. R. 1979. *The foundations of primitive thought.* Oxford: Clarendon Press.
Hertz, Robert. [1909] 1960. The pre-eminence of the right hand: A study in religious polarity. In *Death and the right hand.* Glencoe, Ill.: Free Press.
Hocart, A. M. [1936] 1970. *Kings and councillors.* Chicago: University of Chicago Press.
Isbell, Billie Jean. 1978. *To defend ourselves: Ecology and ritual in an Andean village.* Austin: University of Texas Press.
Lévi-Strauss, C. 1949. *Les structures élémentaires de la parenté.* Paris: Presses universitaires de France.
———. 1956. Les organisations dualistes, existent-elles? *Bijdragen tot de Taal-, Land- en Volkenkunde* 112:99–128.
———. 1962. *La pensée sauvage.* Paris: Plon.

Lieu, Samuel N. 1985. *Manichaeism in the later Roman Empire and medieval China: A historical survey.* Manchester: Manchester University Press.

Lloyd, G. E. R. 1966. *Polarity and analogy: Two types of argumentation in early Greek thought.* Cambridge: Cambridge University Press.

Maybury-Lewis, David. 1967. *Akwẽ-Shavante society.* Oxford: Clarendon Press.

Needham, Joseph. 1956. *Science and civilization in China.* Vol. 2. Cambridge: Cambridge University Press.

Needham, Rodney, ed. 1973. *Right and left: Essays on dual symbolic classification.* Chicago: University of Chicago Press.

————. 1980. *Reconnaissances.* Toronto: University of Toronto Press.

————. 1987. *Counterpoints.* Berkeley and Los Angeles: University of California Press.

Rivers, W. H. R. 1924. *Social organization.* London: Kegan, Paul, Trench, and Trubner.

Runciman, Steven. 1947. *The medieval Manichee: A study of the Christian dualist heresy.* Cambridge: Cambridge University Press.

Schwartz, Benjamin I. 1985. *The world of thought in ancient China.* Cambridge: The Harvard University Press, Belknap Press.

Skar, Harald O. 1981. *The Warm Valley People.* Oslo: Universitetsforlaget.

Whaling, Frank. 1986. Yin yang, Zoroastrian dualism, and gnosticism: Comparative studies in religious dualism. In *Duality,* ed. Emily Lyle, and *Cosmos,* Yearbook of the Traditional Cosmological Society, vol. 1 (1985). Edinburgh: The Traditional Cosmological Society.

Zaehner, R. C. 1967. Zoroastrianism. In *The concise encyclopedia of living faiths,* ed. R. C. Zaehner. Boston: Beacon Press.

Introduction

Dual Organization Reconsidered

Uri Almagor

In the analysis of dual organization, the emergence of structural anthropology, formulated by Lévi-Strauss, was a turning point. One can divide the history of research on dual organization into two distinct periods: before and after Lévi-Strauss. The earlier approaches to this unusual form of organization were put forward as causal explanations. Such explanations can be roughly divided into those that regarded dual organization as a primal and ancient form of organization associated with early stages of social life and those that attempted to analyze the conditions that gave rise to this form of organization. But as is often the case with simple models that try to explain complex phenomena on the basis of a limited number of cases and meager data, the distinction between these two approaches was often blurred. A full exposition of the place of dual organization in ethnological records, the different theoretical emphases given to this form of organization, and their relation to the problems that have preoccupied anthropological thinking at different periods are all intriguing case studies in the history of social anthropology. However, these issues are not the subject of this short introduction. Nor is this the appropriate place to discuss the many philosophical, logical, and methodological controversies surrounding Lévi-Strauss's structural theory in general, and the concept of dual organization, in particular. This was discussed by Maybury-Lewis (1960) and is further elaborated in his introduction to this volume. What is of interest here is the impact his structural theory has had on the analysis of dual organization.

In the structural holistic perspective, the fundamental categories of the human mind, the most important of which are binary oppositions, are also the constitutive elements of culture and the social order. These mental categories are inherent in the human perception of the world and are translated into social practices and forms of thought.

19

Lévi-Strauss stressed that this "deep" or "hidden" structure or "underlying principle" is more real than the apparent order. Ambilineal descent, for example (Pouwer 1974:249), is a surface manifestation of a binary principle expressed through two complementary modalities, horizontal and vertical. But in our perception of the apparent order, and as the structuralists themselves emphasize, the horizontal arrangement dominates. The structuralists argue that surface manifestations conceal the real order. This view was expressed by Lévi-Strauss in his well-known article ([1956]) "Do dual organizations exist?" which became a frame of reference for almost any allusion to dual organization. He questioned whether dual organization really exists as a system in itself and argued that what appears to us as a dual order is actually a tripartite one. In other words, the surface manifestation of dualism is no more than a momentary vision of symmetric relations in systems that are essentially dynamic and asymmetrical.

In my view, it was not Lévi-Strauss's doubts about the existence of dual organization that hampered the development of new perspectives on this subject, for his concepts, terminology, and arguments were taken up by all who studied the subject of dual organization. The very fact that most of the contributors to this volume make extensive use of the conceptual tools brought out in that article shows that it had a stimulating influence. But the association of his structural theory with dual organization hampered the study of this phenomenon from other perspectives, such as those of conflict and power relations, exchange theory, "group interest," symbolic interaction, and the Marxist model. Most of all, the association of structuralism with dual organization created confusion as to what dual organization is all about and how it is related to dualism in general.

Lévi-Strauss's structural theory assigns predominance to the symbolic sphere and assumes an implicit structure that is inherent in culture, in the working of the human mind, and in the social order. In other words, the various expressions of dualism in a society do not stem from organizational or institutional needs or problems, but from this implicit structure. According to this holistic perspective, "social phenomena present the character of meaningful wholes of structuralized ensembles" (Rossi 1974:71), and the fundamental categories of the human mind are those of binary oppositions. No wonder that dualism was seen to be everywhere. A new fashion of "instant dualism" has developed — we could call it the "dualism now movement" — which characterizes almost every domain of social life as dualistic and considers dual classifications as the basic structure of every aspect of the human society. It is possible to present almost any social phenomenon in any society as a dual formation, but that does not mean that the society possesses a dual system or even a scheme of dual classification. As de Josselin de Jong commented on Needham's (1973) essays analyzing the dual symbolism of right and left, it "make[s] one doubt whether the notion of right versus left is really as central to dual symbolic classification as it is made out to be" (1976:172).

Furthermore, frequent references to such terms as the binary character of society, dyadic system, dual categories, conceptual dualism, logical dualism, dual structure, and so on, terms that have been used in referring to different social and symbolic contexts, all indicate that we are exploring unmarked territory and risk falling into a tautological trap. For an orthodox structuralist, it might make sense to combine some of the above in analyzing one society or social phenomena in various societies. Being aware of a variety of oppositions is, in itself, structuring qua perception of order, and bringing together such pairs of opposites is an interesting exercise in structuralism. But for those who are not orthodox structuralists, or structuralists at all, an exposition of dualism at different levels, without an indication of which social, perceptual, or symbolic levels are being referred to, is confusing and is analytically insufficiently refined.

Also, arranging elements in two columns, as is often done, does not necessarily indicate a dual system. As Beidelman states, "The dualistic symbolic classification which I present here is, of course, not an ideological system constructed, as such, by the Kaguru themselves; but this does not mean that the principles behind such a categorization have no meaning for the Kaguru" (1973:153). Meaning is not the issue here, for every dual division has a certain meaning. To constitute a dual organization, the elements must have some social and ideological construction. They must have some degree of what Austin (1975) called "performative utterance." In treating dualism as the basic structure of human nature, culture, and social order, we overlook many possible ways to analyze the different forms of dual organization. All in all, I think Lévi-Strauss's structuralist theory inhibited the study of dual organization by shifting attention away from other potential perspectives. Anyone who has ever written on dual organization in the last three decades has had to negotiate the structuralist hurdle first, and this preoccupation with one theory, however brilliant, left many questions not only unanswered but, worse, unasked.

This volume is neither a debate about structuralism nor is it intended principally to be a challenge to Lévi-Strauss's analysis of dual organization, for we came to praise Caesar. As noted earlier, most of the essays presented in this volume use Lévi-Strauss's theoretical points and elaborate upon them. Even those that do not refer directly to his structural theory portray the impact his analysis has had on the authors' thinking. However, more than just addressing a lacuna in Lévi-Strauss, and expanding both logically and methodologically on the connection between the factual and the normative or formal, where the distinction between "is" and "ought to be" disappears, this volume attempts to go beyond structural analysis and to "unpack" the bundle referred to as dual organization into its various component forms.

Nor is this book an attempt to revive the various theories on dual organization that preceded Lévi-Strauss, although some of the essays refer to diffusion, migration, and conquest because these principles have played a role in establishing dual systems in the societies studied. Also, some essays deal with demographic issues as being clearly connected with change in, or erosion of, dual organizations. In many essays the issues of marriage, reciprocities, and exogamy come to the fore as the basic components of dual organization. Most of them combine critical evaluation with new perspectives on social and symbolic dualism. The emphasis in all the essays presented here is on specifying the mechanisms through which the different features of dualism are related to one another. This is not a simple task if, as Eisenstadt notes in the Epilogue to this volume, these essays taken together show that there is no one-to-one relationship among the social, symbolic, and semantic dimensions of dualism.

Indeed, treating the symbolic, social, and semantic dimensions of dualism as representing different elements in the construction of social order, can help us open up the study of dualism to more articulated explanations of the complicated relationships among these dimensions. Most important, such dissociation may show us how these relationships lead to changes in, and transformations of, dual organization. For as anthropologists who were engaged in intensive fieldwork we cannot afford to ignore the possibility of different realities of dualism.

Finally, this volume does not present a new theory on dual organization that will serve, to use Geertz's (1983:28) expression, as "a form for all seasons." It is doubtful whether a new theory is really needed at this stage to describe phenomena that are so diverse and must contend with so many variables in different social and cultural settings. The existing analytical and conceptual frameworks are sufficient to handle all of these various phenomena and to provide a more balanced picture of dual organization. Our purpose is to explain, through scrupulous attention to context, how the day-to-day operation of dual organization is connected with the awareness of opposites as a mode of conceptualizing life and social processes; how the activities within a dual organization, along with its institutional and symbolic properties, provide nuances of meaning; and how dual division in a society is connected with the regulation and distribution of resources on one hand, and the construction of trust and reciprocities on the other.

Because this volume presents a number of essays, each emphasizing a different approach to dual organization, and each stressing different components of such organization, we thought it would be useful to present the reader with short summaries of the main points in each essay. Fox's essay considers two classic models of dual organization that were elaborated by Lévi-Strauss ([1956]) and van Wouden (1968). He argues that both models actually derive from the Durkheimian tradition of classification through categorization of social forms. As a result, the two models focus on the products, rather than on the processes, of classification. Fox studies these processes by examining five features of dual symbolic classification in eastern Indonesian societies: parallelism, recursive complementarity, categorical asymmetry, categorical reversal, and analogical cross-over. He concludes by examining the relationship between dualism and hierarchy, pointing out that in eastern Indonesia, dualism is a conceptual resource that may be used either as a vehicle for structuring hierarchy or as a device for countering it.

Among the Oromo-speaking people of Ethiopia and northern Kenya, a complex pattern of dualistic opposition provides continuity within seemingly disparate forms of social and ritual organization. Hinnant's essay focuses on one Oromo society, the Guji, whose system of dual organization exists in two temporal orders. During secular time, organizational and ideological oppositions allocate people to different groups, create asymmetries between the groups, and provide a rationale for the system. During the sacred time of ritual, on the other hand, the ideological dualisms become far more dynamic, interactive, and conflictive. The Guji case underscores the importance of analytically separating ideological dualisms, which in this case undergo rapid transformation during ritual, from social organizational dualisms, which are worked through in a far slower historical process. Hinnant points out that it is the alternation between sacred and secular periods in the eight-year cycle of the *gada* generation grading system that creates the full Guji cosmology. The secular periods are devoted to weaving together social relations through complementary oppositions and reconciliation procedures that maintain peace and establish trust. During the lengthy period of sacred time that accompanies the handing over of leadership, the whole set of relations is radically reordered. It is only at this point, Hinnant argues, that the creative content of Guji dualistic thought can be fully grasped.

Aboriginal Australia is notable for the prevalence and variety of forms of dual organization. However, during the last fifty years or so, aboriginal dual organization has been treated in a rather fragmentary fashion and the significance of moieties and cognate divisions has been played down. Maddock's essay takes issue with these trends and attempts to deal with the subject systematically. He redefines dual organization to include cognate divisions of moieties, the criterion for the division being the existence of a dual denominator. Thus semimoieties, sections, and subsections are brought under the same rubric as moieties. Maddock examines three classic questions posed in relation to aboriginal dual organization: its forms, its functions, and its origin and development. Regarding the first question, in addition to arguing that two-, four-, and eightfold systems should be treated together as parts of a larger structure, he shows how we may move from one level to another by means of permutations. Thus, the different varieties of classes are seen as consisting of a single logical system. Regarding the second question, Maddock demonstrates, with reference to ritual and marriage, how logical combinations and recombinations are enacted in aboriginal life. He rejects the view that this pervasive idiom can be treated as a duplication of, for example, egocentric relations of kinship. Finally, in discussing the third question, he argues against a conflation of logical and historical considerations. However, he notes that logical considerations can lead to some limited historical generalizations.

Maybury-Lewis argues in his essay that the dual organization of the Gê and the Bororo of central Brazil are ideologies in equilibrium. According to their world view, human societies are seen as participating in an overall cosmic harmony. Their ideologies govern the social practices of these central Brazilian Indians to such an extent that they have been able to live out their beliefs to a remarkable degree. They combine and recombine binary systems in institutional patterns that have adapted to changing circumstances without ever ceasing to be dual organizations. Dual organization among the Gê and Bororo has survived the pressures exerted by Brazilian society, the shock of the frontier, depopulation, loss of land, and changes in habitat and means of subsistence.

Since the Gê and Bororo dual organizations do not necessarily involve moieties at all, Maybury-Lewis maintains that dual organization, in general, cannot be derived from a theory of reciprocity, or its corollary, a theory of marriage alliance. Reciprocity, he stresses, is a function of dual organization, not its cause. Central Brazilian dual organizations are not characterized by a simple binary symmetry and a static world view. On the contrary, they combine the static with the dynamic, the binary with the ternary, and the symmetric with the asymmetric in systems of dynamic equilibrium. Maybury-Lewis concludes that this degree of complexity is characteristic of dual organization throughout the world and that, therefore, such organization should be studied with a proper regard for the contextual specificity of their binary systems and the processes that relate these systems to each other.

Valeri's essay analyzes three kinds of relationships in the dual organizations of the central Moluccas: the relationship between hierarchy and symmetry, that between social dualism and rivalry in the rites of headhunting, and that between dual organization and complex intertribal and interregional political and exchange networks. His paper shows that the Siwa-Lima (nine-five) dual organization of the central Moluccas is a device for coordinating and normalizing lower-level social processes (see Maybury-Lewis 1979). However, the moieties that constitute this system are territorially discrete confederations rather than segments of a single society. Each moiety ranks itself as superior and, in some way, central to the other, which it ranks as inferior and in some way peripheral. These rankings are repeated in internal rankings within each of the societies. Thus, each society ranks as superior certain ways of producing unity by mediating between oppositions. The outstanding feature of this system is the fact that each moiety has symmetrically opposed views of the hierarchical relationship between moieties. This calls to mind Asad's (1970: chap. 12) explanation of the hierarchical structure and relationships in the Kababish society in the Sudan, where the dynasty of rulers and the ruled commoners have a symmetrically contradictory view of their society; the commoners are content to be dominated simply because they do not see it as domination (see also Black 1972).

Valeri argues that this opposition is a way of symmetrically containing and balancing asymmetries that is compatible with the extreme antagonism between the moieties. In actuality, the moieties are socially complementary, but they do not view themselves as logically complementary. The essay concludes by suggesting that the Siwa-Lima system and similar systems in Indonesia form an intermediate type between the "tribal" moiety systems and "centripetal" political systems.

In my essay I start with a redefinition of dual organization—this in order to distinguish between societies with dual organization and those without it, or between "strong" and "weak" dual systems within one society, and to include East African generation moieties that hitherto were not included in the study of dual organization. I analyze two forms of dual organization among the Dassanetch of southwest Ethiopia, among whom a single principle divides parents and their children into two distinct, but cross-cutting sets of endogamous alternations and moieties. These alternations represent the hierarchical division in the generation-set system and are modeled on kinship structure of fathers and sons. The moiety system, in contrast, is patterned on equality between two groups of affines. Though both sets are governed by the principle of alternate affiliation of kinsmen, the structural implications are different in the short and long run. In the long run, the model of alternations presents a balanced set relation combining a dualistic and cyclical schema. In the short run, or rather in day-to-day life, alternations and moieties variously affect the structure of the individual's social relationships.

In analyzing the Dassanetch, I show how a dual organization actually operates in response to certain basic inequalities in the distribution of resources and power in society and to age, generation, and demographic incompatibilities. However, I argue that an age system usually resolves fairly satisfactorily the control and distribution of resources between individuals of different ages. But in a system that differentiates according to both age and generation, the hierarchical dual division does not successfully reconcile the differences in social standing, resources, and power among individuals of the same age who, according to the explicit ideology of the age-based units, should be equals. The ritual opposition of moieties in various ceremonies is based on principles of exchange that dominate social and economic relationships among men in the middle stage of life. Through repeated visual codes, these ceremonies convey to Dassanetch men that trust among coevals must be constructed through the principles of competition, prominence, and achievement. In this context, ritual drama is a device for translating the macronotion of dual organization as a relationship between somewhat abstract categories into the microlevel of inconsistencies and day-to-day relationships between individuals. I also point out that in a dual generational structure, an individual can counter hierarchy through independent activities that are legitimized in the ritual rivalry of equal moieties through which a dialectic of self and others is expressed.

Yengoyan's essay utilizes ethnographic data from an aboriginal society, the Pitjantjatjara of central Australia, to explore certain features of dual organization in that tribe's social structure, myth, and language. Using Durkheim's notion of the sacred-profane contrast as a point of departure, Yengoyan examines the extent to which Pitjantjatjara concepts of nature and culture are related to their views of the sacred and profane. Through an examination of some grammatical structures and linguistic properties, he develops a theory of cultural coherence (as expressed in their concepts of time, space, and being) for understanding Pitjantjatjara religion, which is also a concept expressive of a cosmological system that maintains closure and forms circumscribed boundaries. Second, the continuity of the mythic past is linguistically conveyed in contemporary ritual activities through the use of the imperfective. Third, by certain linguistic designations, a myth turns elements of the physical world into signs of the spiritual sphere: the spiritual can exist only in terms of a physical referent.

Seeger's essay examines some criticisms of analyses of dualism in the Gê-speaking societies of central Brazil and shows why they are unfounded. One major controversy concerns the nature of dualism itself. His paper shows that for the Suyá, one of the Gê-speaking groups, there are several kinds of relationships among dual elements in different domains. First, is the classification of animals, humans, and states by their odor, an example of "fuzzy sets." Second, is the classification of concentric spatial domains, an example of recursive asymmetrical dualism. Third, is the classification of men by moieties, an example of classical set theory. Each of these types is based on a dual division, but the elements in each set are organized differently. These include a clearer definition of the kinds of dualism present in a society, ethnographic specificity rather than universal statements, a close examination of the different ways sets are formed, and the study of diachronic processes.

The essay by Rosman and Rubel discusses evolutionary aspects of dual organization. Using a structural model, they attempt to explain the relationship between the underlying structure of dual organization and its surface manifestations, such as sister exchange, mortuary rites, kinship terminology, and cosmological and symbolic divisions. They demonstrate that in two different parts of the world (the Northwest Coast of Canada and Melanesia), in totally different contexts of subsistence in contrasting environments, dual organization has evolved into the same complex form. They argue that the nature of the transformation from simple to more complex forms of direct exchange is the same regardless of environment and mode of production. Their hypothesis is that the development of dual organization is linked to the evolution of political power. Among the mechanisms that bring about the transformation are: first, the evolution of the simpler form of reciprocal exchange of women into marriage with members of various groups; second, involvement in long-distance trade and strategic locations on trade networks that is related to the development of rank and more complex structures of exchange; and third, the presence of large surpluses related to ceremonial distribution and exchange.

Lamphear, a historian who collected and recorded the oral traditions of the Jie and the Turkana of East Africa, compares the historical development of dual organization among these two people. He argues that the strong dualism of the Jie system, with its stress on irrevocable generational principles, is a product of their history. Their particular circumstances led to the emergence of a spatially, socially, and politically tight community with an age system in which senior elders are not forced into retirement. Jie origin myths, which represent the Jie at the center of their universe, support this structural conservatism. Thus, in the nineteenth century, these elders were able to withstand challenges to their authority from powerful hereditary functionaries.

In contrast, the historical development of the closely related Turkana led to a quite different generation-set system in which the binary division of alternations seems to be weak. Just as the Jie came to represent the center, the Turkana came to represent the periphery (or expansion into the periphery), and formed an image of themselves as far-ranging pioneers. During their dramatic territorial expansion in the nineteenth century, the Turkana encountered and absorbed many other groups from whom they adopted a time-class system better suited to the circumstances of their expansion. In this process, the Jie model was replaced by a new emphasis on age and coevality. Lamphear concludes that the Turkana system is better seen as a creative adaptation to new circumstances than as an inevitable deterioration of the "unwieldy" Jie system, as some observers have argued.

Zuidema's essay reanalyzes the dual organization of Incaic Cuzco using the newly discovered complete version of Juan de Betanzos's chronicle [1551]. Zuidema seeks to elucidate the ideas behind a system that had cosmological significance, was used in the organization of the calendar, gave meaning to important rituals, and served as an administrative tool for the state. He shows how the peoples of the Inca empire were divided into Incas, pre-Incas (who had inhabited the valley of Cuzco before the ascendancy of their Inca overlords), and non-Incas. The Incas themselves were divided into the upper (Hanan) and lower (Hurin) moieties. These moieties ordered the social and spatial arrangements of the capital city of Cuzco. They were also embedded in the administrative structure of the valley of Cuzco and recognized in the calendar, which was divided into Hurin periods and Hanan periods, with interstitial periods assigned to pre-Incas and non-Incas. Zuidema analyzes Inca rituals and shows that they trace a progression from outside to inside, from non-Inca to Inca, before focusing on the dualistic complementarity of Inca society itself.

He further shows how this intricate system was organized around the political marriages of the Inca himself, who gave his classificatory sisters as wives to lesser lords. Their children, the "sisters' children," became an important category of Inca social and political organization. Zuidema suggests that this enables us to unravel an apparent paradox of Andean social organization. Versions of this Incaic system still persist in contemporary Andean communities. Now, as in Inca times, the Andean peoples speak of reciprocity and intermarriage between moieties, yet these moieties tend strongly towards endogamy. The ideal of symmetry was put into effect through the political marriages of the Inca lords. Otherwise it remained a metaphor that was not put into practice.

Tuzin's essay discusses the Ilahita Arapesh of Papua New Guinea, among whom dual organization provides the framework for nearly all areas of social action and ideology including domicility, subsistence, politics, economics, and ritual, but with the notable exception of marriage.

The Arapesh system, Tuzin believes, underwent a change from exogamous to agamous moieties as a structural shift from "elementary" to "complex" marriage forms occurred. He uses Lévi-Strauss's ([1949]) terminology to propose a typological distinction between "elementary" and "complex" dual organizations based on the presence or absence, respectively, of exogamous moieties. Tuzin considers the relations between the dualistic principle of classification and the social structure in which it is embedded, and he examines the logical, aesthetic, and psychological motives that induce individuals to apply the dualistic principle in their dealings with one another. He finds that Arapesh self and society are mutually determinative by virtue of containing and sharing the dualistic principle. Tuzin's major point is that the dualistic principle is repeatedly joined to the structure of dual organization at the level of social action. Social action also provides a link between moral and aesthetic understanding on one hand, and the legitimation (or reification) of dual organization on the other.

Following Barth's (1959) lead, Spencer analyzes dual age organization among the Maasai of East Africa by invoking the theory of games and, more specifically, the theory of variable-sum (or nonzero-sum) games, where the gains of the winners do not necessarily tally with the losses of the losers. He goes beyond the analogy between politics and games to explore the inherent contradictions of social life, pointing out that the problem of stability and trust in the social system is related to dilemmas at a higher level. Spencer is aware that any attempt to apply theory to ethnographic data is necessarily reductionist and vulnerable to its own limitations. Yet he usefully draws attention to the existence of rules, strategies, and dilemmas in social life that are similar to those found in game scenarios. Dual organizations, like games, reduce social life to two complementary sides. The stability of the two sides cannot be taken for granted in Maasai systems because there are choices and conflicts engendered by dynamics of succession to authority in age-set systems that are not traceable to the manipulation of dual organization per se.

Spencer divides the dual organization of age succession among the Maasai into two models. The southern model is a cyclical process in which the two opposed groups alternately occupy the central arena or the periphery as their members mature. In the northern model, elders and moran (young warriors) are opposed by reason of their different ages: the elders control the center permanently, but face the dilemma of controlling the moran until the latter come to the center as they mature and cross the boundary to elderhood. The logic of the theory of games reduces the dilemmas of the interacting pairs in both models to three or four basic forms, each associated with a vivid scenario in which the players fulfill roles that are, so to speak, larger than life. Indeed, according to Spencer, the players portray stereotypes of symbolic figures in Maasai ritual dramas centering on the inescapable dilemmas of certain roles and transitions in social life.

Traube's essay focuses on dual categories and their realization as hierarchical social forms among the Mambai of eastern Timor. The Mambai use narrative to project the past onto the present, for the persistence of the past in the present defines and maintains the hierarchy. Traube argues that analysis of Mambai dualism must deal with the differential relations of parts to conceptual wholes that the Mambai affirm in narrative discourse. Dual social structures are not conceived as primordial divisions, but as the products of past actions that divide the original totality into asymmetrically interdependent parts. She first examines dual classification in specific social contexts and focuses on the interplay between complementarity and categorical asymmetry. Her essay explores the connection between hierarchy and the ideology of generous giving, which the Mambai carry out mainly through ritual exchanges in which one group represents the past and the original source. Hierarchy rests upon asymmetric exchanges with periodic reminders of the idea of obligation to a source.

In Mambai society, knowledge of ultimate origin is a mark of distinction. Time, in the Mambai view, is divided into ranked categories and knowledge of the distant past is a superior, encompassing, authoritative mode. The essay explores the relational implications of authoritative knowledge in formal ritual contexts. Mambai ritual leaders demonstrate and recreate their status through discursive strategies of allusion and deference. These strategies serve a double purpose: they conceal the content of authoritative knowledge, while advancing claims to its possession. Traube's essay suggests a need for redefining the analytical concepts of structure in a way that incorporates indigenous ideas of temporality.

In the Epilogue, Eisenstadt discusses the implication of the theoretical points presented in these essays from the point of view of some major problems they raise regarding sociological theory, which he has elaborated elsewhere (1977, 1982, 1985). Eisenstadt argues that, as presented here, dual organization has three different components or connotations: as a principle of social organization, as a principle of society's symbolic representation, and as a principle of the semantic view prevalent in a society. These three principles are linked, but not in a one-to-one relationship, to three different aspects of the constitution of social order: the division of labor and exchange, the construction of trust and boundaries of communities, and the regulation of power and construction of meaning. The fact that the three components are not always found together in the societies analyzed in this volume indicates that these aspects of construction of social order are distinct from one another. Furthermore, the three components are expressed by different actors among whom tensions may arise. His analysis indicates the specific ways in which these tensions develop in the societies discussed in this volume. Eisenstadt argues that the various dimensions of dual organization fall mainly along two axes, the cosmological-symbolic and the social-institutional. He concludes by discussing the ways in which dual organizations may develop or become weaker through various combinations of the components of these axes.

The data presented in these essays point out a variety of realities of dualism. Such detailed and original data collected in field research was not available thirty years ago when the debate on the structural analysis of dual organization took place (Lévi-Strauss 1956, 1960; Maybury-Lewis 1960). The overall view that emerges from the essays in this volume is that there are different kinds of dual organization. The complexity of such systems was pointed out in various types of social processes and the production of rules and resources to sustain and transform dual organization. Any attempt to explicate and present dual organization as an easily balanced and systematically structured form that was ideologically neutral, and, above all, based on a single principle of reciprocity, may bypass the complex and contingent relationships of larger social and symbolic forms. Next, the theoretical approach in most analyses is not based on one theoretical orientation but portrays a combination of two or more disparate approaches such as transactionalism, "group interest," symbolic interaction, conflict analysis, cultural analysis, and structuralism. Such a blend of orientations was probably necessary in order to decipher the complex historical processes in social systems that govern the interconnections between various phenomena of dualism and the social order at large.

Such an extension of analysis has its risks and limitations, for it may obscure the issues of dualism with other matters. But one of the purposes of this volume was to illustrate how the principles of dualism operate in a wider context. I therefore hope that the issues, inconsistencies, diversity of viewpoints, and controversies raised here will broaden the conceptual framework of the study of dualism and will generate research into new ways of analyzing this form of organization before it succumbs to change and vanishes into systems that can be reconstructed only through the selective memory of informants.

REFERENCES

Asad, T. 1970. *The Kababish Arabs: Power, authority, and consent in a nomadic tribe.* New York: Praeger.

Austin, J. L. 1975. *How to do things with words*. Ed. F. O. Urmson and Marin Shisa. 2d ed. Cambridge: Harvard University Press.

Barth, F. 1959. Segmentary opposition and the theory of games. *Journal of the Royal Anthropological Institute* 89:5–22.

Beidelman, T. O. 1973. Kaguru symbolic classification. In Needham 1973:128–66.

Black, J. 1972. Tyranny as a strategy for survival in an "egalitarian" society. *Man* 7:614–34.

Eisenstadt, S. N. 1977. Macrosociology: Theory analysis and comparative studies. *Current Sociology* 25:1–112.

———. 1982. The axial age: The emergence of transcendental visions and the rise of the clerics. *European Journal of Sociology* 23:294–314.

———. 1985. Liminality and dynamics of civilization. *Religion* 15:315–38.

Geertz, C., 1983. *Local knowledge*. New York: Basic Books.

Josselin de Jong, P. E. de. 1976. Review of *Right and left*, ed. R. Needham. *Bijdragen tot de Taal-, Land- en Volkenkunde* 132:171–75.

Lévi-Strauss, C. [1949] 1969. *The elementary structures of kinship*. Boston: Beacon Press.

———. [1956] 1963: Do dual organizations exist? In *Structural Anthropology*, 132–63. New York: Basic Books.

———. 1960. On manipulated sociological models. *Bijdragen to de Taal-, Land- en Volkenkunde* 116:45–54.

Maybury-Lewis, D. 1960. The analysis of dual organization: A methodological critique. *Bijdragen tot de Taal-, Land- en Volkenkunde* 116:17–44.

Maybury-Lewis, D., ed. 1979. *Dialectical societies*. Cambridge: Harvard University Press.

Needham, R., ed. 1973. *Right and left: Essays on dual symbolic classification*. Chicago: University of Chicago Press.

Pouwer, J. 1974. The structural approach: A methodological outline. In Rossi 1974:238–55.

Rossi, I. 1974. *The unconscious in culture*. New York: E. P. Dutton.

Wouden, F. A. E. van. 1968. *Types of social structure in eastern Indonesia*. Trans. R. Needham. Koninklijk Instituut voor Taal-, Land-en- Volkenkunde Translation Series, vol. 2. The Hague: Martinus Nijhoff.

Chapter 1

Category and Complement: Binary Ideologies and the Organization of Dualism in Eastern Indonesia

James J. Fox

It is useful to recall that Lévi-Strauss's 1956 article, "Do Dual Organizations Exist?" was written to honor J. P. B. de Josselin de Jong and that it served as a brief, if somewhat belated, recognition of Dutch research on Indonesian dyadic structures. Lévi-Strauss's intention in the article was to draw a comparison between American Indian and Indonesian forms of dual organization, yet the focus of his comparison was curiously incongruent, since it involved a comparative analysis of the specific social structures of the Winnebago and the Bororo on one hand, and a constructed model of an Indonesian-type social structure on the other. This Indonesian-type model, based on five binary oppositions, was characterized by three positive features: nonresidential marriage classes, prescribed marriage, and an opposition between the sexes, thus supposedly resulting in a system of moieties distinguished as male and female in association with asymmetric or generalized exchange.

This model is intriguing but its derivation is difficult to fathom. Moieties of a sort occur throughout Indonesia, but they are not invariably designated as male and female and their function is rarely to regulate marriage. In some Indonesian societies, specific categories of men and women

The research in eastern Indonesia on which this essay is based spans a considerable period. Fieldwork was conducted under the auspices of the Lembaga Ilmu Pengetahuan Indonesia and in cooperation with the University of Nusa Cendana in Kupang on Timor. To both of these institutions I express my thanks. I would also like to thank the participants of the Dual Organization Conference for their helpful discussion of the essay. In preparing the final draft I benefited in particular from valuable comments from Greg Acciaioli, E. Douglas Lewis, and Maureen MacKenzie.

are defined as strictly marriageable, but these categories do not constitute marriage classes nor are they coincident with a particular clan structure. Systems of asymmetric prescriptive marriage do indeed occur in Indonesia, but they are by no means universal. Indeed such systems constitute a minority in a region where marriage is overwhelmingly nonprescriptive. In western Indonesia various Batak groups provide the outstanding example of asymmetric prescriptive marriage, whereas in eastern Indonesia, societies with such systems are found scattered and interspersed among societies with other forms of marriage, primarily on the islands of Flores, Timor, Sumba, and on some of the islands of the Moluccas. Thus, although it is certainly possible to discern the various elements of Lévi-Strauss's model, their combination conforms to no known Indonesian society. Hence it is reasonable to question the relevance of the model for the comparative analysis of dyadic structures in Indonesia. Yet to dismiss this model as irrelevant would be to ignore its relation (and possible derivation from) the more influential model of eastern Indonesian social structure developed by F. A. E. van Wouden in the doctoral dissertation, entitled "*Types of Social Structure in Eastern Indonesia,*" that he wrote under the direct supervision of J. P. B. de Josselin de Jong in 1935 (subsequently translated and published as van Wouden 1968).

Van Wouden, whose work Lévi-Strauss alludes to in his article, attempted to disentangle an accumulation of disparate ethnographic evidence from eastern Indonesia. Like Lévi-Strauss, van Wouden regarded marriage as the "pivot" for social organization, whose categories provided the basis for an all-embracing cosmological classification. He also noted that "ordinary" (MBD/FZD) cross-cousin marriage and "exclusive" (MBD) cross-cousin marriage represented "two opposed systems of affinal relationships between groups" (1968:90). Since van Wouden thought that these types of marriage formed the foundation for the dualistic and triadic patterns of classification that were so evidently interwoven in the cosmologies of eastern Indonesia, he was obliged to construct a model that reconciled them. In his model, which was intended to represent the original form of Indonesian social organization, van Wouden opted for exclusive cross-cousin marriage but in a closed chain of relationships among an even number of clans. By the logic of this model, if the clans are patrilineal there must be an equal number of latent matrilineal groups, resulting in a "double-unilateral" (or double unilineal) system. The limiting case required four clans that would ideally produce a four-clan or "double two-phratry system." In terms of the model, as van Wouden noted, "dual organization . . . is not required by the system, but can very well accompany it" (1968:88).

In retrospect, although it is possible to comprehend both van Wouden's and Lévi-Strauss's model, it is difficult to resuscitate the intellectual ambience that once made these models so compelling. Both models now seem stunningly simplistic. Both are constructed on a simple set of binary oppositions and are thus implicated in a dualism of the sort they are intended to illuminate. Moreover, both models share the same Durkheimian inheritance that ultimately derives classification in general from the categorization of social forms. As a result, both models focus primarily on the products of classification rather than the processes of classification. For this reason in particular, neither model now offers an appropriate starting point for the study of dyadic structures.

Eastern Indonesia: Three Ethnographic Cases of Dual Structures

In eastern Indonesia (and especially in the Lesser Sundas and the Moluccas) comparative research has developed considerably in recent years. When van Wouden wrote his dissertation he had to draw together and attempt to make sense of perhaps a hundred scattered reports of varying lengths and reliability. He had not a single ethnography of note to guide his speculations. Today, however, there are at least a dozen substantial ethnographies on the region and at least another dozen studies now in preparation.[1] The picture that emerges from these studies is somewhat different from the one that van Wouden sketched.

All of these ethnographies, without exception, confirm the prevalence and importance of dyadic structures. Yet the sheer variety and diversity of these structures militate against any conception of a single institution of "dual organization." Nor is it simply the variety of these dyadic structures among the many different societies of the region that makes it difficult to apply the classic models of dual organization; more difficult still is the application of this concept to the diversity of dyadic structures within any single society. To illustrate what I mean by this, I will describe in outline form the dyadic structures of three neighboring island societies on which I have done fieldwork.

The first case is that of Savu. This island has one of the two societies in eastern Indonesia with a bilineal social organization that might be considered to resemble van Wouden's double unilateral model. Together with the tiny offshore island of Raijua, Savu is composed of five ceremonial domains. Each of these domains is, in turn, composed of named, localized, patrilineal clans (*udu*), which are often further divided into lineages (*kerogo*), all of whom recognize the same "origin" village. Cross-cutting

---

1. The ethnographies of the region include a considerable number of doctoral dissertations that still remain unpublished, including Cunningham 1962; Francillon 1967; Fox 1968; Gordon 1975; Traube 1977; Kana 1978; Lazarowitz 1980; Mitchell 1981; Kuipers 1982; Lewis 1982a; Hoskins 1983; and McKinnon 1983. As a result, the remarkable research that is being carried out in this area is not readily accessible to the field of anthropology as a whole.

the particular allegiances of these localized groups is an islandwide system of ranked matrimoieties: *Hubi Ae,* "The Greater Blossom," and *Hubi Iki,* "The Lesser Blossom." These moieties, "The Blossoms," are further subdivided into *Wini,* "Seeds." On Savu, however, there is neither a terminological nor a systematic rule of marriage governing relationships between patrilineal or matrilineal groups. Instead there is a marked tendency, for reasons of status, for the occurrence of internal marriages within each matrimoiety and intermarriage among high-ranking patrilineal groups.

Each ceremonial domain has its own lunar calendar and a native priesthood to conduct ceremonies in sequence throughout the year. The arrangement of the lunar calendar, the cycle of the ceremonial year, the organization of the priesthood, and the allocation of ritual duties to specific priests and clans are all based on a series of interrelated dyadic structures. In the domain of Liae (see Fox 1979a), the ceremonial year consists in an opposition between the planting season and the lontar-tapping season, the period of ritual silence and the period of gongs and drums, the time when the *Deo Rai* from clan Gopo and his priestly council *Ratu Mone Telu,* "The Three Male Priests," preside and the time when the *Apu Lodo* from Napujara and his council, the *Ratu Mone Pidu,* "The Seven Priests," hold sway. During the high ceremonial season that marks the transition between the two seasons, in the month of Bangaliwu Gopo, the *Deo Rai* takes precedence; in the following month of Bangaliwu Rame, the *Apu Lodo* takes precedence.

The progress of each lunar month is also conceived in terms of a set of oppositions: waxing and waning, east and west, life and death, above and below. And during each month a complex ritual dialectic assigns lineages and clans as opposing groups with specific ritual functions. Thus, for example, in the great cockfighting ritual of the month of Bangaliwu Rame, one lineage of Napujara, the *Apu Lodo's* clan, joins Gopo, the clan of the *Deo Rai,* in ceremonial opposition to the clan Nahai, which is joined by an opposing lineage of Napujara. These groups assemble at different village sites, form groups known as "The Male Group" (*Ada Mone*) and "The Female Group" (*Ada Rena*), and then position themselves at the "upper" and "lower" ends of an enclosure on the top of the hill of Kolarae where they conduct ritual combat with their fighting cocks. Other clans take sides with one or the other group, or divide internally into opposing lineages. The essential point to be made here is that this particular configuration of opposing clans holds only for Bangaliwu Rame; other configurations based on different categories occur in other months of the year. The configuration that I observed and described for Bangaliwu Rame in 1973 is neither fixed nor unchanging but, by common understanding, it is recognized to be, in large part, the result of the internal historical dynamics of the development of the clans of Liae. In effect, on Savu there is no single set of concordant dyadic structures, but rather a proliferation of such structures, each fitted to a particular purpose.

The second case is that of the domain of Thie on the island of Roti. Unlike Savu, Roti has only patrilineal or, more precisely, patronymically ordered descent groups; maternal affiliation, however, is acknowledged for three generations, but this acknowledgement does not form the basis for a coherent matrilineal line of descent. Nor is there any terminologically prescribed rule of marriage.

The island was traditionally divided into eighteen domains and, despite administrative consolidation since 1968, these domains still retain their role as primary communities of orientation (Fox 1977a). For centuries each domain, under its own separate ruler, developed distinctive traditions and, except for a few royal and high noble interdomain marriages, each domain has remained largely endogamous, following distinct rules and customary practices. A common set of basic cultural categories is evident throughout the island, but the social application of these categories varies from domain to domain (Fox 1979b).

In the domain of Thie (and in one other domain, Loleh) a system of marriage moieties has developed. Of Thie's twenty-six clans, fourteen are assigned to the moiety of Sabarai, of the *Manek* or "Male Lord," and twelve are assigned to the moiety of Taratu, of the *Fetor* or "Female Lord." In his dissertation van Wouden devoted special attention to Thie, seeing in the domain a phratry system and, on the basis of hints in one source, even a possible eight-class marriage system. However, when examined in more detail, this dual organization dissolves in a variety of disparate dyadic structures (see Fox 1980a). Each moiety is divided into major clans (*leo inak*) and minor clans (*leo anak*), whose status conforms to that of "noble" and "commoner" in other domains. The group of noble clans in each moiety is further subdivided into various ancestral groupings with specific political functions, while the minor clans within the moiety of Sabarai form a ritual group associated with the powers and fertility of the earth. These minor clans also form a separate marriage unit that may marry either with Taratu or with the major clans of Sabarai. Thus, at a further level of specification, an apparent dual organization becomes a triadic structure.[2]

This moiety system dissolves still further, since one clan on each side

---

2. The case of Thie bears comparison with the case of the Winnebago cited by Lévi-Strauss. From the point of view of Taratu, the moiety that marries only with Sabarai, the organization of the whole remains dyadic; whereas from the point of view of Sabarai, the moiety that is subdivided, the organization of the whole is triadic. Indeed, I have heard sharp arguments among people from Thie as to whether the domain is essentially dyadic or triadic.

is exempt from following any moiety rules—in one case because members of the clan originate from an offshore island, and in the other case because the clan's ancestor is said to have arrived late at the ceremonial gathering at which the moiety system was established. These justificatory explanations further highlight an essential conceptual feature of the moieties. They are not conceived of as a primordial structure but rather the reverse: as a formal historical ordering of an untidy process of clan formation undertaken at the behest of one of the later rulers of the domain.

As on Savu, history is given due recognition in Thie. The assignment of groups to a particular dyadic segment is thus considered to be contingent on past events. This becomes clearer when one examines the various ceremonies that were once performed by the moieties. The major clans of both Sabarai and Taratu performed their own origin celebrations. Four minor clans, two from each moiety, also performed individual celebrations. However, the most important ceremonies were performed by the minor, ritually powerful clans of Sabarai. These clans, of which two were associated with the east and three with the west, were obliged to lead an annual ritual combat. At a ritual feast for all the clans, a rice-pounding block would suddenly be tipped over and those who found themselves to the east of the block joined the two clans of the east and those to the west joined the three clans of the west, thus arbitrarily obliterating all other dual structures. Thus, again as on Savu, there is in Thie, despite initial appearances, no single all-embracing dual organization, but instead a host of particular dyadic structures.

The third case is that of the Atoni of west Timor. Dualism among the Atoni, based on such categories as male and female, inside and outside, and "wife-giver" and "wife-taker," has been amply described for the structure of their domains, their descent groups, and their houses (Cunningham 1964, 1965, 1966; Schulte Nordholt 1971, 1980). Unlike the Savunese and Rotinese, the Atoni do have a terminological rule of symmetric marriage, though by preference they tend to arrange particular marriages in an asymmetric fashion. Despite this rule, however, the organization of descent groups defies simple description. In general, domains on the island of Timor are larger than those on Roti or Savu and settlement is more scattered. Moreover, the continual migration of different segments of named descent groups throughout the island has produced a heterogeneous structure within each domain. Thus, a domain whose traditional structure was founded on an idealized set of relationships among certain leading clans, actually consists of a myriad of local relationships among minimal descent groups. Narratives of the wanderings of the ancestors acknowledge these formative processes, all of which create a situation not unlike that of Roti and Savu, where there exist multiple dyadic structures but no classic dual organization.

Faced with the ethnographic situation in eastern Indonesia, certain conclusions can be drawn. Clearly, the classic models of dual organization appear inappropriate, for there is no single organizational form for the variety of dyadic structures that are to be found either within any one society or among the numerous different societies of eastern Indonesia. Furthermore, since the variety of dyadic structures implies an absence of a formal concordance between social and symbolic forms, the study of dual classification risks becoming a typological enumeration of dual structures. Hence I would argue that what is needed is not a further study of the products of classification, but of the processes of classification.

Such a study must be undertaken at two levels: first, at a general, abstract level that focuses on the features that seem to underlie processes of dual symbolic classification, and then at a categorical level that focuses on the way in which specific sets of categories form complex systems of symbolic classification. The first level allows comparison with other societies throughout the world, while the second level can only relate to a reasonably defined ethnographic field of study—to historically related societies that share common linguistic categories. Whereas the first level necessarily requires a degree of formalism, close attention to the second level leads ultimately to an intimate examination of related metaphors for living. Since the two levels are related, however, I shall attempt to examine processes of dual classification in relation to the ethnography of eastern Indonesia, focusing on five features of dual symbolic classification systems in eastern Indonesia: (1) parallelism, (2) recursive complementarity, (3) categorical asymmetry, (4) category reversal, and (5) analogical cross-over.[3]

The Processes of Dual Classification in Eastern Indonesia

Parallelism

Roman Jakobson has argued that the principle of parallelism is implicated in all poetic statements. Jakobson's notion of parallelism is broadly

3. Because at this stage I am primarily interested in describing the classificatory phenomena encountered in eastern Indonesia, I am content to use the term "feature" rather than "principle." Some of these features can occur together, as for example, "recursive complementarity" and "categorical asymmetry." Furthermore, "recursion" and "complementarity" could well be distinguished as analytically separate, though in dual symbolic classification it is precisely their conjunction that is significant. See R. Needham (1980) for an analytic schema in which "duality" is itself a principle.

relevant to an understanding of symbolic statements in general (Fox 1977b: 59–60) and, as I have argued, to ritual performances as well (Fox 1979a: 169–71). Here, however, I will confine myself to the strict form of parallelism known generally as "canonical parallelism," since virtually all of the societies of eastern Indonesia use some form of canonical parallelism for the expression and transmission of ritual knowledge.[4] Generally this parallelism takes the form of a ritual language in which all or most semantic elements are paired in dyadic sets, structured in formulaic phrases, and expressed as couplets or parallel verses (Fox 1971a, 1974, 1975).

As an example of this form of canonical parallelism, I present a brief Rotinese ritual composition by the chanter, L. Manoeain, of the domain of Ba'a.

1 *Sa Lepa-Lai nunun*
     The *waringin* tree of Sa Lepa-Lai
2 *Ma Huak Lali-Ha kekan*
     And the banyan tree of Huak Lali-Ha.
3 *Keka maba'e faluk*
     The banyan has eight branches
4 *Ma nunan mandana siok*
     And the *waringin* has nine boughs:
5 *De dalak ko sio boe*
     Nine roads indeed
6 *Ma enok ko falu boe*
     And eight paths as well.
7 *Fo dala sodak nai ndai*
     The road of well-being is there
8 *Ma eno mamates nai na*
     And the path of death is there.
9 *De suli malamumula*
     Therefore watch with care
10 *Ma mete makananae*
     And look with attention.
11 *Ndanak esa dulu neu*
     One branch points east,
12 *Ma boso musik ndia*
     But do not follow that

---

4. See Fox, ed., 1988. This volume contains ten essays on different ritual languages in the region; each essay examines particular uses to which canonical parallelism is put.

13 *Te fiti-ngge ledon dalan ndia*
> For the *fiti-ngge* on the sun's road is there
14 *Ma telu-ta'e bulan enon ndia*
> And the *telu-ta'e* on the moon's path is there.
15 *De fiti-ngge fiti-fiti*
> The *fiti-ngge* thrusts and thrusts
16 *Ma telu-ta'e tati-tati*
> And the *telu-ta'e* chops and chops.[5]
17 *De nggelo lesuk nai ndia*
> The breaking of the neck is there
18 *Ma ladi puk nai ndia*
> And snapping of the thigh is there.
19 *Ndanak esa muli neu*
> One branch points west,
20 *Boso musik ndanak ndia*
> Do not follow that branch
21 *Te nitu hitu dalan ndia*
> For this is the road of seven spirits
22 *Ma mula falu enon ndia*
> And this is the path of eight ghosts,
23 *De mate nituk nai ndia*
> The death of the spirits is there
24 *Ma lalo mulak nai ndia*
> And the decease of the ghosts is there.
25 *Ndanak esa ki neu*
> One branch points north (left),
26 *Boso musik ndanak ndia*
> Do not follow that branch
27 *Te pila bi'i-late dalan ndia*
> For this is the road of the red goat's grave spider
28 *Ma modo bolau enon ndia*
> And this is the path of the blue-green poisonous spider,
29 *De peta-aok nai ndia*
> The swelling of the body is there
30 *Ma'hina-talek nai na*
> And the festering wound is there.

---

5. *Fiti-ngge* and *Telu-ta'e* are particular named spirits associated with (the temptation to) incest.

31 *Ndanak esa kona neu*
   One branch points south (right),
32 *Boso musik ndanak ndia*
   Do not follow that branch
33 *Te manufui tela dalan ndia*
   For this is the road of forest fowl
34 *Ma kukuha nau enon ndia*
   And this is the path of the four-taloned grass bird,
35 *De o leno kada telas dale*
   You only wander within the forest
36 *Ma o pela kada na'u dale*
   And you only turn within the grass.
37 *Te ndana esa lido-lido lain neu*
   But one branch goes forward toward Heaven
38 *Ma dape-dape ata neu*
   And (one branch) goes straight to the Heights.
39 *Na musik ndanak ndia*
   Then take that branch
40 *Te dala sodak nde ndia*
   For this is the road of well-being
41 *Ma eno molik nde ndia*
   And this is the path of life
42 *Fo nini o mu losa kapa sula soda daen*
   To bring you to the buffalo-horn land of well-being
43 *Ma mu nduku pa-dui molek oen*
   And to the flesh-and-bone water of life.
44 *Dae sodak nai ndia*
   The land of well-being is there
45 *Ma oe molik nai na*
   And the water of life is there,
46 *Fo o hambu soda sio*
   For you will find the well-being of nine
47 *Ma o hambu mole falu*
   And you will find the life of eight
48 *Ma dua lolo ei*
   And with legs outstretched
49 *Ma kala ifa lima*
   And with arms cradled on the lap
50 *Fo ifa limam no limam*
   Cradle your arms upon your arms
51 *Ma lolo eim no eim*
   And stretch your legs over your legs.

This composition shows the power of parallelism to create a cosmology, simply and effectively: the world-*waringin* as the tree of life with its branches as paths leading in different directions. The composition is seemingly traditional: the parallelism is impeccable, and standard formulas (as, for example, "the buffalo-horn land of well-being / the flesh-and-bone water of life") are strictly maintained. Moreover, the cosmology created by the imagery of the composition accords with a common tree-of-life cosmology found throughout Indonesia. The fact is, however, that this cosmology does not conform to the standard cultural cosmology of the Rotinese which, based on imagery of the island as a creature laid out lengthwise, assigns entirely different values to the directions, giving priority to the south and east over the north and west (see Fox 1973:356–58). The blind chanter, "Old Manoeain," who recited this composition for me, was one of the leading Protestant Ministers on Roti and was renowned for his use of Rotinese ritual language in his sermons (see Fox 1983a). His composition, as far as I can determine, is a personal attempt to create a kind of Christian cosmology. The essential point is that it offers an alternative cosmology—another possible world—using the same dualistic linguistic resources that are regularly used to express and uphold the standard cosmology.

The proper use of these linguistic resources requires a minimal knowledge of at least 1,000 dyadic sets. This entails highly specific knowledge of which nouns, verbs, adjectives, and prepositional forms may pair to form "canonical" dyads. Thus, for example, one must know not just that "north" (*ki*) may pair with "south" (*kona*), but that *moi*, which functions as either an adjective or a verb meaning "slick, smooth, to lick" forms a canonical pair with *keni*, "shiny, glossy, to polish"; or that *nafi*, "sea-cucumber," only forms a set with *sisik*, "mollusc"; or that *delas*, the *dedap* tree (*erythina* spp.) must be paired with *nitas*, the *kelumpang* tree (*Sterculia foetida*); or that *melu*, "stomach-cramps," only pairs with *langu*, "headache"; or that *nggio*, which describes the "creaking or scraping" of tree branches, must be linked to *ke*, which refers to "annoyance or teasing"; and so on through hundreds of specific dyadic sets.

This pervasive parallelism, however, is entirely neutral. It may contribute to and sustain a thoroughgoing and highly particularized dualistic perception of the symbolic world, but on its own it is insufficient to constitute the kind of ordered dyadic structures associated with dual organizations and dual cosmologies. A dual cosmology—as indeed any dual organization—is characterized not by a simple pairing of elements but by the analogical concordance of elements within pairs according to some criterion of asymmetry. The rules of parallelism provide no such criterion. Hence dyadic sets are essentially neutral pairs: one element is not superior to another and either element may precede the other in expression. Extralinguistic criteria are required to transform parallel elements into the elements of a dual organization or cosmology.

Moreover, systems of canonical parallelism of the kind that are to be found throughout eastern Indonesia are an overly rich resource of dual categories. Most dual organizations rely on a relatively limited number of categories. Only a selection of categories, rather than all the resources of canonical parallelism, would suffice for this function. In short, the canonical parallelism of the ritual languages of eastern Indonesia may account for the elaborateness of dualistic structures in the region, but it cannot explain them. Thus, the argument must be extended further.

Recursive Complementarity

Dutch anthropology has long insisted on the importance of complementary dualism to the understanding of societies in Indonesia and elsewhere (see P. E. de Josselin de Jong 1977). The complementary categories denoted in these studies are a familiar feature of what is often called two-column analysis: ordered lists of general categories arranged as complementary pairs.

right	left
day	night
sun	moon
east	west
red	black

The possibility of constructing such a table for almost any society and the occurrence of at least some common categories in all such tables limit the usefulness of this kind of analytic exercise. Two-column analysis hardly offers more than a beginning to an understanding of complementary dualism.

In eastern Indonesia the most important and recurrent complementary categories reflect a common Austronesian derivation and a historically shared inheritance of similar metaphors for living. These categories include a variety of directional and spatial coordinates such as north-south, east-west, inside-outside, back-front, right-left, and upward-downward. Equally important are color categories (white-black, red-gold–blue-green), categories for parts of the body (head-tail, or head-buttock), categories for persons and gender (elder-younger, male-female), botanical categories (unripe-ripe, trunk-tip, planted-harvested), and other categories for qualities (cool-hot, bland-bitter). Some of these categories are more than just symbolically associated: they are linguistically synonymous or even identical. Thus, left-right is, in some societies, synonymous with north-south. Similarly, botanical categories which provide the principal metaphors for growth and development may have color or spatial connotations. The complementary colors green-gold may also be synonymous with the categories unripe-ripe, while the categories of trunk-tip imply a spatial-temporal notion of origin and extension.

The major point, however, is that this array of complementary categories represents a relatively small selection from the total resources of all possible canonical pairs furnished by the parallelism of ritual languages. The configuration of this select array of categories varies from one eastern Indonesian society to another, but in each society it constitutes what Needham has described as the set of "primary factors" in that society's symbolic classification (R. Needham 1978:12–13). Moreover, and more importantly, these categories serve as the "operators" of the symbolic system, that is, as organizing elements for the classification of other categories and qualities. In this regard, what is significant is the *recursion* of these categories — the way in which they may be applied successively in various contexts and at many levels of signification.

The categories of male-female provide an excellent illustration of recursive complementarity. On Roti, these categories (*mane-feto*) may apply to persons as well as to certain kinds of trees and plants, to political offices, and, in Thie, to opposing moieties; they may also be applied within descent groups to distinguish client lineages, or between descent groups to indicate wife-givers and wife-takers. These categories may also be applied to different gifts exchanged by wife-givers and wife-takers. At yet another level these categories differentiate between the *sirih* or betel catkin, which is always masculine, and the *pinang* or areca nut, which is feminine — objects mutually offered by both sides in ceremonial exchange.

Forth, in a recent ethnography on the domain of Rindi in east Sumba, indicates how this recursion of male-female categories is extended even further in differentiating articles of bridewealth given by wife-takers. To begin with, all bridewealth objects (which consist of horses plus gold, silver, or tin chains and pendants) are classified as masculine in opposition to the dowry goods (textiles, beads, and ivory bands) given by wife-givers. Internally, however, "masculine" goods are distinguished as male and female: horses as a category are male, whereas metal valuables are female. At a further level, horses are distinguished as male and female and should be given as a pair consisting of a stallion and a mare. The metal valuables are also distinguished as male and female: chains are considered masculine and pendants female, and these categorically feminine pendants are still further distinguished according to their decoration as male or female. Similar distinctions can be applied to the "feminine" goods given by the

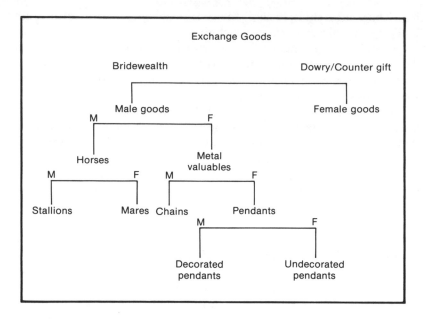

Fig. 1. Male and female exchange goods

wife-givers: textiles must include men's cloths and women's skirts, and so on (Forth 1981:360–61).

By this principle of recursive complementarity, nothing is exclusively of one category; anything that is categorized according to one component of a complementary pair can *potentially* contain elements of its complement.[6] A great deal of the symbolic elaboration of dualistic structures in eastern Indonesia involves playing with this principle of recursive complementarity: male contains female, female contains male; inside contains outside, and outside, the inside; black, white, and white, black. Similarly, wife-givers are also wife-takers, and a group that is classified as elder to one group may be younger to another.

6. This feature of recursive complementarity is not unique to eastern Indonesia. It is the basic idea underlying the ancient Chinese concept of yin and yang. As Maureen Mac-Kenzie has pointed out to me, Joseph Neeham (1956: pl. 16) has reproduced a "segregation table" of the *Book of Changes* deriving from the twelfth century that essentially parallels my diagram of exchange goods on Sumba. As Needham notes: "Yin and Yang separate, but each contains half of its opposite in a 'recessive' state, as is seen when the second division occurs. There is no logical end to the processes but here it is not followed beyond the stage of the 64 hexagrams."

This principle should not be confused with hierarchy, since it is not wholly systematic and it rarely achieves great taxonomic depth. Other factors affect the application of this principle. Thus it is essential to know in any society in eastern Indonesia which sets of complementary categories apply. In Roti, for example, the categories male-female can be applied to distinguish the two unequal halves of the traditional house. Their application, in this case, is coincident with the categories outside-inside. On the basis of this coincidence, however, to apply male-female categories to the "Spirits of the Outside" and the "Spirits of the Inside" would produce a confusion of categories. In effect, no single set of recursive categories is applied systematically throughout the culture.

Categorical Asymmetry

Another feature of those recursive complementary pairs that serve as "operators" for the elaborate dual structures is their asymmetry. In this regard, parallelism is entirely neutral, always consisting of undifferentially paired semantic elements. In Rotinese ritual language, just as there are no criteria to distinguish the verb *ifa,* "to hold on the lap," as, for example, somehow marked in relation to its pair *koo,* "to cradle in the arms or on the hip," so too one cannot differentiate the directional *dulu,* "east," from its pair *muli,* "west." Yet, when east-west are used as recursive complements, east is definitely superior to west. On Roti, where the conflict between traditional and Christian cosmologies has, it seems, prompted a conscious need to justify the traditional, there exist a number of aphorisms that serve as symbolic syllogisms to give "value" to the directional coordinates. Thus, for example, *Dulu nalu muli, te hu ledo neme dulu mai, de dulu ba'u lena muli*: "East is as broad as the west, but the sun comes from the east, therefore the east is much greater than the west." All of the other recursive complements that I have mentioned are similarly distinguished in an asymmetric fashion, although not all are as consciously justified: male is "superior" to female, inside to outside, head to tail, red-gold to blue-green.

This categorical asymmetry is, in some ways, similar to markedness, but whereas markedness pertains to linguistic levels that are largely arbitrary and unconscious, this asymmetry of complementary categories occurs in socially constructed symbolic systems that can be consciously manipulated. Moreover, the category that is "marked as superior" functions as the equivalent of the unmarked category. Thus, in those contexts where one component of a complementary pair is required to stand for the whole, it is the category marked as "superior." Hence "male" may stand for the whole in regard to persons, "inside" for the whole of various bound structures, or "head" in certain contexts for overall authority or precedence. The very existence of such categorical asymmetry, however, creates the possibility of its inversion.

Category Reversal

Category reversal refers to a change in the polarity of any set of complementary categories. This only occurs in special contexts when proper order is subverted and the "world is turned upside down": outside becomes superior to inside, female to male, west to east, north to south, and so on, in terms of the standard dual asymmetries of the culture.[7]

In eastern Indonesia the contexts for inversion are considered "extraordinary" even when they occur with annual regularity. On Savu, category reversal appears to be associated with the transition from one calendar year to the next; on Timor, reversal was crucial to headhunting, which invariably occurred in the dry season (McWilliam 1982); on Roti, minor reversals occur at all funerals, but major reversals are associated with the burial of those who have died a bad death (Fox 1973). More generally, however, some Rotinese characterize the whole period of Dutch dominance over the island as a time of partial inversion of the proper cosmic order. In the Rotinese cosmology, south (right), which is the direction of maximal spiritual power, is superior to north (left), which is the direction of sorcery and bad death. During the colonial period, however, the island was under the spell of the Dutch and the proper order was partially inverted. A symbolic syllogism recorded from the domain of Oepao at the turn of the century is reported as follows: *Ona ba'u i boe, te hu Komponi nai i, de i ba'u lena ona*: "The South (Right) is as great as the North (Left), but the Company (i.e. the Dutch government) is in the North, therefore the North is greater than the South" (Jonker 1913:613). This period, which the Rotinese also describe as a time of native "ignorance" and "lefthandedness," ended with the achievement of independence and the return of symbolic power to the south.

Analogical Cross-over

I use the term "analogical cross-over" to refer to another prominent feature of dual symbolic classification in eastern Indonesia. This feature is

---

7. This is similar to what is sometimes referred to in linguistics as "markedness reversal."

not an aspect of a single set of dual categories but rather pertains to the potential ordering of complex sets of such categories. It is specifically a property of historically developing systems in particular contexts.

Standard two-column analysis of complementary pairs consists in a simple analogical arrangement based upon the asymmetric valence accorded these categories. The result is an apparent concordance. As I have indicated, it is possible to change the valency of any or all of these categories. In eastern Indonesia this occurs periodically at "special" intervals and I have termed this change in valency "category reversal." But it is also possible to retain standard valencies and instead change the analogical association between sets of complementary categories. It is this that I term "analogical cross-over."

An illustration of this feature can be taken from the symbolic classification of the Atoni Pah Meto of Timor. As among the Rotinese, the categories male-female (*mone-feto*) form important recursive complements. In most relational contexts, male is superior to female. *Mone,* for example, is used to refer to the wife-giver and, in any local settlement, refers to the *Atoni Amaf,* the "Father" or "Father Atoni," who represents the founding lineage segment in the area. Those who have come after this founder and have become wife-takers are designated as *feto.* Similarly, the categories outside-inside form another important set of recursive complements; as a set, inside is considered superior to outside. Thus both inside and male are given a positive valency in relation to their mutual complements, outside and female. There is, however, a further factor that affects the analogical association of these pairs. Timorese folk etymology links the word for "male" with a similar word meaning "outside." The combination of these categories leads to analogical cross-over:

$$
\begin{array}{ccc}
\text{male} & : & : \quad \text{female} \\
\text{inside} & : & : \quad \text{outside}
\end{array}
$$

Male, which is superior in certain contexts, is associated with the outside, which is inferior; and female, which is a subordinate category, is associated with the inside, which is superior. The logic of these categories produces a tension that pervades the traditional classification system of the *Atoni,* expressing itself in an ideal model of four political units represented as four "Fathers" grouped around a female center. Like a four-pillared Atoni *lopo,* these male figures "support" a female center but remain subordinate by their outside position.

Schulte Nordholt, who has described the Atoni political system at length (1971), has provided another example of this kind of analogical cross-over in the various permutations of relationships among the four clans in Bikomi and Miomafo. In their affinal relations, Bana and Senak are male; while Atok and Lahe are female. By one ritual division, Lahe and Senak are inside and hence female, while Atok and Bana are male and outside; but by another internal division, Senak represents the immobile center, which is female but superior to Lahe, who represents the active male outside (Schulte Nordholt 1980). A similar form of analogical cross-over seems once to have formed the basis of the sacred hegemony of the "matrilineal" Tetun, whose center was at Wehale (Fox 1983b).

The possibility of analogical cross-over exists in all systems where a variety of complementary categories are applied to the same groups, persons, or objects. The interplay of these categories in different contexts allows the creation of multiple alternative perspectives, or at least marks the contexts where alternate perspectives may apply.

None of the societies of eastern Indonesia appear to have perfectly concordant symbolic systems in which all groups or objects can be classified by categories that define them unequivocally in relation to other groups and objects. The discrepancies between different sets of complementary categories, extended too far for coherence sake, can only lead to evident contradictions. In eastern Indonesian societies, evident contradiction is often avoided by a continual process of mixing metaphors. Instead of allowing any set of complements to be extended to the point of contradiction, other complements are introduced to develop the system.

A brief contrast between Roti and Timor may help to illustrate this point. Roti shares with Timor the same complementary categories of male-female and outside-inside (though in the case of Roti, *mane,* "male," is not linked explicitly to a word for "outside"). Nevertheless, the same asymmetries and associations hold true for these categories, and the potential for analogical reversal of the kind that has become elaborated on Timor is evident in Rotinese symbolic classification. The two halves of the Rotinese house, for example, are classified as male-female and outside-inside, the male half being the outside half. On the other hand, in the political realm, the "Male-Lord" (*Manek*), who is the ruler of the domain, occupies the center or inside and the subordinate "Female Lord" is relegated to the outside. Among the Rotinese, the inconsistencies and potential contradictions in these realms are muted, but a further problem arises in the classification of spirits which are categorized as belonging to two groups: "Spirits of the Outside," and "Spirits of the Inside." "Inside" in this case is in reference to the house and, by analogy with other associations within the house, these spirits might conceivably be considered as "female." This, however, is not done. Instead, a series of other complementary categories (east-west, firstborn–last-born) are commonly applied, and by various associations (inside = west = last-born) the last-born male, who inherits the house, assumes the role of guardian of the Spirits of the Inside.

The point I wish to make is that the possibilities for analogical cross-over in these systems are innumerable, but the ones that are given cultural attention may be relatively limited. The Timorese, as well as the Tetun of Wehale, seem to have fashioned one analogical cross-over into a mystery on which to found a potent political ideology (Fox 1983b).

Conclusions

Before I venture some remarks on the relationship between dualism and hierarchy in eastern Indonesia, it is essential to make clear what is being discussed when these terms are invoked. Dualism, for example, is defined in the *Shorter Oxford English Dictionary* as a "twofold division" or "two-fold condition." Since this definition neither specifies the relations that may hold between dual entities nor makes precise the coherence that may pertain within a dyadic division, it does little to elucidate the complex classificatory phenomena that are generally referred to under the rubric of dualism, particularly in the ethnographic literature on eastern Indonesia. The same might be said of the use of the term "hierarchy," which tends to be used to describe a variety of social phenomena.

Dumont, in his discussion of the Indian caste system, has attempted to give a more precise definition to the term "hierarchy." He defines hierarchy as "the principle by which the elements of a whole are ranked in the relation to the whole," and he goes on to link this "principle of hierarchy" to a single "opposition between the pure and the impure" (1970:66). In turn, this opposition is analytically interpreted as a relation between "that which encompasses and that which is encompassed" (1970:xii).

As useful as this definition of hierarchy may be, an attempt to apply it in eastern Indonesia is problematic for several reasons. The societies of eastern Indonesia do not have the encompassing religious coherence that Dumont has attributed to India; for this reason, hierarchy cannot be described as a single principle nor identified with a specific opposition, such as pure and impure. In eastern Indonesia there are a variety of contending oppositions that are of considerable importance to the definition of hierarchy and it is not one opposition but the interplay among various oppositions that gives rank to elements of a whole in relation to the whole.[8] In

---

8. I take as fundamental Dumont's assertion that judgment must be made in terms of the "whole," but it is pertinent to note that a "whole" organized by various interacting principles appears differently to that of a "whole" organized by a single principle.

these terms, hierarchy is not a principle but an outcome, the result of the application of several principles. By the same token, it is equally problematic to base a conception of hierarchy solely on the analytic distinction between the encompassing and the encompassed. Apart from the fact that the logic of this distinction is, at times, elusive, this is not the only distinction by which "hierarchy" can be generated.

It is possible, however, to derive another lead from Dumont. In a crucial passage in *Homo Hierarchicus,* Dumont refers to hierarchy as "an order of precedence" (1970:75). Adapting this phrase for eastern Indonesia, we may consider hierarchy as consisting of various orders of precedence. The issue, then is to examine the way in which these orders of precedence are categorically structured using prevalent dyadic resources.

The hierarchical use of dual categories depends upon the conjunction of two analytic features: recursive complementarity and categorical asymmetry. With these features, a single set of dual categories can serve as the operator to produce an ordered sequence or graded series. As an example, we may consider the set of dual relative age categories elder-younger, which in eastern Indonesia are generally relied on to define relationships between persons or among groups that are regarded as sharing some aspect of common descent (see Fox 1980b:331). Thus, among the Rotinese, Timorese, or Tetun, these same-sex categories can be used to distinguish a graded series of status segments within a clan, lineage, or birth group. Since a segment in the younger category may be elder to another segment, this series may be represented as follows:

elder	younger		
	elder	younger	
		elder	younger

A similar series based on male-female may be used, as among the Timorese, to define an order of precedence between wife-givers and wife-takers:

male	female		
	male	female	
		male	female

In eastern Indonesia the complementary categories used to create ordered series are the same categories that serve as operators for the system as a whole. Besides elder-younger or male-female, such categories as wife-giver–wife-taker, left-right, inside-outside, or trunk-tip (see Traube, in this

volume) are particularly prominent. In a remarkable analysis of the ceremonial domain, Wai Brama, of the Ata Tana Ai of central east Flores,
E. Douglas Lewis (1982a) has shown how a single line of precedence based
on "origin from the source" constitutes the means for a coherent ordering
of all clans and segments of the domain.[9] In a somewhat different context,
a single royal descent line serves as the ultimate line of precedence for the
hierarchical ordering of lineages and clans in the domain of Termanu on
Roti. In this case, however, the ordered series is not structured by a common set of complementary categories but by a precise and rigidly maintained succession of ancestral dyadic names, each of which—after the first
name—utilizes a component of the preceding name (Fox 1971b:42–47).

This leads to the final point I wish to make in this essay. Dualism is
a prevalent conceptual resource in eastern Indonesia and as such it may
be used either as a major vehicle for the structuring of hierarchy or as a
counter to it. In another essay (Fox 1979b) I have examined in detail the
political and economic differences between the hierarchical structure of
the domain of Termanu and the moiety structure of the domain of Thie.
In analyzing these two domains on Roti, it would be impossible to claim
that there was more use of dualism in one domain than in the other. Both
domains give evidence of elaborate forms of dualism. In Termanu, however, dual categories are utilized socially to form lines of precedence that
foster status rivalry, extend alliance relations, and perpetrate patterns of
relative dependence. By contrast, in Thie the primary conceptualization
of the domain is a dichotomy into moieties that are associated as male-
female. Thus, for Thie, dualism occurs at the highest order of social classification and, though qualified by other dyadic divisions, this primary
dualism has systemic implications for the whole of the domain's system
of classification. Any tendency to form lines of precedence always confronts a primary duality that undermines it. As a result, in Thie a systemic
dualism serves as a counter to hierarchy.

We may therefore conclude with the observation that it is not dualism
per se that defines societies with so-called dual organization but rather the
use of dualism at a general, systemic, level which thus determines the
parameters for other forms of classification.

---

9. Lewis's thesis, which is shortly to be published in revised form in the Verhandelingen of the Koninklijk Instituut voor Taal-, Land- en Volkenkunde, contains a superb discussion of the Ata Tana Ai concept of precedence, and I wish to acknowledge my debt to this
illuminating discussion that has prompted me to see a variety of ways in which the notion
of precedence occurs in the societies of eastern Indonesia. It should be noted, however, that
a similar notion of precedence is implied in Gordon's examination of the "marriage nexus"
among the Manggarai of west Flores (1980:65–67).

REFERENCES

Cunningham, Clark E. 1962. People of the dry land: A study of the social organization of an Indonesian people. Ph.D. thesis, Oxford University.

———. 1964. Order in the Atoni house. *Bijdragen tot de Taal-, Land- en Volkenkunde* 120:34–68.

———. 1965. Order and change in an Atoni diarchy. *Southwestern Journal of Anthropology* 21:359–83.

———. 1966. Categories of descent groups in a Timorese village. *Oceania* 37:13–21.

Dumont, Louis. 1970. *Homo hierarchicus: The caste system and its implications.* Trans. M. Sainsbury. Chicago: University of Chicago Press.

Forth, Gregory L. 1981. *Rindi: An ethnographic study of a traditional domain in eastern Sumba.* Verhandelingen van het Koninklijk Instituut voor Taal-, Land- en Volkenkunde, no. 93. The Hague: Martinus Nijhoff.

Fox, James J. 1968. The Rotinese: A study of the social organization of an eastern Indonesian people. Ph.D. thesis, Oxford University.

———. 1971a. Semantic parallelism in Rotinese ritual language. *Bijdragen tot de Taal-, Land- en Volkenkunde* 127:215–55.

———. 1971b. A Rotinese dynastic genealogy: Structure and event. In *The translation of culture,* ed. T. Beidelman, 37–77. London: Tavistock Press.

———. 1973. On bad death and the left hand: A study of Rotinese symbolic inversions. In *Right and left: Essays on dual symbolic classification,* ed. R. Needham, 342–68. Chicago: University of Chicago Press.

———. 1974. Our ancestors spoke in pairs: Rotinese views of language, dialect, and code. In *Explorations in the ethnography of speaking,* ed. R. Bauman and J. Sherzer, 65–85. Cambridge: Cambridge University Press.

———. 1975. On binary categories and primary symbols: Some Rotinese perspectives. In *The interpretation of symbolism,* ed. R. Willis, 99–132. ASA Studies, vol. 2. London: Malaby.

———. 1977a. *Harvest of the palm: Ecological change in eastern Indonesia.* Cambridge: Harvard University Press.

———. 1977b. Roman Jakobson and the comparative study of parallelism. In *Roman Jakobson: Echoes of his scholarship,* ed. C. H. van Schooneveld and D. Armstrong, 59–90. Lisse: Peter de Ridder Press.

———. 1979a. The ceremonial system of Savu. In *The imagination of reality: Essays on Southeast Asian coherence systems,* ed. A. Becker and A. A. Yengoyan, 145–73. Norwood, N.J.: Ablex.

———. 1979b. A tale of two states: Ecology and the political economy of inequality on the island of Roti. In *Social and ecological systems,* ed. P. Burnham and R. F. Ellen, 19–42. Association of Social Anthropologists Monograph, no. 18. London: Academic Press.

———. 1980a. Obligation and alliance: State structure and moiety organization in Thie, Roti. In Fox, ed., 1980:98–133.

———. 1980b. Models and metaphors: Comparative research in eastern Indonesia. In Fox, ed., 1980: 327–33.

————. 1983a. The Rotinese *chotbah* as a linguistic performance. In *Papers from the Third International Conference on Austronesian Linguistics.* Vol. 3, Accent on variety, ed. A. Halim, L. Carrington, and S. A. Wurm, 311–18. Canberra: Pacific Linguistics.

————. 1983b. The Great Lord rests at the centre: The paradox of powerlessness in European-Timorese relations. *Canberra Anthropology* 5(2):22–33.

Fox, James J., ed. 1980. *The flow of life: Essays on eastern Indonesia.* Cambridge: Harvard University Press.

————. 1988. *To speak in pairs: Essays on the ritual languages of eastern Indonesia.* Cambridge: Cambridge University Press.

Francillon, Gérard. 1967. Some matriarchic aspects of the social structure of the Tetun of middle Timor. Ph.D. thesis, Australian National University, Canberra.

Gordon, John L. 1975. The Manggarai: Economic and social transformation in an eastern Indonesian society. Ph.D. diss., Harvard University.

————. 1980. The marriage nexus among the Manggarai of west Flores. In Fox, ed., 1980:48–67.

Hoskins, Janet. 1983. Spirit worship and feasting in Kodi, West Sumba: Paths to riches and renown. Ph.D. diss., Harvard University.

Jonker, J. C. G. 1913. Bijdragen tot de kennis der Rottineesche tongvallen. *Bijdragen tot de Taal-, Land- en Volkenkunde* 58:521–622.

Josselin de Jong, P. E. de., ed. 1977. *Structural anthropology in the Netherlands.* Koninklijk Instituut voor Taal-, Land- en Volkenkunde Translation Series. The Hague: Martinus Nijhoff.

Kana, Nico L. 1978. Dunia Orang Sawu: Satu lukisan analitis tentang azas-azas penataan dalam kebudayaan Orang Mahara di Sawu, Nusa Tenggara Timur. Ph.D. thesis, Universitas Indonesia.

Kuipers, Joel C. 1982. Weyewa ritual speech: A study of language and ceremonial interaction in eastern Indonesia. Ph.D. diss., Yale University.

Lazarowitz, Toby F. 1980. The Makassai: Complementary dualism in Timor. Ph.D. diss., State University of New York at Stony Brook.

Lévi-Strauss, Claude. 1956. Les organisations dualistes, existent-elles? *Bijdragen tot de Taal-, Land- en Volkenkunde* 112:99–128.

Lewis, E. Douglas. 1982a. Tana Wai Brama: A study of the social organization of an eastern Florenese domain. Ph.D. thesis, Australian National University, Canberra.

————. 1982b. The metaphorical expression of gender and dual classification in Tana Ai ritual language. *Canberra Anthropology* 5(1):47–59.

McKinnon, Susan M. 1983. Hierarchy, alliance and exchange in the Tanimbar islands, Ph.D. diss., University of Chicago.

McWilliam, Andrew. 1982. Harvest of the Nakaf: A study of head-hunting among the Atoni of west Timor. B. Litt. thesis, Australian National University, Canberra.

Mitchell, Instutiah Gunawan. 1981. Hierarchy and balance: A study of Wanukaka social organisation. Ph.D. thesis, Monash University, Melbourne.

Needham, Joseph. 1956. *Science and civilization in China: History of scientific thought.* Vol. 2. Cambridge: Cambridge University Press.

Needham, Rodney. 1978. *Primordial characters.* Charlottesville: University Press of Virginia.

———. 1980. Principles and variations in the structure of Sumbanese society. In Fox, ed., 1980: 21–47.

Schulte Nordholt, H. G. 1971. *The political system of the Atoni of Timor.* Verhandelingen van het Koninklijk Instituut voor Taal-, Land- en Volkenkunde, no. 60. The Hague: Martinus Nijhoff.

———. 1980. The symbolic classification of the Atoni of Timor. In Fox, ed., 1980: 231–47.

Traube, Elizabeth G. 1977. Ritual exchange among the Mambai of East Timor: Gifts of life and death. Ph.D. diss., Harvard University.

Wouden, F. A. E. van. 1968. *Types of social structure in eastern Indonesia.* Trans. R. Needham. Koninklijk Instituut voor Taal-, Land- en Volkenkunde Translation Series, vol. 2. The Hague: Martinus Nijhoff.

Chapter 2

Ritual and Inequality
in Guji Dual Organization

John Hinnant

One of the major problems with the general literature on dual organization is the frequent failure to look at transformations in dualistic systems
of thought and social organization over time. Analyses tend to be concerned with a set of oppositions within a particular social matrix or a particular ideological system as viewed at one moment in time. Observers
generally ignore the developmental cycle of the dualistic system. For example, Lévi-Strauss, in his essay "Do dual organizations exist?" [1956],
by contrasting diametric and concentric models for Winnebego village
organization, attempted to demonstrate that concentric dualism is dynamic relative to diametric dualism in that the former can be transformed
into the latter but that the reverse cannot occur. Here the dynamic aspect is really a rule for transformation between two different kinds of opposition rather than a long-term development within a complex set of
oppositions.

The essays in this volume are devoted in part to correcting the static
atemporal view of dual organization.[1] Tuzin, for example, in discussing
Arapesh dualism, states, "The dual organization is quintessentially both
structure and process, it simultaneously signifies, acts upon, and reconciles the existential disjunction between living wholes and the mundane,
inanimate parts of which they are composed."

Tuzin's statement implies an additional problematic dimension of the

1. I wish to express my gratitude to David Maybury-Lewis, Uri Almagor, and the participants in the conference for their insights and guidance. I am especially indebted to
Richard Werbner, who was the commentator for my essay and who later sent me a detailed
list of suggestions. It was he who pointed out the importance of the incense-bull exchange
(and the Gell article as a source) and brought up several other issues concerning oppositions
and different types of time.

analysis of dualism, namely the relationship between seemingly different systems in a single society. Is there a level at which the disparate dualisms come together in a united system? Are there times when they act on one another?

This essay will attempt to deal with the issues of time and order by analyzing dualism among the Oromo-speaking peoples of Ethiopia and northern Kenya. The expansionist Oromo have built up a network of dualistic institutions over the last four hundred years, the most important of which is a "generation grading" system called *gada*. Within the gada system a world renewal ceremony is periodically performed (ideally, once every eight years) in which the leadership, laws, and even the basic procreativity of the earth and people are literally or metaphorically renewed. During the time between renewals, social organizational and ideological dualisms abound. But at the time of renewal, the order of dualism itself is dissolved and then transformed in a highly charged ritual context. The resulting "new" order provides insights into the meaning behind the dualistic system that was and that will again be.

I will discuss the temporal order in Oromo society on two levels. First, I will analyze dualistic organization and the temporal cycle in a specific group, the Guji Oromo of Sidamo Province, Ethiopia.[2] Then I will discuss the long-term development of dualism among Oromo societies generally, to the extent that the literature permits. My intention is to demonstrate the importance of taking account of time in dualistic systems by showing that a seemingly rigid set of oppositions can go through both cyclical and long-term processes of transformation.

Guji Social Organization and Generation Grading

The Guji consider themselves a loosely knit society of pastoralists organized into a confederation of phratries, each with its own territory and leadership. The only authority uniting the phratries is provided by the External Priest, who lives in his own small territory and whose secular power is limited.[3] There are eight phratries, three in the highlands to the east of the Rift Valley and five others in and around the valley. This paper is mainly concerned with the three highland phratries, each consisting of seven

---

2. This fieldwork was carried out between May 1968 and May 1971 under a grant from the National Science Foundation.

3. The Guji term for the External Priest is *kallu,* apparently from the verb *kallu,* to sacrifice. I have ignored this meaning in translating the term (since he does not sacrifice for the phratries, but the Fathers of Generations do) and have used instead a made-up term that represents his position vis-à-vis the phratries.

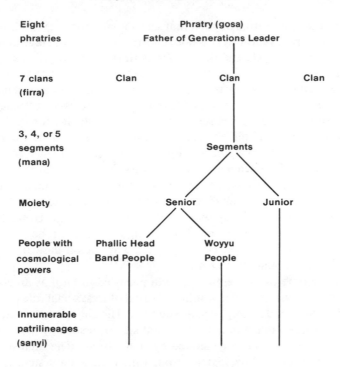

Fig. 1. Divisions within the descent system

nontotemic clans divided into three, four, or five primary segments (see fig. 1). Each clan segment is made up of innumerable patrilineages. There are moieties, which are somewhat unusual in that they cut across the descent system at the level of the clan segment rather than at a more inclusive level of organization. Potentially, each clan in Guji can be made up of segments from each moiety.

A key dimension of social organization for the Guji and other Oromo-speaking peoples is the gada generation grading system. (I have described the Guji *gada* system in Hinnant 1978 and will only outline here the aspects that are essential for understanding Guji dualism.)

Gada superficially resembles an age-grade system of twelve stages, or grades, and final retirement. As will be seen later, the stages of the gada system, taken as a whole, constitute an ideal life cycle, with grades marking childhood, warriorhood, elderhood, and finally priesthood and retirement. Rite of passage ceremonies mark the transition from one stage to the next.

The unusual feature of gada that sets it apart from age-grading is that age per se is irrelevant. Boys do not enter the most junior stage at an early point in their life cycle and then progress through appropriate steps until they die. Rather, they follow their fathers through the set of stages at five eight-year intervals. A boy is, in effect, born into the system at a point determined solely by the position of his father. This forty-year "generation" rule often means that a man is of an inappropriate age for the stage he occupies. If, for example, the father occupies a senior stage when a particular son is born, that son will join his brothers in a stage somewhere in the middle of the sequence and will miss the junior stages altogether. There are social mechanisms for keeping the system in alignment, such as restricting men's legitimate procreation to certain grades so that their sons will be born into the system at the appropriate point. However, gada is ultimately an unstable form of social organization. In fact, one of the anthropological issues concerning gada is why such a basically unworkable system is maintained at all.

At the time of my fieldwork, gada persisted in Guji as an elaborate set of rites of passage and a number of ritual offices; social role play based on gada grades had largely been abandoned. The Guji puzzle, then, is why people devote so much time to the ritual side of a socially inappropriate system and to the offices generated by that system. The dualisms, both social-structural and ideological, from which the gada system is largely constructed, provide a major part of the answer.

Cosmological Dualisms

To explain the Guji system of dual organization, it is necessary to begin with cosmology. The Guji believe in a high god (*waka,* a term that also means "sky"), who created life on earth. Below god are several types of spirits, all of whom are thought to be able to possess people.[4] God offers the Guji a good life based on procreativity and abundance, which are ensured through a variety of social and ritual practices.

The Guji believe that god sent the first External Priest to earth to teach men how to control their destiny and that it was he who told them about the gada system and its rituals. The descendants of that first External Priest, who may never enter the phratry territories, epitomize the force of unrestrained nature, called *woyyu,* symbolized by two species of poisonous

---

4. For a discussion of Guji spirit trance see Bauer and Hinnant 1980.

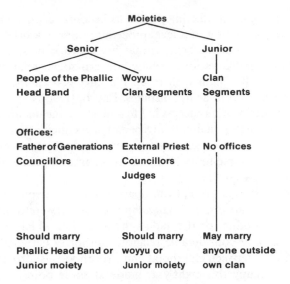

Fig. 2. Moieties and their attributes

snakes, by lightning, and by the relationship between affines, who are said to be "woyyu for each other." The first External Priest brought the snakes to earth, and his descendants and all members of his clan are woyyu. In addition, the segments of certain other clans are woyyu, and the members of those segments are called "people of woyyu." Since woyyu people have the power to curse others, woyyu men frequently are selected to be judges in this society, which lacks incarceration and physical punishment.

The opposite of woyyu is *kayyo,* which symbolizes the forces of nature brought into society and made the predictable basis for abundance through procreativity (see fig. 2). Unlike woyyu, which has no degree — it simply is — kayyo can be good or bad. A man's kayyo is good if he has several wives, many children, and large herds of cattle. Bad kayyo is indicated by lack of abundance, general ill luck, or by illness of people or livestock.

There are no rituals to increase or alter woyyu. By contrast, most Guji ritual involves supplication to god for good kayyo, along with some form of divination to foretell kayyo for the near future. In addition, kayyo also is intimately involved in social relations. For kayyo to be good, people must be in a state of reconciliation with each other. The goal of Guji adjudication is to cause conflicting parties to become reconciled, and after each successful resolution of a legal procedure there is a brief reconciliation ceremony. If someone believes that his kayyo is bad, he will go to an adept whose first questions usually concern social relations. Curing ceremonies generally begin with reconciliation between the sick person and all those with whom he has disputes. Kayyo, then, is apparently seen both as a measure of one's success in life and as the means for controlling one's destiny through ritual and interpersonal reconciliation. The reconciliation procedures, which accompany every dispute settlement and begin many Guji rituals, serve to maintain the trust among people that is considered vital for social life.

Just as the External Priest, living apart from society, epitomizes woyyu, the Father of Generations, (*abba gada*) in each phratry epitomizes kayyo.[5] This office is a product of the gada system, within which the grade of greatest secular and considerable religious authority (situated in the sequence of grades between elderhood and priesthood) is also called gada. All men may occupy this eight-year grade at some point in their lives, but not all can become Father of Generations. The candidates are selected from a small number of specific lineages of segments of certain clans in each phratry. The members of these segments are called "people of the phallic head ornament," a concept that will be discussed later in several contexts.

As men of the appropriate groups progress through the early gada grades, they are watched by senior men, and one is selected as the future Father of Generations long before he takes office. First, the one chosen must be young. Because of the gada generation rule, men of virtually any age may occupy a given grade, but only those who are the appropriate age are considered for the office of Father of Generations. Second, he must be calm, dignified, and adept at reconciliation. Third, he must be physically perfect and in excellent health. The neophyte begins a period of training, during which his general conduct is observed. The qualities he must display are consequences of the concept of kayyo. The major task of the Father of Generations is to sacrifice bulls at various shrines to ensure good kayyo for his phratry. Should there be drought, disease, or unsuccessful warfare, it will be said that his kayyo is bad. This purveyor of procreativity must himself lack defects so that the country will be perfect. After eight years, the next gada rite of passage occurs, and a younger man takes his place. The incumbent thus is always young and vigorous.[6]

5. The term *abba gada* literally means "father of gada."
6. The retiring Father of Generations is promoted to priesthood (*yuba*), from which vantage point he can advise the new Father of Generations.

When a Father of Generations takes office, he marries a wife from a particular clan segment, even if he is already married. Another man consummates the marriage for him to avoid the possibility of failure on the wedding night, which in Guji is conceived of as a pitched battle, with the groom forcibly consummating the marriage. He may then sleep with the new wife of his gada period. He may have no mistresses, although all other men are expected to have them.[7] His principal insignia of office is a phallic ornament that he wears on his forehead, and it is from this obvious representation of his role that the "people of the phallic head ornament" take their name.

The councillors associated with the Father of Generations have a variety of functions. Some are religious and legal advisers, and others are general workers and messengers. These offices, allocated through the moiety system, will be discussed later.

While the most pervasive dualism in Guji culture is that of kayyo and woyyu, there are also subsidiary dualisms within the rich metaphorical meaning of kayyo. For the most part, these cluster around the key distinction between male and female. Men are portrayed in Guji myth and ritual, and in statements of male informants, as the active force in maintaining the well-ordered world that provides good kayyo. Men are associated with god and the sky. The quality of masculinity is explicitly developed in Guji thought; there is no corresponding term for "femininity." Women ideally should be the passive source of fecundity. They are associated with the earth and the sustenance it provides. In Guji mythology, however, women are portrayed as dangerously lacking in passivity, as devious and likely to disrupt the male-generated order.[8] Both women and earth produce unpleasant surprises.

When a child of either sex is born, the midwife touches its head to the earth and says "mother is earth." She then raises its head toward the sky and says "father is god or sky." This distinction is pervasive in ritual, with men actively sacrificing and conducting blessings for kayyo. Women, who do not sacrifice, sit on the ground to receive the blessing from men (who use the blood of sacrifice to anoint themselves and women). A further manifestation of the sky-male–earth-female opposition involves the *gada* leadership. The Father of Generations, whose procreativity must be metaphorically as well as literally controlled, may not dig in

---

7. While I was in the field, one Father of Generations was removed from office for having mistresses.

8. In the Guji creation myth, which is a variant of the Adam and Eve story, Eve participates in tricking the innocent Adam, and when told by God that as punishment her "blood will fall on the ground every three months," she repeatedly asks, "What, every month?" God finally gives in. The story of a queen who ruled Guji relates how the order of society was stood on its head until men asserted their current dominance.

the earth, nor may anyone else do so while within the confines of his homestead.

The male-female dualism has other distinctions. Males and masculinity are equated with the right side or hand, and females with the left.[9] The Guji house is organized in these terms; men occupy the right side (facing the entrance from inside) and women the left. During the ritual a roof support on the right side is the ritual center. This pole is called "the pole of god," and the man who directs the ritual sits before it. On those occasions when women are involved in ritual action, they move to the middle of the house, directly behind the fire.[10] The household shrine is located on the midline in the rear. On the shrine are placed men's ritual implements, along with those of women and the women's milk containers. Under it are placed excised umbilical cords, foreskins, and the hair cut from men's heads during rites of passage.[11]

The final distinction associated with male and female is that of odd and even number. Males are given their childhood names on the fourth day after birth, and they use even numbers (of objects, repetitions, or gestures) to indicate themselves in ritual performances. Women are named on the third day of life and are associated with odd numbers until death.

The sequence of gada grades is a complex commentary on these dualisms. When a male enters the system, after a preliminary stage, he is promoted into *gudurru* grade, adopts the hairstyle of women (gudurru), and is considered to be female. Among the Boran Oromo, according to Legesse (1973), boys in this grade not only are defined as female but also must live apart from society. They are taken from their parents and spend the grade among a people who fish on the Rift Valley lakes and make pottery (a shameful occupation to the Oromo). The boy next passes through the adulthood ceremony, when all his hair is shaved. During the following grade young men take the dry cows of their fathers' herds to the wild lowlands bordering Guji, where they hunt and raid against neighboring pastoral societies. During this grade, for the first time, they may supplicate god for good kayyo. They may pass their bare hands over the back of a sacrificial bull before it is slaughtered and chant their requests for abundance in all things.

---

9. Traditionally, men castrated their defeated enemies. This is called taking masculinity (*dira*) or taking the right (*mida*).

10. In the *makabasa* (name-giving) male adulthood ritual, mothers and their sons gather here before the fire for a brief ceremony in which mothers relinquish their sons as children and reclaim them as men who may someday support their aging mothers ("First I warmed you, and now I call you").

11. Gada ranks are distinguished by different hair styles. In the makabasa adulthood ceremony, the heads of initiates are totally shaved.

The next grade is one of reversal between culture and nature. The initiates remove their clothing, paint red, black, and white lines on their faces, and go into the forest in groups. There they can be heard calling like hyenas. They steal food from Guji houses and fields. If a woman is foolhardy enough to enter the forest, they can rape her with impunity. Men during this grade are said to be like wild animals.

In the following grade men return to society, may marry, and may begin to assume serious responsibility as very junior elders. At the next promotion the initiate receives the long fluted *wudessa* pole that is the ritual implement of the mature supplicant. It is passed along the back of sacrificial bulls before slaughter. The culminating grade (gada) of secular and much ritual power is discussed below.

Another sharp reversal occurs during the grades of priesthood, when the man must give up all secular affairs. He passes his property to his eldest son and stops siring children. The final grades of progressive retirement combine great honor with the license of childhood. At one stage, *jarsa gudurru,* the man is equated with the junior gudurru, including his femininity. The grade of final retirement brings the system full circle. The old man and his wife are virtually the same gender in their symbolic attributes. The man must be treated with great respect, but he may act like a child, and a malicious one at that. He may kill another man's cow on the public path with impunity, but he must employ a knife that only women should use.

Cosmological Dualism or Monism?

Every eight years, when ceremonies are held to replace the gada leadership, kayyo and woyyu confront each other through the actions of the External Priest and the Fathers of Generations of the various moieties. Men of junior rank take office, and the old leaders are promoted to the next rank of priesthood. The process requires a full year, and at one point the retiring Fathers of Generations meet with the External Priest. It is at this point that the relationship between the two sides of the cosmological dualism is most clearly revealed.

The handing over of office begins when the Uraga phratry's Father of Generations, after consulting with a calendrical expert, decides that the year and the day have arrived. He sends small bags of coffee beans (representing cattle in ritual) to the External Priest who gives permission for the ritual to begin. The various Fathers of Generations order people to burn the grass of the country (which they do each year in any case), to complete any marriage arrangements immediately, and to give birth quickly if pregnant. A clear boundary is created between the procreativity of the old leaders and that of those who follow.

The gada leadership of the three phratries gathers at the most sacred of the tree shrines in Guji, where a house with seven doors, representing the phratry's seven clans, has been built for each. Each Father of Generations and his councillors trek to the home of the External Priest, driving a herd of cattle, said to number one hundred, before them. The procession is led by a goat decorated with strings of beads.

When the External Priest hears of their imminent arrival, he puts out poisonous snakes, the representation of his woyyu powers, which have been coated with a mixture of butter and red earth commonly used to represent blood in ritual. A messenger announces the arrival of the gada leaders. Four times the External Priest refuses to accept the messenger, but the fifth time he accepts. Then each group of councillors attempts to drive three bulls into the house (the largest building I saw in Guji). The External Priest's assistants at first block the entrance but finally allow the bulls to be driven in. The Fathers of Generations then enter and hold lengthy discussions with the External Priest concerning the kayyo of the phratries during their time in office.

The final act, following two days of discussion and festivity, is to exchange the herds of the Fathers of Generations for frankincense, which each group of gada leaders uses to infuse the special attributes of the office of Father of Generations in initiates. When those who will eventually occupy this office are first selected as young men, they are required to hold a quantity of frankincense in their mouths throughout an all-night vigil. When they take office, they again must hold the frankincense in their mouths overnight and ultimately swallow it.

Following the encounter with the External Priest, the Fathers of Generations return to the tree shrine and hold a great assembly, at which any man who has passed through the adulthood ceremony may speak. All legal problems of the gada period must be resolved, the organizational rules of gada are reviewed and adjusted, and the retiring leaders declare the end of their "law" (in the broadest sense). Finally, the retiring leaders journey to a great ravine near the spot where, Guji myth relates, the first humans fell from the sky. They build houses on one side of a stream that passes through the ravine and the gadas-elect build houses on the other side. After some days, each new leader crosses to the house of the old one and calls him three times, with no reply. The fourth time the retiring Father of Generations answers, and the successor enters. The actual transfer of power occurs when the initiate crosses to the incumbent, plucks an ostrich feather from his hair, and inserts it in his own.

Each new leader, after proclaiming the beginning of his law, spends a year traveling about the phratry territory, infusing his kayyo into the land through sacrifices of bulls. At present his duties for the eight years in office are primarily ritual, with members of his large group of councillors taking turns in residence with him. When they return home they represent him at ceremonies in their regions.

The rich symbolism of the transfer of office is a particularly revealing example of the relationships between the opposite sides of a dualistic cosmological system. In the myth of the coming of the first External Priest, it was he who created the gada system. In the ritual interaction of the External Priest and the retiring Fathers of Generations, which in its entirety is called *gutu* (full or complete), it is clearly the External Priest who is ascendant. The Fathers of Generations come as supplicants for incense and are met with poisonous snakes and other obstacles. When they finally are allowed to enter the External Priest's house they must bend low and say "The king, the king." Clearly there is a strong barrier between the ultimate representatives of kayyo and of woyyu, and the crossing of that barrier is not simple.

Kayyo, the ultimate metaphor for successfully ordered society, is renewed with each gada period, a process that requires going outside society and encountering the dangerous and largely unknown potency of nature. It should be remembered that woyyu is a power without qualifying attributes, for which people do not sacrifice. It is the dimly glimpsed external power that energizes the fragile realm of human society.

The External Priest is "out of" society. He may not enter the phratry territories, and he alone in Guji does not participate in the gada system of ranks. In a sense he ages "naturally" while all other men age "culturally" through the succession of gada stages. Congruently, he holds office for life and is thus not physically associated with procreativity in the same way as the Fathers of Generations who, with their restricted terms of office, are culturally prevented from aging (and causing the earth to age with them).

Another level of meaning seems to be implicit in the encounter between the two types of leadership. Much of the ritual activity strongly suggests the interaction of affines at the time of marriage. Within a year after a marriage is consummated, the couple visits the family of the bride, who walks ahead dressed in her finest clothing; this is comparable to the all-male gada procession preceded by the goat decked out in beads. The final gift of bridewealth cattle is presented and is accepted with a show of reluctance to indicate that they are not equivalent to the bride. From this moment, relations between the affines are formal and are generally thought to be contentious. It is said that affines are woyyu for one another. Just as society must go outside itself for renewed potency, the lineage must likewise contract marriages with stranger lineages from which the next generation will be born.[12]

In the meeting of the leaders, however, cattle are exchanged not for wives but for frankincense. This is used to create the new generation of gada leadership and to give it the legitimacy and power that ultimately emanate from the realm of woyyu. Incense is not used in any other gada context of which I am aware. It is, however, vital to the two forms of spirit trance found in Guji (see Bauer and Hinnant 1980). The older form, consisting of three key spirits—those of the household shrine, of lightning, and of the songbirds that carry messages between man and god—is hereditary in certain clan segments that are woyyu. In trance meetings frankincense is sprinkled over hot coals so that its perfumed smoke will summon these spirits, and thus it is a marker between the secular world and the spirit world.

In a discussion of the meaning of smell, Gell (1977:27) described it as an escaping essence, both a part of its material source and apart from it, lacking in form, definability, and clarity of articulation. He summarized the usefulness of smell for representing the other-worldly in this way: "There is a profound connection between the olfactory dimension and the dimension of otherworldliness, which is only inadequately expressed in the phrase 'odour of sanctity.' The very words 'spirit' and 'essence' reveal the fact that the vehicle for an ideal or absolute truth which would be, at the same time, concretely within reach, would have to be something like a vapour, a distillate of more mundane reality" (29).

The Fathers of Generations do not burn the incense but instead give it to the future candidates to hold in their mouths overnight and then swallow. In this way the candidates become in part like that other realm of nonsecular power communicating directly with divinity. They themselves become more "generalized" representations of society's relation with the distant forces that must be channeled for human well-being. The ingestion of incense sets them apart from other men and ensures that they "will always speak the truth." The exchange, then, is between the concrete manifestation of secular well-being—cattle—and the substance that, when burned, transfers the unspecified essence of the powers of woyyu.

It is also interesting that the messenger for the Father of Generations must ask the External Priest an odd number of times before being allowed to drive the three bulls into the house, and the Father of Generations–elect

---

12. This level of interpretation is not based on informant statements, but rather seems to be inherent in the logic of the ritual. See Hinnant 1980 for a discussion of Guji marriage and its symbolism.

must ask the retiring leader an even number of times to acknowledge him. The Fathers of Generations are clearly masculine in all their assigned attributes. The External Priest is, like woyyu, somewhat unspecified. In fact, it is possible that woyyu is at least partially like earth, female.[13]

Finally, it appears that there are not two equal cosmological forces but only one, which generates, encompasses, and periodically renews a partially transformed cultural representation of itself. Woyyu stands for all the remote forces that must somehow be transformed into the ordered realm of culture in order for life to be possible. Woyyu is distant and dangerous. If woyyu is a natural product, kayyo is a cultural product. Kayyo can be good only when the cultural realm is properly ordered. It is always vulnerable to disorder. Viewed in this manner, kayyo (good or bad) is the measure of the effectiveness of men in bringing woyyu into culture, thus ordering it.

During the period of the transfer of leadership, when the realm of daily life is left behind, woyyu emerges triumphant. Kayyo is extinguished and can be reborn only with the help of woyyu. The dualism of Guji cosmology is thus resolved into a monism. When the cosmological power is outside culture, it is called woyyu. When, by properly observing the rules of society, men are able to bring this power into culture, it generates kayyo. Divinity controls the transformation. God sent woyyu and the rules of proper behavior to earth at the same time. He judges the extent to which men follow the rules and live in a state of reconciliation and trust with one another. Miscreants experience unrestrained woyyu, and their kayyo is bad. Those who follow the rules experience the good kayyo that is woyyu properly transformed into the realm of culture.

Dual Organization and Marriage Patterns

The cosmological categories kayyo and woyyu interact with Guji moiety organization to form a system of preferential marriage rules upon which the allocation of religious, political, and legal offices also is based (see fig. 3). The moieties, *akaku* and *dalata,* are unequal from their inception. Guji believe that members of the akaku moiety are senior and that the dalata "came later."[14] In the Guji creation myth the first son of the first man and woman, who fell to earth from the sky, was akaku, and the second was dalata.

---

13. See Legesse 1973 for a commentary on the definition of gender for the Boran *kallus.* The Boran are a closely related Oromo people on the southern border of Guji.

14. Initially I thought that the junior moiety might have been the category to which

KAYYO	WOYYU
The good life of abundance	Dangerous potency
In society	Outside society
People of the Phallic Head Band	Woyyu people
Father of Generations — the created	External priest — the creator
Rituals of reconciliation	None
Animal sacrifice	None
Maintain good kayyo	No
Associated dualisms:	Associated dualisms:
male/female	None
right/left	
sky/earth	
active bringer	
of order/passive	
recipient	

Fig. 3. Attributes of kayyo and woyyu

The principle of seniority is crucial in Guji. The first wife is ritually the most important and is the most likely to be married according to the preferential rules. She is also important because she will (or at least should) give birth to the first son, who will inherit all his father's most valued property. He will also be first in line to take over any special status his father may hold. The first son is responsible for the welfare of his siblings and half-

were assigned the many people from neighboring societies who migrated to Guji or were captured. Some informants indicated that this was so but others flatly denied it. I was never able to find independent evidence that might settle the matter. Another puzzling issue concerning Guji moieties is the distinction between *darimu* and *kontoma,* mentioned in Haberland 1963. I asked many informants about these alleged moieties and received no clear or consistent response. Many people had not heard the terms.

siblings and is supposed to use his inheritance to help them. It is therefore not surprising that the akaku moiety, which holds most of the prestigious offices in Guji society, should be considered "senior" or "firstborn."

Within the senior moiety a further distinction has to do with clan segmentation. The clans are composed of a small number of primary segments, which are made up of numerous patrilineages. Most clans have both senior and junior segments. Only the senior segments are further divided into "people of the phallic head ornament" and "people of woyyu." In many clans, then, there are three categories of people: seniors of the phallic head ornament, senior woyyu, and the junior moiety. The clan of the External Priest is an exception; even though there are several segments, they are all senior woyyu.

This system generates preferential marriage rules; it is better for members of the senior moiety to marry seniors of other clans and for phallic head ornament people and woyyu people to marry within their own category of other clans. The following is a statement of the rules by the External Priest:

> The External Priest is from *obitu* clan. Akaku. The External Priest cannot marry people of the phallic head ornament. Certain clans are of the junior moiety, but segments within them can be senior. In *handoa* clan there are senior segments from which Fathers of Generations can be chosen, and there are junior segments from which they cannot. The woyyu people cannot marry people of the phallic head ornament. If a man who is woyyu should do so, maybe either the husband or the wife will not live a long time. If they live, they may not have children. If they have children, the children will not live a long time or there will not be enough cattle for them.
> *Question:* Have there ever been any Guji leaders in the past who were of the junior moiety?
> Maybe some. If the Father of Generations has many assistants, some may be from the junior moiety. If he has many wives, some junior wives may come from the junior moiety.

Within Guji social organization, then, the senior moiety is preferentially endogamous, and the issue of exogamy is irrelevant for the junior moiety (except that it is advantageous to have affinal relations with powerful senior lineages). Within the senior moiety, the cosmological categories that regulate so much else in Guji create preferential marriage rules that direct men to marry into their own side of the cosmological dualism. In fact, the prudent have only two choices: marry their own category or marry into the junior moiety. For example, if woyyu marries woyyu, the children will have woyyu power, which consists of the ability to punish others using illness, snake bite, and lightning. If woyyu marries a member of the junior moiety, the power will be weak or nonexistent.

In practice, the endogamy rule concerning cosmological categories is most likely to be observed by members of particular lineages. Within senior clan segments from which Fathers of Generations have come in the past and might come again, proper (first) marriage is essential to give one's first son the opportunity to be chosen for the office. Since all woyyu people potentially have woyyu power and need no special office to manifest it, all could benefit from proper marriage.

This system taken as a whole has the effect of creating exclusionary categories.[15] People of the junior moiety may not hold any traditional office, except for a few among the "servants" group of the Father of Generations' councillors. Members of the junior moiety may, of course, be honored as great hunters and warriors through their own efforts, and they may become wealthy and be honored. However, they may not participate in the system of leadership. Within the senior moiety roles are strictly apportioned. The one Father of Generations in each phratry belongs to the people of the phallic head ornament, as do his religious advisers and many of his "servants." The position of woyyu people is somewhat different; they are thought to have a close connection with external forces whether or not they hold office. Formal offices among the woyyu include the External Priest and the legal advisers among the councillors. In addition, the elders' courts are often composed of woyyu men. A few non-officeholders within woyyu clan segments are associated especially with the ability to call down lightning. Men of these segments, who are thought to be even more potent than other woyyu, are called upon to perform an elaborate ceremony for people whose property has been struck by lightning.

Dualism in Other Oromo Societies

The Guji are not unique among the Oromo-speaking peoples in having complex systems of dual organization. Among other Oromo groups dualisms abound in social organization, cosmology, and ritual, but unfortunately it is rare to find in the literature more than an occasional allusion to moieties and other dualisms. For this reason I will confine my brief comparative description to the Boran Oromo, whose territory abuts the southern tip of Guji. The Boran have been well studied by Baxter (1954, 1978)

---

15. The gada system also creates restrictions on marriage in terms of the "generations" that are its product. See Hinnant 1978.

and Legesse (1973). Baxter summed up the pervasiveness of dualisms in Boran society as follows:

> Conceptions of unity in diversity, which are expressed through an ordered duality of the familiar left/right type, pervade Boran social structure and metaphysical conceptions: it is almost as if the Boran had a Gallic obsession to impose a seemingly logical set of constructs on the higgledy-piggledy of daily life. Boran representations of their social and ritual organization and activities are intellectually tidy; protuberances are tucked in or covered over. (1978:165)

The Boran have moieties, the *gona* and *sabbu,* but unlike those in Guji, the Boran moieties are balanced. Each has its own External Priest (*kallu*), and each is entitled to roughly half the offices available in the society. The moieties are also exogamous. In fact, they are reciprocating groups that balance the political structure of society between them (Legesse 1973:39–40). The Boran have a gada system, organized somewhat differently from the Guji system but obviously a variant on the same generative principles, including the five eight-year periods separating a father and his sons as they move through the system. The Boran also have elaborate rites of passage. There are no fully detailed descriptions of these rituals, but based on general comments by Baxter and Legesse, cosmological principles similar to those found in Guji seem to be present.

The similarities and variations among the many contemporary Oromo societies can be thought of as the playing out of a structural dialectic in the Lévi-Straussian sense. Disappointingly, the early stages of the dialectic have been lost. Even in the sixteenth century, when the expansionary Oromo peoples invaded the territory of the old highland kingdom of Ethiopia, the only insight into Oromo organization was provided by an Ethiopian Orthodox monk, Bahrey (see Beckinham and Huntingford 1954), who witnessed the accompanying warfare and conquest. His unsophisticated commentary suggests that many aspects of at least the social organizational elements of gada were already in place.

After the sixteenth century the record gradually improves. Oromo groups that conquered new areas settled in a variety of ecological zones and began to change in different ways. Even so, gada persisted in many societies into the twentieth century, and remnants can be found in many contemporary Oromo societies. Variations on the old Oromo cosmology also persisted, except among more northern groups that became Christian and some of the eastern and southern Oromo who converted to Islam.

The phratry organization found throughout contemporary Oromo societies may be the result of long-term segmentation of the original clans of the proto-Oromo. The repetitiveness of phratry and clan names among the various groups tends to support this idea. Other units of social organization are also similar from one Oromo society to another.

I should mention that as late as the nineteenth century the various Oromo societies sent pilgrims to the area of the present-day Boran. They convened on a particular mountain where an oracle (*abba muda,* "Father of Anointing") foretold the destiny (presumably a concept like kayyo) of the new gada period. For this conclave to occur, the many gada systems must have been cycling together. The one element standing above all the disparate Oromo groups apparently was an oracle associated with the very cosmological forces that the elaborate gada systems were intended to influence.

In terms of the structural dialectic, the basic oppositions being played out in Oromo cosmology seem to be contained in this formula: man-woman : : sky (god)–earth : : culture-nature. In the Guji case : : kayyo-woyyu can be added. The formula is dualistic, and the dualisms are forever being manipulated to produce the goal of abundance through procreativity. God, man, and culture are the active forces involved in bringing under control the ideally compliant, but sometimes noncompliant and dangerous, forces of earth, woman, and nature. When things go wrong, people turn to ritual manipulation of this set of metaphorical representations.

Conclusions

It is clear that Oromo societies are largely built on levels of dualistic organization. Each level knits society together through the connections between its oppositions, and at the same time the hierarchical system of asymmetrical oppositions provides a ladder to the ultimate truths revealed during the periods of handing-over of gada leadership and, in the past, during the coordinated visit to the Father of Anointing by representatives of the various Oromo cultures. In these societies the ideologies create the basis for tolerating complex social forms and for continuing the extremely cumbersome gada organizations, with their built-in tendency to misallocate people to grades that are inappropriate to their chronological age. The model for society provided in the cosmologies persisted into the early twentieth century in most Oromo societies and still persists in some.[16]

In Guji there is no strong tradition of secular political leadership. The political power of both the Father of Generations and the External Priest is weak at best. The latter remains outside society and cannot influence secular events directly. The Father of Generations, though stand-

16. For example, Blackhurst (1978) gave a lengthy description of one grade, called *folle,* in the case of highly acculturated Shoa Oromo settlers in Arsi Oromo country. See also Legesse 1973.

ing at the head of the phratry, remains apart from daily affairs. These leaders, instead of controlling the lives of others by secular means, epitomize the dualisms by which the meaningful pattern of life is created.

On the local level the centrality of dualism is manifested both by the asymmetric moiety organization and the sequence of *gada* grades. As initiates pass through gada grades, they live out, alternately, each side of many of the basic oppositions. They experience female and male grades, with final retirement into an amalgam of the two. They become, by turns, men in society and wild animals in nature, secular men and divinity-like men. No one person experiences all of these changes. Because of the generation rule, the grade one is born into is determined by the place of one's father in the system, and one proceeds through the grades from that point. In contemporary gada systems, the total time for transit through all the grades is far longer than a lifetime. Nonetheless, each of the grades is occupied, and the rites of transition are viewed by the society at large.[17]

What is significant is that the vastly complex world of Oromo cultures is played out through dualisms that are first portrayed as totally opposed and inimical forces but are then revealed as dualistic components of principles that must finally be reunited to perpetuate society itself. Clearly, woyyu encompasses kayyo and in fact generates it. The ascendancy of woyyu is also that of nature over culture, of female and affinity over male and lineality, and ultimately of the noumenal realm of sacred time over the phenomenal realm of secular time. The reciprocal exchange between the two realms — bulls for incense — epitomizes the grand dualism. Bulls are at the center of social and ritual life in the periods between interregnums and are used metaphorically to represent the procreativity that is the goal of kayyo. Incense, which is burned in other, nongada contexts, is ingested to incorporate the powers that lack the visible form of the substantial world.

The Guji case underscores the importance of analytically separating ideological and social organizational dualisms and then investigating the relationships between them. In Guji much of social and ritual life is organized around ideological dualisms, but there is clearly an interaction between them and the social organizational dualisms upon which they are based in part and which they in turn justify. Even the exclusion of the junior moiety men from office becomes part of the grand scheme of the cosmos. Analytically the ideological dualisms undergo rapid transformations during ritual, while the social organizational dualisms of the full set of Oromo societies are being worked through in a far slower historical process.

The essential cyclicity of Guji society underscores the importance of

---

17. See Hinnant 1978 for a discussion of the organizational rules of gada and their imperfection in Guji. Legesse 1973 discusses fully the organizational rules of the Boran system.

understanding dual organization as a diachronic process rather than as a static system of classification. It is the alternations between sacred and secular periods in the eight-year cycle that create the full Guji cosmology. The secular period of the regnum is devoted to weaving together social relations through complementary oppositions and through the reconciliation procedures that maintain peace and establish trust among people as a precondition for good kayyo. At the time of world renewal during the interregnum, and the lengthy period of sacred time that accompanies it, the whole set of relations is radically reordered. Woyyu, which was dangerous and remote, comes into focus as the generative force that brings into being the preconditions for human society. It is only at this point that the creativity of Guji dualistic thought can be fully grasped.

REFERENCES

Bauer, D. F., and J. T. Hinnant. 1980. Normal and revolutionary divination: A Kuhnian approach to African traditional thought. In *Explorations in African systems of thought,* ed. C. Bird and I. Karp, 213–36. Bloomington: University of Indiana Press.

Baxter, P. T. W. 1954. *The social organization of the Galla of northern Kenya.* D. Phil. thesis, University of Oxford.

————. 1978. Boran age-sets and generation-sets. In Baxter and Almagor 1978: 151–82.

Baxter, P. T. W., and U. Almagor, eds. 1978. *Age, generation and time.* London: C. Hurst.

Beckinham, C. F., and Huntingford, G. W. B., eds. and trans. 1954. Some records of Ethiopia, 1593–1646, being extracts from the history of High Ethiopia or Abassia by Manoel de Almeida, together with Bahrey's history of the Galla. London: Hakluyt Society.

Blackhurst, H. 1978. Continuity and change in the Shoa Galla gada system. In Baxter and Almagor 1978:245–67.

Gell, A. 1977. Magic, perfume, dream. In *Symbols and sentiments,* ed. I. Lewis, 25–38. New York: Academic Press.

Haberland, E. 1963. *Galla Süd-Aethiopiens.* Stuttgart: W. Kohlhammer.

Hinnant, J. T. 1978. The Guji: Gada as a ritual system. In Baxter and Almagor 1978:207–43.

————. 1980. Guji affinity and the case of a conflictful marriage. Paper presented at the Oromo Kinship and Marriage Conference. Department of Social Anthropology, Manchester University.

Legesse, A. 1973. *Gada: Three approaches to the study of African society.* Glencoe, Ill.: Free Press.

Lévi-Strauss, C. [1956] 1963. Do dual organizations exist? In *Structural Anthropology,* 132–63. New York: Basic Books.

Chapter 3

The Complexity of Dual Organization in Aboriginal Australia

Kenneth Maddock

Kroeber spoke of a "psychological trend towards dichotomization" that found "consistent, widespread, influential and probably ancient expression in a pattern of social structure" in Australia (1952:92). There is a clear affinity between this and Lévi-Strauss's opinion that the aborigines have developed dual organization more subtly than anyone else ([1949]:81–82). I agree with these views, and I hope that one result of my essay will be to establish how refined this form of thought and organization can become in aboriginal hands.

Early anthropologists in Australia were fascinated by dual organization. Fison, Howitt, and Thomas, for example, wrote about it at length. Later anthropologists have addressed themselves, usually more briefly, to the same broad set of questions: What forms does dual organization take? How did they originate or develop? And what are the functions of dual organization?

These perennial questions can, of course, be posed separately, but they do hang together — after a fashion. Thus when Turner suggests that class systems may be especially attractive to aborigines on mission or government settlements, who have to mix more closely with many more of their fellows in conditions of greater tribal diversity than ever before (1980:127), his suggestion has both functional and historical implications. So does the much earlier argument that moieties were instituted to prevent men from marrying their sisters (Fison and Howitt 1880:107, 328).

Even the most cursory survey of the literature shows that answers to the questions conflict too often and too radically for us to be able to speak of an established view of Australian dual organization. It also shows a marked inclination among twentieth-century writers to tackle the questions in a fragmentary way and to play down the importance of class systems in aboriginal life and thought. One of the oddest manifestations of this tendency is seen in attempts to restrict the use of the term "moiety."

Scheffler is a prime example. He distinguishes "genuine" from "spurious" or "so-called" moieties on the ground that the former have proper names (1978:435–36, 476, 522). But this is to exaggerate the significance of nominal criteria. If aborigines divide into two groupings when performing a ritual, the members of one grouping being distinguished from the members of the other by the color of paint on their bodies, the gestures and movements they make on the dancing ground, and the totemic meaning ascribed to their part, and if the division is extensible to the rest of the community, it would be unreasonable to deny that we are in the presence of a case of dual organization merely because the groupings happen to lack proper names.

In her paper on generation moieties, White describes her bizarre experiences with terminology (1981:6 n. 1). Elkin, then editor of *Oceania,* objected to her calling a generation moiety a "moiety." He wanted her to call them "lines." Correspondence with Catherine Berndt revealed that she and her husband Ronald regretted having called these groupings "moieties" — they now favored "alternate generation levels." White tried to coin new words, but after rejecting "altergens" and "zygogens" because they sounded like proprietary drugs, she fell back on (generation) "moieties." She still thinks that a new term would be useful if anyone could devise one. But she misses the point that by calling a moiety a moiety we are reminding ourselves that our subject is dual organization.

Finally, I mention Strehlow's objection to speaking of Australian tribes (or of the Aranda, at least) as divided into moieties, sections, and the like (1965:134–35). These terms imply, he thinks, a system that could not exist in fact and would be unworkable in theory. But Strehlow ignores the lesson of his own examples. A class system is a framework, at once simple, ingenious, and flexible, for ordering things, persons, and relationships, including ones hitherto strange or little known. Because such a system is indefinitely expansible, it is gratuitous to suppose that it cannot exist or function without a definitely bounded tribal structure.

Mine is a broad view of dual organization. Moreover, I extend it to include the fourfold division into classes (sections or semimoieties) that are more exclusive than moieties, and also the eightfold division into classes that are still more exclusive (subsections). This extension, which is probably called for only in Australia, is justified by the dual denominator of a 2-4-8 series. But I require classes to be recognized in some way by the aborigines of the locality concerned. Implicit in the Wolmadjeri subsection are two matrilineal descent cycles structurally equivalent to matrilineal moieties, but the isolation of these cycles "springs from a process of sociological abstraction for which there is no expressed equivalent in Aboriginal thought" (Kolig 1981:92). I would not treat them as moieties, but I would the matrilineal descent cycles of the Walbiri subsection system as described by Meggitt (1962:186, 190–92). On one hand, Walbiri are conscious of the cycles — men "sometimes drew diagrams in the sand for me and pointed out the matricycles, likening them to the revolutions of the vanes on the settlement windmill." On the other hand, the cycles are nominally distinguished — I call the members of my matrilineal moiety *magundawangu* (glossed by Meggitt as "lacking shame") and the members of the other moiety *gundangga* or *magundawanu* ("location or origin of shame," a reference to its inclusion of my actual and potential mothers-in-law).

The Forms of Dual Organization

Often there is more to Australian dual organization than the simple division into two that many writers have described. Lévi-Strauss, for example, says that the term refers to "a system in which the members of the community — tribe or village — are divided into two divisions between which there are complex relations ranging from open hostility to very close intimacy" ([1949]:80; see also Blust 1981:66). But Lévi-Strauss, in criticizing Lowie's "atomism" and "nominalism," suggests that dual organization has to do with "a principle of organization that can be applied very diversely and with varying degrees of elaboration" (1967:86–88). If we think of it in this way, we can better comprehend the existence of cross-cutting dualities on one hand, and of series of less and more inclusive dualities on the other; both are common among aborigines.

In her article on generation moieties, White shows that many peoples in roughly the western half of Australia have a dual organization such that I belong to the same moiety as my grandparents, siblings, and grandchildren; my parents and children are in the other moiety. These divisions are not age groupings; each includes persons of all ages, but persons of adjacent generations (my mother and I, for example) are never of the same moiety. Generation moieties serve diverse purposes for the people who have them, though their precise significance can vary from one society to another. Usually they are endogamous divisions, and commonly they provide a basis for ritual organization (and therefore are relevant to totemic classification), but they can have other functions as well.

By calling these groupings generation moieties, White keeps in view the conceptual linkage between them and the matrilineal and patrilineal moieties that are also common in Australia. The Walbiri, for example, have all three (Meggitt 1972:67–69), while the Mardudjara (Tonkinson 1978:56–57) and the Wolmadjeri (Kolig 1981:101–4), who both lack matrilineal moieties, have the other two varieties. But White does not ask about deeper relationships among them, nor about relationships between them and the fourfold and eightfold class systems.

I believe that a simple structural description can be given of the different kinds and varieties of classification. Because we are not, at this stage, concerned with questions of origin or development, it will be convenient to start from the two varieties of fourfold division.

One variety consists of sections for which it has become usual to substitute the letters A, B, C, and D for the aboriginal proper names. Assume that sections are paired off. Figure 1 shows that three varieties of moiety organization are logically possible. Reading from left to right they are patrilineal moieties, matrilineal moieties, and generation moieties. One variety or any two or all three may be recognized in a particular society.[1]

The other variety consists of semimoieties (literally halves of halves) for which it has become usual to substitute the letters P, Q, R, and S for the aboriginal proper names.[2] Assume that semimoieties are paired off. Figure 2 shows that three varieties of moiety organization are logically possible. On the left we have patrilineal moieties, but the other two varieties cannot be straightforwardly described in lineal or generational terms. They are no more than combinations (or recombinations) or semimoieties.

Taking together the section-based and the semimoiety-based varieties of moiety, we can see that five varieties of dual organization (in the literal sense of a twofold division of the totality) are logically possible. Patrilineal moieties occur in each set (being symbolized as AD-BC and as PQ-RS), but the other two varieties in each set are unique to it.

The point about uniqueness can be expressed in another way. Think of a class (of whatever kind or variety) as embracing a constellation of ego's kin. If I am ego, I find that A, B, C, D, P, Q, R, and S are unique constellations of my kin, in the sense that not one of these classes comprises the same set of my relatives as any of the others. Similarly AB, CD, AC, BD, PR, QS, PS, and QR are unique constellations. But AD is the same as PQ, in the sense that each comprises the same set of my kin, and BC is the same as RS.

The distribution of relatives is shown in figure 3, which is also a portrayal of a subsection system, in this case, a division of the totality into

---

1. For maps and discussion of the geographical distribution of classes, see Thomas (1906:37–41), Radcliffe-Brown (1930:37–42), Elkin (1954:89–107) and Berndt and Berndt (1964:45–60); these sources also include information on rules of marriage and descent between classes.

2. Kolig uses W, X, Y, and Z instead of P, Q, R, and S (1981:164). He gives no reason for his innovation, which is to be regretted as potentially confusing.

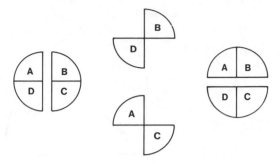

Fig. 1. Varieties of section-based moiety

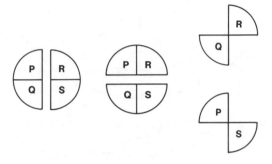

Fig. 2. Varieties of semimoiety-based moiety

eight that comprises the least inclusive classes. Numerals from 1 to 8 are used instead of the aboriginal proper names. The pairing of subsections into sections on one hand, and semimoieties on the other, is shown in figure 4. By comparing it with figure 3 we can work out the kin constellations peculiar to each variety of class system.[3] I have not attempted to show the logically possible combinations of classes at the eightfold level into classes at the fourfold or twofold level. Assume that we are interested in moieties, that each moiety comprises four subsections (as is, in fact, usual) and that I belong to subsection 8. Simple calculation will show that there are sixty-nine ways of combining my subsection with (three) others to produce

---

3. I have used English kin terms for convenience, but they must be understood in a broad sense to accommodate aboriginal classificatory usage. Readers curious about the class distribution of aboriginal kin terms could consult such sources as Berndt and Berndt (1964:72–76), Hiatt (1965:44–49), and Meggitt (1972:68–70, 75) who deal with Gunwinggu, Gidjingali, and Walbiri respectively.

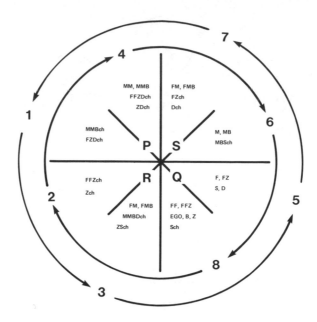

Fig. 3. Subsections and the distribution of relatives. Arrows show matrilineal descent cycles; relatives are distributed on the assumption of ideally preferred subsection marriages, but the fact of many alternative marriages means that each specification shown will be found in the two subsections equivalent to a section.

a moiety. Reference to figures 1, 2, and 4 will show that only five of these combinations have been used (AD or PQ = 1458; BD = 2468; CD = 3478; QS = 5678; and QR = 2358).

Thus far I have sought to bring out logical relationships between class systems of the two-, four-, and eightfold kinds. Classes at a more inclusive level have been treated as products of the fusion of less inclusive classes, and conversely the less inclusive classes have been treated as products of the fission of classes at a more inclusive level. I would not, at this stage of my argument, want to be taken as implying that these processes of binary fission and fusion, of combination and recombination, correspond to any historical course of events.

In the next part of my essay, I describe the part that classes play in aspects of thought and organization of southern and central Arnhem Land aborigines. The people with whom I am concerned have no name for themselves, but I shall call them Dalabon. This is actually the name of a language, but I apply it not only to members of the patrilineal clans

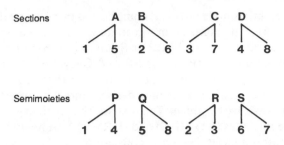

Fig. 4. Pairing of subsections into sections and semimoieties

having land in the area traditionally associated with that tongue but also to aborigines belonging to clans having land in nearby areas associated with other languages (Djauan, Maiali, and Rembaranga, for example). Speakers of all these languages (or people whose immediate forbears would have spoken them) have been living on what is now the Beswick Reserve or in its neighborhood since before the Second World War. In spite of their language differences they show many resemblances in social and religious organization.[4]

Dual Organization in Action

The Dalabon have subsections, semimoieties, and three varieties of moiety. The semimoieties and two varieties of moiety are activated in the two great ceremonies, Gunabibi and Yabuduruwa, which were being performed alternately each year during the 1960s, the main period of my research in this region. In an earlier article I discussed the relation in design-plan between these ceremonies (Maddock 1979a); here I shall limit myself to the Yabuduruwa.

Both patrilineal moieties (Duwa or PQ and Yiridja or RS) have parts to play in a Yabuduruwa ceremony—PQ as *djungkayi* and RS as *gidjan*. What is the difference between these roles (which are reversed in the Gunabibi)? Most of the dancing is by men who are gidjan, and most of the totemic imagery seen during the ceremony is of their moiety. But they cannot stage the ceremony on their own. The performance is arranged and the program settled by men who are djungkayi. It is they who make the dancing grounds and most of the paraphernalia, who paint designs on the bodies of gidjan, and who play the gongs that symbolize one of the founding figures of the Yabuduruwa. In addition, the djungkayi take part in some of the dancing and they officiate when gidjan dance.

---

4. For discussion of aboriginal life under reservation conditions, see Maddock 1977.

This apparently simple picture is complicated by a second duality cutting across the first. It results from a recombination of the semimoieties (Walugar or P, Mambali or Q, Budal or R, Gwiyal or S) into what I have called ceremonial moieties (Budal or PR and Gwiyal or QS) (see fig. 2).

The picture is further complicated by the fact that complementarity and opposition are manifested not only *between* moieties, whether PQ-RS or PR-QS, but also *within* them. The system, that is to say, must be expressed by the formulas (P-Q)/(R-S) and (P-R)/(Q-S). I am not suggesting that such anthropological algebra is consciously in the minds of Yabuduruwa actors, yet it is embodied and made visible in the colors they wear, the movements and gestures they make, the totemic significance of their parts, and so on. These points can be illustrated by analyzing four ritual episodes: Fat, Milky Way, Grasshopper, and Honeybee.

In Fat the actors are painted red from head to foot, with ovoids of glossy red (the ochre having been mixed with fat) outlined in white on chest and upper arms. Men of the ceremonial moieties PR and QS form lines across the western end of the rectangular dancing ground, QS in front (as one faces east) and PR behind. Men of the patrilineal moiety PQ officiate, either playing gongs or giving dancers cues with the wands they carry. (PQ has djungkayi responsibilities in the Yabuduruwa, but the example shows that some of its members join with gidjan to form the ceremonial moieties and to dance.)

In the first phase of the dancing the dancers run by ones or twos to the other end of the ground, QS going first and PR afterwards. There they again form lines across the ground, QS in front (as one faces west) and PR behind. In the second phase the dancers, rising from a kneeling position, advance along the ground, shaking the green leaves they carry in the hand, grunting, stamping hard down to make clouds of dust rise, and driving the gong players before them.[5] The neat lines dissolve and the gong players and wand bearers are caught up in the crowd. Massed together at the western end, the men seem to surge to and fro before moving eastwards again. When half or more of the way back, they utter a sudden shout and throw themselves to their knees to the fast tattoo of the gongs. The totemic part of the PR moiety is kangaroo (or tortoise), of QS goanna and of PQ honeybee.

Actors in Milky Way are painted as in Fat, except that two men of the R semimoiety may have black facial marks, as may those PQ men who officiate (as distinct from those who, aligned in ceremonial moieties, join in the dancing). These officiants may have their legs painted yellow to just

---

5. The first and second phases in this and the succeeding episodes are distinguished by the arrival at or near the dancing ground of novices or women.

above the knee. The paraphernalia is also the same—green leaves in the hand for dancers, gongs or wands for officiants. The ceremonial moieties form in lines across the western end of the ground, but their relative positioning is the reverse of Fat, for PR is in front and QS behind.

In the first phase the dancers run to the eastern end of the ground, PR going first and QS afterwards (again the reverse of Fat). There, instead of forming lines *across* the ground, they form a line *along* the ground, QS men being in the front segment (as one faces west) and PR behind (which restores the relative positioning of Fat). In the second phase, the dancers, rising from a seated position (kneeling in Fat), advance westwards as a column, keeping good order until they reach the end of the ground, where they become bunched together and surge to and fro in a mass together with gong players and wand bearers. The finish resembles that of Fat. The totemic part of the PR moiety is sometimes said to be Nagaran (an anthropomorphic hero who used to fly through the air), the part of QS is sometimes said to be heavy rain, and that of PQ is said to be honeybee (as in Fat), though quite often the whole ritual episode, is simply said to "mark" (signify or symbolize) the Milky Way.

Milky Way is quite close to Fat in its class basis. The ceremonial moieties PR and QS are activated, as is the patrilineal moiety PQ, and there is no role for RS; however, one semimoiety (R) is stressed. Positional patterning is more varied; there is a line along as well as lines across the dancing ground, and the ceremonial moieties rotate front and back positions. Totemic symbolism shows a shift upward, with Nagaran, Milky Way, and heavy rain replacing kangaroo and tortoise.

Grasshopper departs from the pattern of Milky Way more radically than Milky Way from Fat. It is held in the late afternoon, whereas the latter two are staged in the early morning, and the ceremonial moieties (PR/QS) are not activated. Once more PQ officiates, but the dancing is by gidjan only, with the R and S semimoieties being distinguished from each other.

Men of the patrilineal moiety PQ are painted as in Fat. Those of RS are black with white spots over most of the body; arms to just above the elbow and legs to just above the knee are red for men of the R semimoiety and yellow for S. As in Fat and Milky Way, the PQ officiants bear gongs or wands; the RS dancers have green leaves in the hand, and those who are S wear green leaves at the ankle and have sticks symbolizing water lilies up their backs (compare Milky Way, in which a step is taken to stress R). The dancers congregate at the western end of the ground, but not on it (in contrast to Fat and Milky Way), R being clustered by the southwest corner and S by the northwest.

In the first phase the dancers run to the eastern end, R going first and

S afterward. There they form lines across the ground (as in Fat), with S crouching on their haunches in front (as one faces west) and R standing behind. The R men are relatively sedate, shuffling about and making little jumps, but the S men bob and gyrate energetically, leaping upright when a tattoo sounds on the gongs and then dropping back on their haunches. In the second phase the dancers advance along the ground, with the S men at first continuing to bob up and down as they go; but soon they, too, are standing up, and the dancing becomes indistinguishable from Fat and Milky Way. The totemic part of R is a grasshopper called *djadeidei* and of S, a grasshopper called *leidjleidj,* respectively reddish and yellowish under the wings; PQ's part is honeybee. A crouching dancer signifies a grasshopper on the ground, while a standing dancer signifies that the insect is in flight. Perhaps we could see this episode of the Yabuduruwa as "mediating" in symbolism between earthbound Fat and sky-oriented Milky Way.

Honeybee, which begins by night and ends by day, is performed entirely by men of the patrilineal moiety PQ (djungkayi for the Yabuduruwa), there being no role for RS or for the ceremonial moieties.

Actors in Honeybee are painted like the dancers in Grasshopper, with men who are P having legs and arms red to just above knee and elbow (like R in Grasshopper) and men who are Q painted yellow (like S in Grasshopper). But both P and Q wear green leaves at the ankle and have sticks symbolizing water lilies up their backs (only S have these items in Grasshopper). In the first phase the actors stay for several hours in an inward-facing circle towards the eastern end of the ground (Fat, Milky Way, and Grasshopper start at the western end), uttering cries to percussion accompaniment. During the later part of this phase they bob up and down and gyrate, but the circle is kept. In the second phase, in which the dancers hold green leaves in the hand, the bobbing and gyrating are intensified, with occasional springs into an upright position, before the men rise to their feet and advance westward. The rest of the dancing resembles that in the earlier episodes. The men of both semimoieties play the part of honeybees, there being no species distinction among them (contrast Grasshopper). When the men squat, the bees are on the ground; when the men are on their feet, the bees are in flight (compare Grasshopper).

My description of a sequence of episodes from the Yabuduruwa, brief though it is, shows that classes are not abstractions made by anthropologists or aborigines. They are a basis of organization of ritual action. Moieties and semimoieties are shuffled, permuted, combined, and recombined — call the process what you will — and their changing pattern is made vivid and alive through color and design, movement and gesture, objects worn or carried, totemic symbolism, and other indications that I have left out of the account.

In each episode certain classes are stressed, but stresses change from one episode to the next. In Fat the ceremonial moieties PR and QS have parts, and so does the patrilineal moiety PQ. This pattern continues in Milky Way, but is elaborated to allow attention to be focused on R. In Grasshopper the ceremonial moieties have no parts, but the patrilineal moiety PQ stays on the scene and is joined by RS, within which R and S are distinguished. Honeybee provides a part only for PQ, within which P and Q are distinguished. Thus the succession of episodes is also a progression from a broader to a more constricted focus.

It has become commonplace for anthropologists to see classes as significant in ritual and totemism, and for them to reject the earlier view of classes as important for marriage. The latter institution, it is now widely thought, is governed by the finer discriminations of kinship, whether conceived genealogically or categorically (see, for example, Radcliffe-Brown 1931:440, 443; Meggitt 1962:169; Scheffler 1978:4). Obviously I would not deny the ritual significance of classes, for it can be demonstrated from other episodes of the Yabuduruwa and also from other Dalabon ceremonies. Their totemic significance, too, is easily demonstrable, with nearly all species being classified by semimoiety. But I think there is more to be said for the role of classes in marriage than is usually thought.

Dalabon most often talk about the regulation of marriage in terms of kin categories or of subsections. Ego finds his or her spouses among the members of the *gagali* category, which includes such genealogical specifications as mother's mother's brother's daughter's child. It is the only marriageable category. Or, in subsection terms, ego finds his or her spouses among the members of two subsections (each of which includes some of ego's gagali). Which two are marriageable depends, of course, on ego's subsection. The system may be shown in this way (numerals replacing proper names):

Husband's class	1	2	3	4	5	6	7	8
Wife's class	2,6	1,5	8,4	7,3	6,2	5,1	4,8	3,7
Child's class	4,8	3,7	2,6	1,5	8,4	7,3	6,2	5,1

If I am 8 and marry 3, my children will be 5 (which pairs with my subsection to form Q semimoiety), but if I marry 7, my children will be 1 (which pairs with 4 to form P semimoiety). Now the Dalabon prefer a man to make the marriage that will put his children in his semimoiety. To take a wife of the other subsection (shown in each case to the right below his number) is not wrong, but it puts his children in the other semimoiety of his patrilineal moiety. If male, they will be unable to follow exactly in his ritual footsteps (the dominant totemic ordering being by semimoiety), and where dancing is organized by semimoiety or ceremonial moiety, they will find themselves disjoined from him.[6] There is thus a rational preference for marrying into one of the two permitted subsections, even though women of the marriageable kin category will be found in both. This is not to see in such a preference a causal force in choice of marriage partner in individual cases; it is rather that aborigines can make statements in class terms that are not simply reducible to statements in kin terms.

The third variety of moiety found among the Dalabon is the matrilineal. These moieties, named Madgu or Marawar and Ngaraidjgu or Rerwondji, are structurally equivalent to matrilineal descent cycles in each of four subsections (1357 and 2468); sections are not recognized by the Dalabon. I did not find that the matrilineal moieties had any ritual or totemic significance and, although they are spoken of as exogamous, statements in this idiom add nothing to our understanding of causation or rational preference in marriage choices.

I have shown, selectively and far from exhaustively, that Dalabon classes are more than a system of logical relations. They enter into the ordering or regulation of totemism, ritual, and marriage (and of other aspects of thought and organization with which I have not dealt here). In addition, as is implicit in all I have said, they provide aborigines with conceptual means by which to grasp, express, and manipulate (if only imaginatively and symbolically) some of the most general features of nature and culture. Quite similar accounts, allowing for differences of detail and emphasis, could be given of many other aboriginal peoples (as, for example, the Walbiri; see Meggitt 1972). These considerations lead to questions of a historical kind.

Origin and Development of Classes

Class systems are so widespread in Australia, and written records of aboriginal life so recent, that an impenetrable mist may seem to hide the history of this form of thought and organization. Yet from the earliest days of anthropological interest in aborigines up to the present, accounts of form and function have been accompanied by hypotheses about the rise, development, and spread of classes. The usual approach has been to see

---

6. These consequences follow, in the Dalabon case, because their subsections are indirectly matrilineal in descent and a woman's subsection determines the semimoiety of her children. The consequences can be avoided by relaxing the relation between semimoiety membership and ritual-totemic representation, or by having children belong to their father's semimoiety regardless of their mother's subsection.

explanatory force in relations of kinship and marriage, classes having somehow been produced by or derived from them, but the theorists who take this line often conflict with one another.

In that early classic, *Kamilaroi and Kurnai,* Fison and Howitt argued that classes arose from the segmentation of an original "undivided commune" into two intermarrying halves, the motive being to prevent men from marrying their sisters (1880:27, 33, 35–37, 328). Later these primary classes themselves divided in two, thus producing a fourfold system (though the possibility was also entertained that such a system arose from the amalgamation of two tribes with moieties), and later still the same "orderly process of evolution" saw an eightfold system result from the segmentation of the quarters.

When Howitt returned on his own to the same great theme (1904:88–90, 142–44), he admitted that the original commune was "hypothetical" and that aboriginal myths explaining how it came to be divided in two have "no historical authority." As a general rule, however, aborigines were found to be divided into exogamous moieties. From this baseline, divergencies occurred: on one hand, segmentation into four and further segmentation into eight classes; on the other hand, atrophy of the classes and the appearance of an "anomalous" system in which local groups regulated marriage.

Shortly afterward, Thomas drew an unfavorable contrast between Fison and Howitt's "reformation theory" and his own "development theory" of moieties (which he called phratries) (1906:55, 65, 69–72). As he pointed out, it is highly unlikely that early aborigines saw inbreeding as harmful, and if they did, why allow cross-cousins to marry while forbidding parallel cousins to do so? Thomas thought that moieties originated from the custom whereby a man took his wife from one particular group with which his own had come to be friendly. The two intermarrying groups drew in smaller ones, and their names became moiety names in the newly formed aggregate, the largest unit known at that stage of social evolution. As to the fourfold division, Thomas thought it a priori probable that it succeeded the twofold and was in turn succeeded by the eightfold.

In our own day, Fox has propounded a very similar theory (1967:182, 194). Two local groups began by exchanging women; growth in membership caused them to split up; but since the portions retained their original identity, the local groups became transmuted into moieties. The more elaborate forms of reciprocal exogamy found in Australia are derived from the logic of this simple situation of intermarrying groups.

The strength of these explanations is that they presuppose the unity of class systems. Their weakness is that they conflate a logical sequence (2-4-8) with a process of historical growth. Moreover, in stressing exogamy or the desire to marry out, they ignore the widespread existence of the endogamous generation moieties (discussed by White 1981). Logically there is no "*a priori* probability" that they arose as part of the "orderly process of evolution" that saw four- and later eightfold divisions developing from exogamous matrilineal or patrilineal moieties. This difficulty does not arise with the PR/QS or PS/QR varieties, schematically represented in figure 2 as resulting from combination or recombination of semimoieties.[7] Because they are neither lineally nor generationally based, it is reasonable to suppose that they appeared after semimoieties, being historically as well as logically semimoiety combinations. Therefore we need see no special significance in the fact that they cut across the exogamy-endogamy distinction. (Comparison of figures 2 and 3 with the subsection marriage table shows that, with both varieties of moiety, a man finds some of his potential wives in his own and the rest in the other moiety.)

Another wing of the approach I have been discussing is represented by Scheffler, one of whose aims is to perform a kin (ultimately a genealogical) reduction on moieties and cognate divisions. He derives them from kin "superclasses" ("class" here refers to what would more usually be called a category), many of which are covert in the sense of not being recognized by the aborigines who have them (1978:4, 522, 524). The Pitjantjatjara, for example, purportedly have a covert superclass "parent" divided into the subclasses *mama* and *nguntju,* which are said to be focused on ego's actual father and mother respectively (Scheffler 1978:95).

In deriving classes (in the sense of moieties, etc.) from kin categories, Scheffler rejects the opinion that they are best understood in relation to one another. He thinks that this view is disqualified by the fact that a society may have sections, for instance, but not moieties or only one variety of moiety (1978:432–35). But this is to use historical or sociological considerations to score a point in formal analysis. There is little reason to believe that classes of a particular kind or variety have always been derived either from other classes or from the kin categories of the community in which they are, at present, to be found. Such a belief would have the extraordinary consequence of committing us to suppose that independent geneses occurred by the score.

I have no objection in principle to attempting to derive classes from kin categories. Scheffler puts matters too strongly, however, when he writes that classes "are derived" (453), with its suggestion of historical origin. He should have written "are derivable" or "can (or could) be derived," since these expressions make it clear that logical relations are at stake. But

---

7. Semimoiety combinations are also discussed by Kolig (1981:164–66). In his notation (see n. 2 above) the patrilineal moieties are WX and YZ; by recombination, WY is opposed to X and Z, and XZ to W and Y. Elsewhere I have discussed a possible PS/QR combination among the Mara (Maddock 1969, 1979b; see also Heath 1978).

if we are on the level of logical description, it is clear that classes of any kind are more elegantly understood when set in a larger structure to which all classes belong. The larger structure shows a process of binary fission and fusion, and obviously lends itself to the combinations and recombinations that are so evidently a feature of Australian class systems.

That kin categories may be correlated with classes is beyond dispute (see fig. 3). But I am not impressed by Scheffler's formulas for getting from one to the other. For example, he explains the derivation of subsections from kin categories as "the product of assigning priority to the AGA (alternate-generation agnates) and AGU (alternate-generation uterine) rules in relation to the parallel-cross status-extension rule, and of providing these rules with certain auxiliary rules" (457)! He seems to think that this is not merely a possibility in the self-enclosed world of formal analysis, but that it actually explains the emergence of subsections among aborigines. The formula is so contrived that one puzzles to work out what connection it could have with the historical events by which aborigines, at different times and in different parts of the country, acquired the class divisions we find among them today.

Turner's theory that moieties and other classes are derived from a local organization consisting of "patri-groups" linked by relations of marriage (1980:126–27) is open to much the same sort of comment. Logical considerations are conflated with historical. And whether the derivation is from kin categories or patri-groups, we are left wondering why the 2-4-8 sequence. Because the derivations are so clearly cast in this mold, it is hard to escape the conclusion that dualism is as deeply rooted in aboriginal thought and organization as the supposedly more basic considerations of kinship and local organization. But I fully agree with Turner that once classes have been instituted they take on a life of their own.

Finally, we may consider the attempts that have been made to explain not the derivation but the distribution of classes. Howitt foreshadowed an approach that was later developed by Yengoyan and accepted by Godelier when he noted that the atrophy or extinction of classes was most evident among coastal tribes, for they are smaller, more isolated, and occupy land better supplied with food and water than inland tribes (1904:143).

Writing more than half a century later, when far more data were available on aboriginal societies, Yengoyan (1968; see also Godelier 1975:3–13) argued that survival under harsh conditions requires the maximum mobility of land-using groups and some means of linking large numbers of individuals and groups so as to facilitate expansion and contraction in response to environmental variability. Sections and subsections provide the means. He stated that tribes with the eightfold division are the largest in membership and territory and have the lowest population densities; moreover, as the number of classes decreases from eight to four to two, tribal territories and memberships also decline and population densities rise. But as McKnight (1981) has convincingly shown, these correlations will not survive critical scrutiny; accordingly we must reject survival as the prime mover of the complexity of class systems. It is noteworthy, for example, that the Dalabon, in a relatively rich and well-watered part of northern Australia, have a class system at least as elaborately shaped as that of the Walbiri of the arid interior. It is also striking to notice the evidence for a growing importance of classes, including subsections, under modern conditions in which aborigines enjoy an assured food supply and live together in larger numbers than would ever have been the case in the past (see Kolig 1981:91, 95, 99; Turner 1980:127).

McKnight himself agrees with Kroeber (1952:213, 217) that classes are not basic but secondary phenomena, from which he infers that there can be no all-embracing explanation for their distribution.[8] The best we can do is take each case as it comes. Now it is true that it might be hard to find a common denominator in the various instances of adoption of classes reported in the literature: for example, the spread of subsections in and around the Aranda area (Strehlow 1947:72; 1965:130-31), of subsections and patrilineal moieties to the Gunwinggu (Elkin, Berndt, and Berndt 1951:258-61; Berndt and Berndt 1970:204-5), and of subsections to the Murinbata (Stanner 1936:196-202). But all of these occurred in an environment in which classes were already known. Indeed, by the time these borrowings were made, classes of all kinds were well established in many parts of Australia. It is unlikely that explanations of their distribution or of the motives behind modern instances of diffusion would throw light on the origin and development of class systems.

Conclusion

Australia may seem a good place in which to study dual organization. A number of kinds and varieties exist — often the same community has several — and usually it is easy to see their significance for thought and action. But the difficulty for anyone interested in historical causation or sequence is that aboriginal societies are broadly similar in their main institu-

---

8. That Kroeber was not always of the same opinion about classes can be seen from several of the essays brought together in his *Nature of Culture* (1952: esp. 91-92, 213-17, 220). McKnight is quoting from an article originally published in 1938, but articles first appearing in 1942 and 1943 show Kroeber moving away from the idea that "phenomena of formal social organization" are "secondary and often unstable embroideries on the primary patterns of group residence and subsistence associations" (Kroeber 1938:308).

tional features, at least when compared with the Indian societies of the Americas, with their marvelous range from minuscule communities of hunter-gatherers to urban and imperial civilizations. It is as though Australia presents us with variations on a theme that never developed.

For the same reason, it is more difficult than, say, in Indonesia to study the relation between dual social organization and dualism as a mode of thought. The second, which can exist perfectly well without the first, has been abundantly documented for many parts of the world (see Needham 1973 and 1979, for example). It manifests itself in varying degrees of strength and coherence, ranging from elaborate schemes of symbolic classification (often associated analogically with handedness) to a fugitive life in modern western politics (think of all those melodramas in which "right" is opposed to "left," "wet" to "dry," and "hawk" to "dove").

Yet some threads can be drawn out from the tangled skein of a hundred years of ethnography and woven together. It is indisputable that classes show family resemblances. From this it is fair to infer that, regardless of their kind or variety, they should be treated together as a system, albeit one that may never have been realized anywhere in its entirety. It is after elucidating the properties of this system that we can go on to explore its connections with other systems (of kin relations and categories, for example, or of intermarrying local groups).

What is really striking about the system was only partly caught by earlier writers who spoke of progressive "subdivision," "segmentation," or "dichotomization," and who tended to think of these as steps taken in history. The processes are reversible, as the phrase "binary fission and fusion" brings out. Neither movement to less inclusive classes nor movement in the reverse direction should be treated as though it only belongs in historical time. I see an analogy with segmentary lineage systems, in which — according to occasion and often in the very short term — lineally defined sets expand by fusion and contract through fission. The likeness is only partial, of course, for in Australia the processes are expressed in binary fashion (which would be exceptionally rather than generally the case with segmentary lineages) and the occasions on which they come into play have the flavor of eternal recurrence (the episodes of the Yabuduruwa and other ceremonies, for example). If we then compare the Australian with other class systems we see that chains of fission and fusion are lacking or little developed in the latter; hence they are hardly in a position to practice the recurrent reshuffling of segments into different combinations that is so evident among some aborigines.

Although it is essential not to confuse logical with historical processes, I suspect that a consideration of the former can lead us to some likely historical and sociological hypotheses. For example, the question of which came first, the two- or the fourfold division, seems unanswerable when posed with such generality (though for heuristic reasons we may wish to give a certain order to our exposition). However, if we look at the moiety varieties that are logically possible on a semimoiety basis, it is reasonable to assume that only one of them, the patrilineal (PQ/RS), could have antedated semimoieties. The others (PR/QS and PS/QR) do not conform to any of the three basic conceptions of relations between members of the same set. First, their members cannot be thought of as belonging to a continuous uniline (whether patri- or matrilineal); second, they cannot be thought of as belonging to a generationally discontinuous uniline (in which persons of the same line are disjoined if of adjacent generation); and third, they cannot be thought of as having all their potential spouses either within their own set (endogamy) or without it (exogamy). The first and third of these principles are operative in the case of patrilineal moieties. The other two moiety varieties would seem to become possible after the recognition of semimoieties; conceptually they are simply semimoiety combinations.

No such hypothesis can be raised regarding the moiety varieties that are logically possible on a section basis, because each of them conforms to the third principle and to either the first or the second. Accordingly, there is no reason to suppose that any of them must postdate the recognition of sections.

The operation of the three basic principles may also be appealed to in order to explain what might otherwise seem puzzling: why have so few of the sixty-nine moiety varieties logically possible on a subsection basis been empirically realized? The answer, I suggest, is that the variety of moiety that maximizes aboriginal satisfaction is one that complies with the third principle and with either the first or the second. The pleasure is intellectual: confusion of categories is avoided.

It would, of course, be astonishing if any society were crisscrossed by sixty or seventy pairs of moieties. Three, four, or five varieties seem as many as can usefully be operated; apart from problems of memory span there is the small size of the traditional social universe to be considered. Would it, for any individual, have included more than five hundred or a thousand people at the most? But allowing for these constraints, the frequency with which a few varieties of moiety recur shows that subsections cannot, in general, be regarded as randomly combined into twofold divisions. This conclusion lends support to my earlier point about the historical precedence of semimoieties over certain varieties of moiety.

I doubt our ability, in Australia at any rate, to get much further with explanation, as distinct from elucidation and ethnographic description.

No doubt we can speak, with Kroeber, of a psychological trend to dichotomize or with Needham, of a natural proclivity to binary classification; such suggestions seem, indeed, to have an intuitive rightness about them. But so far as anthropology goes, they leave one with an "end-of-the-road" feeling.

REFERENCES

Berndt, Ronald M., and Catherine H. Berndt. 1964. *The world of the first Australians.* Sydney: Ure Smith.
———. 1970. *Man, land and myth in north Australia.* Sydney: Ure Smith.
Blust, Robert. 1981. Dual divisions in Oceania: Innovation or retention? *Oceania* 52:66–79.
Elkin, A. P. 1954. *The Australian aborigines: How to understand them.* 3d ed. Sydney: Angus and Robertson.
Elkin, A. P., R. M. Berndt, and C. H. Berndt. 1951. Social organization of Arnhem Land, I, Western Arnhem Land. *Oceania* 21:253–301.
Fison, Lorimer, and A. W. Howitt. 1880. *Kamilaroi and Kurnai.* Melbourne: Robertson.
Fox, Robin. 1967. *Kinship and marriage.* Harmondsworth: Penguin Books.
Godelier, Maurice. 1975. Modes of production, kinship and demographic structures. In *Marxist analyses and social anthropology,* ed. Maurice Bloch, 3–27. London: Malaby Press.
Heath, Jeffrey. 1978. Mara 'moieties' once again. *Mankind* 11:468–79.
Hiatt, L. R. 1965. *Kinship and conflict.* Canberra: Australian National University Press.
Howitt, A. W. 1904. *The native tribes of south-east Australia.* London: Macmillan.
Kolig, Erich. 1981. *The silent revolution.* Philadelphia: Institute for the Study of Human Issues.
Kroeber, A. L. 1938. Basic and secondary patterns of social structure. *Journal of the Royal Anthropological Institute* 68, n.s., 41:299–310.
———. 1952. *The nature of culture.* Chicago: University of Chicago Press.
Lévi-Strauss, Claude. [1949] 1967. *Les structures élémentaires de la parenté.* 2d ed. Paris and The Hague: Mouton.
McKnight, David. 1981. Distribution of Australian aboriginal 'marriage classes': Environmental and demographic influences. *Man* 16:75–89.
Maddock, Kenneth. 1969. Necrophagy and the circulation of mothers: A problem in Mara ritual and social structure. *Mankind* 7:94–103.
———. 1977. Two laws in one community. In *Aborigines and change,* ed. R. M. Berndt, 13–32. Canberra: Australian Institute of Aboriginal Studies.
———. 1979a. A structural analysis of paired ceremonies in a dual social organization. *Bijdragen tot de Taal-, Land- en Volkenkunde* 135:84–117.
———. 1979b. Poor ethnography, careless writing and unwise extrapolations about Mara moieties. *Mankind* 12:61–71.

96   *The Attraction of Opposites*

Meggitt, M. J. 1962. *Desert people.* Sydney: Angus and Robertson.
———. 1972. Understanding Australian aboriginal society: Kinship systems or cultural categories? In *Kinship studies in the Morgan centennial year,* ed. Priscilla Reining, 64–87. Washington: Anthropological Society of Washington.
Needham, Rodney. 1979. *Symbolic classification.* Santa Monica, Calif.: Goodyear.
Needham, Rodney, ed. 1973. *Right and left: Essays on dual symbolic classification.* Chicago: University of Chicago Press.
Radcliffe-Brown, A. R. 1930. The social organization of Australian tribes, part 1. *Oceania* 1:34–63.
———. 1931. The social organization of Australian tribes, part 3. *Oceania* 1:426–56.
Scheffler, Harold W. 1978. *Australian kin classification.* Cambridge: Cambridge University Press.
Strehlow, T. G. H. 1947. *Aranda traditions.* Carlton, Victoria: Melbourne University Press.
———. 1965. Culture, social structure and environment in aboriginal central Australia. In *Aboriginal man in Australia,* ed. Ronald M. Berndt and Catherine H. Berndt, 12–25. Sydney: Angus and Robertson.
Stanner, W. E. H. 1936. Murinbata kinship and totemism. *Oceania* 7:186–216.
Thomas, N. W. 1906. *Kinship organisations and group marriage in Australia.* Cambridge: Cambridge University Press.
Tonkinson, Robert. 1978. *The Mardudjara aborigines.* New York: Holt, Rinehart and Winston.
Turner, David H. 1980. *Australian aboriginal social organization.* Atlantic Highlands, N.J.: Humanities Press.
White, Isobel. 1981. Generation moieties in Australia: Structural, social and ritual implications. *Oceania* 52:6–27.
Yengoyan, Aram A. 1968. Demographic and ecological influences on Australian aboriginal marriage sections. In *Man the hunter,* ed. Richard B. Lee and Irven DeVore, 185–99. Chicago: Aldine.

Chapter 4

Social Theory and Social Practice: Binary Systems in Central Brazil

David Maybury-Lewis

The Gê-speaking peoples of central Brazil first became well known to anthropologists through the works of Curt Nimuendajú (1939, 1942, and 1946). At about the same time (1942) the Salesian fathers Colbacchini and Albisetti published a book on the closely related Bororo. These works described peoples quite unlike the better known Indians inhabiting the tropical forests of lowland South America. The Gê and Bororo speakers traditionally occupied the *cerrados* (savannahs) of the central Brazilian plateau, where they lived by hunting and gathering, with agriculture playing a variable but usually secondary role. They did not in any case grow and process bitter manioc as most of the tropical forest peoples did, but relied on the traditional American staples of maize, beans, and squashes. Nevertheless, these seminomadic peoples with rudimentary technology and relatively underdeveloped agriculture lived in communities that were on the average considerably larger than those of their neighbors in the tropical forests. At the same time they were reported to have complex social systems, centered around multiple sets of moieties, and the Salesians documented the richness of Bororo philosophical and cosmological thought. These accounts led some scholars to speculate that these elaborate social systems might have been diffused to the savannah dwellers from more advanced civilizations (Haekel 1939; Lévi-Strauss 1944). Alternatively, the parallel was noted between the central Brazilians and the Australians, for whom a similar conjunction of complex social organization and simple technology had long been known (Kroeber 1942; Lévi-Strauss 1949). Yet in spite of these speculations, the central Brazilian systems themselves remained poorly understood.

Subsequent research in central Brazil (see Maybury-Lewis 1979) has served to clarify many of the issues that remained obscure in the pioneering monographs.[1] Nimuendajú, Colbacchini, and Albisetti gave the impression that the dual organization of the central Brazilians revolved around exogamous moiety systems that were matrilineal among the Northern Gê, patrilineal among the Central Gê, and matrilineal again among the Bororo (see fig. 1).[2] We now know, however, that the Northern Gê do not recognize unilineal descent and that their kinship systems are bilateral. Yet recent ethnographers have confirmed Nimuendaju's sense of the importance of binary systems among these peoples. Their dual organizations are clearly not grounded in exogamous moieties, which are not found among the Northern Gê. They do not, in fact, depend on the existence of named moieties at all; for as Turner (1979) and Bamberger (1979) have shown, the dual organization of the Northern Kayapó is a matter of insistence on two men's houses in a properly constituted village, or of having two opposing men's factions in a village that is reduced to a single men's house. If binary systems are a striking and characteristic feature of central Brazilian societies—and all ethnographers agree that they are—and if they do not depend on exogamous moieties or even any moieties at all, then what is their underlying rationale and how is one to analyze it?

Social Theories of the Gê and the Bororo

I suggest that we can understand these binary systems better if we do not start the analysis by focusing on moieties—whether they are present or absent, whether they are exogamous or agamous, and so on. These dual divisions have attracted much anthropological attention and have preempted and confused the analysis of dual organization in central Brazil. I propose instead that we begin with a consideration of the village. The Indians themselves regard the arrangement of the village as a paradigmatic representation of their society. The villages of the Northern Gê and the Bororo are circular, those of the Central Gê are semicircular. I shall not discuss the reasons for this difference here, for that would involve too much of a digression. Instead I want to emphasize that all of these societies, irrespective of the paradigmatic shape of their villages, make a distinc-

---

1. For other recent works on the Indians of central Brazil see Carneiro da Cunha 1978; Da Matta 1982; Lopes da Silva 1986; Melatti 1972, 1978; Seeger 1981; Vidal 1977; and Viertler 1976.

2. In table 1 and throughout the text of this essay I use the newly agreed upon, standard spellings of the names of tribal peoples. The Xerente and Xavante are thus the same peoples to whom I referred in my earlier writings, published before this convention had been established, as the Sherente and the Shavante.

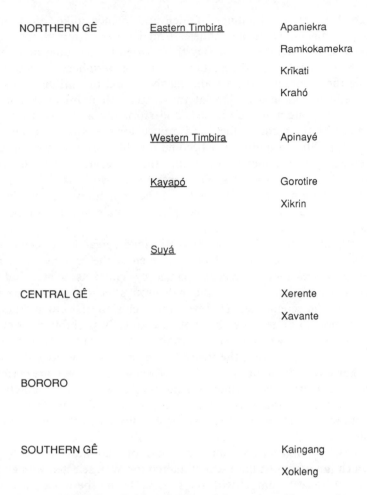

Fig. 1. Linguistic affinities of Gê- and Bororo-speaking peoples

tion between the center of the village and the periphery, which is correlated with the distinction they make between the sexes. The symbolic and
social functions of men are clearly distinguished as being antithetical to
those of women. These distinctions are reflected in the fact that the center
of the village is thought of as a male sphere opposed to the periphery of
the village, which is a female sphere. In the center there is a men's house
or men's houses (as among the Kayapó and the Bororo) or men's meeting
places. These are contrasted with the huts at the periphery which, al-

though they are the dwellings of men and women alike, are thought of as preeminently a female sphere. Females grow from childhood to maturity at the periphery and stay there, often in the same household, throughout their lives. Males start off at the periphery in childhood and are then separated from it during the period of initiation in order to be reintegrated into society at the center. All political and public matters are brought up, discussed, and (formally at least) decided at the center by the men. In fact, as I argued for the Xavante (Maybury-Lewis 1967:179), no matter can become a public issue unless and until it is taken up in the men's forum, and this is generally true for all of the central Brazilian societies. The central male world is therefore also the place where all the public affairs of the community are conducted. In contrast, what happens in the peripheral, female world is supposedly of only domestic concern.

The public affairs of the community include a great deal of ceremonial activity, which is carried out largely by men at the center.[3] Such male groups may occasionally be accompanied by female associates, but this does not alter the fact that it is the male groups themselves that are seen to perform the ceremonies. However, the exclusion of women from the center is not absolute. They are not categorically prohibited from approaching the men when they are attending a meeting in the center of the village, nor from entering the men's house (in those societies that have men's houses), though they rarely do so. Even when the men are performing esoteric ceremonies or using instruments that women are theoretically prohibited from seeing, there does not appear to be the same categorical prohibition on female approach as there is in some other parts of the world.

The most important Xavante ceremony, for example, is the *wai'a*, during which initiated men have sexual intercourse with selected women and then go on to seek contact with the spirits. During the wai'a performed at initiation, it is the age-set of newly initiated men who have intercourse with the women. Afterward the men dance around the village, while the women in the village are obliged to stay inside the huts. Women may not, in theory, see the dance or the ceremonial items that men brandish while they dance, and men speak luridly of the gang rape that would be the punishment for a woman who flouted this prohibition. Yet most women have seen parts, if not all of the ceremony, and the women who have just had intercourse with the men are actually painted in the male paint styles and

---

3. Men often perform rituals that involve moving round the periphery of the village, but they come from the center to do this and return there when it is done.

accompany the men who dance around the village. The point is that women are not *supposed* to see this ceremony. Men establish this unequivocally but do not seem to mind much whether the women actually do or do not.[4]

This demonstrates a fundamental principle of central Brazilian culture. It is the male world that is at center stage. It is the social world and the focus of the symbolic life of the community. Men, who are considered the only fully social beings, enter this social world by means of initiation and through the names that are bestowed upon them.

Names distinguish humans from animals, giving each human their social persona and linking them to other people. Central Brazilians consider that there are two separate aspects to each individual personality. There is the social self, inculcated through names, and the physical self, which is acquired biologically. The distinction is more important for men than for women, because the social aspect of a man will eventually be perfected through initiation and enable him to take part in the public and ceremonial life of the community. He will eventually achieve a bifurcation between his social persona and its corresponding roles at the center of the community, and his physical person which functions at the periphery. No such sharp separation will ever be achieved by women, whose social potentialities will remain forever relatively undeveloped at the periphery.

Among the Northern Gê, the central forum is not only a political place where the public affairs of the community are decided, but it is also a ceremonial place where the social dramas of the community are played out. In these societies men are allocated to moieties by a variety of means. The names bestowed on them carry membership in moieties, which I shall call "name-based moieties."[5] Men are assigned on the basis of age to age-sets or age-grades and these, in turn, are ordered in age-based moieties. Men are also allocated arbitrarily to pairs of moieties that function only for specific ceremonies, or classes of ceremonies. It is through these binary systems that community rituals are performed that emphasize complementarity, balance, and harmony. Conflict and disharmony, meanwhile, are associated with kin groups and kinship ties. All the Northern Gê are cognatic and uxorilocal so that males at the periphery come together in informal domestic clusters grouped around matrilines of women. A man is said to belong to such groups through his physical self. That whole aspect

---

4. This contrasts strikingly with the attitude of the men in some Melanesian societies, where they take the view that if women were to enter the men's house or see the sacred objects forbidden to them, this would be the end of their religion and the world as they know it.

5. The Bororo hold similarly that their clans are name-based groups (see Crocker 1979, 1985).

of his persona, that whole aspect of society, which is built out of such relationships is relegated to the periphery where, according to the prevailing ideology, it is secondary and trivial. The energy and attention of the society is focused on harmony at the center, while an attempt is made to control disharmony by banishing it to the periphery where it is ideologically unimportant. Such attempts are not always successful, as we shall see in the next section when we move from social theory to social practice.

The Central Gê take a different approach. They do not focus on name- or age-based moieties at center stage while downplaying kin groups at the periphery. Instead they have patrilineal descent groups, though still maintaining uxorilocality. Their dual organization therefore operates, sometimes with moieties, sometimes without, at both the center and the periphery. The Central Gê thus lack some of the contrasts characteristic of Northern Gê culture: they have neither the contrast between moiety systems at the center that have nothing to do with kinship and kinship groups at the periphery that are not ordered in moieties; nor that between name-based systems on one hand, and descent systems on the other. Among the Central Gê, names are associated, instead of contrasted, with descent groups that operate at all levels of the system.

The Central Gê seek balance and harmony in their systems, not by contrasting name- or age-based ceremonial moieties with kin-based political groups, but by seeking to establish an equilibrium between different sorts of binary institutions. On one hand, they have moieties constructed out of lineage-based factions, rooted in an ideology of patrilineal descent; on the other hand, they have sporting moieties and particularly age-moieties. Names are associated with the first dichotomy which is, in the minds of the Indians, a model of conflict. That conflict model, however, is counterbalanced by institutions that are, in the minds of the Indians, models of complementarity. These are the moieties based on age-sets and the sporting moieties.

It is significant that the log races essential to all major rituals are carried out among the Xavante by age-moieties and among the Xerente by sporting moieties. Two lengths of palm trunk are cut at some distance from the village. A member of each moiety then runs (or staggers) toward the village with the log on his shoulder. When he is tired, he rolls the log onto the proffered shoulder of one of his fellow moiety members. In this way the two teams "race" their logs to the village and dump them on arrival in the mature men's meeting place at the center. The performance, however, is not a race in the ordinary sense of the word. The Indians engage in heated postmortems after such ceremonies, not about who won, but about who ran well and who ran badly, in effect about whether or not the ceremony was well performed. Their idea of a very good performance is one in which everyone exerts himself to the full, runs well, the logs are never dropped, and above all, *the logs arrive simultaneously in the center of the village.* Log races are thus performances explicitly designed to show that equilibrium and harmony can be created out of the disorderly and continuous flow of events. Furthermore, the Indians are conscious of the way they manipulate these binary systems and are eloquent about the dualisms, which they see permeating their society because such dualisms are immanent in the universe.

The Bororo, finally, have an all-pervasive dual organization that is at once cosmic, symbolic, and social (see Crocker 1985). It is expressed through the two major classes of spirits that exist in Bororo cosmology: the *Aroe* and the *Bope.* The Aroe are associated with essence and pure form, as opposed to the Bope who are associated with process and flux. The Aroe are thus static, where the Bope are dynamic. The Aroe are associated with order, the Bope with disorder. The Aroe are comparatively sterile, as compared to the Bope who are associated with both creativity and destruction.[6] The Aroe are rather distant, whereas the Bope are immediate and their influence is both sought and felt.

The whole social order of Bororo moieties and clans belongs to the order of the Aroe. The Bororo hand down name-sets in a manner similar to that found among the Northern Gê, and Crocker (1979) has argued that Bororo clans are more correctly thought of as name-based corporations than as matrilineal descent groups. In any case, names here reinforce the system of descent as they do among the Central Gê. Names are associated then with the Aroe form of Bororo society.

Bororo social theory thus emphasizes the supremacy of the social over the physical. Bororo social life can be seen as an endless social drama in which the Bororo insist on the classic Aroe form and attempt to control the entropic Bope form. The Bope are dangerous, except under special circumstances, and have to be approached with care so that their generative powers can be obtained without the concomitant visitation of their destructive influence. Bororo philosophy elaborates the Aroe-Bope distinction. Bororo religion tries to reconcile the two principles. Bororo social theory attempts to enshrine the Aroe principle in society and to act it out, while controlling and neutralizing the entropic and destructive aspects of the Bope principle.

This discussion of central Brazilian social theories has had to be very

---

6. Compare this with the analysis of the two kinds of power, generative-sexual and destructive-aggressive, sought by the ceremonial moieties performing the Xavante wai'a ceremony (Maybury-Lewis 1967:266, 299).

brief, but the outline I have presented is enough to show that the peoples of this part of the world use a common set of contrasting principles out of which they construct their philosophical schemes. It is out of such contrasts as male-female, center-periphery, name-body, social-physical, ceremonial-instrumental, culture-nature, structure-process, and the relations between these ideas that they build their social theories. Central Brazilian dual organizations can thus be seen as ideologies of equilibrium derived from a theory of a cosmic harmony in which human societies of necessity participate, since they too are part of the scheme of things. Of course the central Brazilians are not alone in believing (or insisting) that there is harmony in the universe and that this harmony stems from the interaction of opposing principles that dialectically establish the balance of things. The idea is so firmly rooted in the great philosophical schemes of the East, and also in much of Western philosophizing, that it may even be for this reason that the central Brazilians were once considered so anomalous. If this is also a central tenet of central Brazilian philosophy, then we must admit that these ideas can be independently developed by societies much less technically sophisticated than our own. Yet the remarkable thing about central Brazilian societies is not so much that they develop these philosophies, but rather the extent to which they have succeeded in living out their beliefs. Their dual organizations are not like smoke screens, as Lévi-Strauss once suggested (1956), but rather ideologies. Like the "cold" societies, which Lévi-Strauss so brilliantly discussed in *La pensée sauvage* (1962), central Brazilian societies see themselves, their past, and their future contained in categories that are immutable and impervious to change. The paradox that they face is that they insist on the timeless nature of their systems while at the same time struggling hard to protect them from erosion. I shall show, however, that this is not as paradoxical as it seems, for the central Brazilians do not take a static view of their dual organizations but think of them rather as systems of dynamic equilibrium.

Social Theory and Social Practice

What, then, are the forces that threaten to undermine or explode these systems of dual organization? Lave (1979) has described how the Krĩkatí suffered depopulation to the verge of extinction in 1935 and then reconstituted themselves as a distinct people, nowadays much influenced by the highway linking Brasília with Belém. In the course of these changes Krĩkatí age-sets and age-moieties vanished and their functions were taken over by the naming system. As a result, the name-based moieties, which had previously coexisted with the age-moieties, emerged as the dominant institution in Krĩkatí society. Da Matta (1982:14–34) described a similar process among the Apinayé. In spite of depopulation and acculturation, resulting from close contact with neighboring Brazilians, name-based moieties remained the dominant institution in Apinayé social theory and practice. Seeger (1981) showed that the Suyá, who suffered even more severe decimation and were regrouped at the time of his study in a single village, similarly maintained their name-based moiety system.

Among the Northern Gê peoples, it is the Gorotire Kayapó who seem to have come closest to abandoning their dual organization. Traditionally they used to allocate males to two opposing men's houses in the center, while downplaying the role of consanguinial groups at the periphery. But this did not succeed in curbing factionalism, which erupted chronically in the central, ceremonial sphere and led to the breakup of village after village. Consequently, when Turner and Bamberger were with the Gorotire Kayapó in the late 1960s, they found that although the Indians claimed that a properly constituted village should have two men's moieties occupying two men's houses, all their communities had for some time been one-moiety villages (see Turner 1979:209). Nevertheless, the Gorotire continued to insist on the moiety system as the proper institutional framework for their society and tended to establish moiety divisions within a single men's house where there was only one such house in a community. Meanwhile Vidal (1977:195–98) described how the Xikrĩ, another branch of the Kayapó, revised their traditional system of two pairs of male moieties, in the senior and junior age grades respectively, and instituted men's moieties that cut across age-grade boundaries.

These examples show the remarkable durability of Northern Gê moiety systems. They do not depend on any specific population size or any particular mode of production for their continuance. They are systems that were generated when the Northern Gê peoples lived in relative isolation. At that time they were adapted to the traditional subsistence economies of these societies and served as the framework for their independent political systems. Yet they did not become obsolete as the economic circumstances of these societies changed, as their populations fluctuated wildly, and as their politics were dramatically altered by contact with the Brazilian frontier.

It might seem, from the Kayapó examples, that Northern Gê dual organization came closest to disappearing in precisely those societies that used their moieties as their major political institutions. Nevertheless, the Kayapó still think in terms of moieties and are still explicitly recreating moiety systems. I suggest that they do not do this because of the material conditions of their present existence, but rather because they think that this is the proper way for their societies to be constituted.

We should in fact beware of assuming that politics may explode dual organization in central Brazil. This is simply to accept the thinking of many of the central Brazilians about their own societies. Our studies show that this is often their fear and concern, but that dual organization appears to be as durable in societies that use it for political purposes as it is in those that explicitly separate their binary associations from political action.

The Xavante are a case in point. When I revisited them in 1982, I discovered that they had waged a successful battle for the demarcation of their lands. They are now engaged in intensive, tractor-powered rice cultivation for the market. They also have a wide network of contacts in Brazilian society through which they seek economic favors for their villages. They are relatively successful in obtaining their benefits, because they have become famous in recent years as the proud Indians who stood up to the government's Indian agency. Xavante chiefs often appear in the Brazilian press or on television, making speeches (sometimes in the Xavante language) about Xavante rights in particular and the Indian question in general. It is therefore not surprising that the first Indian ever to enter the Brazilian Congress as a federal deputy is a Xavante who was elected in Rio de Janeiro in November 1982. In spite of these dramatic changes from their relatively isolated, hunting and gathering way of life only twenty-five years ago, the Xavante still maintain the traditional form of their villages. These continue to be laid out in semicircular fashion and the men's councils and men's ceremonies are still held in the "center."[7] Furthermore, the categorical opposition between "people of my side" and "people of the other side," which I described as the central principle of Shavante society (Maybury-Lewis 1967), still structures their thinking and serves as a matrix for their politics. Thus both the Xavante and the Kayapó, societies that made great political use of their binary systems, have shown that these are derived from social theories that can accommodate the most dramatic changes and still continue to determine social practice.

---

7. All Xavante are still clearly agreed on how a proper, semicircular village should be arranged, and many Xavante villages are indeed set out this way. In fact, the village of Pimentel Barbosa, which I know best, has recently returned to a more clearly demarcated semicircle of traditional, conical houses, replacing the square Brazilian-style houses that some people had begun to put up. But there are nowadays more and more problems with making the actual village plan conform to the ideal one (see Lopes da Silva 1983:49).

After this it will come as no surprise to learn that the Bororo, who have suffered much in recent decades, have nevertheless retained a version of their dual organization (Viertler 1976). It has survived the disappearance of some Bororo communities and the temporary, despairing decision of another village to go out of existence by not having children. It has survived the vicissitudes of the Bororo being regrouped in mission villages and has even survived the rampant alcoholism that affected them.

The remarkable thing about the dual organizations of central Brazil is their extraordinary resilience. They are so adaptive that they do not change (or are not changed) to the extent of losing their binary character altogether. Central Brazilian societies have experienced depopulation, the breakup of their communities, and their reconstitution under different circumstances, all under the impact of the frontier of Brazilian settlement; they have abandoned some of their institutions, revised others, and reorganized the relations between them; and all this while maintaining their dual organizations in one form or another. It seems that, in the short run, contact with the Brazilian world leads the Indian peoples of central Brazil to emphasize their own ways in self-defense and thus to accentuate their dual organizations.

The Xerente have probably come closer than any other central Brazilian people to abandoning their dual organization. The history of this process is therefore worth considering in a little more detail. They have been in constant contact with Brazilians for well over a century. The area that they inhabit, in the north of the state of Goiás, is remote and was until recently relatively inaccessible. Nevertheless, when Nimuendajú studied them in the 1930s, he said that he found Xerente culture "in a state of collapse" (1942:8). He attributed this largely to the disappearance of the men's associations (age-sets). My wife and I visited the Xerente in 1955–56 and again in 1963, and on the basis of our observations I came to a rather different set of conclusions concerning Xerente culture and society. I suggested that their way of life had shown surprising persistence. Their age-set system was indeed moribund, but moiety and clan reckoning still persisted. I concluded therefore that the associational or age-set system was less vital to Xerente culture than Nimuendajú had supposed, and that this culture was being maintained in a self-consciously Xerente fashion on the basis of "moieties as a conceptual matrix and the clans as potential factions" (Maybury-Lewis 1979:221). At that time, then, the Xerente were reacting, like the other central Brazilian societies I have discussed, to the profound changes affecting them. They were maintaining their sense of themselves by incorporating these changes into their own dualistic view of how Xerente society should properly be constituted.

When we visited the Xerente again in 1984, we found that the situation had changed.[8] It is now only older Xerente who remember how their society should properly be organized according to their ancient traditions. Younger Xerente have a keen sense that their traditional culture is disappearing, but only a hazy idea of how it used to be. Young adult men do not know their clan affiliations, for they are less interested in Xerente politics than they are in Brazilian affairs.

Xerente politics are themselves no longer conducted in traditional fashion. When the Xerente saw their villages as paradigmatic representations of their world, their communities expressed the binary division that was essential to their cosmology and social theory. But it was a dialectical opposition, producing in society a dynamic tension that had to be constantly mediated. So the "people of our side" would meet the "people of the other side" in the nightly councils held at the center of the village, where the opposition between them could be both reaffirmed and transcended. Nowadays these councils take place, if at all, in the house of a chief, and they are routinely attended only by his own faction.

The intimate relationship between the spatial arrangement of the village and the Xerente way of life is further illustrated by another interesting development. Three communities have made a conscious effort to revive Xerente tradition by rebuilding their villages according to the old plan. Yet they have constructed circular, rather than semicircular ones. The elders in these communities are aware that traditional Xerente villages were semicircular, but they go along with the circular ones (imitating their Northern Gê neighbors) because such villages are aesthetically pleasing, feel traditional, and, above all, provide the sharpest contrast with Brazilian hamlets. Small Brazilian settlements in the interior are built along a single street and Brazilians refer to any township as *a rua* (the street) irrespective of its shape. For the Xerente, the contrast between the *rua* and the Indian village (*aldeia*) sums up the contrast between two ways of life, between modernity and tradition, a contrast that is sometimes also thought of as between progress and backwardness. Even in those Xerente villages that had been rebuilt in a circle, there were plenty of Indians who said it would have been better and more progressive to build them as a street.

In the most traditional Xerente village we visited, the elders have arranged it so that one chief from each moiety lives on each side of the circle in houses approximately facing each other. Only one of these chiefs is knowledgeable about Xerente tradition or about clan and moiety membership. And yet moieties are essential to certain ceremonies that the Xerente still perform, notably log races and the boys' name-giving. On these occa-

8. I gratefully acknowledge the funds provided by the Ford Foundation as part of a consultancy in Brazil which made it possible for us to return to the Xerente in 1984.

sions, participants are organized into two named opposing groups, but nowadays people are allocated to the two sides on an ad hoc basis at the time of the ceremonies so that the moieties have little consistency outside of the ceremonial context.[9] In this way the binary structure of the ceremonies is maintained, even when the membership in the moieties that perform the ceremonies is neither constant nor remembered. Among contemporary Xerente, then, their traditional culture is becoming a matter of essentially folkloric interest. Yet even as they cease to live it, they remember its dualistic properties, for which the recollection of their moiety systems serves as a mnemonic device.

It should now be clear why dual organizations in central Brazil are so adaptable and so durable. It is because they are independent of particular institutions or practices. They are views of society or perhaps theories about society that can be used to generate a variety of different institutions and different patterns of relationship between these institutions. A society subscribing to such a theory can undergo considerable change without having to abandon it. Such a society merely reorganizes its institutions to reflect its enduring vision of the binary nature of things. It is only when its members abandon their traditional culture that they lose interest in the binary world view that informed it. Yet as the Xerente example shows both clearly and poignantly, it is the dualism of their ancient traditions that remains for them the most compelling memory of their past and the last one to fade.

Theoretical Implications

Now that it is established that the dual organizations of the Gê and the Bororo are preeminently social theories, I will discuss some of the more immediate implications of that conclusion, while leaving the discussion of more general issues for the Introduction to this volume.

It is now clear that these systems are not rooted in descent; nor are they functions of kinship. On the contrary, many central Brazilian societies take pains to stress the antikinship nature of their moieties. So, among the Apinayé, it is a *surrogate* father (no relative) who is required to sponsor a boy when he acquires the names through which he enters the name-based moieties. Similarly, among the Kayapó, it is a surrogate father who is required to sponsor a boy when he enters the men's age moieties. Among the Xavante, age moieties are explicitly contrasted with kin-based dual organization. Among the Bororo, a system of apparently matrilineal moi-

---

9. I cannot be sure that the allocation to moieties on ceremonial occasions is completely ad hoc. Some men do know their moieties and may make sure that they line up correctly with them. Many, however, do not, and their numbers appear to be growing.

eties is considered by the Indians themselves to be a system of name-based moieties. Descent or kinship is thus only one of a variety of principles used by the central Brazilian peoples for recruiting people into their moiety systems. In fact, the Indians do not apparently feel the need for any independent principle of recruitment at all. If necessary they simply assign people (usually males) to permanent or temporary pairs of groups that function as moieties in specific situations.

The central Brazilian systems cannot therefore be accounted for by the sort of theory that Lévi-Strauss put forward in *Les structures élémentaires de la parenté* (1949), where dual organization is explained in terms of reciprocity and marriage alliance between descent groups. Similarly, Lévi-Strauss's (1952) reinterpretation of the central Brazilian systems was based on faulty premises. He pointed out that these societies were neither comprehensively binary nor rigidly symmetric and, through an analysis of these supposed "anomalies," came to the conclusion that they were actually asymmetric systems masquerading as dual organizations. But we have seen that the central Brazilian systems are highly complex. Not only can they accommodate asymmetry and disequilibrium, they presuppose it. Their raison d'etre is in fact to express and control these tendencies — something which they do without necessarily resorting to exogamous moieties. We are not therefore dealing with inherently asymmetrical societies pretending to be symmetric, or inherently dynamic ones pretending to be static. The societies of central Brazil cannot usefully be categorized in such either/or terms. I have elsewhere called them dialectical societies because such oppositions are contained within their systems (Maybury-Lewis 1979). They are conscious of them, and their social theory and social practice is a constant attempt to synthesize them.

Nor am I convinced by the argument of Lévi-Strauss's famous paper (1956), in which he questioned whether dual organizations in general (and the central Brazilian ones in particular) existed. This is not the place to continue my debate with Lévi-Strauss on such matters,[10] but certain points in that discussion have to be mentioned, since they bear on the thesis I am presenting here. The first concerns concentric dualism. It is obvious that the central Brazilian Indians make much use of this idea, as reflected in my discussion of their systems. It was one of Lévi-Strauss's great contributions to the analysis of dual organization to have perceived the importance of concentric dualism and to have embarked on an analysis of its significance. I think, however, that he misunderstood its significance in central Brazil and that he was incorrect about its formal significance elsewhere.

---

10. The original exchange is found in Maybury-Lewis 1960 and Lévi-Strauss 1960.

Lévi-Strauss contrasted concentric with diametric dualism. He called diametric the form where, for example, moieties are held to be diametrically opposed either physically or conceptually to each other. He called concentric the form where, for example, the center of the village is contrasted socially and symbolically with the periphery. He argued that diametric dualism was essentially binary, symmetric, closed on itself, and inert. Concentric dualism, on the other hand, was asymmetric, for its very conceptualization required surroundings—a third term, logically speaking—beyond the periphery. It was thus inherently ternary and dynamic, offering prospects for change in the system and eventually for transformation of a dual organization into something else.[11]

There is however no formal reason for diametric dualism to be a closed and static system while concentric dualism is open and dynamic. Neither system exists in a vacuum. The significance of either system depends therefore on how people use it, on how they "situate" it, both cosmologically and sociologically. It follows that the meaning and the implications of these systems can only be properly understood in their ethnographic contexts. This requires the sort of total analysis that I have outlined in this essay.

There are therefore no formal grounds for accepting Lévi-Strauss's suggestions concerning the meaning of concentric and diametric dualism. Furthermore the ethnography does not support them. Central Brazilian societies employ both forms of dualism. They often consider the diametric form (e.g., when expressed through kin-based moieties) to be dynamic, indeed too volatile for comfort. At other times they consider the concentric form (e.g., when expressed through the symbolic opposition of male/center and female/periphery) as an eternal and essentially timeless complementarity. In their thinking, both diametric and concentric dualisms can be either static or dynamic. It depends on the content of the particular dualism and the context in which it is expressed.

I have outlined my reasons for thinking that Lévi-Strauss's discussions of central Brazilian systems were too formal and simplistic because the discussion helps us to understand some salient features of those systems. The dual organizations of central Brazil make use of an impressive variety of binary ideas and institutions, whose significance can only be understood in context. Seeger (this volume) emphasizes this point and argues that the Suya Indians of central Brazil not only manipulate an array of dualisms in their culture, but they use many of them in quite specific

---

11. The structure of this argument parallels that of the thesis developed in Lévi-Strauss 1949, where he suggests that dual organization is a form of restricted exchange, symmetric and closed in upon itself, in contrast to generalized exchange, which is open and asymmetric.

contexts. It follows that any analysis of such systems requires an understanding of such contexts as well as the pattern and dynamic of the relations between them.

Central Brazilian systems are thus complex and difficult to analyze. Their elements are regularly combined into models that inform the thought and actions of the Indians. Each society uses a number of such models, so the analyst needs to know when they are used and in what combinations. The total system of such a society juxtaposes tendencies that are frequently antithetical to each other (see Almagor, this volume).

It is now clear (and demonstrated in various essays in this volume) that such a dialectic between alternative or opposing models is quite common in dual organizations. It could almost be said to be characteristic of them. So too is asymmetry and imbalance, both within the oppositions that go to make up a dual organization and, at any given moment, within the system as a whole. This characteristic of dual organization is also amply documented in this volume, but it has not always received sufficient emphasis in the past. Too much of our theorizing has been mesmerized by the idea of dual organization as perfect equivalence, with the corollary that, where there is hierarchy or imbalance, these ideas and their implementation tend to undermine the binary system. Hierarchy, like concentric dualism, is neither logically nor sociologically incompatible with thoroughgoing and persistent dual organization. We need only look as far as the Inca empire to see that this is so. Moreover, it is formally obvious that a hierarchical arrangement of paired categories or groups is perfectly consistent with dual organization.

The idea that hierarchy is somehow subversive of and ultimately incompatible with dual organization seems to derive from two separate contentions. First, it is held that differential (hierarchical) evaluation of categories and groups in a binary system would necessarily undermine it. But we have seen that the differential weighting of complementary categories is fundamental to the resilient central Brazilian systems and we know that this is frequently found elsewhere. On the other hand, where hierarchy involves categories or groups of people, then the ranked strata can easily be bifurcated to maintain a dual organization. The second argument about the incompatibility of hierarchy with dual organization derives from the idea that dual organization is essentially a system of reciprocity between equals, probably involving the exchange of spouses. Here again the central Brazilian data demonstrate that dual organization is not necessarily rooted in reciprocal exchanges between groups and certainly does not depend on intermarriage between them. Reciprocity is a logically necessary attribute of any system with only two elements in it, but it has sometimes been thought that it was the reciprocity which gave rise to the system, whereas in central Brazil (and often, I would suggest, elsewhere) it is the system which creates the reciprocity. This is demonstrated by the central Brazilian data that show how the terms of the reciprocity can change drastically without destroying the system. Reciprocity, in short, is a function of dual organization, not a cause of it.

We have established that the elements of central Brazilian social theories and the moiety systems associated with them are often unlike and unequal. These dual organizations are thus far from being mere binary systems of classification, imposing some sort of glacial order on an inert universe. The central Brazilians do feel that there is order in the cosmic scheme of things and that their own communities are part of that order, but they are not passive parts. They have to work hard to synthesize those complementary and competing forces that might balance each other in the long run but could easily unbalance and destroy a community or a people in the short run. Their systems, then, are thought to be in considerable tension, held in precarious equilibrium.

This brings me back to central Brazilian concepts of time. As we have seen, the Gê and the Bororo are quite conscious of process in their scheme of things. They also have a lively sense of history (see Seeger, in this volume); but they separate history from structure. In this they differ from most of the societies discussed in this volume, who incorporate their own visions of time into the structure of their systems. The central Brazilians have no concept analogous to the aboriginal dreamtime (see Yengoyan, in this volume). They do not, in the manner of some of the Ethiopian peoples, see their existence as oscillating between sacred time and profane time (see Hinant, in this volume). Their views are perhaps furthest of all from those of the Indonesians, who conceive of the past as projected into the present and at the same time consider their dual organizations to be the historical outcomes of imposing order on the untidy process of clan formation (see Fox, Traube, and Valeri, in this volume). Unlike the Indonesians, who see their present systems as resulting from the reordering that necessarily took place when their original state of undivided plenitude was shattered, the central Brazilians conceive of their dual organizations as timeless in two senses: they are given in the scheme of things, but they are also set apart from and thus impervious to the flow of events.

This imperviousness is perhaps their most striking characteristic, especially when we consider how relatively small the central Brazilian Indian populations are and the potentially shattering events that have overtaken them in recent years. Yet it is a characteristic shared by many other systems of dual organization.

Andean dual organization is a case in point. The Incaic worldview was a model that could be used to organize an empire or to determine the arrangement of individual villages (see Zuidema 1964). It has survived the vicissitudes of the Spanish conquest and the political and economic changes visited upon the Andean people as a result of it, and can still be found operating in the organization of present-day Andean villages (see Flores 1971; Isbell 1978; and Sklar 1981).

The Australian systems have been similarly persistent. Although their dual organizations are frequently rooted in their kinship systems (see Maddock, in this volume), the aborigines can and do change and experiment with those systems without undermining the dual organization itself. Indeed as Yengoyan (in this volume) shows, kin-based moiety systems are not essential to aboriginal dual organization. The system is essentially a social theory that requires neither a certain institution nor a certain kind of institutional arrangement for its expression.

Some East African dual organizations appear to be different in that their dual organization is indeed rooted in a particular kind of institution, the age-set system (see Almagor, Spencer, and Lamphear, in this volume). In this connection Spencer develops an argument that takes Barth's (1959) essay on game theory and the Swat Pathans as its starting point. Barth suggested that, given the rules of the political game among the Pathans, if each player pursued his own interests, then the outcome would tend to produce contrasting political factions that were stable over time. Spencer similarly argues that men in Maasai age-set systems cyclically reproduce their dual organization by following their own self-interest.

This kind of dual organization appears to contrast with those I have previously been discussing, where there is an ideological commitment to binary organization, which is given cosmic justification. One type of dual organization is the outcome of self-interested actions, while the other is an ideological matrix for such actions. Yet the consequences seem to be remarkably similar in both cases. One might reasonably expect that the seemingly "utilitarian" dual organizations discussed by Spencer would be unstable, for circumstances could well force the modification or abandonment of the age-set systems that served as their vehicle. Yet the Maasai and the Samburu have confronted changing circumstances without abandoning their age-sets. I suggest that this is because their age-set systems have more than an instrumental role to play in their societies. This raises the interesting question as to why some East African societies maintain their age-set systems in the face of change, while others allow them to wither. The answer could well be related to the notion of ideological commitment versus instrumental convenience that I have been discussing here. I suspect that some East African peoples are more ideological while others are more utilitarian in their approaches to age-set systems.

This brings us back to the argument I have been making for the dual organizations of central Brazil, which stresses their ideological nature. They are comprehensive social theories, linking cosmos and society and giving the cultures of the Gê and the Bororo their characteristic stamp. While it is difficult to say much about how these systems arose, it is not so difficult to see how and why they endure. They do so because they are not dependent on political, demographic or ecological circumstances and are thus insulated from changes in those circumstances. Furthermore, central Brazilian systems are dependent on no particular institution. They are capable of generating new institutional arrangements when and where it may be necessary. These dual organizations are therefore likely to survive until the Gê and the Bororo die out or abandon their cultures.

REFERENCES

Bamberger, Joan. 1979. Exit and voice in central Brazil: The politics of flight in Kayapó society. In Maybury-Lewis, ed., 1979, 130–46.
Barth, Fredrik. 1959. Segmentary opposition and the theory of games. *Journal of the Royal Anthropological Institute* 89:5–22.
Carneiro da Cunha, Manuela. 1978. *Os mortos e os outros*. São Paulo: Hucitec.
Colbacchini, Antonio, and Albisetti, Cesare. 1942. *Os Bororos orientais Orarimogodogue do planalto oriental de Mato Grosso*. São Paulo: Companhia Editora Nacional.
Crocker, J. Christopher. 1979. Selves and alters among the Eastern Bororo. In Maybury-Lewis, ed., 1979, 249–300.
———. 1985. *Vital souls: Bororo cosmology, natural symbolism and shamanism*. Tucson: University of Arizona Press.
Da Matta, Roberto. 1982. *A divided world: Apinayé social structure*. Cambridge: Harvard University Press.
Flores, Salvador. 1971. Duality in the socio-cultural organization of several Andean populations. *Folk* 13:65–88.
Haekel, Josef. 1939. Zweiklassensystem, Männerhaus und Totemismus in Südamerika. *Zeitschrift für Ethnologie* 70:426–54.
Isbell, Billie Jean. 1978. *To defend ourselves: Ecology and ritual in an Andean village*. Austin: Institute of Latin American Studies, University of Texas.
Kroeber, A. L. 1942. The societies of primitive man. *Biological Symposia* 8:205–16.
Lave, Jean. 1979. Cycles and trends in Krĩkatí naming practices. In Maybury-Lewis, ed., 1979, 16–44.
Lévi-Strauss, Claude. 1944. On dual organization in South America. *America indigena* 4:37–47.
———. 1949. *Les structures élémentaires de la parenté*. Paris: Presses universitaires de France.
———. 1952. Les structures sociales dans le Brésil central et oriental. In *Indian*

tribes of aboriginal America, ed. Sol Tax, 302–10. Selected papers of the Twenty-ninth International Congress of Americanists. Chicago: University of Chicago Press.

———. 1956. Les organisations dualistes, existent-elles? *Bijdragen tot de Taal-, Land- en Volkenkunde* 112:99–128.

———. 1960. On manipulated sociological models. *Bijdragen tot de Taal-, Land- en Volkenkunde* 116:45–54.

———. 1962. *La pensée sauvage.* Paris: Plon.

Lopes da Silva, Aracy. 1986. Nomes e amigos: da prática Xavante a uma reflexão sobre os Jê. Antropologia 6. São Paulo: Universidade de São Paulo.

Maybury-Lewis, David. 1960. The analysis of dual organizations: A methodological critique. *Bijdragen tot de Taal-, Land- en Volkenkunde* 116:17–44.

———. 1967. *Akwẽ-Shavante society.* Oxford: Clarendon Press.

———. 1979. Cultural categories of the Central Gê. In Maybury-Lewis, ed., 1979, 218–46.

Maybury-Lewis, David, ed. 1979. *Dialectical societies: The Gê and Bororo of central Brazil.* Cambridge: Harvard University Press.

Melatti, Julio Cezar. 1972. *O messianismo Krahó.* São Paulo: Herder.

———. 1978. *Ritos de uma tribo Timbira.* São Paulo: Atica.

Nimuendajú, Curt. 1939. *The Apinayé.* Washington, D.C.: Catholic University of America.

———. 1942. *The Šerente.* Los Angeles: The Southwest Museum.

———. 1946. *The Eastern Timbira.* Berkeley and Los Angeles: University of California Press.

Seeger, Anthony. 1981. *Nature and society in central Brazil: The Suyá Indians of Mato Grosso.* Cambridge: Harvard University Press.

Skar, Harald O. 1981. *The warm valley people.* Oslo: Universitatsforlaget.

Turner, Terence. 1979. Kinship, household, and community structure among the Kayapó. In Maybury-Lewis ed. 1979, 179–214.

Vidal, Lux. 1977. *Morte e vida de uma sociedade indígena brasileira.* São Paulo: Hucitec.

Viertler, Renate. 1976. *As aldeias Bororo: Alguns aspectos de sua organização social.* São Paulo: Museu Paulista.

Zuidema, R. Tom. 1964. *The Ceque system of Cuzco.* Leiden: Brill.

Chapter 5

Reciprocal Centers:
The Siwa-Lima System in the Central Moluccas

Valerio Valeri

The central and southern Moluccas are famous for a moiety system that once encompassed all societies from Seram to Aru in the southeast, and that even now is ideologically important. I call this the Siwa-Lima system because one moiety is identified with the numerical index nine (*siwa*), and the other with the numerical index five (*lima*).

These two indexes are prefixed or suffixed to different words in different areas. In Seram they are suffixed to the word *pata* or *fata* and sometimes, especially in the past, to *uli*. They are also prefixed to the word *taun*. In Amron the two numerals are suffixed to *uli*, and in Banda, Kei, and Aru, to the corresponding words *ur* or *uri*, (van Hoëvell 1890; Sachse 1907:60; *Seran* 1922:33; Duyvendak 1926:77–78; de Vries 1927:144; Jensen 1948:152–58; Nutz 1959:89; Cooley 1962:13–18; Barraud 1979:62; Valeri, field notes).

Uli is glossed as "sibling" or "again and again" or "people," so Ulisiwa means "nine-phratry" or "nine times" or "nine-people" (see sources quoted by Duyvendack 1926:77 n. 2). "Nine-people" is also the meaning given to Patasiwa by Jensen and Niggemeyer (1939:72). Duyvendack (1926:78 n. 2) connects *pata* with *hata-i* or *pata-i* in the language of Paulohi (western Seram), a word meaning "tree trunk" or "tribe," but he acknowledges that the Malay word *badan* ("body") may have become fused with the original Seramese word. He also reminds us that an early eighteenth-century source, Valentijn ([724–26]), gives *patan* the meaning "assembly" (see also Ludeking 1868:56). Thus Patasiwa may mean "nine trunks" or "nine tribes" or "nine assemblies" (Duyvendack 1926).[1]

---

1. A folk etymology from western Seram derives *pata* from the Malay *patah*, "broken," and therefore emphasizes that Siwa and Lima are the two parts of an allegedly original whole (Krayer van Aalst 1920:98–101).

117

The word *taun* is used mainly in the Taluti area of southern central Seram, where it means "set" or "confederation" (Valeri, field notes). I shall call one moiety "five-moiety" or "Lima moiety" or simply "Lima"; the other, "nine-moiety" or "Siwa-moiety" or simply "Siwa." Each society included in a moiety will be referred to as "five-group" or "Lima group" if it belongs to the five-moiety, or as "nine-group" or "Siwa group" if it belongs to the nine-moiety. I shall also say—following the people of central Seram, among whom I have done my fieldwork—that a group is "Siwa" or "Lima," meaning that it belongs to the Siwa or Lima moiety.

Apart from their numerical indexes, the moieties have or had other symbolic marks, such as "male" and "female," "inside" and "outside," "landward" and "seaward," "autochthonous" and "immigrant," and—less often—"right" and "left," "life" and "death," "black" and "white," and so on. The same marks are not always associated with the same moieties in all areas. For instance, it is reported that in western Seram "male" is associated with the Siwa moiety and "female" with the Lima moiety (Jensen 1948:46, 53, 56, 72, 231–32). But in Ambon and central Seram, societies in both moieties agree that Lima is "male" and Siwa is "female" (Manusama 1977:34–35; Valeri, field notes).

Analogously, both in the central and the southern Moluccas the Siwa groups are usually connected with the "inland" direction because they are considered "autochthonous," while the Lima groups, as paradigmatic "immigrants," are connected with the seaward direction (van Ekris 1861:319; Riedel 1886:90; Jensen 1948:50, 57; Ribbe 1888:172; Valeri, field notes). But some sources claim that the opposite correlations exist (Duyvendack 1926:72).

The traditional location of Siwa and Lima groups on most islands lends support to the view that in former times the frequently used contrast Siwa = "autochthonous" versus Lima = "immigrant" was not purely arbitrary. The Lima were often located in coastal areas, as in southeastern Seram, or in areas directly involved in trade, as in the Hitu Peninsula in Ambon and in northern Seram. That the Lima are sometimes located between two Siwa areas, as in Seram and Kei Kecil (Duyvendack 1926:136), suggests that they wedged themselves in. On the other hand, in the most commercialized areas, such as the Hoamoal Peninsula in western Seram or the Banda islands, both moieties were equally involved with the outside and lived close to the coast. It is therefore impossible to view the autochthonous-immigrant, landward-seaward contrasts as mere reflections of an actual situation.

Until the arrival of the European colonial powers, both moieties included pagans, but Moslem groups were in the Lima moiety, as befits its connection with the "outside." In contrast, the Siwa moiety was said to include mostly pagans. But when the Portuguese established their strong-hold in Ambon in Siwa territory in the sixteenth century, and members of the nine-moiety cooperated with them and even converted to Christianity, that religion became associated with the Siwa. The association was strengthened after the Dutch established their domination of the central Moluccas and allied themselves with the Siwa of Seram (Valentijn [1724–26]: 2:821; van der Crab 1862:212–13; Tiele and Heeres 1886: 1:196, 204, 244; Duyvendack 1926:81–82; Wessels 1934:29–30; Jacobs 1980:11–12; Rumphius, n.d., 191).

These symbolical and factual associations of Islam with Lima and of Christianity with Siwa conditioned the history of conversion in the central Moluccas, where nine-groups have tended to convert to Christianity, five-groups to Islam. The Lima (and pagan) Huaulu of central Seram, among whom I did most of my fieldwork from 1972 to 1973, still believe in these connections between moieties and religions. They repeatedly told me, "We have no intention of converting, but if we have to, it should be to Islam not to Christianity, because we are Lima." Elsewhere I was told that Europe, being Christian, is Siwa. This echoes the seventeenth-century Seramese view that the Dutch were Siwa (Rumphius 1910: 2:84).[2]

It is important to realize that the relationship between a moiety and the group it encompasses is conceived as a type/token relationship. In other words, a group is classified as five or nine because it is supposed to exemplify a number of features associated with the five- or nine-moiety. The principle of these features is the numerical one, which is realized in various forms in actual societies.

A frequently held view, as I shall show in greater detail later, is that a nine-group consists of nine units (or can be analyzed as such in some way), while a five-group consists of five units. Also common is the view that rituals, music, dances, and so on, are organized by five-part schemes in the five-groups and by nine-part schemes in the nine-groups (see *Seran* 1922:288; Valentijn [1724–26]: 2:87; van Rees 1866:106; Tichelman 1922; Duyvendack 1926:78–79).

The numerical indexes therefore give the basic rhythms that, at least

---

2. Banda seems to be an exception to the view that Siwa is religiously "traditional" or Christian, and Lima Moslem; when the Europeans first visited it, all Bandanese were Moslem. Yet a myth on the origin of Banda, which survived — probably with many transformations and borrowings from Ambonese culture — the uprooting of much of the original population by the Dutch in the seventeenth century, displays the opposition found elsewhere. The myth says that five siblings — called Urlima like the five-moiety (van Ronkel 1945:126) — travelled to Mekkah, whence they brought Islam to, as the text puts it, "our land Negri Ursiwah, which means Negri Sembilan ['Nine Villages' in Malay V.V.]" (van Ronkel 1945:127). Thus an opposition is made between the originally pagan, "aboriginal" Siwa and the Moslem and originally "immigrant" Lima. (The expression *Negri Sembilan* is also used in a palace chronicle from Bacan to refer to the Siwa of western Seram; see Coolhaas 1923:447, 481, 506.)

in theory, organize social action in each moiety. More generally, all the features associated with each moiety are the basic cultural categories ascribed to the societies that belong to them. In this respect, Siwa and Lima must be seen as the two most general categories — and therefore types — of groups. At the highest level, then, the opposition of Siwa and Lima is a categorical opposition. Yet this opposition is applied to the relationship between discrete territorial groups in each large island or archipelago; at this level, the opposition is one of groups. Indeed, each archipelago (such as Kei, Aru, or Banda) or island (such as Ambon or Seram) was divided into a Lima territory and a Siwa territory. I call these "local sections" of the moieties.

Potentially, Siwa groups of different archipelagoes could combine their forces against an analogous combination of Lima groups. But there was no Athens or Sparta in the southern Moluccas. Local solidarity and the difficulty of developing and maintaining interinsular alliances without a centralized system of power seem to have checked this possibility. Nevertheless, until the Dutch defeated it in the mid–seventeenth century, the community of Hitu, which led the Lima moiety in Ambon, had been developing a system of interinsular ties over much of the central Moluccas and beyond. Thus Hitu had political connections with the Lima of southern Seram (Valentijn [1724–26]: 1:240, 2:69–70; Rumphius 1910: 1:83) and with the Lima of Banda (van Vollenhoven 1918: 2:792). Furthermore, one of the ruling houses of Hitu had kinship ties with the ruling lineage of Lisabata, leader of the Lima in northern Seram, as well as with an important lineage of Luhu, a Lima principality on the Hoamoal Peninsula in Seram. These kinship ties also implied ties with the northern Moluccan sultanates of Jailolo or Bacan (depending on the versions; see Valentijn [1724–26]: 1:236, 270–71; 2:55–56; Manusama 1977:21), which were influential in the central Moluccas. Hitu had also established a political alliance with the sultanate of Ternate, again in the northern Moluccas (Rijali 1977: chap. 8; Valentijn [1724–26]: 2:240). No comparable network seems to have developed among the Siwa. On the other hand, the Dutch were able to mobilize the Siwa on a vast scale for military purposes, thanks to the influence of three Siwa "kings" — Sahulau, Sumit, and Siseulu — in western Seram (see de Vlamingh van Oudtshoorn 1650–51:119; Valentijn [1724–26]: 2:72–75, 78–79, 80–84).

Although rather vast regional networks seem to have developed before the Dutch established effective political control in the Moluccas, the really important networks were at a more restricted level, in each archipelago or large area. Each discrete territory classified as Siwa or Lima seems to have belonged to some form of confederal order. In the areas most involved with trade, certain groups tended to become leaders of these confederations, in an embryonic process of political "centering," rather than centralization. Let us consider these confederations beginning with western Seram. There all the Siwa were members of a large confederation, the Three Rivers, which had special meeting places and leaders at least until the beginning of this century (*Seran* 1922:278–88; Duyvendack 1926; Jensen 1948:80–125; Leirissa et al. 1982:45–54).

East of the Three Rivers confederation live the majority of the tribes that affiliate with the Lima moiety in Seram. Those in the north were for a long time under the influence of the rulers of Lisabata and indeed were often exploited by them (Valentijn [1724–26]: 2:55–56, 58; Rumphius, n.d., 111–112, 113, 114, 115). These Lima also had a meeting place — similar to those of the Three Rivers confederation — on the Sapalewa River in north central Seram (Valentijn [1724–26]: 2:59; Valeri, field notes). East of these Lima is a second section of the Siwa moiety. This was under the somewhat tenuous leadership of the Lord of Manusela, although in the south the Siwa were hegemonized by the powerful community of Taluti (Valeri, field notes; Röder 1948).

Southeastern Seram is again Lima territory. These Lima were under three rulers (Kilmuri, Tobo, Werinama) and were connected with the Lima in south central Seram through a fourth ruler, Sepa. These four Lima rulers were collectively called *Raja Empat* ("four kings" in Malay) and were themselves unified by their common reference to a "fifth," an external sultan (Valeri, field notes; see Röder 1948:24).

In Ambon, as already mentioned, the Lima were dominated by Hitu; in Banda, each of the two local sections of the moieties was closely knit, and the Lima seem to have been led by four kings, analogous to the four Lima kings of southern Seram and the four Lima rulers (*perdana*) of Hitu.[3] In Aru, each moiety was supposedly led by a trader-ruler (Kolff 1840:194–95; Brumund 1845:288–90; van Eijbergen 1864:557–58; van Eijbergen 1866: 199; Muller, n.d.). Influential rulers successively claimed control of all Siwa or of all Lima in Kei as well (Bosscher 1855:23–26; van Eijbergen 1866:254, 268–69).

These few facts suffice to indicate that the Siwa-Lima system presupposes the existence of metatribal, territorially discrete confederations. The confederations, in turn, presuppose a system of trade (see van Leur 1967).

---

3. On the four kings of Banda, see Valentijn [1724–26]: 3:29, 290–91; Beschrijuinge 1855:78. These kings are mentioned in the first contract (1602) between the Dutch East India Company and the Bandanese (de Jonge 1862–1909: 2:536; Heeres and Stapel 1907:23; van der Chijs 1866:169–70). One king was the ruler of the "towns" of Dender and Rosengein; the others ruled Labetaka, Waier, and Salama. Since in a somewhat later and more accurate report (Beschrijuinge 1855), these "towns" are all said to be Lima, except Labetaka, which in the meantime had become Siwa, I infer that the four kings were all Lima at the time of the first contract.

Thus the historical evidence seems to indicate that this sytem of moieties developed as an application of the culturally pervasive dualistic principle to the regional alliances and conflicts induced by the ancient trade in the spices (cloves and nutmeg) that grow in this area. Moreover, the very contrast between peoples directly connected with coastal trade and those living inland seems to have partly motivated, at least originally, the partition into moieties.

Some ancient observers (Rumphius, n.d., 197, 201; Valentijn [1724–26]: 1:249) recognized that the Siwa-Lima system was connected with political processes induced by trade but were reluctant to view it as an autonomous development. They preferred to postulate that it had originated in the extension to the southern Moluccas of the rivalry between the two northern Moluccan sultanates of Ternate and Tidore. They compared the Siwa and Lima to the Guelfs and Ghibellines of medieval Europe, which corresponded to the papacy and the empire, respectively. Although the sultanates were involved in the Siwa-Lima system,[4] this view cannot be accepted for at least two reasons. One is that the influence of the sultanates never extended to Banda, Kei, and Aru, where the Siwa-Lima system also existed (see van der Chijs 1866:73–74). Another is that the Siwa and the Lima did not form merely a "political two-bloc system" (Barth 1981: 2:72)

---

4. Those who maintain the theory I am criticizing usually imply that one moiety was associated with the index "nine" because the corresponding sultanate was divided into nine units, while the other was "five" because of the fivefold structure of the sultanate matched with it (Rumphius 1910: 1:16; Ludeking 1868:56). This supposition is patently false. In the first place, the sultanates seem to have changed sides in the course of time. Originally, Ternate was associated with the Lima, Tidore with the Siwa (Tiele and Heeres 1886–95: 1:7; Rumphius, n.d., 83, 191, 201; Valentijn [1724–26]: 1:239, 249; Brouwer 1612, in van der Chijs 1886: 62; see also van Ekris 1861:314). Later, however, the opposite connection was reported (see Riedel 1886:88). Moreover the sultan of Ternate, at least after he became an ally of the Dutch, claimed sovereignty over the members of both moieties, as testified by his letters or proclamations to central Moluccan chiefs (Tiele and Heeres 1886–95: 1:150–51; 3:154–58, 204, 209–10; de Jonge 1862–1909: 3:317–18; de Vlamingh van Oudtshoorn 1650–51:7).

Second, although little is known of the internal structure of Tidore, there is no reason to doubt that it was similar to that of Ternate (see van der Crab 1862:319–20; on Tidore, see *Encyclopaedie van Nederlandsch-Indie,* s.v. "Tidore").

In the third place, Ternate combined five and nine in its structure. From Valentijn's account ([1724–26]: 1:241–43) it appears that the Ternatan state was dualistic at various levels. The main opposition was between the Soa Sio — the "nine divisions" of the Ternatan people — and the Fala Baha ("the four of the house") plus the sultan and three other officials. At first, this seems to be an eight-nine opposition. But the sultan and his three associates together represent a single unit, sovereignty. Thus one moiety of the state (the ruling one) is characterized by the numerical index five (the "four of the house" and sovereignty); the other moiety is characterized by nine. This system agrees with the Siwa-Lima system in that nine symbolizes the people (the autochthonous), and five symbolizes the rulers (the immigrants). This structure is further subdivided, but I cannot discuss it here in full.

but rather a true system of moieties, because they were and are the two indispensable parts of a whole. Indeed, as Duyvendack (1926:82) noted, the ancient formulas and songs, as well as the letters and treaties of the seventeenth century, all use the Siwa-Lima couple in the sense of "all people without exception," or "totality." (For examples see de Jonge 1862–1909: 3:317–18; Tiele and Heeres 1886–95: 1:150–51; 3:154–58, 204, 209–10; de Vlamingh van Oudtshoorn 1650–51:7.) That Siwa and Lima form a moiety system is also indicated by their association with polar opposites such as right and left, male and female, which are cosmological, not simply political, in nature.

Although Siwa and Lima form a moiety system, it is a moiety system of a peculiar kind. For instance it emphasizes, much more than moiety systems at the tribal level do (see Davy 1922:5–6), the agonistic and conflictive relationship of the moieties. Siwa and Lima may be conceptually complementary, but they do not seem at first to be complementary in terms of social action. Indeed traditionally they were endogamous, and no peaceful exchanges or transactions of a positive kind normally existed between them. On the contrary, they were said to be "eternal enemies" that related only through war (see van der Crab 1862:212; Tiele and Heeres 1886–95: 1:204; Ludeking 1868:59).

In what sense, then, did each moiety necessarily contribute to the existence of the other? I will attempt to give a brief answer to this question, by way of a tentative and somewhat hypothetical reconstruction. It is impossible to do otherwise, not only because of the implicit or even unconscious character of some of the relations involved, but also because the Siwa-Lima system has largely ceased to function. Further, the kind of evidence needed to construct a totally satisfactory model is lacking and indeed unlikely to be obtained ethnographically at this point because of profound changes that have occurred in the system.

I have developed a model on the basis of my direct knowledge of a traditional Lima society, the Huaulu of central Seram, and of its place in the Siwa-Lima system. I assume that the Huaulu view is structurally related to the views of other societies in the system; that is, I assume that each society's view reflects its position in the system and, most important, the fact that it belongs to one moiety instead of the other.

Considering the Huaulu view as one instantiation of the Lima permutation of the system, I attempt to reconstruct, on the basis of the available evidence, the Siwa permutation, or at least a variety of it. My model presupposes that the Siwa-Lima system has been generated by and coexists with the societies it encompasses because its structure is in some way related to the internal structure of these societies. This relationship should also explain why the system is functional; that is, why the reproduction of the Siwa-Lima systems contributes to making possible the internal reproduction of the societies within it.

"Male" Inside and "Female" Outside in a Lima Society

The Huaulu cultural order is characterized by a strong opposition between the "inside" and the "outside" of the village. The inside represents the most ordered social state, while the outside represents a less ordered state of social relations or mere disorder, although, as I have shown elsewhere (Valeri 1989) the two states are dialectically related.

One aspect of the disorderliness associated with the outside is that it connotes the incompatibility of the principal defining activities or states of the sexes: hunting and headhunting for the males, menstruating and childbearing for the females. Indeed these activities or states, which must occur outside the village, imply a separation of men and women. Men who engage in headhunting and to some extent in hunting must be separated from women because they endanger their life-giving function, while contact with women who menstruate or give birth makes men unable to be successful in the above-mentioned activities (cf. Valeri 1989).[5]

That Huaulu culture associates a state of incompatibility between the sexes with the disorderly world outside the village indicates that it associates social order in the inside with the compatibility of man and woman and indeed with their productive association. On the other hand, and somewhat paradoxically, the inside is viewed as male because men are most responsible for the maintenance of social order, and are therefore the unmarked term in the male-female opposition as it occurs inside the village. Conversely, the female is the unmarked element in the opposition as it occurs outside, since women are supposed to have a closer affinity with the disorderliness of the wild.

Let us not forget, in the course of this discussion, that the contrast between male inside and female outside is always a function of the inversion of the marked-unmarked opposition when we move from inside to outside or vice versa. In other words, the contrast of male and female is at this level the contrast of the signifiers of two states of the relationship of the sexes: one mediated, the other unmediated.

Although there is a global opposition between "female" unmediated relationships in the outside and "male" mediated relationships in the inside, the inside is itself differentiated in various levels that are sexually marked. The highest level is represented by the center of the village, which is also its most male part, since it is the place where men dance alone. Yet even this place is male in the sense that it is associated with a media-

---

5. Women must menstruate and give birth in special huts outside the village (Valeri 1989; R. Valeri 1977:62), and men must kill animals and humans outside the village. No animal that lives in the village may be killed or, if it is killed, may be eaten by a Huaulu. The latter rule extends to wild animals that have penetrated into the village.

tion of male and female: indeed, women are admitted to it when men dance, in order to honor them with gifts. The male dancing ground is at any rate inseparable from the communal house adjacent to it, which symbolizes the mediation of male and female at the level of the global society.

This collective mediation is represented — during the great *Kahua* feast — by a dance in which men and women are associated. Although the dance involves both sexes, it takes place on the "male" veranda of the house. Thus at the level of the global society, represented by the communal house, the mediation of male and female is associated with the male category. This reflects the fact that men make the feast possible by their ritual and political activities.

In both communal house and "private" house the veranda (*ha ha*) is male and the kitchen (*tuka*) is female. Yet in various contexts it is the female kitchen, not the male veranda, that is the unmarked element in the private house. Indeed the kitchen is the "inside" of the house, where the heirlooms representing the identity of a lineage and even the trophies of male hunting (i.e., the lower jaws of wild pigs and deers) are preserved. This inversion as those discussed by Dumont (1978) and Tcherkézoff (1983) might indicate a hierarchical difference between two levels of mediation (see fig. 1); but it should be kept in mind that in other contexts, particularly when the alliance relations between two houses are considered, the unmarked part of the house is the veranda. In this case, though, one house (that of the wife-giving group) is itself opposed to the other (that of the wife-takers) as "male veranda" (*haha mana*) to "female veranda" (*haha pina*) (cf. Valeri 1975, 1976, 1980).

The inversion of the unmarked element, male or female, of the house might reflect a hierarchical contrast between an "outward-looking" and an "inward-looking" view of the house. Indeed houses are defined both by the relations, which are made by men through exchange, and by their internal productivity, which is associated with female fertility and to some extent female work. It is beyond the scope of this essay, however, to discuss these questions in full.

External and Internal Relations

How can the above help us understand the Siwa-Lima system? The thesis I would like to defend is that in Huaulu there is an implicit equivalence between the opposition of the most encompassing social level and the disordered outside on one hand, and the opposition of the Lima and the Siwa moieties, on the other hand.

We have already seen that the moieties are opposed as male and female, inside and outside. But I have also shown that the contrast between

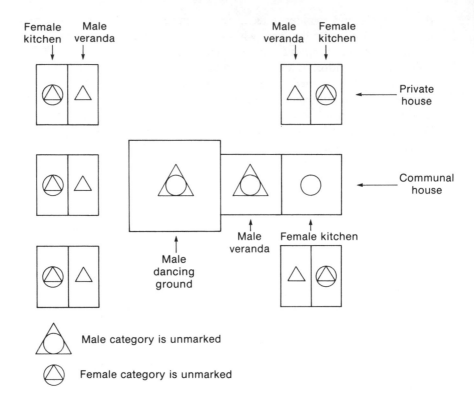

Fig. 1. The structure of gender values inside the village

male inside and female outside in Huaulu society is to a large extent equivalent to the contrast between two states of the male-female contrast itself: one in which the contrast remains unmediated and runs the risk of being dissolved by a confusion of the male in the female (i.e., the pollution of the male by the menstruating or child delivering female); the other in which the contrast is fully mediated. Is this also the case for the male-female opposition applied to the moieties?

In much of central Seram the undivided Lima moiety, identified with maleness and center, is opposed to a female and outer Siwa moiety, which consists of two opposite sections, one called "black," the other "white." The contrast of colors displayed by Siwa versus the neutralization of this contrast displayed by Lima would suffice to establish a formal analogy between local level (as illustrated by the Huaulu case) and moiety level, since at both levels the outside is opposed to the inside as a contrast to its neutralization. But there is probably an even stronger connection between the two levels, since the opposition black-white is equivalent to the opposition male-female, although there are different views as to which color corresponds to which sex. Some stress the fact that black refers to the tattoos of male initiates in western Seram and therefore conclude that black is male and white is female (Jensen 1948:52). But from a central Seramese point of view, black seems to refer to the autochthonous people (Röder 1948; Jensen 1948:57), who are also viewed as female (like Earth itself); thus black is female and white is male.

The crucial fact is that the male Lima, in its unity, may be viewed as neutralizing the contrast of male and female that seems to define the female Siwa. There is thus an analogy between the local level (where the male inside, which socially mediates the opposition of male and female, is opposed to the female outside, which does not) and the global level (where the male moiety, Lima, fully mediates the opposition of male and female by neutralizing it, while the Siwa moiety does not, because it is divided into a male and a female section).

The same analogy of internal relations at the local level and of moiety relations at the global level is found in an even more direct way in the contrast between the numerical indexes of the moieties. Both these indexes (five and nine) and their contrast seem unmotivated until we realize that they must be seen as the result of operations that are the most general schemes of the symbolic processes defining each moiety.

Five is analyzed as four plus one (see Jansen 1977; Manusama 1977), to indicate the special status of the unit that embodies the totality. This unity can be viewed as the "fifth" (when the process of attainment of the totality is emphasized) or as the "first" (when rank is emphasized).

An example of the first case is given by the Huaulu ritual formula "one, two, three, four . . . five," which marks the conclusion of several ritual processes (for instance, that of the marriage rite). In this formula the "five" is pronounced after a brief pause and more emphatically than the other numbers, to indicate that a process has been completed, a fullness has been reached.

The way in which the structure of a five-group is often represented furnishes the best example of the second case. Indeed, very often the "unity" of the group is represented by the "first" unit, which is ideally at the center of four surrounding units. This center symbolizes the totality because it is the point at which the opposition of the four surrounding units is neutralized. The four points are oriented to the cardinal points (or their subdivisions) and often are associated with other opposites as well.

An example of neutralization by the center is given by the central unit in the four-plus-one structure which characterized the five-group of Hitu-lama in Ambon in the sixteenth and seventeenth centuries. Latu Sitania, the lord who was at the center of the group's four *perdana,* or rulers, com-ing from as many groups, wore all of the colors separately associated with each perdana and forming pairs of oppositions. As the spatial center, Latu Sitania also neutralized the north-south, east-west opposition that ordered the relationships between the perdana (see Manusama 1977:35).[6]

In Huaulu we find a very similar structure. The society consists of four basic units: Huaulu, Tamatay, Allay, Peinisa. But the Huaulu unit is in fact divided into two autonomous sections, called Huaulu *potoa* (senior Huaulu) and Huaulu *kiita* (junior Huaulu), respectively. Huaulu potoa furnishes a "male" ruler, called *Kamare* and sometimes Latu Ama ("father ruler") and is therefore the first unit, corresponding to the center of the society and mediating its external oppositions.[7]

Sometimes, particularly in Ambon, the four-plus-one structure is a shorthand for an anthropomorphic metaphor of the society. In this meta-phor, the units associated with even numbers are represented by the limbs on the right side of the body; those associated with odd numbers are represented by the limbs on the left; and the unit that symbolizes totality (and that also furnishes the headman) is represented by the head (Jansen 1977; Röder 1939).

Nine is analyzed as (four plus four) plus one. This makes clear that a nine-group (or any other social or ritual instantiation of the nine for-mula in the societies of the Siwa moiety) is conceived as the result of a duplication of the four units surrounding the central unit in a five-group (see Holleman 1923:14). It also implies that the four-plus-one structure is common to both moieties. Valentijn remarked that quadripartition was fundamental for both Siwa and Lima (1862: 2:34, 36), but he failed to see that there is no quadripartition without an explicit or implicit central unit, so that four plus one and not simply four is the element common to both moieties.[8] (see Manusama 1977; 25, 32, 34, 77-78).

---

6. On the structure and history of Hitu, see Rijali 1977; Rumphius, n.d., 10-25; Val-entijn [1724-26]: 2:104-15; Manusama 1977.

7. Note that the core territory of the Huaulu, and the tribe itself, are called *Seke-nima,* which they translate "five segments" (*nima* is interpreted as a corruption of Lima, "five").

8. It is worth stressing that both in central Seram and in Ambon there is a certain consensus that the Siwa moiety includes or should include or did include four-plus-four-plus-one groups, and the Lima moiety, four-plus-one groups. For instance, I was told by Siwa informants in the Taluti area of southern Seram that the Nuaulu people (the southern cousins of the Huaulu) "in the past" had a four-plus-one structure. The historical documents from the sixteenth and seventeenth centuries show that this theory corresponded to practice in Ambon and in the Uliaser Islands (see Rumphius, n.d.; Valentijn [1724-26]; see also Jansen

It thus appears that the contrast of five and nine is not arbitrarily associated with the contrast of the two moieties. The "elementary political structure" is, as it is elsewhere in Southeast Asia, and particularly in Indonesia, the four-plus-one structure (see van Ossenbruggen 1918; Schulte Nordholt 1971; Fox 1982). This structure is reduplicated—four plus four plus one—to form its opposite, that is, the class of nine-groups. The duplication of the four-plus-one structure equals nine, not ten, because by definition there is only one central unit in a group: central units or "heads" are never added to one another.

The two sets of four in a nine-group are often opposed to each other as male to female, both in central Seram and in Ambon. In central Seram, perhaps the best example of this phenomenon is offered by the community of Maraina, which lies at the geographical and social center of the Siwa of that area of the island. Maraina is divided into two moieties, one named Ilela *potoa* (senior Ilela), the other named Ilela *kiita* (junior Ilela). Each moiety is divided into four units, which are further opposed as couples. The highest-ranking unit in Ilela potoa furnishes the Latu Nusa, Lord of the Land (also called Latu Ina, Lord Mother) for the entire community. This unit, therefore, is both part of the moiety system and, as its totalizing center, above it. In this respect, it counts for two, explaining why the eight units form a nine-group. In sum, we find here an instantiation of the four-plus-four-plus-one structure.

This structure is made visible, as it is in Ambon as well, by two associated stone tables, which together represent the society and on which heads hunted were formerly put as sacrificial offerings.

The main table belongs to Ilela potoa, and the smaller one to Ilela kiita. The four feet of the main table belong to the four units of Ilela potoa, while the four feet of the smaller table belong to the four units of Ilela kiita. The tops of both tables belong to the Lord of the Land, who is also the owner of the foot at the northeast (the superior direction) of the main table (Röder 1948:16–17; Valeri, field notes). Hence the Lord of the Land is at the center of both groups and at the same time above them as a symbol of their unity.

Unfortunately, when I visited Maraina and was shown the tables, I did not ask if the two moieties are opposed as male to female. But everything indicates that this is the case. In the first place, Ilela potoa furnishes the Lord Mother and must therefore be considered female. In the second place, Ilela potoa is supposed to be more autochthonous, if one may say

---

1977 for orally transmitted views of this fact). In Seram, too, this often seems to have been the case. For instance, a society not far from Huaulu, which ceased to exist long ago, namely Permata, can be interpreted as having had a four-plus-one structure according to data given by Valentijn [1724–26]: 2:59). As in Huaulu, the central unit gave its name to the whole and had a double value.

so, than Ilela kiita, which arrived "later" at the place where Ilela potoa was already settled (see Röder 1948). Since the autochthonous, or first-comer, is equivalent to female, and the immigrant, or last-comer, is equivalent to male, Ilela potoa must again be opposed to Ilela kiita as female to male. Finally, and more decisively, in Piliyana, a community closely related to Maraina, Ilela potoa is opposed to Latumutuani (which functions there as the "other" moiety) as female to male.

Maraina is by no means unique in central Seram in displaying a (four-plus-four)-plus-one structure in which one set of four is opposed to the other as male to female. Old Taluti seems to have had the same structure, at its core at least. There the structure was represented by a single stone table. Each of its four feet was connected with two groups, while the top belonged to the "female" Lord of the Land. This structure was clearly concentric, since the most important set of four units included the groups that arrived first in Taluti; therefore this set was closer to the center than the second set of four. Again, it seems that the first set, being closer to the female center, is itself female when opposed to the outer set, which is in that respect male (Valeri, field notes; Röder 1948:9–14).

Whether or not they have a structure of (four plus four) plus one, other groups in the Siwa moiety in central Seram seem to be divided into moieties or "sides" classified as male and female. In one case at least — the above-mentioned Piliyana — these internal moieties are exogamous. In Ambon, too the two moieties of a Siwa group are usually classified as male and female (Jansen 1977:103). Furthermore, as in central Seram, the central unit (that is, the unit that represents the society as a whole) of a Siwa group is female and identified with *ina,* "mother," in contrast to the central unit of a Lima group, which is male and identified with *ama,* "father" (Manusama 1977:33).

Whether we consider the relationship between entire moieties or the relationship between five-groups and nine-groups taken individually, then, we see that the Lima term may be opposed to the Siwa term just as the male symbolic neutralization of the male-female contrast (which implies mediation) is opposed to its female neutralization (which implies absence of mediation). This explains why, from a Lima point of view much as that of the Huaulu, it is possible to equate the outside state of male-female relations in a five-group with the relationship between male side and female side in any nine-group or in the Siwa moiety, as a whole, when it is divided into a "male" and a "female" territorial section. This equation implies that the Siwa are more disordered than the Lima, and therefore inferior in the latter's eyes as female is to male. Of course, this is only one aspect of the asymmetry of the two moieties as perceived by the Lima (fig. 2).

It goes without saying that this Lima view differs from that of the

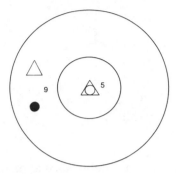

△ Male neutralization of the male/female opposition
● Female neutralization of the male/female opposition

Fig. 2. Siwa-Lima contrast as seen by the Lima

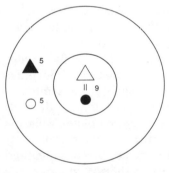

▲ Male neutralization of the male/female contrast
● Female neutralization of the male/female contrast

Fig. 3. Siwa-Lima contrast as seen by the Siwa

Siwa. Indeed, several statements from Ambon — which seem to be applicable to central Seram as well — make it clear that the Siwa point of view is the opposite of the Lima view just discussed (fig. 3). For instance, Manusama (1977:33–34) reports that the female nine-groups are self-reproducing (and therefore complete), while the male five-groups are sterile because they arc

incomplete. Far from realizing a superior mediation of male and female, therefore, the five-groups realize no mediation at all. This point comes out even more clearly from the theory summarized by Jansen:

> In these systems, five is the complete being; man is five: This being, however, is sterile on its own and cannot be the origin of other beings; for this purpose two beings are needed, a male five and a female five. Together they become nine, for the units of the female five and the male five (*uru ulu*) merge into each other (*ulisiwa*) to form a complete and most perfect unit. (Jansen 1977:103)

Clearly this theory completely reverses the Lima theory. Indeed the nine-group is defined as the union of two five-groups of opposite sex and therefore considered superior to their nonunion "outside" society. This view, then, negates the idea that a single five-group can ever mediate male and female categories: on the contrary, it identifies five with sterility, of which the male is the most appropriate symbol, since men do not bear children. Thus the male neutralization of the male-female opposition is viewed as inferior (sterile and incomplete), while the female neutralization is viewed as superior (fertile and complete).

That the Siwa and Lima perspectives are inverted at least in parts of central Seram is confirmed by the existence of a striking inversion between Huaulu, on one hand, and several Siwa societies farther east. In Piliyana, Maraina, and Taluti the superior, central position is given to the symbolically female ruler (Latu Ina), while the inferior, outside position is given to the "male" ruler (Latu Ama). The opposite happens in Huaulu, where the Latu Ama has the central position while the Latu Ina has the outside one. Indeed a myth makes him an immigrant, originally an animal transformed into a human by a warrior hero.

That the symbolically female ruler at the center of Siwa societies is actually a man shows that the Siwa qualification of the inside as female does not imply that women as such are responsible for bringing about social order. Moreover, in both societies the passage from outside to inside is connected with the transformation of disordered activity into ordered activity and the same basic activities or states are evaluated as ordered and disordered. But the Lima emphasize in the inside the dimension of transformative *action,* which is paradigmatically male; in the inside, the Siwa, in contrast, emphasize the *result* of the transformation, that is, reproduction, which is best viewed as female, since it is women who bear children. On the outside the opposite is true. The Siwa emphasize action, which is male, but since the action takes place in the outside, it is disordered and inferior. The Lima emphasize reproduction, but again, since it is in the outside, it is reproduction in its unfinished, incomplete aspects and is therefore viewed as inferior to male action.

Why are opposite aspects of the same process emphasized? Why do the Lima emphasize the positive aspect of action while the Siwa emphasize the positive aspect of reproduction, of fertility? I believe that these differences result from the fact that the Siwa, who consider themselves autochthonous, emphasize fertility as a property of female land, while the Lima, who consider themselves immigrant, emphasize action as a property of the male conquerors of the female land. These opposite emphases are enshrined in each moiety's conception of its relative value and are reflected in the evaluation of the inside-outside, mediated-unmediated oppositions in the actual societies in each moiety. More specifically, they may be reflected in the inverse hierarchy of the Lord of the Land and the Lord of Force among the two groups. I might add that in central Seram the Siwa emphasize the female Earth in the cosmological pair, Father Sky–Mother Earth, and the Lima emphasize the male Sky, for instance addressing Sky more often in prayers.

This pattern confirms that there is a definite correspondence between moiety level and local level and that each society therefore must conceptualize its superior state as it conceptualizes the moiety to which it belongs, and its inferior state as it conceptualizes the moiety to which it does not belong. The difference between societies in opposite moieties is only a difference as to which value — maleness or femaleness — signifies the mediation of male and female categories and therefore the social totality, but native consciousness must misconstrue this as the opposition of two unequal degrees of mediation or even as the opposition of mediation and nonmediation. Otherwise, each moiety's assimilation of its outside with the other moiety's inside would not be possible.

Although I have emphasized the logical distinction between female and male as symbolic values, on one hand, and men and women, on the other, I must report that the association of social totality (the inside) with female may reverberate on the status of women. I was struck by the fact

that among the Siwa of central Seram the male war dance at the center
of the village is accompanied by a female dance, which is totally absent
and in fact explicitly forbidden in Huaulu. Also striking is that shamanic
practices are reserved for men in Huaulu, while they are open to women
in the Siwa tribes farther east. Moreover, phenomena connected with female fertility (menstruation, childbirth) on the whole seem to be more
positively evaluated among the Siwa of central Seram than among the
Lima of the same area. Indeed all the Siwa tribes, with the exception of
the Nisawele, allowed women to menstruate and give birth in the house,
albeit in a special area, even before their conversion to Christianity (Tauern
1918:33, 165, 184–85; Valeri, field notes). This custom seems to be in agreement with the connection established between female fertility and inside
among the Siwa. On the other hand, the logical disjunction between female reproduction as a symbol and actual processes of reproduction in
women is underscored by the case of the Nisawele tribe. This Siwa society
excludes from the village the women who menstruate or give birth, just
as their Lima neighbors do.

Among the Siwa of western Seram one finds more pronounced variations in the states of menstruation and childbirth than among the Siwa
of central Seram. In some areas, menstrual huts are located outside the
village, sometimes far away from it; in other areas, women are allowed
to menstruate under the house. Interestingly, in one case the Lima structure found in Huaulu seems to be completely reversed, since the menstrual huts are located *inside* the village (Jensen 1948:139). Perhaps in
this case the saliency of femaleness (which in the matrilineal societies
of western Seram is very great) in the definition of inside has resulted
in giving women the inside position precisely when they manifest their
power to generate and become signifiers of fertility. Unfortunately, this
is only a speculation; no details are known on this particular case.

Probably these variations in the status of women among the Siwa are
an index of their somewhat contradictory situation: on one hand Siwa
privilege female values, on the other hand they separate these values from
actual women. The different degrees of this separation in different societies corresponds to different degrees of pollution attributed to women.
Yet rarely in Seram are women considered pollution-free, so the Huaulu
ideas on female pollution (see Valeri 1989) manifest in extreme form views
shared by most Seramese societies.

Although I do not have any precise information on this score, there
may also be variations among the Lima with regard to the intensity of the
pollution attributed to women when menstruating or giving birth. At any
rate, those Lima who have converted to Islam usually have abandoned the
custom of the menstrual hut.

Some Reflections and Provisional Conclusions

In an important sense, the perspectives of the five-groups and the nine-groups are perfectly inverse and symmetrical. Each group conceives its relationship to the other as a part-whole relationship, articulated processually and temporally: *wo Lima war, soll Siwa werden; wo Siwa war, soll Lima werden.* In other words, each group perceives in the other a lower state of totalization, which coincides with its conceptualization of the state of male-female relations in the outside. Each group therefore furnishes to the other the image of what it must necessarily be at some level (for instance, when engaged in activities that take place in the outside) but which it must transcend to be fully a group, to be a totality. This is, essentially, the contribution each moiety makes to the other's existence.

The moieties are not conceived, therefore, as complementary opposites pure and simple, which together would make up a harmonious whole or would give each other, through exchange, needed opposite qualities. Indeed, at the end of this analysis we must conclude that what appeared at first to be complementary opposites (male-female, inside-outside) are in fact marks of the inverse hierarchy between the very opposites they appear to be. These opposites are already present in each moiety; they need not be exchanged. But each moiety is dependent on the inverted image of the hierarchy of these elements (an image realized by the opposite moiety) to reproduce its own hierarchy.

In sum, it is not sufficient for a society to reproduce itself by a positive reference to a type that it must instantiate; it also needs a *negative* reference to a type that it must not instantiate (or rather, must not continue to instantiate, insofar as it inevitably instantiates the type at some level at some time). In this respect, the relationship between Siwa and Lima reminds me of the relationship between the Eaglehawk and Crow moieties in Australia as recently reinterpreted by Testart (1978). Testart has shown that the opposition between the two birds in fact is between hunter and carrion-eater (95–96), an opposition underlying other pairs of animals associated with moieties in Australia. More profoundly, all these oppositions symbolize the opposition between proper behavior and transgression as conceived in a hunter society. The moieties, therefore, become identified with the two complementary aspects of reproduction of the moral order: one with the direct enunciation of that order, the other with its inverse (i.e., representation of transgression). Hence the hierarchical difference between moieties (see Testart 1978:102–8).

The relationship of Siwa and Lima is somewhat analogous to that of Eaglehawk and Crow, but it differs on a fundamental point: in the Moluccas, each moiety gives itself the superior, prescriptive role and gives the other the inferior, transgressive role. The moieties thus differ more because of the inverse relationship between their points of view than because each moiety has a role acknowledged by both. I say "more" because in the central Seramese and Ambonese variants of the Siwa-Lima system analyzed here, there is some agreement as to the features that characterize each moiety, although not as to their signification and value. Yet the system can do without even these elements of agreement. Indeed, as I have mentioned, in certain cases both Siwa and Lima claim to be male and maintain that the opposite moiety is female. In this case the moieties share only the view that male is superior to female: to claim a status superior to that of the opposite moiety, each moiety must claim male status.

But whatever form it takes, the Siwa-Lima system emphasizes the contrast between inverted *judgments* as to the relationship between terms (or as to their reference to the moieties) over the simple contrast of *terms* associated with the moieties. Consequently, complementarity exists more on an interactional and processual plane than on a simply logical one. Each moiety needs an Other to which it can attach the negative terms of its own system of oppositions; the reciprocal relation between moieties consists in each moiety being the Other of its own Other, although it refuses to acknowledge the fact. Each moiety denies its contradictory value affirmed by the opposite moiety, yet, insofar as a moiety is inseparable from the system and therefore inseparable from the affirmation of that contradictory value, the moiety tacitly admits its contradictory value in the very act of negating it. All this goes to show that socio-logical relations cannot be immediately identified with logical ones.

We can also grasp the profound difference between this system of "political" moieties and the "galactic" polities (as Tambiah 1976 calls them) of Southeast Asia. The difference is made more striking by the fact that both use the same basic four-plus-one mandala-like structure and its correlated oppositions: inside-outside, center-periphery, and sometimes male-female (see Holleman 1923:14).

The galactic polities are based on an indefinite multiplication of the peripheric set (four or otherwise) around a single center, as for instance in the *mancapat* system of Java. Thus the center is defined by its opposition to an indefinite number of outer and inferior Others which it is able to subordinate.

In contrast, in the Siwa-Lima system there is only one Other. This is linked with the fact that by definition there are only two kinds of mandala-like structures: (four)plus one and (four plus four) plus one. The single duplication of the periphery (the four-unit set) that is allowed does not produce the encompassment of an Other; on the contrary, it implies identification with it, the passage to the category in which it is included. In other words, if a five-group adds to itself a second periphery it becomes simply the opposite of itself. At the same time, each moiety conceives the opposite moiety as equivalent to a part, or rather state, of itself, for the reasons discussed above.

The Siwa-Lima system, therefore, confronts us with the symmetrical relationship between two opposite hierarchical evaluations: it combines the claim of encompassment of the Other, which characterizes the galactic polities, with the reversibility of that claim, made possible by the dualistic structure of the system. The system can therefore be viewed as typologically intermediary between the purely tribal dual organizations and the purely centralized galactic polities. It is significant, in this respect, that the Siwa-Lima and similar systems in outer Indonesia have developed at the periphery of centralized systems.[9] Unfortunately, too little attention has been paid to this phenomenon and, more generally, too little relevance has been given to these regional systems of moieties in the discussion of Indonesian political systems.

I would like to conclude by pointing out that the greatest paradox of the Siwa-Lima system — the equivalence established between the Other moiety and the lower level of order in each society — is inextricably linked with the concrete form of the moieties' interaction. As we have seen, they are supposed to interact through war alone. But war implies headhunting, that is, the translation of an enemy from the opposite moiety into the center of one's society. It seems that this translation represents and realizes the connection between the various levels implied in the system. The head of the enemy is at first a metonymic sign of the opposite moiety. It is also a sign of the condition of its acquisition: of violent and disordered male hunting outside society and therefore of the unmediated contrast between male and female categories. Thus in the head the equation of opposite moiety and lower level of order is concretely realized.

But the killing of the enemy also implies the subordination and mastering both of the opposite moiety and of the outer state of one's society. It therefore makes possible the transcendence of that state and consequently the full social mediation of male and female, symbolized by dancing around the hunted head in the communal house at the center of the village.

Thus the ritual makes clear in what sense the reproduction of the hierarchical relationship between one's moiety and the opposite moiety co-

---

9. See, for instance, the Demon-Padzi system of the Solor Islands (Vatter 1932:285; Arndt 1938), the Wetu Telu–Waktu Lima of Lombok (Cederroth 1981; van der Kraan 1980), and the Koto-Piliang and Bodi-Caniago of Minangkabau (de Josselin de Jong 1952:71 n). Interestingly, both in the Solor Islands and in Lombok, the moiety paradigmatically associated with Islam is, as in the Moluccas, the moiety indexed by five.

incides with the reproduction of a hierarchical relationship between two levels of order in one's society. The other moiety, symbolized by the head, truly constitutes the most encompassing social order, symbolized by the productive conjunction of man and woman in the circular dance.[10]

The rite reveals that the center of one society does indeed revolve around a hidden center: the opposite moiety. In this sense, both moieties are correct in viewing themselves as the center of the other. The rite appropriates one moiety's view of itself as center to create the opposite moiety's center.

ACKNOWLEDGMENTS

Renée Valeri and I undertook the fieldwork on which this essay is partially based in 1971–73 under the sponsorship of the Indonesian Institute of Sciences (LIPI). The work was supported by grants from the Wenner-Gren Foundation and the Association Franco-Suédoise pour la recherche. The published and unpublished materials used in the essay were collected in Holland in 1974, thanks to a scholarship from the Dutch Ministry of Education. Additional archival research was done in 1983 through a Guggenheim Fellowship, to which I also owe the year of free time when this essay took its first shape.

I am also extremely grateful to these institutions and to those individuals who gave me the opportunity of presenting drafts or summaries of the essay to very competent audiences: to David Maybury-Lewis and Uri Almagor, who invited me to the Conference on Dual Organizations (June 1983) and to the Department of Anthropology of the University of Leiden, which asked me to read another version at its seminar (September 1983). Finally, I wish to thank my colleague Terence Turner for his useful comments on yet another version.

Postscriptum: Since this essay was completed, I have returned three times to Seram for additional research (1985, 1986, 1988). Although I have obtained additional data on Huaulu views of the Siwa-Lima system and on its present modifications, it has not been possible (nor has it seemed advisable) to incorporate them in this essay. I hope to return to the subject in a monograph on Huaulu culture.

---

10. Hence the extreme respect shown to the head when it is introduced into the village. If not enough respect is paid to it, I was told, the society's existence is threatened.

REFERENCES

Arndt, P. 1938. Demon und Padzi, die feindlichen Brüder des Solor-Archipels. *Anthropos* 33:1–58.

Barraud, C. 1979. *Tanebar-Evav: Une société de maisons tournée vers le large.* Cambridge: Cambridge University Press.

Barth, F. 1981. *Selected essays of Fredrick Barth.* Vol. 2, *Features of person and society in Swat: Collected essays on Pathans.* London: Routledge and Kegan Paul.

Beschrijvinge. 1855. Beschrijvinge van de eilanden Banda. *Bijdragen tot de Taal-, Land- en Volkenkunde van Nederlandsch-Indië* 3:73–85.

Bosscher, C. 1855. Bijdrage tot de Kennis van de Keij-Eilanden. *Tijdschrift voor Indische Taal-, Land- en Volkenkunde* 4:23–33.

Brumund, J. F. G. 1845. Aanteekeningen, gehouden op eene reis in het oostelijke gedeelte van den Indischen Archipel. *Tijdschrift voor Neerland's Indië* 7:39–89, 251–99.

Cederroth, S. 1981. *The spell of the ancestors and the power of Mekkah.* Gothenburg Studies in Social Anthropology, no. 3. Göteborg, Sweden: Acta Universitatis Gothoburgensis.

Chijs, J. A. van. 1866. *De Vestiging van het Nederlandsche Gezag over de Banda Eilanden.* Batavia: Albrecht.

Cooley, F. L. 1962. *Ambonese Adat: A general description.* Cultural Report Series, no. 10. New Haven: Yale University, Southeast Asia Studies.

Coolhaas, W. P., ed. 1923. Kroniek van het Rijk Batjan. *Tijdschrift voor Indische Taal-, Land- en Volkenkunde* 43:474–500.

Crab, P. van der. 1862. *De Moluksche Eilanden.* Batavia: Lange.

Davy, G. 1922. *La foi jurée.* Paris: Alcan.

Dumont, L. 1978. La communauté anthropologique et l'idéologie. *L'Homme* 18:83–110.

Duyvendack, J. P. 1926. *Het Kakean-genootschap van Seran.* Almelo: Hilarius.

Eijbergen, H. C. van. 1864. Korte woordelijst van de taal der Aroe- en Keij-eilanden. *Tijdschrift voor Indische Taal-, Land- en Volkenkunde* 14:557–68.

———. 1866. Verslag eener reis naar de Aroe- en Key-eilanden in de maand Junij 1862. *Tijdschrift voor Indische Taal-, Land- en Volkenkunde* 15:220–72.

Ekris, A. van. 1861. Verslag betreffende de zending op Ceram. *Mededeelingen van wege het Nederlandsche Zendelingsgenootschap* 5:287–329.

Fox, James J. 1982. The great lord rests at the center: The paradox of powerlessness in European Timorese relations. *Canberra Anthropology* 5:22–33.

Heeres, J. E., and F. W. Stapel, eds. 1907. *Corpus diplomaticum Neerlando-Indicum,* vol. 1. The Hague: Martinus Nijhoff.

Hoëvell, C. W. W. C. van. 1890. De Kei-eilanden. *Tijdschrift voor Indische Taal-, Land- en Volkenkunde* 33:102–59.

Holleman, F. D. 1923. *Het adat-grondenrecht van Ambon en de Oeliassers.* Amsterdam: Molukken-Instituut.

Jacobs, H., ed. 1980. *Documenta Malucensia II (1577–1606).* Rome: Jesuit Historical Institute.

Jansen, M. J. 1977. Indigenous classification systems in the Ambonese Moluccas. In de Josselin de Jong 1977:100–15.

Jensen, A. E. 1948. Die drei Ströme. Leipzig: Harrassowitz.

Jensen, A. E., and Herman Niggemeyer. 1939. Hainuwele: Volkserzählungen von der Molukken-Insel Ceram. Frankfurt am Main: Klostermann.

Jonge, J. K. J. de. 1862–1909. De opkomst van het Nederlandsch gezag in Oost-Indie, vols. 1–13. The Hague: Martinus Nijhoff.

Josselin de Jong, P. E. de. 1952. Minangkabau and Negri Sembilan. The Hague: Martinus Nijhoff.

Josselin de Jong, P. E. de, ed. 1977. Structural anthropology in the Netherlands. Koninklijk Instituut voor Taal-, Land- en Volkenkunde Translation Series, vol. 17. The Hague: Martinus Nijhoff.

Kolff, D. H. 1840. Voyages of the Dutch brig of war Dourga. Trans. G. W. Earl. London: James Madden and Co.

Kraan, A. van der. 1980. Lombok: Conquest, colonization and underdevelopment 1870–1940. Kuala Lumpur and Singapore: Heinemann.

Krayer van Aalst, H. 1920. Van wee en van vree - Twee schetsen uit het leven der Alfoeren op Ceram. The Hague.

Leirissa, R. Z., Z. J. Manusama, A. B. Lapian, and P. R. Abdurachman, 1982. Maluku Tengah di masa lampau. Jakarta: Arsip National Republik Indonesia.

Leur, J. van. 1967. Indonesian trade and society. The Hague: van Hoeve.

Ludeking, E. W. A. 1868. Schets van de residentie Amboina. The Hague: Martinus Nijhoff.

Manusama, Z. J. 1977. Hikayat tanah Hitu. Ph.D. diss., Leiden University.

Muller, F. N. N.d. Reise gedaan in 1833 van Banda naar Goram, Aroe, Key, Tenimbar. . . . H146, KITLV Library, Leiden.

Nutz, W. 1959. Eine Kulturanalyse von Kei. Düsseldorf: Zentral-Verlag für Dissertationen.

Ossenbruggen, F. D. E. van. 1918. De oorsprong van het javaansche begrip montjapat, in verband met primitieve classificaties. Verslagen en mededeelingen der Koninklijke Akademie van Wetenschappen, Afdeeling Letterkunde 5 (3): 6–44.

Rees, W. A. van. 1866. De pionniers van der beschaving in Neerlands Indie. Arnhem: Thieme.

Ribbe, C. 1888. Die Aru-inseln. In Festschrift zur Jubelfeier des 25 jahrigen Bestehens des Vereins für Erdkunde zu Dresden, 153–201. Dresden: Huhle.

Riedel, J. G. F. 1886. De sluik- en kroesharige rassen tusschen Selebes en Papua. The Hague: Martinus Nijhoff.

Rijali, H. T. H. 1977. Hikayat tanah Hitu. Malay text and Dutch translation in Manusama 1977.

Röder, J. 1939. Levende oudheden op Ambon. Cultureel Indië 1:97–105.

———. 1948. Alahatala. Bamberg: Meisenbach.

Ronkel, Ph. S. van. 1945. Een Maleisch Geschrift, met nautische illustraties, over de geschiendenis van Banda. Cultureel Indië 7:123–30.

Rumphius, G. E. 1910. De Ambonse Historie. 2 vols. The Hague: Martinus Nijhoff.

————. N.d. *D'Ambonsche Land Beschryving.* VOC 11245 (copy dated +/– 1700), Algemene Rijksarkief, The Hague.

Sachse, F. J. P. 1907. *Seran en zijne bewoners.* Leiden: Brill.

Schulte Nordholt, H. G. 1971. *The political system of the Atoni of Timor.* The Hague: Martinus Nijhoff.

Seran. 1922. *Seran.* Encyclopaedisch Bureau, no. 29. Weltevreden: Kolff.

Tambiah, S. J. 1976. *World conqueror and world renouncer.* Cambridge: Cambridge University Press.

Tauern, O.D. 1918. *Patasiwa und Patalima.* Leipzig: Voigtländer.

Tcherkézoff, S. 1983. *Le roi Nyamwezi, la droite et la gauche: Revision comparative des classifications dualistes.* Cambridge: Cambridge University Press.

Testart, A. 1978. *Des classifications dualistes en Australie: Essai sur l'évolution de l'organisation sociale.* Paris: Editions de la maison de sciences de l'homme.

Tichelman, T. L. 1922. Aanteekeningen betreffende Ceramsche Alfoeren-eeden. *Koloniaal Tijdschrift* 11:520–28.

Tiele, P. A., and J. E. Heeres. 1886–95. *Bouwstoffen voor de geschiedenis der Nederlanders in den Maleischen Archipel,* vols. 1–3. The Hague: Martinus Nijhoff.

Valentijn, F. [1724–26] 1862. *Oud en Nieuw Oost-Indien.* Ed. S. Keijzer. Vols. 1–3. Amsterdam: van Kestaren.

Valeri, Valerio. 1975. Alliances et échanges matrimoniaux à Seram central (Moluques), pt. 1. *L'Homme* 15:83–107.

————. 1976. Alliances et échanges matrimoniaux à Seram central (Moluques), pt. 2. *L'Homme* 16:125–49.

————. 1980. Notes on the meaning of marriage prestations among the Huaulu of Seram. In *The flow of life: Essays on eastern Indonesia,* ed. James J. Fox, 178–92. Cambridge: Harvard University Press.

————. 1989. Both nature and culture: Reflections on Huaulu gender ideology. In *The Paradox of Gender: Essays on Power and Difference in Island Southeast Asia,* Stanford: Stanford University Press, ed. Jane Atkinson and Shelly Errington.

Valeri, R. 1977. La position sociale de la femme dans la société traditionnelle des Moluques centrales. *Archipel* 13:53–78.

Vatter, E. 1932. *Ata Kiwan: Unbekannte Bergvölker im tropischen Holland.* Leipzig: Bibliographisches Institut.

Vlamingh van Oudtshoorn, A. de. 1650–51. Verhael of daghregister, gehouden bij . . . op zijn voijage . . . van Batavia naar de Moluccos . . . . H 742, KITLV Library, Leiden.

Vollenhoven, C. van. 1918. *Het Adatrecht van Nederlandsch-Indie.* 2 vols. Leiden: Brill.

Vries, G. de. 1927. *Bij de Berg-Alfoeren op West-Seran.* Zutphen: Thieme.

Wessels, S. J. 1934. *Histoire de la mission d'Amboine (1546–1605).* Louvain: Museum Lessianum.

Chapter 6

The Dialectic of Generation Moieties in an East African Society

Uri Almagor

The anthropological literature abounds with descriptions of societies that are on the borderline between a dyadic system, in the most general meaning of the term, and pseudo-dual organization, with only traces of some kind of symbolic dualism. Jeffreys (1946), Haekel (1950), and Jensen (1953), for example, mention several dozen tribal societies in Africa whose relation to dual organization is dubious. Almost any set of social values can be presented as a set of dual elements, but this does not mean that the system itself must be dualistic. What makes a social system dualistic, first of all, is a set of beliefs about the natural, social, and supernatural worlds constructed in a dual symbolic schema that gives logic and meaning to people's activities and to natural and cosmological phenomena. Second, such a system implies that the members of the society perceive their system in dual terms and that their perception of reality, as well as their activities, is based on a binary world view. But all of this is too general. How are we to distinguish between societies that have a dual organization and those with only a pseudo one? Or those with "strong" and "weak" dual systems? Can we speak about dual organization "without an ideology of dualism," as was said about some East African age systems at the 1983 conference on dual organization in Jerusalem? Most East African age-system societies have elaborate symbolic systems with different aspects of dualism ruling different levels of their cosmology, religion, and rituals.[1] In order to include East African dual systems in what is called and analyzed as dual organization we must have some kind of a definition that will integrate the spheres of dual ideas and of dual social activities and

---

1. See, for example, Peristiany 1951; Spencer 1959; Hinnant 1978, and in this volume; Almagor 1983c, 1985a, 1985b, 1987a, 1987b.

show how these spheres superimpose upon one another in a mutual relationship. But to define the various and variable phenomena of what is known as dual organization, is to run the risk, as is usually the case with composite definitions, that they may be inherently self-defeating. Yet not to define the notion of dual organization and to leave it in its broadest usage of the term, so that any rhetorical use of binary opposition could be taken as a hint of dual organization, would dilute the concept beyond usefulness. Thus, in order to distinguish between societies with dual organization and those without it, or between "strong" and "weak" dual systems within one society, I shall suggest several pervasive components that seem to be the central ones in native models and from which any analysis of dual organization should start.

Dual organization, it seems to me, has six major components.[2] The first is a dual cosmological system divided into a number of complementary, binary categories. The second is a clear division between center and periphery, which can also be expressed as a cyclical, or pendulum-like movement that, over time, changes the hierarchical relations between two halves. Third, the society is divided into one or more sets of halves: an individual's identity and the meaning of his life cycle are determined to a large extent by his affiliation with these sets of halves. Fourth, various ritual events give the dual cosmological beliefs some tangible dimension: the symbolic expression of dual elements strengthens the collective identity of each part, but it also reiterates their unity and interdependence through the sharing of space and time. Fifth, the commitment to social and symbolic dualism includes the sense that the whole is more important than any of its parts. And sixth, there are social carriers who articulate, interpret, and often represent the idea of dual divisions.

Such a definition may enable us to include East African generation moieties that hitherto were not included in the study of dual organization.[3] Furthermore, such a definition may facilitate the examination of both the symbols expressed in action and the purposive nature of dual organization as expressed in some ritual performances.

East African Generation Moieties

Most of the anthropological literature on generation moieties examines the Australian systems of dual organization, concentrating mainly on the

---

2. Some of these points are made by Eisenstadt in his essay in this volume, but I have reformulated a few of them and have explicated their meaning in a slightly different manner.

3. The early approaches treated exogamous moieties with unilineal descent as if this were the only type of dual organization in existence. They ignored all other forms, even when information about them was available, as it was, for example, for the *gada* system of the Galla people of East Africa (Rivers 1924).

institutional-organizational and evolutionary aspects of the social structure. Such literature primarily demonstrates the ways in which generation moieties are related to, and evolve from, different forms of marital alliances. Various detailed studies maintain that the principles of marital alliances and kinship division are the core elements of alternate generation moieties. However, little attention, if any, has been given to the meaning of moiety structure for the individual as an actor and, especially, to the basic codes that the opposing principles of moiety division entail for ordering a person's social interaction throughout his life cycle.

In this essay I first analyze the system of alternate and endogamous generation moieties among the Dassanetch of southwest Ethiopia as a case study of East African dual organization. I shall attempt to show how the concrete institutional order of two types of moiety division and the mechanisms of their continuation, combined with the meaning derived from the opposing principles of the moieties, sheds light on the relationship between the level of organization and the level of individual behavior. I shall elaborate on the ways in which the structural and symbolical properties of moiety divisions shape elements of individual behavior.

A generation moiety is based on the principle of alternate affiliation of kinsmen with two genealogical lines, so that a person belongs to the opposite moiety of his parents and children, but to the same moiety as his grandparents and grandchildren. Such a division establishes an opposition between generations and introduces a structural distance between parents and their children.

Although this moiety structure divides kinsmen into two distinct categories, the moiety itself consists of people of all ages, most of whom are not kinsmen. A feature common to societies divided into generation moieties is that the people perceive them as sui generis (White 1981). However, where the people order the generations or genealogical levels into a hierarchy, an incompatibility between a person's generational level and his actual age is likely to arise. This is most obvious in an age system that divides fathers and sons into distinct hierarchical categories but at the same time organizes persons according to the principle of common age. Here, where polygyny leads to a protracted period of procreation, it is by no means unusual for a young boy to belong to a senior generational category and for an old man to belong to a junior one.

East African age systems have handled such incompatibilities either by separating the two principles and allowing them expression in two distinct subsystems, as adopted, for example, by the Galla people in the form of the respective *gada* and *harriya* systems (Legesse 1973; Baxter 1978), or by giving clear priority to one principle over the other. And so the second point I examine in this essay is how such incompatibilities are resolved through the principles projected by a double set of generation moieties and how these affect the individual's social relationships by striking a balance between the principles of age and of generation in a single system.

The third point I seek to elucidate concerns the schisms between individuals in terms of control over resources, access to resources, and social standing. In an age system in general, and in a generation-set system in particular, access to resources and their utilization in the process of social exchange are contingent upon the respective ages of the parties involved. The basic dual feature of an age system enables the senior generation to control the flow of resources which, as Spencer (1978:147) puts it, "interferes with a natural process . . . associated with age and maturation"(cf. Radcliffe-Brown 1950:27–28; Almagor 1985c). In other words, the common institutionalized division into "fathers" and "sons," elders and moran, and so on, and the structural distance between the divisions, makes it possible for the senior generation to exert effective control over the redistribution of scarce resources along a generation and age ladder that appears natural and is accepted as "given." Nevertheless, my argument is that the age system does not successfully reconcile the differences in social standing, resources, and brokerage power among individuals of the same age who, according to the explicit ideology of the age-based system, should remain equals (Almagor 1978b). The ethos of equality that is ascribed to coevals is limited to a short period in the individual's lifetime, for during most of their lives, coevals compete for scarce resources. In the following sections, I shall examine how the principles of hierarchy and equality, expressed in the idioms of kinship and affinity, are related to two sets of generation moiety and, particularly, how these notions are demonstrated in various rituals and collective ceremonies that provide cultural "guidelines" and legitimation for a person's activities and relationships, especially competition among coevals.

The three points referred to above are interlinked. They bear on the broader subject of the meaning of dual organization in an age-stratified society and the oscillation between symbolic management and certain organizational predicaments as expressed in the dialectical relations between two kinds of generational dual divisions.

Alternations and Moieties

The Dassanetch, who number about 15,000, inhabit the area north of Lake Turkana. They exhibit dual features in almost every sphere of their society and environment. The Omo River splits their country into left and right banks. Their economy is divided between flood-retreat cultivation and transhumant pastoralism. Residential units are either permanent settlements or mobile, temporary camp sites. The people themselves apply dichotomies by affiliation, according to their origin (tribal sections that are Dassanetch "proper," i.e., share a common origin, versus sections said to be derived from diverse origins) and according to whether they belong to the "original," holy clans (*nyerima*) or to assimilated "latecomers" (*mezatich*). Above all, the structure of generation moieties forms the basic foundation of Dassanetch social organization.

The Dassanetch have two sets of moieties representing two distinct forms of a single complex. One moiety structure operates in the age system, dividing all its members into two classes: "fathers" (*izam*) and "sons" (*umo*). These are socially named categories rather than biological descriptions. The other moiety structure divides society into two halves: "outside" (*badiet*) and "womb" (*gerge*), symbolically connoting "male" and "female," respectively. In the following passages, I shall use male and female for the sake of simplicity, but here, too, the terms do not refer to sex differences, but to socially named categories that include both men and women. Again, to simplify this exposition, I shall call the first type of moiety "alternations" and the second, "moieties," though both are governed by the same principle. Affiliation with an alternation or a moiety is based on patrilineal linkage in that every individual is automatically born into the opposite alternation and moiety of his father. For example, if one's father is affiliated with the sons' alternation and with the male moiety, one will be affiliated with fathers and female. This principle, through which kinsmen find themselves on opposite sides of the dual system, is an expression of a fundamental and consistent schism between genealogical generations in Dassanetch society. Though I have elaborated on this subject elsewhere (Almagor 1978a), here I shall describe briefly the two independent and cross-cutting dual systems, starting with alternations, the more complex of the two.

"Alternation" is a term coined by Gulliver (1958:902-4) to describe the division of the Turkana into two halves. Dassanetch alternations differ from those of their Turkana neighbors in that the Turkana's consist of more or less coevals, whereas the Dassanetch are ranked hierarchically in spite of a great deal of overlapping in ages. This combination of generation moieties, ranked by seniority with the overlapping of ages between alternations, can be explained by the structure of a Dassanetch alternation, which consists of three ranked generation-sets. Since a generation-set is a temporal unit, based on both a predetermined genealogical affiliation and a limited period of recruitment, the age system as a whole displays these two features most prominently.

Let us look at these two features in the structure of the generation-set systems in greater detail. A person's generation-set is determined at birth. He joins one of six named sets that are arranged in three pairs. Each pair forms a vertical line of patrifilial descent through which a man and his descendants pass in alternate affiliation. Thus, a grandfather and his grandsons belong to the same named generation-set, whereas a father and his sons belong to opposite affiliations. The three pairs are independent of one another, not only because they are genealogically unrelated, but also because each pair of alternate generation-sets recruits its members independently. In fact, a generation-set is inaugurated as soon as the first child is born to its parent (opposite) set, regardless of whether or not other sets in other pairs have ceased to recruit members.

An alternation is composed of three permanent generation-sets, one from each pair. Thus, each generation-set in an alternation has its counterpart in the other alternation. Since each line (pairs in sequence) begets children without regard for the other two lines, ages overlap across the three vertical lines. The three permanent generation-sets that make up an alternation are ranked in order of seniority. The relative position occupied by each set relates to the relative age of its members, but because of the overlapping of ages across sets, the age difference between any two adjacent sets is fairly slight (eight to ten years). It only becomes evident when comparing the ages of the oldest and the youngest in each set or between sets.

To illustrate the relative position of generation-sets, I will refer to each alternation by a single letter and to the generation-sets in it by number:

$$A_1 \qquad A_2 \qquad A_3$$
$$B_1 \qquad B_2 \qquad B_3$$
$$(A_1) \qquad (A_2) \qquad (A_3)$$

Each number represents a line of vertical continuity, but the sequential order of seniority follows the line of alternations (horizontally from left to right): A_1, A_2, A_3, B_1, B_2, B_3, (A_1), and so on.

The termination of recruitment into a generation-set is determined by the number of circumcision ceremonies performed independently by that set. Each generation-set holds its own series of ceremonies independently of the others. Men are circumcised late in life, in their late twenties or early thirties, which is usually the age at which they first marry. Consequently, a set's first circumcision ceremony may take place as long as thirty years after the set was opened. The interval between ceremonies ranges from four to six years. Each set holds four ceremonies. Recruitment ceases after the fourth circumcision. I shall return to this subject later, but it is important to note at this stage that the age differences between members of different sets inevitably affect the opening and closing of sets. Since the inauguration of a generation-set depends entirely on the time at which members of the alternate set start fathering children, the more senior a generation-set, the earlier its alternate set is opened. By the same token, a set that starts its recruitment earlier will cease to recruit earlier than sets that started later. Hence, the age differences between the oldest and youngest persons in successive generation-sets are perpetuated.

The genealogical principle on which the structure of the generation-set system is based creates large age differences between members of a generation-set, which can span several decades. This is self evident. Since procreation is a continuous process, and polygyny commonplace, the age span of a man's progeny can be fairly long. Yet, all his sons belong to the same generation-set, no matter what the age difference between them. Furthermore, since the members of a generation-set are not genealogically related, apart from a few clusters of agnates, its wide age span is expanded even further. Each generation-set is internally differentiated by principles of age and comprises ranked cohorts (age sets). Age sets comprise men who underwent the ceremony marking social maturity within the same four-year period. Each age-set is further differentiated by "annuals" and within each annual there are several "cliques" consisting of ten to fifteen age peers. Annuals and age-sets are not distinct or cohesive groups. They rarely, if ever, meet, and the solidarity a man feels with them is patently weak. They do, however, represent the sequence through which men of different ages are incorporated into the adult section of their generation-set.

In contrast, cliques are formed at an early stage, during the period boys are peers tending cattle in temporary camps. Dassanetch society imposes a long period of disengagement on its youth. The young man who has left his natal household spends more than ten years "outside society" with other young herders. The solidarity, ethos of equality, and reciprocal relationships among them are developed and reinforced throughout their youth and early manhood. At this time in their lives, when they are virtually cut off from their households and settlements, associating with other boys of the same age and sharing common needs and problems becomes paramount. It fulfills an important function in a period of transition, when the boys' commitment to their fathers' households declines as they enter the stage of manhood and independence (see Eisenstadt 1956). At the end of this period, upon "reengaging" with society, the young man is expected to construct new social relationships that are different from the relationships that dominated the period of disengagement. He is also expected to build up a new network of social ties that will differ from those of his agnates. Here the young man moves from one social reality to another, from one dominated by an ethos of equality (Almagor

1978b) and the suppression of individuality, to one that plunges him into intensive economic activity and new responsibilities as the head of an independent household.

The hierarchical structure of the age system is expressed in the fact that the senior alternation is always "fathers." When a particular generation-set in an alternation dies out, the alternation is left with only two sets (or one, if the first two sets have died out), with no possibility of filling in the vacant slots from the following alternation ("sons"). Thus, sons remain in their junior position until all three generation-sets of fathers die out, which can take a fairly long time. In Almagor 1985a and 1985b, I have shown the various repercussions of the infrequent succession of generation sets in what I referred to as a "stagnant" system, so called because the lifetime of an alternation exceeds that of an average individual.

All in all, Dassanetch alternations are not, strictly speaking, generation divisions, because they do not correspond to demographic generations, which are usually defined as the period of time it takes for a father to be succeeded by his son, or as an accepted average span of years between parents and their children. Here the concepts of genealogical generations at the level of alternate pairs of generation-sets in a single line is extended to alternations that embrace the entire population, dividing it into two hierarchically ranked halves.

Dassanetch alternations are endogamous, which seems rather puzzling. The units of the age system contain only men and the age system as a whole is considered "the world of men," with political and social features concentrated in men's activities. The principle of affiliation with age categories, however, also applies to women who, like men, enter a predetermined generation-set at birth according to patrifilial lines of descent, which at the same time affiliates them to a particular alternation. However, women's divisions, unlike the men's, are purely nominal and are not expressed in the actual grouping of women into age group units within generation-sets.[4] The main importance of a woman's affiliation in the age system lies in the rules of alternation endogamy. All the Dassanetch, men and women, belong to one or the other of two alternations and each must find his or her spouse within his or her own alternation. Alternation endogamy also means that a man may marry a woman belonging to his own generation-set, provided she is not related to him genealogically or in any other way that precludes marriage.

Like the alternations, the male and female moieties — the other form of dual system among the Dassanetch — are also alternate and endoga-

---

4. Women's divisions are nominal, apart from the formation, during their second decade of life, of local groups of unmarried girls of the same settlement and generation-set. For more details, see Almagor 1983b.

mous generation moieties, based on the same principle of dividing parents and children into two opposing halves. But unlike alternations, moieties are not differentiated further and have nothing to do with the age system. Nor do the divisions into alternations and into moieties overlap. A person's moiety affiliation is totally unrelated to his own or his father's generation-set affiliation. The two divisions are independent of one another. They were established far in the past and the Dassanetch themselves are unable to offer any explanation as to why moiety division cuts across the division into alternations. The ultimate result is that each alternation consists of people from both moieties and that each moiety consists of both "fathers" and "sons" of both sexes.

This cross-cutting of endogamous alternations and moieties establishes four matrimonial divisions, each an endogamous quadrant. Since the quadrant within which a person may select a marriage partner is the one opposite that with which his parents are affiliated, there are two axes of generational exchange, each linking two quadrants for the purpose of exchanging spouses. Children are placed in the counterpart quadrant to that of their parents, and grandchildren are assigned back to their grandparents' quadrant (fig. 1). Thus, a man belonging to a given quadrant is expected to avoid any form of sexual intimacy with women from the other quadrants. These women are said to be either "mothers" or "daughters," according to their genealogical generation in relation to the man's moiety and alternation.[5]

Although moiety affiliation is determined by generational linking, an individual's age is irrelevant to his moiety. Moieties neither begin nor end; they recruit members continuously and simultaneously, so that each contains persons of both sexes and of all ages. Hence, moieties are permanent and nonhierarchical. This is not true of alternations, which are time units, since they are based on an affiliation with subunits (generation-sets) that are themselves temporal units with beginnings and ends. Although both alternations recruit members simultaneously, one is always senior to the other. The hierarchical structure of alternations and the changing relations between them rest on the notion of a generation as a temporal unit. Within this concept, "sons" advance from a position of subordination to become "fathers" wielding domination over others.

Hierarchy, Equality, and Sociotemporal Order

Let us assume for the moment that the symmetry suggested by figure 1 indeed describes a real-life situation in which each quadrant is roughly

---

5. The women in a man's moiety and alternation are obviously not called "sisters." The women referred to as sisters are either one's close cognates or other women with whom, for various reasons, one cannot have sexual relations or marry.

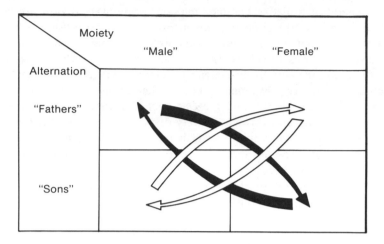

Fig. 1. The two axes of generational exchange

equal in numbers to the others. As far as the moieties are concerned, the division of the population as a whole into more or less equal halves is unaffected by demographic variations, by the practice of polygyny, or by the few irregular instances of exogamous marriage.[6] This is so, because moieties are not time-based units. For the same reason, moiety affiliation does not create the sort of age incompatibilities that the alternation system does. The hierarchical structure of alternations is based, among other things, on the ages of the individuals in its units. More specifically, the range of ages in each unit is a function of the stage of its recruitment. Here demographic changes (and, more importantly, polygyny) could disrupt the pattern on which the end of recruitment and, thus, the span of the time unit, are based. If all of a man's sons, irrespective of their ages, joined this alternate generation-set, the generation-set system would lose much of its temporal character. The age range and, hence, the duration of a generation-set would be so broad that its position vis-à-vis other generation-sets with similar age ranges would be virtually the same. It is here that the incompatibility between age and generation is most apparent. Indeed, in the alternation system, mechanisms have emerged through which the youngest members of each generation-set are relegated to more junior sets.

Unlike most African age systems in which circumcision marks the in-

6. The endogamous moiety affiliations are, on the whole, maintained in intersection marriages. Two tribal sections (Koro and Randal), whose moiety affiliations are purely nominal, are ignored for purposes of endogamous marriages (see Almagor 1972).

auguration of an age-set, Dassanetch circumcision ceremonies are not connected to set inaugurations or to the initiation of new members. At most, when considered from this point of view, circumcision ceremonies mark stages in the termination of recruitment of a generation-set. All uncircumcised children, and those born into a generation-set after the fourth circumcision ceremony, are relegated to the set that is alternate to the one into which they were born. Men are usually anxious for their sons or younger brothers to be circumcised in time to be admitted into the generation-set of their birth. At the crucial, "last chance" fourth circumcision ceremony, therefore, the age of initiates can range from thirty years or so down to ten years or even less.[7]

The relegation of a boy born into, say, generation-set B_1 to set (A_1) creates an anomaly in the pattern of affiliation within the age system. This is especially evident in the relegated boy's household, as the moieties and alternation affiliations of its members overlap. An act of relegation may result in both a father and his son belonging to the same named generation-set and alternation, while brothers may be divided between two alternate generation-sets. However, it should be noted that once a child has been relegated to another set, he starts a new line of patrifiliation for his descendants. From this point, affiliations are determined in relation to the relegatee's new generation-set.

Returning to the four matrimonial divisions, the changes of affiliation between parents and their descendants over generations, as a result of relegation, can be described schematically as illustrated in figure 2. The relegation of boys to another generation-set is a necessary adaptive means of adjusting the relationship between age and generation. This mechanism limits the duration of generation-sets sufficiently to ensure that change can occur in the positions occupied by each set to bring about, in due course, a transformation in the alternations' relative positions.

It is interesting to note that there is a difference between the practice of relegating boys and that of relegating girls. The relegation of girls is far less rigidly bound in the sense that a late-born girl can more easily "slip" into her predetermined generation-set, which is in the interest of her father and brothers.[8] Her brothers, in particular, are keen on maintaining her original generation-set affiliation in order to ensure that they will have a say in influencing her future marriage ties. This discriminatory practice

---

7. This extension of the recruitment period is given so that boys can be included in the last age-set of a generation-set, thereby widening the age range of the generation-set's members. This practice is also found among the Karimojong (see Dyson-Hudson 1966:196–99; Stewart 1977:73–75).

8. Girls are circumcised earlier than boys, when they are about eight to ten years old. A girl's circumcision ceremony is not held publicly, but individually, at the hut of the girl's mother.

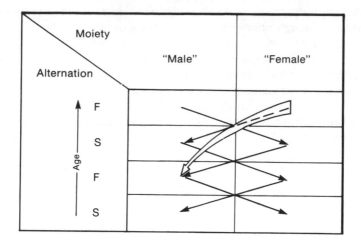

Fig. 2. Relegation and changes of moiety and alternation affiliation over generations. The white arrow represents boys whose moiety affiliation is opposite that of their fathers but who were relegated, so that their alternation is henceforth the same as that of their fathers.

also tends to bolster existing lines of seniority and control over access to recourse in the hierarchical structure of the generation-set system. It means that at least some potential competitors for nubile girls and affinal ties will inevitably be relegated to more junior alternations, to the advantage of elders in the senior alternation who seek brides (from the same alternation) who will help them establish (or expand) their polygynous households.[9]

The line of continuity joining a father and his son is severed by the principle that assigns them to different social categories, for the emphasis on different generational affiliation is a legitimation of a son's distinct social, political, and economic interests and the newness of social relationships that he is obliged to establish. The exchange relationships and social ties he builds up are roughly divided into those that emphasize hierarchy and dependence, and those in which equality and independence are of primary importance. These emphases vary at different stages in the individual's life cycle. Let us now see how the content of these relationships corresponds to the principles of moieties and alternations.

The model of kinship is the core element in the hierarchical nature

9. This subject is connected with what I have called the "structural scarcity" of nubile girls, which follows the lines of generation-set seniority and is elaborated upon in Almagor (1983b).

of the alternation system. Almost all the ingredients that are relevant to this context and that exist in the household are found in the age system. These include the general subordination of sons to their fathers and, particularly, the tensions and antagonisms between fathers and sons over access to, and control of, resources (which are dominated by fathers). Until he marries, a man formally belongs to his father's household, fulfilling various tasks in its economic activities—mainly tending livestock in temporary camps. The young man's own livestock, the basis of his future herd (whose nucleus is a cow and several head of female small-stock that he was given when he was born), are kept with, and form a part of, the household herd, although he retains rights to all his own beasts and their progeny. When a man marries, he withdraws all these beasts from his father's herd and establishes an independent, neolocal household that is distinct from those of his father and his brothers. The economic and social interests of father and son reflect the quality of relations between them. On one hand, sons depend on their fathers because unmarried men cannot own a bull, so the increase of their herds depends on the services of their fathers' bulls. On the other hand, fathers and sons conflict regarding the purpose for which the household herd is to be used, because sons would rather keep as much as possible of the herd intact for the time when they marry, rather than slaughter it for ritual purposes (for more details, see Almagor 1978a: chap. 3).

This conflict of interest stands in contrast to the affinity in name, affiliation, and quality of relationship between grandfathers and grandchildren. Just as the passage of time plays a major role in the household sphere, in the change from dependency to independence and having dependents, so the principle of changeability operates in the age system where "sons" become "fathers" and juniors become seniors who control access to resources.

In contrast, the model of affinity, like the moiety structure, juxtaposes two distinct groups in terms of equality and, above all, complementarity.[10] Unlike the alternation system, in which one alternation has political hegemony over the other and in which political consciousness is well developed, the moiety structure involves no hegemony or control of resources that might generate tension and antagonism.

The moiety structure is timeless, in contrast to the alternation structure. As illustrated in figure 2, the shift in affiliation over a long period of time is from side to side without any regard for individuals' age differences and without one moiety being superior or inferior to the other. The

---

10. See Maybury-Lewis (1974:108) for the notion that affinal relations express relationships of equality. See Legesse (1973:39) for a similar notion of relationships between moieties.

main attribute of the moiety structure is the reciprocal relationship between the two sides, based on their equality and expressed symbolically in their collective ceremonies. This will be discussed in the following section. Here I will only note that these attributes are felt most keenly in connection with affinal relations. It should also be noted that in a mixed economy such as that of the Dassanetch, no household can be self-sufficient in labor. The main preoccupation of the head of a household is with obtaining cultivable land, labor to tend livestock, and with fostering cooperation with other households. Thus, each man endeavors to weave a network of social relationships that can be used in times of need. In these networks, various types of social ties are used, including those based on neighborhood and common age, but affinal ties and individual bonds play the crucial roles.

Affinal ties contribute preponderantly to the independence of a newly established household and consolidate a man's social and economic status. The very pattern through which the Dassanetch allocate bridewealth, in gradual transfers over a prolonged period of time, accentuates the fact that affinity, if it is to be effective, must be carefully cultivated and nurtured. Among the bride-givers, it is mainly the young brothers-in-law, who are of the same genealogical generation and who share a common affiliation with the husband, with whom the husband must develop reciprocal relationships in this gradual allocation of bridewealth. The immediate, or at least short-run, advantages of such relationships lie in the direct and equal cooperation between affinally related households. In the long run, the advantage is future cooperation between brothers-in-law as they become elders together linked by ties of long standing.

Although some of the bride-givers with whom a man collaborates are senior to him in age and are affiliated with the opposite moiety, and although some affinal ties may prove temporary and relevant only to immediate expediencies, they are, as a rule, based on equality and reciprocity. The overall picture is one in which men, in the middle stage of life, are engaged in reciprocal relations both as coevals and as competitors between whom temporary alliances and bond partnerships play a major role.

The individual's development cycle significantly involves a movement from one hierarchical relation of dependence and cooperation, centered on the father's household, to another hierarchical scheme in which the man is the head of a household and others are dependent upon him. This shift from being a son (subordinate) to being a father (in a position of authority) is a natural process in which time plays a major role. The development of alternations is parallel to this shift: when one dies out, the other takes its place. The filial terms "fathers" and "sons" express the notion that the differences between the two opposite aspects of dependence lie in differences between generations, rather than between ages.

However, in the intermediate stage in the individual's life cycle, the emphasis is on relationships with affines and bond partners. While they entail competition and rivalry, such social relationships, mainly established between coevals, are nevertheless characterized by a strong need for cooperation and reciprocity. It is at this stage that the terms "male" and "female" and the importance of moieties arise. These terms do not refer either to sexuality, as such, or to sex differences between siblings. Rather, they stress biological differences on one hand, and equality on the other, since the simplest way in which equality and complementarity can be established is by invoking the equal contribution of the sexes in nature to procreation and to the continuation of life. Indeed, the middle stage in life is marked by marriage and fertility, both of which are symbolically expressed in the main ceremonies a man undergoes in the transition from being a junior to becoming an elder.

A central question arises regarding the ways in which different structural properties of the dual system provide meaning for the individual in weaving social relationships. One possible answer is that binary oppositions have a cultural significance and are used as sociocultural guidelines to show how social relations should be shaped at different stages in life. But this is too general and obvious. If the fundamental principles of generation moieties are shaped on the models of kinship and affinity, they represent an extension of the relationships in which an individual is engaged throughout his life cycle: moving from those dominated by kinship to those of affinity and then back to those crystallized through kinship ties.

It is interesting to note the ways in which the intrinsic relationships between father and son and those between husband and wife, which have different qualities of complementarity, reciprocity, and opposition, are conveyed to individuals through rituals that express and focus on the differences in relations between generations and between moieties. Let us now see how these various attributes, especially those of moieties, which emphasize the middle stage in life, are encoded in a simple formula that relates back, in rituals, to the individual protagonist.

The Ritual Opposition of Moieties

Most Dassanetch ceremonies mark stages in the individual's life cycle. Every individual undergoes a series of ceremonies that can be seen as milestones in his life. The ceremonies vary in scope and social context. Some are collective tribal affairs, some are limited to members of a particular generation-set, and some are conducted by individual households. However, the dual divisions of society figure prominently in all ceremonies. They provide meaning through symbols and symbolic acts, codes, and ritual dramas and exemplify how social relations should be organized throughout a man's life cycle.

The first two ceremonies a male undergoes emphasize the hierarchical principles of generation-sets and alternations. The first is the name-giving ceremony in which a man, usually an age-mate of the child's father, bestows his name on the newborn child. This name-giving ceremony establishes a bond partnership between an adult from one alternation and a boy from the other. It is the strongest of all bond relations a man is likely to have and is expressed in kinship terms (Almagor 1978a: chap. 4). The second ceremony is held when a man attains physical maturity. This is the *uru* ("smearing") ceremony in which an adult, belonging to the same generation-set as the boy and usually chosen by the boy's father, establishes a bond with the boy. Although both partners belong to the same generation-set, the difference in their ages is significant.

These two bonds are unbreakable and are characterized by patronage relations. However, just as relations between alternations are modified as time passes, so, too, the junior partner in these bond relationships eventually becomes an elder himself, a name-giver to a boy belonging to the opposite alternation, and a senior partner in uru bonds with young boys from his own or his grandchildren's generation-set. But unlike a junior partner, who is connected with only two senior partners, an elder, as patron, can give his name to any number of newborn boys and be a senior partner to numerous boys as they undergo the rites of initiation. The sheer number of bonds entered into clearly distinguishes between the two stages in the life cycle, for an elder's social standing rests on the accumulation of bond ties and serves, among other things, as his power base and an indication of his social prominence.

The principle of vertical continuity is the central theme in these two kinds of bond relationships established at the very early and at a later stage in a man's life. In name-giving, the kinship quality of the relationship between the partners symbolically expresses the line of continuity from generation to generation. In the "smearing" bond the chyme smeared on the boy's body symbolizes a blessing for his future fertility: the boy will beget children affiliated with the alternate generation-set (to himself and his uru partner), with which new bonds will be established. Here, too, the senior-junior dichotomy between the partners in terms of age, as well as the vertical line linking pairs of generation-sets, is clearly emphasized.

Circumcision, marriage, and *dimi* are the three main ceremonies in the middle stage of life. The focus in these ceremonies is on moieties and equality. The question arises why the three most important ceremonies in a man's life, which are held within a span of about ten years, should emphasize one kind of dual system rather than the other. Part of the answer may lie in the fact that inequality and distribution of social power and authority, all of which derive from the age system, are implicitly and explicitly displayed in everyday life. In the notion of "fathers," seniority is presented in various domains: in places where the elders meet (the central yards of the settlements), in separate dining occasions, and in dress and ornamentation (for more details, see Almagor 1983b and 1985b). Furthermore, the daily references to the senior alternation as "fathers" is evidence of the legitimation of the moral authority of the social hierarchy that is based on a "natural" hierarchy. As Schwartz (1981:5–6) notes, "vertical categories are not conceived; they are lived. Or perhaps, more precisely, they are conceived because they are lived." The generation-set system, in other words, is capable, as Fortes notes, of resolving and mobilizing" for the services of society the tensions and potentials for conflict intrinsic to the relations of successive generations of fathers and sons" (1984:117).

In contrast, the notion of equal moieties is not displayed in everyday routines, nor is the opposition between the two moieties made explicit in different meeting places or dress. Yet the three major ceremonies of a man's life recreate moiety distinctions in sociospatial categories. Two questions remain. Why is there a ritual recreation of the opposition of moieties in these ceremonies? What does this opposition represent at this stage in the individual's life? Before discussing these questions, let us see how moiety opposition is ritually enacted in the three ceremonies.

Circumcision, as noted, is a generation-set affair. Age peers of both moieties are circumcised together, usually when they are in their twenties or thirties. The ceremony lasts three or four weeks, during which time all the peers who have been circumcised live in a big hut specially built for the occasion. During this period, the circumcised peers are divided into two groups according to their moiety affiliation. Each peer is armed with a bow and four arrows with which he will attempt to bring down specific birds that are identified with neighboring enemy tribes. Each moiety group goes away from the hut in a different direction, spreading out over different areas in their attempt to kill as many birds as possible. At the end of the day, they return to the circumcision hut and each moiety tallies the birds it has brought down. The moiety with the largest kill is pronounced winner for that day. The contest is repeated daily until the ceremony is over. The symbolic connotation of this ceremony, especially where killing birds is concerned, is not relevant to the present discussion (see Almagor, n.d.), but the element of competition between the two moieties in this context is obvious. In fact, the spirit of competition dominates the atmosphere during this ceremony, even when the moieties are not busy with the bird hunt. For example, peers of one moiety will joke about the poor performance of their rivals the day before or adorn themselves with feathers to brag about their successful hunt.[11]

The second ceremony in which the distinction between "male" and "female" moieties is ritually expressed is marriage. The notion that marriage is individually contracted and not an alliance between groups of kinsmen is expressed in the way the marriage ceremony is conducted. None of the kinsmen, including those from the couple's parents' generation, participate in the ceremony. They may be present, since the ceremony is held in the bride's father's household and they may join in the meat-eating festivities, but they fill no role in the ceremony per se, which is performed by the groom's generation-mates. The climax of the ceremony is the "opening" of the bride's heavy metal anklets, part of the ornaments worn by every unmarried Dassanetch girl, which are then usually presented to one of the groom's unmarried sisters. This ritual begins with the bride sitting inside her mother's hut with her legs stretched out through the entrance. The groom's generation-mates deploy in two groups. The men belonging to the "male" moiety stand on the right side of the hut (customarily the side of a spear that is associated with men), while those belonging to the "female" moiety stand on the left, where a large Y-shaped stick (fig. 3) symbolizes femininity.[12]

The bride's leg lies between two small upright Y-shaped sticks behind which the members of the two moieties assemble. Leather thongs, tied to the anklets and leading to either side, are pulled by the moiety groups to open the rings. When all the rings have been opened, the Dassanetch say, "The marriage is open," i.e., formally contracted (Almagor 1978a:220). In

11. It is interesting to note that whenever competition and counting are involved in ceremonies of circumcision, marriage, and *dimi,* each moiety uses numbers (from 1 to 10) which have a purely ritual purpose as follows:

Number	Moiety	
	Gerge ("female")	Badiet ("male")
1	tatacho	tantio
2	tanama	nanie
3	marachiro	ilerbe
4	bibiyo	ilmoriet
5	bi-armaj	darolay
6	armaj-sile	holetoro
7	kolomotcho	iromure
8	kutchhalak	irolay
9	kutch-nama	nasito
10	tshalamutch	nas

12. See Legesse 1973:43. For more details on the symbolic meaning of the Y-shape, see Almagor 1983a.

Fig. 3. A bride awaits the opening of her anklets.

this ritual, in which the physical division into moieties is acted out, it is the equality of the parties, their joint coordinated effort, that is symbolically accentuated. Coordination is conceived as symbolizing the way in which reciprocal affinal relations should operate. Its aim, among other things, is to achieve a balanced harmony. Thus, uncoordinated or unbalanced tugging on the leather thongs in this ceremony would result in the anklets breaking, just as imbalances in affinal relations may cause rifts.

The third ceremony in which moiety division assumes prominence is the *dimi* ceremony. *Dimi* ("planting a tree in a barren land") is an annual event performed by, and on behalf of, those men who have fathered a daughter some eight to ten years previously. Dimi is a ritual obligation to which every father must bring his first daughter to be blessed for her future marriage. The blessing is extended to all his daughters, including those not yet born. Although the celebrant of dimi gains a great deal of prestige, the ceremony requires him to slaughter almost his entire herd and plunges him deeply into debt because of the obligation to entertain a multitude of guests.

The ceremony is held during the dry season, a time of food shortages, and lasts about six weeks. Dimi provides an opportunity to alleviate the harshness of the dry months, since it is based on regular daily consumption of meat and grain and the conspicuous and extravagant consumption of tobacco and coffee. In fact, the routine life of the tribe ceases and most of the tribal section's population assembles for a prolonged feast. The men undergoing dimi perform rituals, dance, and entertain guests, while their families are constantly engaged in preparing and serving food.

The rule of eligibility for dimi is inflexible: a man must have fathered a daughter. Hence, the dimi ceremony publicly recognizes an individual's potential ability to contract affinal ties through his daughter.

Two separate and identical villages, one for each moiety, are built especially for the dimi ceremony. The "men of dimi," as those undergoing the ceremony are called, are divided into these two villages according to their moiety affiliation. Although the two villages are juxtaposed in terms of the fathers' respective moieties, their daughters, who are affiliated with the counterpart moiety of their fathers, nevertheless stay in the same dimi village as their fathers (as do the girls' brothers and cognates).

The relevance of the "male" and "female" principles in marriage and fertility is accentuated in the recreation and juxtaposition of the two distinct, but equal, cooperating categories, rather than in a division according to genealogical generations of kinsmen. Although there is an element of competition between the two moieties, in that "men of dimi" in each moiety village strive for ever greater prestige by providing more and more lavish entertainment to impress their guests (from both moiety villages), the main significance of the ceremony lies in the realm of exchange.

Toward the end of the ceremony, the notion of exchange of women between moieties is dramatized. The "Bulls," the powerful elders of the senior generation-set, who were hitherto divided between the two villages according to their moiety affiliation, perform a symbolic blessing over the girls. The Bulls from each moiety depart from their village and cross to the other moiety village to bless the girls of their own moiety for their future marriage and fertility. Note that the visiting Bulls bless the girls who are affiliated with the Bulls moiety, even though the girls reside with their fathers during the dimi ceremony. Thus, the blessing is a ritual accentuation of the endogamous principle governing moiety structure. But the sociospatial opposition of moieties in the dimi ceremony brings out the features of exchange in affinal relationships. First, it stresses the equality of potential bride-givers and bride-receivers in a milieu of competition. Second, it points out that although the endogamous principle and the division into alternations divide potential affines into hierarchical generations, marriage will turn affines into equal and cooperating groups. Third, by staying with their fathers in the moiety village constructed for the fathers, the girls indicate the direction in which women are transferred: fathers give their daughters to men who dwell in opposite moiety village.

Finally, the Bulls, who visit the other moiety village to bless the girls, also go to each "man of dimi" (the girls' fathers) and select from the herds presented to them the specific beasts to be slaughtered after the ceremony is over. The fact that potential affinal relationships, expressed in blessings, are symbolically connected in one ritual act with the slaughtering for various social purposes, is highly significant. It shows that redeploying one's herd and slaughtering stock to offer guests food are part of the exchange relations in which a man is engaged. These practices are designed, among other things, to widen and deepen his affinal relationships.

All told, the generation moieties facilitate the temporal ordering of life into sections. Yet the individual's movement from one stage in life to the next involves what Benedict (1956) called "discontinuity in cultural conditions." This occurs first when boys detach themselves from their natal household. Such discontinuity is most severe at the time of the second movement, after young men have disengaged from society for more than a decade and have entered into new kinds of relationships that will dominate their lives until elderhood. However, the structuring of social life based on the generation-set system is not rigidly controlled. The structure of the age system creates temporal units, but individuals seek and establish networks of social ties that extend beyond their prescribed groups and sets. The outcome is that the age system does not operate effectively with regard to differences in resources, brokerage power, and social standing developed by coevals or people who are, and should remain, equals, at least in theory. There is a paradox here. The Dassanetch accept the notion that people who were born at the same time, or whose early childhood, youth, and adulthood coincided, can also be differently located in the hierarchical structure of the age system. Yet there are no norms of behavior, guidance, references, or concepts relating to social and economic differentiation among coevals. How is this paradox resolved?

The three ceremonies described above are rites of passage. One of the functions of these rites is to bring the individual into close contact with the values and symbols by which various aspects of his life are ordered and derive meaning. The dualistic aspects, which are expressed in these rituals of confrontation, are based not on organic parts of the body, which are exploited by culture (cf. Hertz 1960; Schwartz 1981:21), but rather on a form that expresses opposition and correspondence, or the distinctness and complementarity of whole organisms. These relationships are between a man and a woman, a father and a son. The notion here is that of the relationship between one organism and another. Being a man or a father means little in itself without the counterpart, a woman or a son. Similarly, for example, the notions of "male" and "female" say little in themselves. Their meanings depend on how they are interpreted.

The ritual and symbolic opposition of moieties underlines the basic principles on which the new social relationships are based. As Schwartz (1981:8) notes, "The manner in which society divides up and represents the world is not simply a projection of its own division and union: it is rather a system of conceptions to be used by members in their day-to-day dealings with one another." As head of an independent household, a man's interests often shift at this middle stage in life and he competes with others (mainly coevals) through investing and manipulating his limited resources in order to enlarge and consolidate his networks of social relationships. Although these relationships are interwoven mainly with affinal and bond-partner relationships, they manifest themselves in different spheres through codes that derive from ritual confrontations. In these rituals, signals about competition (circumcision), cooperation and reciprocity (marriage), and exchange (dimi) are conveyed through the ritual opposition of moieties. These codes serve as guidelines for new kinds of relationships between individuals. The trust, cooperation, and reciprocity engendered through these rituals do not negate the competition, prominence, and achievement that exist in these relationships. Furthermore, these forms of confrontation teach Dassanetch men not only that competition and inequality among coevals are possible, but that they are essential.

It is in this context that the ethical aspects of social interaction, what Ekeh (1974:58) calls "the morality of social exchange," are reflected in ceremonies. These condensed and repeated codes are the fundamental principles of social relationships, extending beyond the specific situations of exchange. They are the moral codes that permeate society as a whole.[13]

The Dialectic of Self and Other

The very existence of two sets of dual organization expresses a fundamental dichotomy in an individual's life. He is at once and the same time both

---

13. For a comprehensive analysis of the reconstruction of trust in society, see Eisenstadt and Roniger 1984.

inside and outside the age system. In every Dassanetch man there is something of the Durkheimian notion of *homo duplex,* not so much in the sense of the inherent dualism of human nature, but in terms of two worlds, two realities, and two different individualities that exist in every adult person. Basically, these dualities refer to differences in social milieu or context, which give different contents to the concept of person. As I have noted, the hierarchical structure of alternations represents a temporal framework of generational continuity, while the moiety system is timeless. The hierarchical structure emphasizes the collective aspect of society and the demarcation of boundaries, while the moiety principles are infused into the microlevel of social relationships of self-selected, flexible networks. Between these antithetical principles, which respectively accentuate the group or the isolated individual as the unit of reference (Fortes 1984), there is a dialectical process that is expressed at two different levels.[14]

The first level is that of alternations. Because the moiety structure is timeless and stands for a different order of trust from that in the relations of fathers and sons or that among coevals sharing an ethos of equality, it does not remain in the minds of the Dassanetch, in the long run, as a model that permeates their society. It is significant to note that time is connected with alternations in a way that eventually renders the generation-set system a cyclical dual structure of permanent order between alternations that are related to one another in the same way that points on a circle are related to each other (fig. 4).

The structure of alternations undergoes a transformation and is eventually abstracted from kinship and age distinctions and lacks the hierarchical character of the temporary subordinate relations of fathers and sons. It becomes a model of set relations displayed in a symmetrical mode which the Dassanetch conceive as being based on identical time intervals. In other words, the movement through time of opposites in alternating sequence, in a process of similar repetitions, establishes a balance between symmetrical units in a cyclical order that had hitherto been asymmetrical in power, age, and seniority. The "diachronic consciousness" of the continuity of generations is converted into a schema which is a meaningful referential mode that not only transcends time, but also combines the basic elements of relationships such as pairs, cycles, and alternations.[15]

---

14. The moiety principles exist in form and content outside the structure of the age system and thus can be said to represent an antistructure element which is most vividly expressed during the liminal rite of passage ceremonies. See also Almagor 1983c for the activities of young men among the Dassanetch that expose the discrepancy of symbols at the center, activities which could bring about the breakdown of the age system.

15. For more details on Dassanetch cyclical order, see Almagor 1985b.

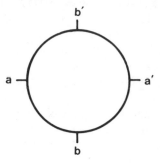

Fig. 4. The cyclical order of alternations

The second level of the dialectical process inclines heavily toward the moiety structure and is expressed in terms of self and other. This is so because the reciprocal nature of social interaction is inevitably a dialectical frame of reference and the public and open rivalry between moieties ritually institutionalizes this process of reciprocity. The comparison with alternations is revealing here. Unlike the age system in which units are contrasted in terms of *time* and are differentiated in their rules of behavior according to age, while sharing a commitment to a centralized authority, the moiety structure, especially during ritual confrontation, contrasts the different interests of self and other in terms of *space*. However, they all share time in the sense that rivalry exists simultaneously. Nevertheless, in spite of this contest, the members of both moieties are committed to the same rules of manipulation and performance. Unlike the age system, in which there is a spectrum of differentiated privileges, in the ritual confrontations of moieties, self must struggle, compete, and intermingle with other in order to achieve and anchor privileges.

Finally, there is a message in these confrontations that goes beyond simple reciprocities. The different contexts in which the we-they or self-other oppositions take place indicate that it is not the identity of moiety which is at stake, but the principles of exchange, moral responsibilities, and the notion of personhood. The notion of equal moieties only provides the public, ritual setting in which these principles come to the fore, but these principles are expected to govern the proper dialectical interplay between self and other in nonritual and more negotiable situations. The symbols that express such an interplay between equality and competition are not only a device to counter the hierarchy of the age system, but also operate to shape the ways social actors see, feel, and think about their relationships with others and thus produce social transformation among them.

Conclusion

The various levels of dualism discussed in this essay point to another option of dual organization that is not that of the holistic view which structural anthropology has advocated. They do not derive from a single "deep structure" and there is no apparent relationship between them. Though the two levels of dualism (i.e., alternations and moieties) share the same principle that divides each of them into two halves, each level stands on its own in that one set of dual elements does not represent other elements or relations, nor does the invocation of one dual set necessarily invoke the other. Each level of dualism is founded on a specific dualistic schema that consists of a variety of formulations that build up dynamically and develop in the social and symbolic systems. The difference between alternations and moieties is expressed in the number of components and their combinations that makes a dual organization as a whole "weak" or "strong," not in artificial separation between the spheres of ideas and social action. In each level of dualism there are various elements of opposition, reversibility, contrast, asymmetry, or analogy that are differently expressed in various contexts. But it is not only the number of components in each level that makes such a dual system "strong" or "weak" but the institutionalized relationship between the elements that establishes a specific profile of a dual organization. Thus, in a moiety system we lack the second component of center-periphery, but the fourth component of symbolic expression in rituals is stronger in the moiety system than it is in alternations. On the other hand, the carriers of the moiety division are not those who occupy the center, and perhaps due to these various combinations of components the moiety system seems to be weaker than that of alternations. Yet one cannot say that the viability of the dual organization depends on the integration of the six elements and their institutionalized relationships. For both alternations and moieties lack the first element of a dual cosmological system (which exists at other levels), hence the feeling that such a dual organization lacks an ideology of dualism. Nevertheless, there is an unclouded "utterance" of dualism in East African societies, especially in those with age systems, so much so that dual organization is an undeniable realm of these people's reality. Furthermore, and paradoxically, their dual organization is viable and endures much more than dual organizations in other parts of the world where an ideology of dualism, or what I have called a dual cosmological schema, is firmly connected to its organizational manifestations.

All told, the Dassanetch case shows that not only may there be partial profiles of the six elements, but that the arrangement in which these partial profiles are articulated may vary even within one society. Furthermore, within one society we have several levels of dualism that may seem inconsistent or even explicitly contradictory in different contexts. Quite often one can see within these levels a dialectical interaction between the sets of dual organization whose morphology and content may be different. We do not know yet why certain elements develop and combine with specific components in one particular dual system but not in another. A systematic elucidation of possible combinations and conditions that give rise to these different combinations of alternations and moieties is still ahead of us. All we can do at this stage is point out how the people use the same principles of dualism, expressed in different combinations and relationships between the components of dual organization, to respond to some disparate social incompatibilities that are in tension with each other.

References

Almagor, U. 1972. Tribal section, territory and myth: Dassanetch responses to variable ecological conditions. *Asian and African Studies* 8:185–206.

———. 1978a. *Pastoral partners.* Manchester: Manchester University Press.

———. 1978b. The ethos of equality among Dassanetch age peers. In Baxter and Almagor 1978:69–94.

———. 1983a. Colours that match and clash: An explication of meaning in a pastoral society. *Res—Anthropology and Aesthetics* 5:49–73.

———. 1983b. Alternation endogamy in the Dassanetch generation set system. *Ethnology* 22:93–108.

———. 1983c. Charisma fatigue in an East African generation set system. *American Ethnologist* 10:635–49.

———. 1985a. A generation after *From generation to generation:* Coevals and competitors in "cattle complex" societies. In *Comparative social dynamics: Essays in honor of S. N. Eisenstadt,* ed. E. Cohen, M. Lissak, U. Almagor. Boulder, Colo.: Westview Press.

———. 1985b. The bee connection: The symbolism of a cyclical order in an East African age system. *Journal of Anthropological Research* 41:1–17.

———. 1985c. "Long time" and "short time": Ritual and non-ritual liminality in an East African age system. *Religion* 15:219–34.

———. 1987a. The structuration of meaning in a "Primitive Religion." In *Gilgul: Evolution, revolution, and permanence in the history of religion: Essays in honor of R. Z. F. Werblowsky,* ed. S. Shaked, D. Shulman, G. Stroumsa, 11–34. Leiden: Brill.

———. 1987b. The cycle and stagnation of smells. *Res—Anthropology and Aesthetics* 13:107–21.

————. N.d. Birds of fertility and of the Afterworld: The structuration of symbolic domains in an East African Society. In *Fertility, continuity, and oneness,* ed. A. Jacobson-Widding. Uppsala: Uppsala University Press.

Baxter, P. T. W. 1978. Boran age-sets and generation-sets: *Gada,* a puzzle or a maze? In Baxter and Almagor 1978:151–82.

Baxter, P. T. W., and U. Almagor, eds. 1978. *Age, generation and time.* London: C. Hurst.

Benedict, R. 1953. Continuity and discontinuities in cultural conditioning. In *Personality in nature, society and culture,* ed. C. Kluckhohn, H. Murray, and D. Schneider. 522–31. New York: Knopf.

Dyson-Hudson, N. 1966. *Karimojong politics.* Oxford: Clarendon Press.

Eisenstadt, S. N. 1956. *From generation to generation.* Glencoe, Ill.: Free Press.

Eisenstadt, S. N., and L. Roniger. 1984. *Patrons, clients and friends.* Cambridge: Cambridge University Press.

Ekeh, P. 1974. *Social exchange theory.* London: Heinemann.

Fortes, M. 1984. Age, generation and social structure. In *Age and anthropological theory,* ed. D. I. Kertzer and J. Keith, 99–122. Ithaca: Cornell University Press.

Gulliver, P. H. 1958. The Turkana age organization. *American Anthropologist* 60:900–922.

Haekel, J. 1950. Die Dualsysteme in Afrika. *Anthropos* 45:13–24.

Hertz, R. 1960. *Death and the right hand.* Trans. R. and C. Needham. London: Cohen and West.

Hinnant, J. T. 1978. The Guji: Gada as a ritual system. In Baxter and Almagor 1978: 207–43.

Jeffreys, M. D. W. 1946. Dual organization in Africa. *African Studies* 5:82–105, 157–76.

Jensen, A. E. 1953. Dual-systeme in Nordost-Afrika. *Anthropos* 48:737–59.

Legesse, A. 1973. *Gada.* New York: Free Press.

Maybury-Lewis, D. 1974. *Akwĕ-Shavante society.* New York: Oxford University Press.

Peristiany, J. G. 1951. The age system of the pastoral Pokot. *Africa* 21:186–206, 279–302.

Radcliffe-Brown, A. R. 1950. Introduction. In *African systems of kinship and marriage,* ed. A. R. Radcliffe-Brown and D. Forde. London: Oxford University Press.

Rivers, W. H. R. 1924. *Social organization.* London: Kegan, Paul, Trench, Trubner.

Schwartz, B. 1981. *Vertical classification.* Chicago: University of Chicago Press.

Spencer, P. 1959. The dynamics of Samburu religion. Paper presented at a conference sponsored by the East African Institute of Social Research, Kampala.

————. 1978. The Jie generation paradox. In Baxter and Almagor 1978:131–50.

Stewart, F. H. 1977. *Fundamentals of age group systems.* New York: Academic Press.

Turner, V. W. 1967. Betwixt and between: The liminal periods in rites de passage. In *The forest of symbols,* ed. V. W. Turner, 93–111. Ithaca: Cornell University Press.

White, I. 1981. Generation moieties in Australia: Structural, social and ritual implications. *Oceania* 52:6–27.

Chapter 7

Language and Conceptual Dualism: Sacred and Secular Concepts in Australian Aboriginal Cosmology and Myth

Aram A. Yengoyan

I suspect that virtually any anthropologist who has either read the ethnographic and theoretical literature on Australian aboriginals or who has done fieldwork in aboriginal societies has been puzzled by the existence of dualism and dual organizations and the nature of the sacred-profane contrast. Does dualism really exist in society and how is it manifest? How do dualistic principles relate to dual organization? Can one exist without the other? Are these concepts empirically verifiable or are they theoretical implantations devised by generations of anthropologists and projected on the "native"? Is it simply a French problem or as some would have it, a French disease? When I first worked among the Pitjantjatjara of the western desert, all of these questions flooded my consciousness, leading to my attempts to determine what kinds of cultural content the Pitjantjatjara labeled within a dualistic framework. Approaching this issue while trying to learn Pitjantjatjara, I found that one way to get at a problem was through language structure and discourse. Throughout the 1960s and into the early 1970s, one of the major issues pertaining to aboriginal languages, especially those in central Australia, was whether or not they had the past

This essay was completed while the author was a fellow at the Center for Advanced Study in the Behavioral Sciences (Stanford, California) during the year 1984–85. The final rewriting was done during the 1987–88 year as part of the work done under a fellowship from the John Simon Guggenheim Memorial Foundation, whose support I gratefully acknowledge. I am also grateful for financial support provided by the National Science Foundation grant number BNS – 8011494 and by the University of Michigan, Ann Arbor. I also want to thank David Maybury-Lewis, Robert McKinley, and Karen Ito for their critical and constructive reading of earlier drafts of this essay.

tense. One argument claimed that some of the languages did have the past tense and that it could be considered a linguistic universal. Others maintained that the "past tense" was somewhat unusual and that in most cases it was embedded in the contrast between transitive and intransitive constructions. Not being a trained linguist, but having a strong interest in language, I realized that arguments of this type were beyond my expertise and that I would do better to try to work out how the Pitjantjatjara dealt with the dualistic contrasts and the past construction in terms of categorical imperatives, namely, to use the static approach. At least this would be a good start and might provide me with a few clues or hunches in terms of my own methods of inquiry.

The impact of our intellectual ancestors on our contemporary theoretical thinking is such that we find it difficult to divorce any particular expressions of dualistic thinking from the larger frames of analysis that they developed earlier in their attempts to understand the problem of the persistence of dualism. Prior to Durkheim, most writings dealt with dualism and dual organization as totalities, in that they were recognized as the arena in which particular expressions of cultural content existed. The early writing of Fison, Howitt, Lang, Frazer, van Gennep, and to a certain extent Spencer and Gillen all stressed the meaning of dualism and what could be inferred from it regarding the workings of aboriginal society. In one sense there are few, if any, aspects of these cultures in which dualism is not expressed as either an organizational or a conceptual framework.

Durkheim, whose writings influenced the thought of later writers on this question, accepted dualism as a given while focusing on the sacred-profane contrast and the articulation of that contrast as religious symbolism. Thus we see the start of a tendency that no longer focused on dual organization per se, but moved the analysis to what dual organization embraced. For Durkheim this was found in the realm of religion, and for later writers such as Elkin, Radcliffe-Brown, Stanner, Ronald and Catherine Berndt, and Strehlow the discussion revolved around the infinite variety of complexities that existed in kinship, marriage rules, moieties and semi-moieties, sections and subsections, and so on. Throughout these approaches, almost no reference is made to what dualism is as a totality or as a whole philosophy, or as a philosophical resource which provides the underpinnings for the internal variance and complexity characterizing aboriginal cultures. Thus, in effect, all anthropological work has assumed an underlying dualism which becomes more extreme and involuted as one is attempting to understand the reality of any particular institutional feature.

In the past thirty years, Lévi-Strauss's (1958, [1949]) work has provided the major thrust for theoretical analysis in demarcating the dualistic nature of aboriginal kinship and marriage. Following from Lévi-Strauss, von Brandenstein (1982) analyzed the multiple interconnections between totemic affiliation and section-subsection systems in various societies, concluding that dualistic categorization continuously underwrites the whole system of action, organization, and thought from the most exclusive taxonomic categories to those that are the most general, inclusive, and all-embracing. However, minute ethnographic analysis of later ethnographers blurs the critical importance and impact of dualistic principles. Most anthropologists who have worked on such problems have tacitly assumed its importance, with only a few addressing inquiries directly toward the nature and philosophical implications of dualism and dual organization.

In this essay, my concern is to show how dualistic principles operate within the semantic domain of language. The persistence of contrastive oppositions both in myth and native taxonomies is an expression of an underlying logic of dualistic features that operate primarily in the lexical sphere of language. In this case, I will focus on Pitjantjatjara; however, many features that relate to semantics are also found throughout other aboriginal languages. Since most previous work has dealt with social life and symbolism in aboriginal dualism, delimiting the problem to semantics should add another critical dimension to understanding how dualistic properties establish the arena of action and thought throughout aboriginal Australia.

Semantic domains as they express generalized features of dualism or dualistic organizations are best exemplified by an analysis of another anthropological dogma that has also emerged from the study of the Australian aboriginal, namely the existence of the sacred and profane contrast. Again, we must detour back to Durkheim, who essentially combined the sacred-profane dichotomy with dualism and dualistic organization. At best dualistic principles were understood as a *conceptual phenomenon,* while the sacred-profane was an aspect of *organizational dualism.* Although I will attempt to demarcate one from the other, in actuality the distinction between conceptual and organizational is difficult to sustain within theory, and even more within the ethnographic realm. For while the Pitjantjatjara can and do understand conceptual principles, virtually all of their discussions start and end in the way they are organized on the level of content and the extent to which that content is contextualized. The sacred-profane contrast probably provides the best example of this, though there are others. My own reason for considering this an essential example is that the contrast does exist in the thinking and actions of the Pitjantjatjara; the dichotomy is one of the most basic means by which individuals intellectualize systems of structures and symbols of which they are a part. In the conclusion of my analysis I will return to why Durkheim and Mauss dealt with the sacred-profane as they did, and the kinds of problems that emerged as a result.

The Pitjantjatjara within the context of Aboriginal dualism

If dual organization is a universal tendency, as Lévi-Strauss ([1949]:80–88) would contend, the aboriginal version in terms of both dualism and dual organization is probably the most complex and extreme in structure as well as content. Ken Maddock's essay in this volume provides an illuminating analysis of this complexity. Polar thinking in terms of extreme reversals and acute lexical inversion is an expression of an inner logic that permeates most aspects of aboriginal symbolic and structural life. Although Lévi-Strauss (1958) noted a long-term weakening of opposition in reversals and inversions, in reality aboriginal societies consciously work toward maintaining and enhancing polarization.

The Pitjantjatjara are one of the largest language groups in the western desert, from Warburton east to Ernaballa, north to the western MacDonald ranges and south to Ooldea and Yalata. Much of this vast geographic spread started in the 1920s and 1930s, when, as Elkin, Tindale, and others noted, there was movement from the west and northwest toward the east and southeast. Currently most of the Pitjantjatjara live in small communities in a chain of mountain ranges extending from the Musgraves on the east to the Petermanns and Tomkinsons on the west, and most recently residing on small settlements in western Australia. Traditionally they had a classic hunting and collecting economy, but over the past five decades they have shifted toward a mixed cash economy of wages, a mild to extreme form of dependence on social welfare funds emanating from Canberra and Adelaide, and occasional entrepreneurial activities fostered by governmental assistance agencies.

In spite of these economic transformations and the demise of hunting and collecting as full-time activities, the social and religious segment of Pitjantjatjara society has remained intact. Initiation rituals are followed with precision and are emphatically supported through both internal means, such as the denial of a potential marriage partner, and external means, such as red ochre ceremonies, which move throughout the Pitjantjatjara lands.[1] Religious rituals as well as the totemic system are still the essential source of all human activity. In fact, rituals of different scales of intensity are conducted with much greater frequency than in the past. During a period of sixteen months in 1966–67, at least 150 to 200 ceremonial

---

1. Red ochre ceremonies are basically male initiation rites whose purpose is to ensure that males go through the full cycle of initiation prior to marriage. The aim is not to maintain the structure of marriage, but to reinforce the idea that the greatest violation of the system is when males circumvent initiations and marry prior to the stage when they are considered "complete men." Such ceremonies are performed by individuals who normally do not live in the area of Ernaballa and Amata. They might come from as far as western Australia or from distant southern towns like Port Augusta.

activities and initiation rites were performed in Amata (a Pitjantjatjara settlement in the Musgrave Ranges). The increasing sedentarization of the population, along with the recent improvements in mobility resulting from the use of motor vehicles instead of camels, has resulted in more "leisure" time for ritual reproduction. Mobility also makes it possible to take part in rituals taking place at a great distance from home. One can safely conclude not only that the ritual life of the 1960s and 1970s is probably as rich as that of the precontact past, but also that the intensity and frequency of performances have now reached new heights which none of the tribal elders could have anticipated.

Another factor in the contact process in Pitjantjatjara culture, especially in the religious realm, is the role and impact of Christianity. In the late 1930s a Presbyterian mission was started at Ernaballa as a buffer between the Pitjantjatjara to the west and the encroachment of European influences from the east and south. Since that time, the mission has successfully cared for the needs of the people by providing them with gasoline and mechanical assistance for their vehicles, medical aid, and provisions through its store. However, the number of conversions to Christianity has always remained low; in fact, one might argue there are no more than a dozen or two "true" converts. The same situation is found in Yuendumu (Walbiri country) to the north, where the pastor indicated in 1970 that he had only one convert over a twenty-one-year period.

Marriage regulations are closely adhered to in the Amata area. A section system was introduced in conjunction with the Pitjantjatjara expansion. Most marriages now conform to this system, which was adapted to the Aluridja kinship framework, so that over eighty percent of all marriages are licit ones. This is because marriages are regulated both in terms of structure (or rule) and practice. Structurally speaking, a particular marriage rule is linked to myth, which provides the moral justification for its existence. In practice, when a person contracts a marriage that is wrong according to the rule, then the marriage is redefined. Kinship connections and genealogical ties are reordered and changes occur in the kinship terms employed, which in turn make the marriage "correct" or at least "optionally" acceptable. Furthermore, the marriage structure is maintained in and through a well-defined set of moral imperatives which are never compromised. At the end of this section, I will present further discussion of the connection between structure and event.

In many cultural and structural aspects, the Pitjantjatjara are characterized by extreme forms of dualism. However, the Pitjantjatjara, along with the neighboring Yankunytjatjara, also lack some dualistic features which are normally present among most western desert and central Australian aboriginal cultures. Hamilton (1979:301) characterized the Yankunytjatjara society, which also has an Aluridja-type kinship system, by "the absence of vertical exogamous moieties, either patrilineal or matrilineal; the absence of section or sub-section systems, except where these have recently arrived; the absence of a great variety of kinship terms, or the paucity of terms; and finally, most importantly, the failure of the system to make any 'proper' terminological provision for cross-cousins or the children of cross-cousins, and the classification of these together with brothers and sisters."

Over the past forty years or more, sections have come in from the west and northwest, both the more typical four-section system and the local variant of a six-section system, which is elaborated in the western regions, such as the Warburton Ranges. Section terms are essentially designations for kin categories, and in most cases individuals, especially if they are relatively new to a community, are referred to by section terms. However, among individuals who are both socially and spiritually "distant," section terms are also used, unless specific genealogical relationships are recognized by both parties.

Section groupings not only regulate kinship interaction but also provide a canopy for relationships between various totemic groupings for ceremonial purposes. In many Pitjantjatjara local rituals, the enactment of particular rites depends on how certain totemic groups are related to each other. Usually the ritual connection between totems and totemic members is expressed in terms of how sections are related to one another. If a particular man who represents a certain totem is absent, thus jeopardizing the ideal performance of the ritual, a man of another totem will enact the role only if the two men are grouped within the same section category. The structure of the ritual performance is maintained, even though the specific totemic member is absent. Although section terms and categories are not pivotal in terms of regulating kinship behavior and marriage and are not essential to ritual performance (unless a particular person is absent), my own interpretation is that sections are primarily an index or a shorthand calculation for simplifying the internal complexity of the system to permit the structure to operate on the ground. Everyday contingencies, such as the presence or absence of certain individuals, situations which are increasingly common because of the high mobility of the population, are overcome by structural substitutions without violating the moral and structural principles that underwrite the totality of social and religious life.

Section categories also regulate how individual families arrange themselves in the camps. Each section is related to different compass directions, which are maintained on the ground. According to the symmetrical patterning, those sections that have the closest kinship connections are adjacent to one another, and those groups whose members one could marry are normally located directly opposite. Dual organizational principles are the essential key to understanding how the contrasts are constituted and how each segment is related to the others.

Hamilton also noted that exogamous moieties, which are common throughout central Australia, are also absent. However, the Pitjantjatjara, like the neighboring Yankunytjatjara, possess what Hamilton (1979:310) regarded as the major structural feature that dominates most of the Aluridja kinship area, namely, alternate-generation-level endogamous moieties that are not only named categories but are also egocentrically linked to particular individuals. One's own group is named *nganantarka,* "our bone" or "we bone," while the opposite category, to which ego does not belong, is named *tjananmiltja,* "their flesh" or "they flesh." As merged alternate-generation moieties, ego's own generation is merged with one's grand-parents as well as grandchildren as the "we bone," while the "they flesh" opposition includes the generation of one's father(s), mother(s), mother's brothers, father's sisters, sons, daughters, nephews, and nieces. Marriage is always in one's nganantarka, but only with individuals who are spatially and genealogically distant, though they might have some totemic affinity. In theory, a nganantarka male could marry into an alternate generation, especially one that contains grandchildren, or a category such as ego's sis-ter's son's daughter. Within the four-section system, the latter is a permis-sible marriage; however, there is a wide divergence of opinion on this mat-ter. Elder males claim that it is the law, while younger men on the verge of marriage claim that it is allowable but should not be done. The latter statement is apparently based on the assumption (empirically supported) that marriage with a sister's son's daughter is done only to enhance one's polygynous state. But it also reflects the feeling of young men that such marriages simply take away available wives, which in turn creates more tension, camp fights, and interpersonal disputes over the control of women and the possibility of obtaining a spouse. At least in this case, the fit oc-curs between the marriage system and those principles of marriage ex-pressed in the structure of alternate-generation-level moieties.

In the case of Pitjantjatjara, one of the major structural themes is the interconnection between structure and rules, on one side, and be-havior and events, on the other. I have discussed this subject in other works (see Yengoyan 1976, 1978, 1979a, 1979b, 1980), so a short note on the issue here will suffice. Pitjantjatjara rules, especially those that pertain to kinship behavior, marriage regulation, ceremonial and ritual activities, and interpersonal relationships, are nearly always dominant and anterior to the kinds of behaviors that are expressed. By dominant, I mean that the rule or structure not only generates and governs behavior, but in theory the rule itself cannot be negotiated. Since rules and structure are paramount, there is a basic assumption that action and behavior are the logical extension of the rule, and that the rule is an expression of a moral imperative or a cultural truth. Yet behavior can and does diverge from rules, both verbal and nonverbal. When behavior diverges, the event of that behavior is changed or modified to fit and reaffirm the rule. However, divergence from the rule and its reworking are dealt with in different ways, depending on the importance of the issues to the Pitjantjatjara. For example, when one marries a person who is not in the correct category, the marriage is sanctioned by a change in kin terms going back at least one or two generations. A change of this type makes it "correct." However, if adult males think that too many of these wrong marriages are occurring and too many are made "correct," they may stop the next case, which usually results in interkin disputes and ill feelings. The question of marriage leaves room for events that do not conform to the rule, but these "wrong" or "correct" marriages do not nullify the rule. In other matters the rule cannot be negotiated. Thus, if a male marries before completing the full cycle of rituals leading to adulthood, all social pressures are invoked to stop it. Either the boy is physically forced to terminate the marriage, or, if the married couple runs off (as happens in most cases), a group of elders may track them down and spear the boy. In some cases, the father of the boy is speared in retaliation, but also as a warning to parents that it is their job and concern to make sure that all males complete the initiations. The extreme of this pattern is to invoke red ochre ceremonies, which from time to time sweep through the Pitjantjatjara country. One of the primary functions of the red ochre ceremony is literally to hunt down males who have left as a result of initiation violations.

Myth and the Eternal Logic

The system of contrast, in terms of undeterminable oppositions as well as the combining of opposition at different levels of complexity, runs through kinship, ritual, myth, and cosmology, as well as epistemology. In trying to understand how certain stories were linked with the constellations of stars, I soon found that almost all astronomical knowledge and all accounts of stars and planets are highly differentiated as male or female knowledge. For instance, the Southern Cross is men's knowledge, as is the Big Dipper, but accounts of Venus are almost all female knowledge. Even if males possess knowledge of Venus (and I am not sure whether they do or do not), I was unable to obtain any such information from them. Pitjantjatjara males would relate only knowledge they knew was theirs and would make no attempt to deal with other kinds of information, which they considered inferior since it belonged to women. Because of my limited contact with women, almost all the gaps in my information on the galaxy and the constellations fall along gender lines. Throughout the culture, dualistic contrasts and oppositions are the basis of almost any organization of group structure and knowledge, which are based on principles of inclusion and exclusion. Gender differentiation is the best example of this principle, but it is also important in other realms, such as the contrast between adult males and young novices and children. The whole system of initiation rites and socialization can be expressed through dualism. Maddock (1982) noted that dualism is a fundamental feature of all aboriginal societies.

Yet myth must unite any contrast and opposition at all levels of structure and discourse. Since religion is essentially mythic, the structure and idiom of myth are the pivotal points for understanding how Pitjantjatjara cosmology and ontology relate to social structure and other forms of human activity. The sacred-secular contrast is best characterized by two features that articulate with myth as a means of maintaining continuity through time. The cosmological system can be characterized as a world of closure in which contrasts exist at all levels of categorizations but in which, at the extreme poles, unity is achieved. The concept of eternal logic refers to the belief that all human creation belongs to the most ancient past, so that creativity itself is cast in an eternal mold. Human beings are therefore passive. They merely play out their roles in a drama whose plot was created once and for all time. The vehicle for propelling the past into the present as a form of continuity is found both in language and in the physical environment. All creativity is attributed to the Dreamtime, and the Dreaming is expressed and contained in totemic powers that are in the ground as well as above it. Although other accounts from northern Australia, as well as from the south and southeast, stress the prevalence of belief in transcendental powers as well as totemic powers, such beliefs in transcendental powers do not occur among the Pitjantjatjara.

Figure 1 is a schematic diagram of the secular and sacred contrast in Pitjantjatjara. In many central Australian languages the term *tikiliyi* is used for the idea of sacred. Since the term is widespread, it is almost a blanket concept, covering a range of events including the most sacred of songs, which can be sung on both sacred and secular occasions, since their sacredness depends almost purely on the context. The five terms in figure 1 contain material objects, events, activities, and thoughts that express increasing degrees of sacredness and increasing degrees of secularity. Thus an implement is secular if used in everyday activities, but the same implement is partly sacred if used in sacred activities. Songs also follow the same pattern, but as one moves toward more sacredness, the songs are

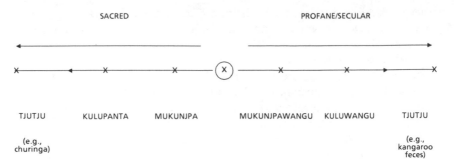

Fig. 1. Pitjantjatjara contrastive lexical terms for degrees of sacredness and profaneness

identified as more sacred. The center X is the mundane, which Stanner (1966, 1967) discussed; however, the Pitjantjatjara have no term for this, and it is not crucial, since almost all activities fall on either one side or the other or are some combination of the two sides. In reality the center X should be regarded as a heuristic device for drawing this contrast.

What do sacred and secular mean in this context? Secular things and activities are those that have a greater amount of natural entity. Natural entities are those events and thoughts in which culture has a low degree of involvement. Thus the sacred is perceived as events and thoughts that are primarily cultural; things and thoughts that have been created primarily by humans are ascribed to the Dreamtime which was established in the most ancient past. As the degree of human creation and intervention decreases, the natural increases correspondingly. In many ways these categories support Stanner's observation that the profane contains elements that are combined in terms of their commonness, minor sacredness, or even antisacredness.

An increase in sacredness is directly related to an increase in the cultural derivation of that object or event. Culture is thus the expression of all things that have been humanly created in the past, and consequently the role of nature is minimally developed in explaining how and why this cultural object came into existence. The sacredness of any object is highly charged in terms of its mythic properties. The realm of nature is set up as a contrasting category, and nature by definition means that human thought and action have played almost no role in its existence. Thus an increase in nature means that human involvement is either absent or minimal.

At both ends of the continuum, the category labeled *tjutju* exists for those things that are purely cultural, such as the *churinga,* and those things that are purely natural, such as kangaroo feces. The natural category would also include rocks that have no use to humans, vegetation that is never consumed, and objects for which there is no cultural construction, namely those with which there is absolutely no human involvement. The use of the same term for both extremes means that the differences in what the category contains are really secondary to what the category means. The common feature in both uses of *tjutju* is partly derived from how the category is formed. The category is based on one principle, and thus all cultural items and all natural terms express a single principle. In this sense they are pure, since they are never conditioned or modified by contextual factors. The theoretical implications of this form of contrast and convergence is best illuminated by Steiner (1956).

How is one to interpret the fact that both extremes of the continuum are characterized by the same lexical item? One can view it as a closed system in which all events, actions, and thoughts are placed within a single framework. This is not an expansive framework whose structure might be changed by possible future events, but rather a constant one, which implies that all knowledge from the ancient Dreaming is always cast into the present and the future. Knowledge is thus not cast for a return, but new events are interpreted and fitted into an established frame that is seldom modified. Although the Pitjantjatjara invoke a form of linear causality to explain most daily secular actions, the ongoing continuity of their world has its eternal source in the Dreaming.[2]

However, the contrast of secular and profane categories is only a reflection of where the cosmos ends. The next major issue is to understand the internal dynamics that maintain the reproduction of myth. Although all religion is myth, the nature of myth places marked constraints on the nature of religion and its operation in terms of ritual and everyday activity. All myths, regardless of their intratribal, intertribal, and extratribal scope, have a physical referent which is vital to understanding why and how myth persists. For all social and spiritual purposes, the Dreaming unifies the social with the spiritual; also, however, Dreaming tracks employ only land and physical referents as icons. The sky is never used as iconic marker. Most of the environment is carved and demarcated with the tracks of mythic heroes and ancestral beings who move from locality to locality. Some of these tracks are on the surface of the earth, but most

---

2. In 1970, while in the field, I noted the use of *tjutju* for both extreme sacredness and extreme profaneness. I though that this had not been recorded before, but on returning to Ann Arbor, I realized that Roheim, who was a fine ethnographer, had also referred to this finding, though he used the contrast for highly different purposes (see Roheim 1942, 1945).

are below the surface. In relating stories, Pitjantjatjara males underscore the drama by stating what happened at a particular locality, where the events moved to, and all the intricacies of how each event relates to all other events. These tracks and movements are a means of coding and maintaining a myth; also, each story reflects a particular moral and shows how this moral forms part of Pitjantjatjara existence. Each step or track is a signifier of a story, myth, or legend. By a signifier, I mean that the track or physical form emblematically expresses what is happening in a highly overt and literal way. The symbolism is always there, and from this symbolic expression a number of accounts can be unpacked for each physical referent. But the symbolic constitution is not the heart of expressive culture; consequently the environment and what it means are what trigger the kinds of rituals that must take place. Even more important is the fact that certain rituals can be enacted only in the appropriate physical context; since the meaning of a ritual or of a larger ceremony has a physical referent, nearly all physical and environmental features also possess a spiritual counterpart.

This interlocking of myth and nature means that everything that comes in from outside must establish itself within a dual system of referents. Stories and myths borrowed from the Walbiri or from the Yankunytjatjara are linked to the context. However, most aspects of Christianity cannot be incorporated within this tightly knit system of interdependency. Christian concepts like God, the holy Trinity, holy water, and so on, are simply not accepted because they lack the force of possessing a physical referent. The sociological facts of conversion testify to this inability to deal with Christianity as a meaningful system of belief. The closure of the religious system which is based on the ancient myths not only unifies the past with the present and the future, but it also provides a single unifying theme that embraces all humanized nature and naturalized humans.

Language in Myth and Everyday Life

Earlier, I mentioned that one issue in the study of aboriginal languages in central Australia is the question of the past tense—whether or not it exists and how it is used. In trying to analyze this problem among the Pitjantjatjara, I found no single linguistic construction that could be labeled the "past tense." What is commonly regarded as the past implies a completed action; the continuity of that action has ceased. But for the Pitjantjatjara, many activities and thoughts have no beginning and no end. The major features of Pitjantjatjara humanity, such as myth, ritual, and kinship, are part of a continuous, almost unbroken existence from the ancient past as unfolded in the Dreaming.

In the recording of myths and sacred stories, the past is completely absent. Most mythic and religious accounts are narrated in the imperfective and continuing imperfective, which stress the continuity of action as a stream of events. Thus, in versions of the eaglehawk myth, the narrative is given as "eaglehawk was falling off the branch," as opposed to the more pure form of the past, "eaglehawk fell off the branch." In the first version the imperfective is used as aspect and not as tense. The stress is on the continuity of myth from the most distant past into the most recent past and into the present. These stories are expressed in a way that connotes that the action is still continuing. It has not ended, and thus myths and other sacred stories are always propelled into the present and into the future. Using the past tense for myths and sacred accounts would imply that the action has ended and will never recur. If the past were used in sacred contexts, it would mean that once the event transpired, its impact on the present would be marginal, and over time it would have no impact or meaning in religious thought and action. Not only is this kind of linguistic construction absent in mythic narrative, but culturally it would not be tolerated. The combination of the imperfective as aspect and the utilization of physical referents for all mythic accounts may be interpreted as a collective means of maintaining religious value in the present, even though its source is in the most distant past. Thus all of the sacred has a particular form of linguistic structure, and this structure continuously maintains itself in the realm of the present.

However, the past tense is utilized for nearly all activities that might be labeled as secular or profane. Thus all activities in the daily realm of human interrelationships, like eating, going on a trip, seeing another person, and so on, are conveyed in the past. "I saw him four days ago" represents a completed action, but it also means that the action itself will never recur. Actions of this type have no impact on structure, and it might be concluded that such actions are part of recent history. As history, secular actions are not subject to the structure of religion and myth. The past tense is often used for events that have occurred within living memory, and these events are commonly pegged to particular historical events. For one of my elder informants, the events during and just after the First World War established his sense of historical time. He placed other accounts in this context and discussed each account as something that had happened once.

It would be ideal if all sacred events (myth and religion) were cast in the imperfective, while all secular events were expressed in the past. This pattern of difference does exist, but certain other forms of narrative may occasionally serve to modify it. However, it remains safe to assume that for the basic contrast between structure and history, between the sacred and the secular, and between different expressions of time and historical time, the use of the past as tense and the imperfective as aspect does allow the Pitjantjatjara to maintain the sacredness of their existence.

Conclusion

Distinctions between sacred and secular among the Pitjantjatjara are expressed through language, through the use and meaning of the physical environment, and through a worldview that stresses the continuity of myth and cosmology as they emanate from the most ancient past. In my ethnographic analysis, I have attempted to demonstrate that the sacred-secular contrast has a well-defined empirical existence; however, Stanner's (1967) critique of Durkheim is essentially valid in that the dynamics of the static concepts must be understood in the realm of everyday life. Although the distinction is based on the assumption that each of the static concepts possesses its own inherent properties, the vitality and creativity of the sacred and the profane as a force in social action is best understood when we focus on what each category does for the other. If we assume that some expression of reciprocity, either symmetrical or asymmetrical, is essential to maintaining dualistic organization, we must go back to Durkheim and ask why he insisted on demarcating the sacred realm as a world within itself.

For Durkheim and Mauss, the structure of a category was inherently linked to the principles that constitute the category. Thus the structure of the sacred was based on its own principles and not on how the sacred functioned nor what the sacred did. Function was an expression of structure, thus the basis of the categorical imperative or the structure must be understood within itself. The world of the sacred exists "out there" as a quasi-natural entity, and the task of the analyst is to enter that world with the aim of explaining it.

Throughout most of Durkheim's work, especially after 1900, the role of the metaphysical in structuring and giving logical coherence to religious behavior was a dominant issue. The social milieu was the arena of action, and although it might influence religious categories and thought, Durkheim always assumed that the milieu would be the "playing out" of the rules and structures coded in moral thought and metaphysics. In some ways the Australian aboriginal was the ideal case, yet as Stanner reminded us, Durkheim's sociocentric fixation could never accept myth and religious thought that was not linked to society and social institutions. Among the Pitjantjatjara, like other central Australian aboriginal societies, both features are dominant. Rules and structures are based on moral imperatives and cultural givens which may have no social counterpart; but at the same time, much of the mythic past is closely connected to ritual which is eminently social.

The concern in this particular case has been with dualism as a conceptual phenomenon, as opposed to the issue of organizational dualism. Organizational dualism seems almost secondary for Pitjantjatjara and is manifest and expressed through a number of conceptual oppositions that are reproduced in myth and in cosmology as part of linguistic demarcations encoded in the language. In regard to conceptual dualism, a proper understanding of the Pitjantjatjara material suggests that Durkheim's development of the sacred-profane contrast was excessively sociocentric on one hand, and inadequately relational on the other. Throughout the analysis, Durkheim (1915) tended to equate the profane with the social (as opposed to the religious) and the everyday (as opposed to the special) aspects of human life. This understanding of the contrast must be seen as part of the larger opposition in Durkheim's thought where the social is to the individual as the sacred is to the secular or profane. Thus the social-religious opposition seems at cross purposes to Durkheim's main theme even if it is an assumption that guided his reading and understanding of aboriginal ethnography. For the Pitjantjatjara, the degree of sacredness of any object or event is defined by the degree of cultural elaboration associated with it rather than in terms of its membership in a distinct religious domain segregated from everyday life.

This kind of conceptual dualism, which is different from the Durkheimian version of the opposition between sacred and profane, is also the basis of totemic and kinship organizations among the Pitjantjatjara, which are certainly based on dualistic principles. But given the particular moral, mythological, and conceptual principles of Pitjantjatjara dualism, the social forms of dualism are not autonomous, "secular," or primary organizational phenomena, but are simply extensions into social life of more basic, abstract, and overarching ways of conceptualizing the world. To show in detail the complex links between this ontology and the specifics of aboriginal social organization would require a more lengthy treatment.

Apart from the significance of the contrast between conceptual dualism and organizational dualism, one may still be puzzled why relatively little current anthropological writing on aboriginal cultures and societies addresses the issue of dualism and dual organizations as the central generating concepts that constitute the basis of an infinite variety of social and religious contrasts as well as being the central unity that gives rise to social processes which bind aboriginal societies to their cultural underpinnings. To a certain extent we are still focusing on what dualism and dual organization embrace, as opposed to dualism apart from its empirical existence. Two examples are critical in understanding why this tendency which started with Durkheim, Radcliffe-Brown, and Elkin has continued to the present. In 1978, Hiatt edited a volume under the title *Australian Aboriginal Concepts,* based on a symposium presented at the 1974 meetings of the Australian Institute of Aboriginal Studies. In the index, categories such as dualism, dual organization, binary opposition, reciprocity, and complementarity do not appear. Yet virtually all the essays deal with these topics of analysis or at least assume their existence, although no single work addresses itself specifically to any of these issues. It appears that organizational dualism, though not explicit, is an underlying, unstated theme. By focusing on the ethnographic detail or an analysis of particular institutions, the various contributors to this volume (of which I was one) dismissed the importance of conceptual dualism either by simply accepting it as a given, which might or might not require explanation, or simply rejecting it.

However, the problem also evokes another kind of dilemma that seems to limit our understanding of how an all-embracing dualism structures a particular society. In a brilliant rethinking and reanalysis of his Walbiri work, Meggitt (1972) creatively develops a set of linkages between the various facets of Walbiri religion and cosmology and the realm of kinship by asking to what extent Walbiri kinship groupings are connected to other cultural categories that permeate society. By developing the contrast between noumenal and phenomenal, Meggitt (1972:71) shows that the existence of this distinction is basic to comprehending how totemic myths are recounted, how songs are expressed and what they express, how Dreamtime heroes are named, and so on. But what is critical is that noumenal acts and thoughts also define the pattern "to which the phenomenal world conforms." As Meggitt correctly stresses, these patterns and linkages are the Walbiri "gloss" of what Durkheim meant by the sacred and profane. The contrast of noumenal-patrimoieties-sacred on the one side is balanced by phenomenal-matrimoieties-secular on the other. Not only does dual recognition extend throughout kin groupings, cosmology, myth, gender, and the Dreamtime, but the environment is also recognized as both icon and material resource (Meggitt 1972:80).

In reading this imaginative piece of reanalysis, one is puzzled why Meggitt does not focus on dualism per se, since virtually every distinction is an expression of an underlying conceptual dualism which is the general principle behind the myriad of distinctions that the Walbiri have utilized to deal with their physical, social, and cultural worlds. Dualism is expressed not simply as contrastive categories, but also by how the contrast is held together. The interdependence of each half or section is expressed through the Walbiri concepts of reciprocal interaction, complementarity, and equivalence (Meggitt 1972:71). It is this interdependency that maintains the whole and is expressed in contrastive opposition. Durkheim, in his insistence on interpreting each half or category as a world within itself, misunderstood what circumscribes the whole as a oneness.

Meggitt, however, seems to skirt the issue of dualism per se and in passing validly criticizes Lévi-Strauss for his analysis of aboriginal totemism. Although one can readily interpret Meggitt's analysis as the best of structuralism, it is structuralism without admitting to structuralism or addressing itself directly to what Lévi-Strauss understood by dualism and dualistic properties.

In both the Hiatt and Meggitt examples, one is left with the conclusion that dualism as an underlying theme in aboriginal culture is not discussed for a number of possible reasons, one of which is the potential for being tagged as a structuralist or a Lévi-Straussian. But the ethnography of the Walbiri and the brilliance of Meggitt's analysis illuminate the vividness and provocativeness of a conceptual dualism that circumscribes Walbiri "structuralism," and also indicate what Lévi-Strauss and other analysts are trying to accomplish: an approximation or a reading of a way of thought and action that existed prior to any form of structuralism in Western philosophical traditions.

Throughout aboriginal Australian cultures, the combinations and permutations existing in binary opposition and reciprocity are all expressions of a dominant and pervasive logic of dualism and dualistic principles which lie at the core of aboriginal social structure and cosmology. In attempting to comprehend the totality of the dualistic system, I think it is appropriate to recognize three levels of expression, covering the range from overt everyday cultural statements to more abstract sets of constructions which permeate the system. Dualism and dualistic properties lie at the broadest and deepest basis of unity. The intermediate expression of dualism is in binary oppositions, structural inversions, and reciprocity. Most expressions of these intermediate principles occur in taxonomic systems that possess meaning for cultural participants, but which have the virtue of not succumbing to social pressures, change and everyday activities. At the most overt expression of dualistic principles, we find moieties, sections and subsections, ritual exchange and opposition, elaborate variations in totemic groupings and affiliations, as well as mythic inversion and unity. Over the past four to five decades, most of our social anthropological fieldwork has dealt with the most overt and expressive aspects of dualism without attempting to relate these features either to intermediate principles or to the underlying logic of what constitutes dualism.

The dual system of referents, such as myth and nature, are expressive of what the logic of dualism is, and it must be kept in mind that the recognition of the pervasiveness of dualism as a generative principle is simply not an expression of structuralism or a Lévi-Straussian fantasy. In fact, many ethnographic and historical accounts of aboriginals in the last century recognize the widespread existence of dual organizations; thus we simply cannot dismiss the dominance of dualism as an expression of structuralism. The dualistic features and propensity not only give structure and meaning to those social institutions that embrace aboriginal life, but they are encoded within particular cultural ontological axioms as well as language.

What has been demonstrated in this essay is that dualistic tendencies are not merely a creation of anthropologists, nor are they only overt expressions of aboriginal culture. In the case of the Pitjantjatjara, language is the codification of the system in which dualistic contrasts are expressed as nature and culture, the sacred and the profane, the past and the present, and structure and history. As a conceptual phenomenon, dualism in language persists at the lexical and grammatical level of linguistic structure. To a certain extent, the isomorphic connection between the social sphere and the cosmological sphere is ruptured in rapidly changing societies; however, the extent of the break would vary from case to case. It is true that in most cases, the social sphere weakens faster, but I am convinced that in most aboriginal Australian cultures, which are still demographically intact, this kind of severe change normally would not occur. Not only are these cultures resistant to external changes, such as Christianity, but the kinds of changes that are accepted are always reworked within the context of the cultural structure. The unity of the social and cosmological sphere of dualism is connected to the dominance of dualistic properties from the most abstract underlying principles of society through intermediate features, and eventually to those features of cultural form and content that are the most overt and expressive, namely, those features that are the empirical evidence for anthropologists as well as what life is all about for aboriginals.

Are dualistic principles, categories, and exchanges culturally based or are they ideological frameworks that support a hegemonically based social structure? Without going into detail, I contend that dualism in all its aspects, from supreme abstractions to concrete actions and groupings, is the very basis of cultural givens which are partly codified in language. As givens, these cultural statements are ballast; they are not questioned, they are the basis of behavior, and they provide coherence and continuity for cultural reproduction. If ideology is defined as the ability of a group of individuals to utilize cultural symbols for certain willfully designed ends, mostly conscious, it might be possible to conceive how married men in classless society, like aboriginal Australia, may utilize cultural symbols to maintain domination of women and young men. However, the very essence of dualism, in all its expressions, is so ingrained in the cultural structure as well as in the language structure, that it would be most difficult to comprehend how ideological mystification would be perpetuated, let alone created. Dualism and dualistic structures ranging from everyday realities to abstract principles not only dominate aboriginal cultures, but their persistence is also a testimonial to the vitality and creative abilities of a cultural form that is far from cultural death.

The universality of conceptual dualism in aboriginal cultures must be understood apart from its particular manifestation. Moiety structures do exist which might not reflect conceptual dualism; however, these cannot be accepted as a refutation of the universality of conceptual dualism in aboriginal cultures. To argue that gaps in a particular cultural system are a denial of the universal is simply wrong, for in many cases the universal exists in forms that are distorted or embedded in other cultural practices which might mask the appearance of the universal (Yengoyan 1978). The problem of embeddedness of one form or concept in another is critical and widespread in the ethnography of aboriginal Australians, and anthropologists must devise means for analyzing how this process operates. Again, Meggitt's rethinking of Walbiri kinship is a critical opening. Most anthropologists including myself have assumed a position that if a cultural structure is not apparent, it is nonexistent, as opposed to assuming that the universal exists as a concept and attempting to realize how the process of embeddedness operates in masking and altering appearances.

In summary, dualism, either conceptual or organizational, is the very basis of a process of intellectualization that permits the Pitjantjatjara as individuals to comprehend how the parts all fit and also allows them the ability to step outside of the system in a way that brings forth particular expressions of creativity and thought that transcend the rigors of everyday life. The complexity of social, mythic, and cosmological forms is the living testimony of how a cultural system has been intellectualized far beyond what is humanly necessary.

REFERENCES

Brandenstein, C. G. von. 1982. *Names and substance of the Australian subsection system.* Chicago: University of Chicago Press.

Durkheim, Emile. 1915. *The elementary forms of the religious life.* Trans. J. S. Swain. London: Allen and Unwin.

Hamilton, Annette. 1979. Timeless transformation: Women, men and history in the Australian western desert. Ph.D. diss., University of Sydney.

Hiatt, L. R., ed. 1978. *Australian aboriginal concepts.* Canberra: Australian Institute of Aboriginal Studies.

Lévi-Strauss, Claude. [1949] 1967. *Les structures élémentaires de la parenté.* 2d ed. Paris and The Hague: Mouton.

———. 1958. La geste d'Asdiwal. *Annuaire de l'Ecole Pratique des Hautes Études, section des sciences religieuses,* 3–43.

Maddock, Kenneth. 1982. *The Australian aborigines: A portrait of their society.* 2d ed. Ringwood, Victoria: Penguin Books.

Meggitt, M. J. 1972. Understanding Australian aboriginal society: Kinship systems or cultural categories? In *Kinship studies in the Morgan centennial year,* ed. Priscilla Reining, 64–87. Washington: Anthropological Society of Washington.

Roheim, Geza. 1942. Transition rites. *Psychoanalytic Quarterly* 11:336–74.

———. 1945. *The eternal ones of the dream.* New York: International Universities Press.

Stanner, W. E. H. 1966. *On aboriginal religion.* Oceania Monograph no. 11. Sydney: University of Sydney.

———. 1967. Reflections on Durkheim and aboriginal religion. In *Social organization: Essays presented to Raymond Firth,* ed. Maurice Freedman, 217–40. London: Frank Cass.

Steiner, Franz. 1956. *Taboo.* London: Cohen and West.

Yengoyan, Aram A. 1976. Structure, event and ecology in aboriginal Australia: A comparatisystem perspective. In *Tribes and boundaries in Australia,* ed. Nicholas Peterson, 121–32. Canberra: Australian Institute of Aboriginal Studies.

———. 1978. Culture, consciousness, and problems of translation: The Kariera system in cross-cultural perspective. In Hiatt 1978:146–55.

———. 1979a. Cultural forms and a theory of constraints. In *The imagination of reality: Essays in Southeast Asian coherence systems,* ed. Alton L. Becker and Aram A. Yengoyan, 325–30. Norwood, N.J.: Ablex.

———. 1979b. Economy, society, and myth in aboriginal Australia. *Annual Review of Anthropology* 8:393–415.

———. 1980. Myth and ontology in aboriginal Australian society. *American Anthropologist* 82:839–43.

Chapter 8

Dualism: Fuzzy Thinking or Fuzzy Sets?

Anthony Seeger

It was in studies of the Gê and Bororo societies of Brazil, among others, that dualism as an analytic tool was developed and applied with particular salience. Dualistic analyses for this ethnographic area have also been strongly criticized. Rather than ignore the criticisms, this essay will respond to some of them in order to clarify what analyses of dual organization in Brazil have tried to do. Since one fundamental issue involves the nature of the categories themselves, this essay will discuss three different forms of dualism involving different aspects of category, or set.

Lévi-Strauss's ground-breaking articles "The Social Structures of Central and Eastern Brazil" (1952) and "Do Dual Organizations Exist?" (1956) were discussed in Maybury-Lewis's "The Analysis of Dual Organizations: A Methodological Critique" (1960) and defended in "On Manipulated Sociological Models" (Lévi-Strauss 1960). The Harvard–Central Brazil Project, under the direction of Maybury-Lewis, then restudied the Northern and Central Gê in an effort to "set the record straight" (see Maybury-Lewis, in this volume), and a number of other researchers who had not been part of the original project contributed to the burgeoning ethnographic record. The ethnography on the Gê today is quite rich, theoretically sophisticated, and international.[1]

Many of the reanalyses of the Gê argue for a fundamentally dualistic interpretation of their social organization and social processes. This is all the more impressive as the authors differ on many other aspects of these

---

1. Rather than discuss the literature in detail, I refer the reader to Maybury-Lewis (in this volume). In addition to the studies cited there, a few others are worthy of note. These are Goncalves 1981; Vidal 1977; Werner 1980, 1984; Urban 1978; Ferraz 1983; Sa 1982; Silva 1980; and Novaes 1979. Dissertations by Vanessa Lea (Museu Nacional, Rio) and Stephen Schwartzman (University of Chicago, in progress), and others will further enrich our understanding of these groups.

societies. Maybury-Lewis (1967) described his ethnography as an argument that Xavante society can best be understood in terms of a dichotomy between *Waniwihã* and *Wasi're'wa*. Melatti (1970) saw Krahó as basically dualist, with the added feature that each pole of the dualism contains within it part of the other pole. Da Matta (1982) argued that Apinayé dualism is fundamentally complementary, as opposed to other possible forms, and I have presented an extended analysis of the Suyá in terms of their own dual models (Seeger 1981).

At the outset it is important to distinguish between *dual forms of social organization* and *dualism*. Dual organization had often been used to refer to dual forms of social organization—moieties; exchange of goods, services, or women between two groups; age grading; and so forth. Dualism refers to the principles that organize not only social relations, but also concepts of time, space, person, and the cosmos. Some societies that possess dualistic institutions may not be good examples of cosmological dualism. Examples include the Northwest Coast groups discussed by Rosman and Rubel (in this volume) and some African societies. Other societies which are fundamentally dualist do not have the exogamous moieties which were long considered the sine qua non of dual organization.

It seems useful to distinguish among societies where dual institutions exist without a dualist cosmology, those with a dualist cosmology but without dual social institutions, and those with both dualism and dual organization. The institutional and cosmological features of these three categories of societies—representatives of each of which are discussed in this volume—are quite distinct. The Suyá Indians of Mato Grosso are a good example of a society in which both social forms and cosmology are fundamentally dual. They share these features with the Eastern Timbira groups, the Apinayé, and to a lesser extent with the Northern Kayapó.

A dual principle of differentiation is found in many social and cosmological domains of Suyá society. It is present in their classifications of space, time, animals, food, bodies, and each other. It is expressed in their villages, their body ornaments, their myths, their songs, their perceptions of political process, and their statements about the efficacy of their ceremonies. They use the principle dynamically and creatively to interpret new situations and to reinterpret past ones (Seeger 1981).

The principle is best expressed as the contrast between animals (*mbru*) and adult men (*me mbu yi*). In a more general way these terms can be conveniently glossed as "nature" and "society."[2] Nature, in Suyá terms, is

---

2. Considerable confusion has resulted from the translation of what is happening in Brazil into the terms of "nature" and "culture." I use the word "society" instead of "culture" to stress that what is opposed to the forces of the nonhuman world is human society— specifically in its most "social" form, adult men. Further, "nature" is a category constructed

powerful and transformative; society, its opposite, is usually transformed. Nature and society cannot, however, be represented in a table containing two columns of opposed pairs of elements. Such a view is essentially static and distorting. Instead, there are gradations of socialness in society and of naturalness in nature. This allows for a dynamic, context-specific contrast that provides for the creation of new metaphors, new activities, and new interpretations. Although I have described this elsewhere (Seeger 1981), what is important here is to define more exactly the kind of dualism the Suyá use in different situations.

Nature, Society, and Fuzzy Sets

One of the principal problems with analyses of social and conceptual categories is that they either make the categories appear rigid or they are contradicted by apparent inconsistencies in the ethnographic record. This is a problem anthropology seems to share with mathematical models; the models are logical enough, but is there any evidence that people use logic the way mathematicians (or anthropologists) use it?

Needham has discussed anthropological assumptions about categories in a number of publications (see especially Needham 1983). Anthropologists have generally not examined their use of the concept of "category" in any systematic way, and to do so involves a radical critique of the discipline. Another problem seems to be, as Fox (in this volume) suggests, that anthropologists appear to be analyzing the products of classification rather than their principles relating categories to each other.

The concept of "fuzzy set" may help us out of some of the logical dilemmas created by studies of social categories (and of mathematical sets). The analysis of the contexts in which certain concepts are used will help address the issue of "principles of relationship" and remove any doubts about the flexibility of the products of classification. The fuzzy set concept comes from mathematics, where attempts to deal with the realities of the phenomenal world rather than the abstractions of the logically constructed world required a kind of set theory that was quite different from the traditional one. In classical set theory, membership in a set is defined by a particular trait, which is either possessed or not possessed. Something is either a table or it is not a table. In a fuzzy set, on the other hand, membership is not necessarily an absolute but may be a question of degree.[3]

---

by the Suyá: just as they define themselves, so they define nature. Neither their society nor their nature are the same as Western philosophical (especially romantic) concepts of "nature" and "culture." Finally, what is important in this argument is not so much the definition of the terms as the relationship between them.

3. There is an extensive bibliography on fuzzy sets. The journal *Fuzzy Sets* is in its

A cursory examination of the literature indicates that the concept of fuzzy sets became crucial when attempts were made to stimulate human thought processes with computers. Humans, it was discovered, think "fuzzily." Classical set theory could not adequately.model this human facility. There were theories for randomness, but fuzziness could not be equated with randomness. The theory of fuzzy sets was developed as a logic that would simulate, rather than present an idea of, human thought processes. One of the foremost exponents of fuzzy set theory summarized it as follows:

> The theory of fuzzy sets may be viewed as an attempt at developing a body of concepts and techniques for dealing in a systematic way with a type of imprecision which arises when the boundaries of a class of objects are not sharply defined. . . . Membership in such classes is a matter of degree, rather than an all or nothing proposition. Thus, informally, a fuzzy set may be regarded as a class in which there is a graduality of progression from membership to nonmembership. Or, more precisely, in which an object may have a grade of membership intermediate between unity (full membership) and zero (non-membership). (Zadeh 1977:325–26)

The theory of fuzzy sets was born from the confrontation of classical mathematics and the imprecision of the real world. Fuzzy set theory, combined with other principles, can help us to understand how the dualism in a cosmology such as that of the Suyá can find expression in a spectrum of concrete things which may be multiple, may be situationally defined, and may not all be equal among themselves. Anthropologists as well as mathematicians have to a certain degree been imprisoned within the constraints of their concepts of category and set. In the Suyá cosmology, some things are "more" or "less" natural, powerful, and transformative. The question of *degree* is fundamental, because it allows for all kinds of subtleties, for manipulations, and for creativity. When their ethnographic context is considered, the set of "natural" things is quite fuzzy.

Other ethnographic cases may not present a group of features which can be grouped according to degree.[4] In this case another kind of relation-

---

twelfth year, and a tremendous amount of energy and sophisticated mathematics have gone into developing aspects of the concept.

4. The case of women is a little more complicated. Moiety membership is given by a person's names. Most women's names do not belong to sets at all and have no moiety affiliation. Some women have names that *are* affiliated with a name set, and they may participate in certain clearly defined ways with other bearers of names in the name set in moiety activities. But with women it is not a case of being either *Ambanyi* or *Krenyi*, for they may also be neither.

There is a more or less explicit desire in some Northern Gê groups that the names "be ship is needed. Fox (in this volume) has presented a typology of dualisms, one of which is particularly appropriate for the Suyá case. Using Fox's terms, the relationship between nature and society is an example of *recursive symmetry* ("they may be applied successively in various contexts and at many levels of signification") and *categorical asymmetry* (an "asymmetry of complementary categories . . . that can be consciously manipulated") (see Fox, in this volume). Here the relationship between elements is more important than the degree to which they belong to a given set. The complementarity is as important as the asymmetry, for many things are defined by their complementary contrast. Seen from one perspective, nature is powerful and transformative; seen from another, society is valued more highly by the Suyá, and itself transforms natural things, using items said to come from the animal domain. Animals, men, and all the other contrasted figures in Suyá cosmology are mutually defining and mutually transformative. Much of Suyá myth, ritual, song, and interpretations of the life cycle and social processes involves these transformations.

Some sets are neither fuzzy nor recursive and may be said to resemble the situation posited by classical set theory. In some cases — Suyá men's moieties are a good example — all members of a set *do* equally possess a given trait, while those that do not possess it are members of another set. No one is any more or less a member of a moiety than anyone else.

There are, therefore, at least three kinds of dualism among the Suyá. These are fuzzy dualism, recursive and asymmetric dualism, and nonfuzzy dualism. When the three are confused, as they sometimes are in analysis, the entire concept of dualism is often considered to be faulty. But instead of dismissing the existence of dualism, we should investigate which kinds of sets are involved in which domains.

To the idea that there are fuzzy, nonfuzzy, and recursive expressions of dualism, I would add the consideration of context. Fuzziness and nonfuzziness are abstract propositions. But in social life, every action, including the act of classification, is part of a specific context. That context is essential to an interpretation of the act. In a given context a set may include certain items, while in a different context different ones would be included or excluded. In an abstact sense the set seems fuzzy or nonexistent. But the specificity of a context may allow the analyst (with the help of the people he or she is studying) to determine which items will be mem-

---

returned" to the house of the sister who gave them (or had them) (Ladeira 1982). Moiety membership is not, however, in any way simply lineal. It is the units of the village circle that are important, not descent, even here.

bers of which set under which conditions. The indeterminate nature of something may refer only to the set abstracted from its contexts. The specific situation would reveal whether a specific configuration was customary or brilliantly innovative. Different specific situations, however, may often involve the operation of similar principles. The Suyá categories of smell, space, and moiety will serve well as illustrations of the three kinds of dualism, and these examples can be compared with the other expressions of dualism in this volume. The reader wishing fuller ethnographic details for the Suyá can consult my earlier descriptions (Seeger 1981).

Odor

The Suyá use discriminations of odor to classify edible animals and to indicate the degree of restriction that applies to eating them. They also use the same terms to classify members of certain age grades, people in certain temporary states, and herb medicines. The use of odor as a means of classification has rarely been described in anthropology, although Lévi-Strauss (1964) indicated the importance of odors in his analysis of South American mythology. The Suyá's attribution of odors to animals and humans may be less a mode of "objective" olfactory classification than a way of expressing the power, force, or dangerousness to (other) human beings of a certain animal, person, or state.

There are three main degrees of odorousness. The strongest is *kukumeni*, which I have translated as "strong-smelling." In addition to classifying animals, the word is used to describe sexual excretions and slightly tainted, but not rotten, food. The next most powerful odor is *kutu-kumeni*, "pungent." In addition to animals, it is used to describe sweat, perfume, and mosquito repellent. The third important word is *kutwa-kumeni*. This can be translated as "bland" or "tasty," although it can also be used to mean "without odor." There are also other terms, such as *kraw-kumeni* (rotten), which are used for specific items.

Among the animals called strong-smelling are the jaguar, the tapir (specifically before it is cooked), and the deer. In the pungent group are the wild pigs, anteaters, and some armadillos. In the bland group are mice and rats, all bats, monkeys, most birds, and most fish. Different dietary restrictions apply to the animals in the different groups. Animals in the bland category may be eaten by both sexes of all ages unless they are under some extreme kind of restriction. Animals in the pungent category may be eaten by most people most of the time. Animals in the strong-smelling category either may not be eaten at all, as in the case of the jaguar, or may not be eaten by a large part of the population; the deer, for example, is prohibited to the parents of babies from the time they are born until they can crawl.

Odor is associated with the natural domain. Strong-smelling things are powerful and potentially dangerous. The contact of human beings or adult men with the strong-smelling and strongly natural is filled with restrictions. Initiated adult men, uniquely among human beings and animals, are said by some (men) to have no odor at all. Others say they are bland (kutwa-kumeni) (again uniquely among human beings, women and infants are strong-smelling, old men and women are pungent). There is thus a continuum of "naturalness" from those animals, persons, and states that have the strongest smell to those that have the least.

The Suyá attribution of odor to things can be considered a kind of fuzzy set. Every item is more or less a member of the group "odorous." Those that are most members are strong-smelling and those that are least members are bland. This continuum is not broken up into just three or four groups. Nearly all of the herb medicines the Suyá use are described as pungent. However, a medicine may be "truly pungent," "pungent," or "slightly pungent." These distinctions are not usually used when discussing animals. What is a single group for animals is divided into three subgroups or smaller areas of the continuum.

If all animals, persons, and states comprise some kind of fuzzy set, the same is not true of the domains of space. There some other mechanisms are at work.

Space

The example of space is especially appropriate, since it is fundamental to Northern Gê cosmology and has also been the subject of considerable analysis (for example, Lévi Strauss 1956; Da Matta, 1982; Maybury-Lewis, in this volume).

The most important contrast is between the center, which is social, and the periphery, which is natural. But the Suyá have at least five named degrees of peripherality, as shown in figure 1. Any one of these degrees can be used to establish a distinction between the social and the natural, with the more central representing the social and all of the more peripheral domains representing the natural. For example, the plaza (1) may be contrasted with the uxorilocal houses (2), but in a different context both may be considered social domains contrasted with the wasteland in back of the houses (3), which in turn may be considered social in contrast to the gardens (4). The entire village space, wasteland, and garden region may in another circumstance be contrasted with the forest, the domain of wild animals (5). In myths about monsters or distant peoples or at the farthest point of named landmarks in forest or river, the closer and known forest is contrasted with the distant forest, abode of the truly terrifying

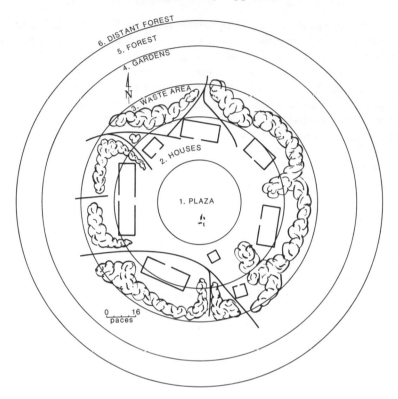

Fig. 1. Suya village plan showing concentric spatial domains

and anomalous. The point of contrast is movable, a kind of sliding scale. The only points that do not change are center and periphery: that contrast is never abandoned, though the scale it operates on has at least six principles.

Can these spatial domains be further subdivided? Is there a difference between the close gardens and the distant gardens? Perhaps. At least the principle allows for its invention. Every spatial area can potentially be divided into more central and more peripheral. At times the geographic center of the plaza (the point of intersection of imaginary straight lines drawn from the door of each house to its opposite on the village circle) is contrasted with the peripheral paths connecting the doors of the houses around the circle. Among the linguistically closely related Eastern Timbira groups, that is frequently an important contrast; among the Suyá it is rare. There is nothing fixed about the number of items; it is the way they are contrasted that is fixed. The "set" of what is natural and what is social is thus apparently fuzzy: things that are members of one pole (natural) may be social in a certain context. More exactly, however, space is an example of recursive dualism, since every subdivision of it reproduces the general contrast between central and peripheral. Whatever the specific features, the contrast is much the same.

As one might expect in a dual society, space has a second aspect, a nonfuzzy dyadic feature. That is that there are only two directions, east and west. North and south are called "the edges of the sky."

Moieties

There is nothing fuzzy about Suyá moieties. There is no continuum: if you are a man and you are not *Ambanyi*, you are *Krenyi*. You are never both, and you are never neither. Since the two moieties have nothing to do with the domestic sphere, Suyá dyadic space is limited to the center of the spatial diagram. There is, however, even here a slight tinge of asymmetry between the moieties. One moiety sings songs of game animals at a slower tempo while the other sings songs of inedible animals at a faster tempo. In the Gê case, asymmetry is absolutely essential if there is to be complementarity.

A pair of social groups is associated with two directions. Two ceremonial moieties are located on the eastern and western sides of the central plaza, but they are not marital or residential. They are groups that paint, dance, sing, exchange ceremonial food, and initiate children together, always acting in the plaza or oriented toward it. They are usually represented by the Ambanyi to the east and the Krenyi to the west. The two groups are fundamentally reciprocal: Ambanyi wear long macaw feathers, Krenyi wear shorter macaw feathers; Ambanyi sing slowly, Krenyi sing fast, Ambanyi walk counterclockwise around the village when they sing, Krenyi walk clockwise. There is only a slight asymmetry between them.

Confronting the Critics

Various objections have been raised to the analyses of Northern Gê dualism. By addressing these objections, I hope to clarify some issues which must be faced if we are to use dualism as an analytic tool. The six criticisms most frequently mentioned are as follows.

1. The first reaction of many ethnographers who work in lowland South America is that the dualism described for the Gê cannot be applied to the ethnographer's own group of study. "It is not Tupi," they object. As soon as anyone suggests a general form for the analysis of a group of societies, another anthropologist rushes in to say that it is different some-

where else (in Brazil this group includes the Tupi, Arawak, and Karib language families). This kind of criticism has been an excellent defense against hasty generalizations throughout the history of anthropology. The appeal to the ethnographic record on other societies is particularly frequent in discussions of dualism, because Lévi-Strauss's (1956) argument that the human brain and its thought processes are dualistic has been used as a basis for arguing the dual nature of human thought in general.

With respect to human concepts and social process, however, the "It is not Tupi" criticism is absolutely correct. Tupi social morphology is apparently far less concerned with making distinctions on the order of "us" and "other" or even of establishing relationships between nature and society. Instead of stressing distinctions, the Tupi groups tend to negate them and to unite poles. In the case of cannibalism, the "other" is incorporated into the "us," and the difference between them is abolished. Among the forest Tupi, especially, there are no complex, cross-cutting social groups such as those found among the Gê, but instead spirits (hundreds of them), which are not necessarily ordered in a binary way (Viveiros de Castro 1984).

The upper Xingú Indian communities, a group of societies that live close to the Suyá but that speak different languages and possess different social and cosmological organization, also cannot be as fruitfully analyzed using a pervasively dual model as by searching for other models. Dualism simply does not work in space (Viveiros de Castro 1977), music (Bastos 1977), kinship (Basso 1973), social organization (there are no intragroup moieties), or other domains. The triad nature-society-supernature, proposed by Dumont (1976) for the Panare, seems to be more appropriate than the nature-society contrast, which works well for the Suyá (Viveiros de Castro 1977).

Rather than being a destructive criticism, the observation that some societies do not apply a coherent, extensive, dualistic scheme to their world is encouraging. It suggests that we are not facing a universal fact resulting from the binary nature of human thought, but a social fact which can be related to other social facts and studied comparatively. In other words, anthropologists should be entirely competent to deal with the kind of variation we have found. In arguing that the Gê apply a systematic dualism to their world, most Gê ethnographers are happy to leave the analysis of other societies to people who are studying them. Those others, in fact, should compare their societies with the rich Gê ethnographic data. When this is done we will reach a better understanding of what dualism is and what it is not.

2. Another objection to analyses of Gê dualism, leveled most often by ethnographers working in other parts of the world, is "They are too

neat." Anyone who dares to engage in some kind of structural analysis often hears this complaint. The comment is so frequent that it probably deserves some analysis in itself. It seems to be an article of faith in some anthropological circles that human societies are not "neatly organized" and that their cosmologies are not logically related to their social processes. One could be malicious and suggest a subtle kind of prejudice: natives cannot be neat. The complaint, however, often seems to be an intuitive distrust rather than a clearly formulated analytical rebuttal.

One can ask, "What is wrong with neatness?" When a critic says something is too neat, he or she seems to be arguing that the dualist analysis takes into account more than the critic intuitively believes possible and that the analysts must have swept something under the rug. Instead of picking up the rug to look for dust, the critic expresses a general distrust of the whole enterprise. I suggest, however, that the "rug" under which everything else is swept is in fact often the fabric of the critic's misconceptions.

Examples of this kind of criticism are legion. A case in point is a criticism (Shapiro 1982) made of an earlier work of mine (Seeger 1981) for my failure to recognize that the dietary taboos of childbirth do not entirely follow the classification of animals by odor. Far be it from me to deny the specificity of Suyá metaphors. The transformative power of a strong-smelling animal is dangerous to any person in a weakened state. But even bland-smelling animals that undergo violent death spasms are dangerous to newborn children, who are prone to convulsions. The parents of a newborn child, therefore, eat neither strong-smelling animals nor animals with violent death convulsions. In fact, the principle in both cases is the same and unites them: avoidance of the dangerous and transformative proximity that would result from eating these animals. The richness of the Suyá system is precisely in its specificity of application. But common principles are involved. The objective of structural analysis is to present the common principles; the purpose of ethnography is to describe the specificity with which these are applied in such a way as to illustrate the simultaneous application of multiple principles. It would have been difficult for me to have systematized the data on Suyá dietary restrictions without recognizing the specificity of childbirth restrictions.

3. Another criticism of dualistic analysis is that not everything comes in pairs. The critics argue, "There aren't two, there are five." It has often been observed that institutions, objects, and concepts do not always appear in pairs in societies described as dyadic. This is the problem that the concepts of fuzzy set and recursive dualism are designed to resolve. It does not matter whether there are two or three or five if the relationship among them is either of degree or of contrast.

As I have described above, the Suyá have six (and potentially more) concentric categories of space, five types of person, and four categories of smell. Each of the categories of smell can be further subdivided (although only some of them in fact are) into "more X," "X," and "a little X" by adding common suffixes. The division is always into greater or lesser degrees of something. Thus one thing — for example, "periphery" — when in a polar contrast with something else — in this case "center" — can easily become three or five or any number. The question to ask is not how many there are, but what principle or principles apply to however many distinct things the group is made up of. Dualism does not necessarily mean that everything must come by twos, as in some strange anthropological Noah's ark.

Lévi-Strauss's famous article (1956) in which he demonstrated that dualism is transformed into a triad through the introduction of hierarchy is only one example of the formal ways in which dyads become the basis for other forms. Other ways include those described in this essay and in Fox's essay (in this volume). The issue is not how may things there are, but how they are ordered.

4. Anthropological studies of dualism have been criticized as being "idealist," because dualism is applied to cosmological domains rather than to the material aspects of life and is thus considered to be unimportant. This criticism has come from those who prefer a materialist analysis and from some Marxists who distrust the attention given to myth, ritual, and symbol. As with the distrust of "neatness," these criticisms stem from the orientation of the critic and do not necessarily reflect on the adequacy of the analysis for the questions it has posed.

Anthropologists have repeatedly criticized the practice, in "commonsense" and social science both, of distinguishing between a "symbolic" and a "real" world. Yet from the criticisms leveled at dualism, one can only assume that these arguments have fallen on deaf ears. It is necessary to repeat at each presentation that the "symbolic" and the "material" are virtually indistinguishable in any social process. The "material" is "symbolic," and the "symbolic" is "material" (see Sahlins 1976).

The Suyá, for example, divide their year into two parts, a dry season and a rainy season. The two moieties engage in different types of songs and rituals and different subsistence activities during the two seasons. The year itself, however, is neither as regular as the ritual calendar nor as exclusively dual. The Suyá describe quite a few shorter "seasons" that occur between the height of the dry season and the height of the flooding rainy season. In a sense they impose order, through their moieties, on the processes of raining and drying out. The social and cosmological dualism is not derived from the "objective" constraints of their habitat, since other groups in the region that have very similar environments (the Upper Xingú groups, for example) have neither moieties nor dualist cosmologies.

5. The charge "You don't account for origins," which is related to the previous one, criticizes the distance between conceptual structures and the nitty gritty of social processes. Structuralism has often been accused of being ahistorical. The accusation, while sometimes pertinent, is not necessarily true. Different peoples' histories may have different structures, and one social form may generate another one. Sahlins's discussion (1976: 19–47) of Moalan dualism is a case in point. There he argued that certain social forms contain the dynamics to produce their own future transformation. This may well be the case of the Gê. One can see in the different Northern Gê societies different specific dual patterns, which could arguably be related to an earlier form.

There is virtually no archaeological record for the Gê, however, to confirm any reconstruction. Although ethnohistorical work is being done, little has been published as yet. The contact of the Gê with Europeans is relatively recent and has not been extensively documented. So far there is little data with which to work, and for this reason the sorts of questions that have been addressed are those that can be examined in the ethnographic present. In other parts of Amazonia historical studies are being done (for example, Wright 1981).

The Gê do not deny either time or history, as has sometimes been suggested as a defense against criticisms of analyses that do not deal with the origins of certain social forms. All the Gê have a dramatic oral history. The Suyá Indians have both a concept 'of diachrony and a place for it in their cosmos, their oral literature, and the socialization of their children. But the locus of diachrony is outside the village—in the forest and distant forest. Changes occurred "to the east" (occasionally in other directions), outside of the village plaza, or in other villages. These events are remembered and geographically located. The peripheral is also the temporal. The past is in a sense engraved on the forest and rivers through place names (Seeger 1977; 1981:75–78). In contrast to these peripheral events in time, relationships that the Suyá define as being constant throughout history (at least since names were learned from enemies living underground) are located in the plaza. If diachrony has not been central to our analyses, it should be noted that origins and history are peripheral to the Suyá, and probably to most of the Gê, themselves. History, although discussed and often used in interpreting the present, is banished to the margins.

Various kinds of structural histories are found in dual societies. Suyá dualism is quite different from that described by Valeri (in this volume). In Seram, an initial unity becomes a dual contrast. In the Suyá case, the terms of an initial dualism are simply redefined. The membership of certain things changes from one pole to the other, but most institutions and concepts are dual from the start. Raw and cooked meat always existed, but at one time only the jaguar had fire and cooked its meat; humans ate raw meat heated in the sun. Today humans eat cooked meat and jaguars do not. The moietics always existed—there is no origin myth for them—but at one time there were only two names: one for all Ambanyi and one for all Krenyi. More names were obtained, but there was never a time when the moieties were not distinguished by personal names. Dualism is taken for granted in Suyá myths.

Structure and history are not entirely incompatible. Events never simply happen; they are interpreted and fitted into some kind of pattern by the people experiencing them. Structuralism should be able to deal with interpretations of history and the tranformations involved in social processes just as it deals with short-term social processes.

6. The criticism of structuralism is also extended to situations involving the confrontation of radically different societies. Thus critics have said of dualistic analyses in Brazil, "You can't account for social change." This charge is made partly to accuse the analyses of the sin of synchrony and partly to argue that they overlook the most important event in some other analysts' perception of Indian life: the arrival of the Brazilian frontier.

In fact, the Gê societies seem to fit their experiences with and observations of the whites into their existing cosmos. To the Suyá, the urban poor are remarkable for living in strong-smelling or rotten-smelling houses, for being ill and oversexed, and therefore transformative and dangerous in ways that they understand. I have argued elsewhere that their relationship with whites has been oriented from the start by their own myths. They interpret the invaders as powerful possessors of desirable things, similar to the jaguar from whom they obtained fire, the enemies from whom they obtained their names, the Upper Xingú Indians from whom they obtained women and pots, and so forth (Seeger, n.d.). How else can one understand the way they stole things from the first non-Indian they saw—the explorer Karl von den Steinen, who camped on a sandbank across the river from the Suyá village in 1884? One of the Timbira groups has apparently been very successful in adapting to the arrival of the Brazilians and the market economy; a study of this group has argued that their model for Brazilians is that of a monster, described in their myths, that always threatens society (Ferraz 1983).

Structural analyses that study native interpretations of social processes are not necessarily doomed to ignore social change. They can, indeed, provide a different perspective on it. The understanding of social change they provide may lessen the Eurocentrism of the histories and studies of change that have been produced for most of these groups.

Gê societies possessing a coherent cosmology characterized by a dual cosmos confront the Brazilian frontier at a dramatic moment. Each group enters the other's history at a different point and from a different perspective. While many features of the larger society determine the future of the tribal societies so encountered, as Ribeiro (1977) has convincingly argued, the perspective of the groups themselves on the process is certainly part of the encounter and is intricately related to their own social processes and their cosmology.

Conclusions

In this essay I have suggested that distinctions should be made among those societies with dual social institutions but lacking a strongly dual cosmology, those societies with dual cosmologies but lacking strongly dual social institutions, and those societies that have both dual institutions and dual cosmologies. Since not all societies are organized on dual principles, dualism is a social fact that can be addressed comparatively by anthropologists. Most of this essay was devoted to an analysis of dualism among the Suyá Indians of central Brazil, which have a strongly dual cosmology and some dual features in their social organization.

I argue that among the Suyá there are at least three kinds of dualism: fuzzy set dualism, where membership in a group is a question of degree; recursive symmetrical dualism, where the relationship between the elements is more important than the degree to which they participate in a given set; and nonfuzzy dualism, where a person or thing either is or is not a member of a set. Each of these forms appears in Suyá social organization and cosmology. I described the fuzzy set of things odorous, the recursive asymmetric dualism of space, and the nonfuzzy dualism of moiety membership. In each case there are dual features, but they are ordered differently. When the three forms of dualism are confused, as they sometimes are, critics have tended to believe that this was grounds for rejecting dualistic analysis and discounting dualism as a principle of organization.

Criticisms of dualist analysis have often foundered on basic misconceptions. Not all societies use a dual principle to organize groups of people or concepts; within South America there are a number of other forms of organization. In strongly dual societies not everything comes in pairs; dual principles are capable of organizing things in sets of three or more. The neatness of structural analysis does not necessarily hide data or involve sleight of hand; rather it reveals the operation of similar principles in apparent diversity. Dualistic analyses do not by definition ignore the material, the temporal, and relations of power. If certain dualistic analyses have done so, that is not a result of the approach itself but of a tendency in much of anthropology, which is found in nondualistic analyses as well. The six common criticisms of dualistic analyses have tended to obscure the possibilities of addressing dualism in a comparative way.

There are probably more forms of dualism than the three I have described for the Suyá. Some of them are suggested in other essays in this volume. By refining our discussions of dualism through the analysis of the different ways dual principles organize sets, we can go beyond the statement that a given society is characterized by dualism and begin to specify the forms of dualism found in it. By eschewing fuzzy thinking and considering fuzzy sets, recursive dualism, and other forms, we can develop an adequate, comparative way of analyzing dual forms of organization around the world. This should also throw some of the nondual principles of organization into relief and advance the comparative study of general principles of social and cosmological organization.

ACKNOWLEDGMENTS

This essay owes a great deal to careful readings given earlier drafts by Eduardo Viveiros de Castro, David Maybury-Lewis, Uri Algamor, and students in one of my courses on social organization. I was directed to the concept of fuzzy sets by Pierre Maranda, to whom I am very grateful. Many fruitful ideas developed in conversations with Roberto Da Matta, and I was greatly stimulated by the conference participants. None of these are responsible for the form this essay has taken.

REFERENCES

Basso, Ellen B. 1973. *The Kalapalo Indians of central Brazil.* New York: Holt, Rinehart and Winston.

Bastos, Rafael. 1977. *A musicologica Kamayurá.* Brasília: Fundacão Nacional do Indio.

Da Matta, R. A. 1982. *A divided world.* Cambridge: Harvard University Press.

Dumont, J. P. 1976. *Under the rainbow: Nature and supernature among the Panare Indians.* Austin: University of Texas Press.

Ferraz, I. 1983. Os Parkateje das matas do Tocantins: A epopéia de um líder Timbira. Master's thesis, University of São Paulo.

Gonçalves, J. R. S. 1981. A luta pela identidade social, o caso das relações entre índios e brancos no Brasil Central. Master's thesis, National Museum, Rio de Janeiro.

Ladeira, M. E. 1982. A troca de nomes e a troca de cônjuges: Uma contribuição ao estudo do parentesco Timbira. Master's thesis, University of São Paulo.

Lea, Vanessa, 1986. Nomes e nekrets kayapó: Uma concepção da ripueza. Ph.D. diss., National Museum, University of Rio de Janeiro.

Lévi-Strauss, Claude. 1952. Les structures sociales dans le Brésil central et oriental. In *Indian tribes of aboriginal America*, ed. S. Tax, 302–10. Proceedings of the Twenty-ninth International Congress of Americanists, Chicago. Translated and reprinted in Lévi-Strauss 1963.

———. 1956. Les organisations dualistes, existent-elles? *Bijdragen tot de Taal-, Land- en Volkenkunde* 1122:99–128. Translated and reprinted in Lévi-Strauss 1963.

———. 1960. On manipulated sociological models. *Bijdragen tot de Taal-, Land- en Volkenkunde* 116(1):45–54. Translated and reprinted in Lévi-Strauss 1975.

———. 1963. *Structural anthropology.* New York: Basic Books.

———. 1964. *Le cru et le cuit.* Paris: Plon.

———. 1975. *Structural anthropology II.* New York: Basic Books.

Lopes da Silva, Aracy. 1986. Nomes e amigos: da prática Xavante a uma reflexão sobre os Jê. Anthropologia 6, São Paulo, Universidade de São Paulo.

Maybury-Lewis, D. 1960. The analysis of dual organizations: A methodological critique. *Bijdragen tot de Taal-, Land- en Volkenkunde* 116:17–44.

———. 1967. *Akwē-Shavante society.* Oxford: Clarendon Press.

———. 1974. Preface. In *Akwē-Shavante society.* New York: Oxford University Press.

———. 1979. *Dialectical societies.* Cambridge: Harvard University Press.

Melatti, J. C. 1970. *O sistema social Krahó.* Ph.D. thesis, University of São Paulo.

Needham, R. 1983. *Against the tranquility of axioms.* Berkeley and Los Angeles: University of California Press.

Novaes, S. C. 1979. Mulheres, homens e heróis: Dinâmica e permanência atravéz do cotidiano da vida Bororo. Master's thesis, University of São Paulo.

Ramos, A. R. 1977. O mundo unificado dos Apinayé ou o mundo dividido dos antropólogos. *Anuário Antropológico* 76:263–82.

Ribeiro, D. 1977. *Os índios e a civilização.* Petrópolis: Editora Vozes.

Sa, C. 1982. Aldeia de São Marcos: Transformações na habitação de uma comunidade Xavante. Master's thesis, University of São Paulo.

Sahlins, M. 1976. *Culture and practical reason.* Chicago: University of Chicago Press.

———. 1981. *Historical metaphors and mythical realities: Structure in the early history of the Sandwich Islands Kingdom.* Ann Arbor: University of Michigan Press.

Seeger, A. 1977. Fixed points on arcs in circles: The temporal, processual aspect of Suyá space and society. *Actes du quarante-deuxième congrès international des americanistes* 2:340–59.

———. 1981. *Nature and society in central Brazil: The Suyá Indians of Mato Grosso.* Cambridge: Harvard University Press.

————. N.d. Thieves, myths and history: Karl von den Steinen among the Suyá, 3–6 September, 1884. To appear in a centenary volume marking the 1884 visit of Karl von den Steinen to the Xingu, ed. V. P. Coelho.

Shapiro, W. 1971. Structuralism versus sociology: A review of Maybury-Lewis's *Akwẽ-Shavante society. Mankind Quarterly* 8:64–67.

————. 1982. Review of *Nature and society in central Brazil,* by Anthony Seeger. *American Anthropologist* 84:478–80.

————. 1983. Review of *A divided world,* by Roberto Da Matta. *American Anthropologist* 85:675–76.

Urban, G. 1978. A model of Shokleng social reality. Ph.D. diss., University of Chicago.

Vidal, L. B. 1977. *Morte e vida de uma sociedade indígena brasileira.* São Paulo: Hucitec and University of São Paulo.

Viveiros de Castro, E. B. 1977. Indivíduo e sociedade no alto Xingú: Os Yawalapiti. Master's thesis, National Museum, Rio de Janeiro.

————. 1984. Araweté: Uma visão da cosmologia e da pessôa Tupi-Guaraní. Ph.D. thesis, National Museum, Rio de Janeiro.

Werner, D. 1980. The making of a Mekranoti chief: The psychological and social determinants of leadership in a native South American society. Ph.D. diss., City University of New York.

————. 1984. *Amazon journey: An anthropologist's year among Brazil's Mekranoti Indians.* New York: Simon and Schuster.

Wright, R. 1981. History and religion of the Baniwa peoples of the Upper Rio Negro. Ph.D. thesis, Stanford University.

Zadeh, L. A. 1977. Set theory. *Encyclopedia of computer science and technology* 8:325–63. New York: Marcel Dekker.

Chapter 9

Dual Organization and Its Developmental Potential in Two Contrasting Environments

Abraham Rosman and Paula G. Rubel

This essay is concerned with the evolutionary possibilities of dual organization. Two sequences are presented which show how dual organization evolved into more complex forms in two different parts of the world. The methodology used involves the building of structural models using data on ceremonial exchange, social structure, and symbolism. Our approach is predicated upon the important distinction between surface phenomena and underlying structure. This distinction is the same as that made in linguistics by Ferdinand de Saussure between *parole*, the speech behavior of individuals, and *langue*, the grammar of a language. The underlying structure of a society constitutes a model for that society. The structural models we develop derive from an analysis of material goods exchanged, the social relations of the exchangers which form part of a larger system of social relations, and the cultural meanings of the goods and of the actions of the exchangers which form the symbolic system. The underlying structure or structures of a society account for as many aspects of surface behavior as possible. Integration here means that different aspects of surface phenomena are all explained or subsumed within a single theoretical model. The notion of an explanatory hierarchy is also important. First there is explanation at the level of behavior—what people in a society actually do. At a higher level of abstraction statements of the rules of what people should do in different cultural realms. The third and most abstract level is that of the theoretical model or models that encompass different cultural realms.

We will use the concept of dual organization to illustrate the nature of the relationship between surface phenomena and underlying structure.

Dual organization as a structural model may have a wide variety of surface manifestations in various cultural domains. Communities may be divided into two parts that may be named or deictic ("us" and "them"). These are usually referred to in the anthropological literature as "moieties." A settlement may be physically divided into two sectors that perform various ritual services for one another at rites of passage such as birth, initiation, and death. They are then recompensed for their services with goods or feasts. Sometimes the two sides merely exchange goods or feasts ceremonially without the performance of services for one another. Women may be exchanged between the two sides of the community so that the sides stand as affines to one another. This exchange of women may be expressed by one or more marriage rules such as: moiety exogamy, sister exchange, bilateral cross-cousin marriage, or marriage with someone in the general category of cross as opposed to parallel relative. Dual organization may be expressed in kinship terminology through the distinction between parallel and cross relatives, as is found in Dravidian or Iroquois terminologies. The dual division may be reflected in a division in the cosmology and in other symbolic, cognitive, and ideological realms.

None of these manifestations of dual organization is more basic than the others; they are all equally manifestations of the structure of dual organization; not all of these may be found in any single society. It can be said that dual organization is the underlying structure, structural model, or dominant structure for a society when this model serves to integrate more surface data from different cultural realms than does any other model. We argue later in this essay that dual organization is not necessarily the dominant structure wherever named moieties are present (as for the Tlingit and Haida) and that dual organization nevertheless *may* be the dominant structure where named moieties do not exist (as in the Slave or in Tanga).

The marriage rule of a society is merely one of the manifestations of a structure. It has no special status. However, since marriage rules serve to align groups in relationship to one another, such a rule frequently serves as a basis for a hypothesis about the underlying structure of a society. Sometimes mortuary rites or ceremonial food exchanges may be the focal point for a society, serving to align social groups in relationship to one another in the same way that marriage rules do. In such instances, these can form the basis of hypotheses about the underlying structure of the society. In both areas of the world that we will be considering in this essay, mortuary rites are of central significance, and the dominant structure is revealed in them.

Some analysts make a distinction between preferential and prescriptive marriage rules and consider this difference to be critical. To us, a preferential rule as to whom one ought to marry is as important as a prescriptive one. We are in agreement with Lévi-Strauss, who notes, "If I have employed the notion of preference and obligation indifferently, even at times in the one sentence, for which I have been reproached, it is because, in my opinion, they do not connote different social realities, but rather, correspond to slightly differing ways in which man envisages the same reality"([1969]:xxxi–xxxii). The critical point is whether or not that marriage rule is in accord with other expected manifestations of a particular structural model, not whether it is preferential or prescriptive.

Structuralism has been accused of being atemporal, of ignoring process. However, a number of avowedly structuralist analyses have tried to deal with this question. The structuralist Marxists, for example, have attempted to show how structures unfold through time in the process of reproducing themselves, or alternatively how the social reproductive process involves change or alteration in the structure when intersystemic contradictions develop. The changes that have taken place leave their traces. As Roman Jakobson has noted for language, the diachronic process is contained within the synchronic description. Similarly, in the synchronic analysis of societies, one can find clues about their prior structures. Such clues enable one to formulate hypotheses about how prior forms changed into present forms. We refer to these processes of change as transformations. An advantage of viewing such changes as transformations is that the concept of transformation implies reversibility at the level of the model. The view we are adopting here is that "synchronic" is only a frame of reference, and that the Saussurian distinction between synchrony and diachrony is one which had heuristic value in Saussure's time but at present should be seen as only artificial. Sahlins has convincingly argued from a similar point of view, that structure and history must be seen as continuously interrelated since historical events are always ordered by existing structures and structural description encapsulates previous history (Sahlins 1981, 1983).

In this essay, then, we will examine synchronic descriptions for clues about diachronic process. We will begin with relatively complex societies for clues regarding their simpler antecedents. We will then show how the dual organization of the matrilineal Athapaskan societies was transformed into the more complex social forms of the matrilineal societies of the Northwest Coast of North America, specifically the Haida and Tlingit. In the second part of this essay, we will examine Trobriand structure for clues to its antecedents, and then demonstrate how societies of New Ireland and the Solomons with structures of dual organization resemble the antecedents of and are in a transformational relationship to Trobriand society. In comparing these transformations in two different parts of the world, we will examine the processes involved as dual organization changes, and the conditions under which the transformation to more complex forms takes place.

The Evolution of Dual Organization on the Northwest Coast

The Haida and Tlingit, both having ranked chieftainships, are identical in underlying structure. They share the following features. They are matrilineal in descent. In both, inheritance of leadership positions is from the mother's brother to sister's son. Postmarital residence is avunculocal. Both have named moieties. In Haida, they are named Eagle and Raven; in Tlingit, Wolf and Raven. These moieties are exogamous, but do not have any other function. Both societies have kinship terminologies of the Crow type. In both, father's sister's daughter and mother's brother's daughter are terminologically separate. Haida and Tlingit both have preferential rules for marriage with father's sister's daughter. Murdock states the marriage rule for the Haida in the following fashion: "In any case, the preferred marriage is with a *sqan* (father's sister's daughter) of the same generation, though not necessarily a first cousin"(1934:364). Sqan is the Haida term for father's sister and for father's sister's daughter, and is generally applied to women of father's clan. That women referred to as sqan, and of one's own generation, are the preferred mates demonstrates how a Crow kinship terminology can sort relatives in such a way as to reflect a preferential rule for marriage with father's sister's daughter. This marriage pattern, given matrilineal descent, generates the structure illustrated in figure 1. In our earlier work we presented extensive ethnographic evidence in support of this as the dominant structure in Tlingit and Haida (Rosman and Rubel 1971:34–68). We will provide only a brief summary of that information here. This dominant structure is a three-sided one, with each group intermarrying with two other groups.

Swanton presents information indicating for each Haida group the two in the opposite moiety with whom it is allied in marriage (1905). The Tlingit genealogies collected by Durlach demonstrate a preference for marriage with two groups in the opposite moiety (1928). One implication of this structure is that ego and his father's father are in the same matrilineal clan. In support of this, we are told by both Swanton (1905) and Murdock (1934) that the Haida believe that a man is a reincarnation of his father's father and inherits his name from that individual (Rosman and Rubel 1971:45). Details of events at Haida and Tlingit potlatches also attest to the existence of this three-sided structure. Haida and Tlingit share an identity of structure but their potlatching differs in one important respect. The Tlingit hold only one major type of potlatch—the mortuary potlatch—at which the heir of the deceased succeeds to his new position, the members

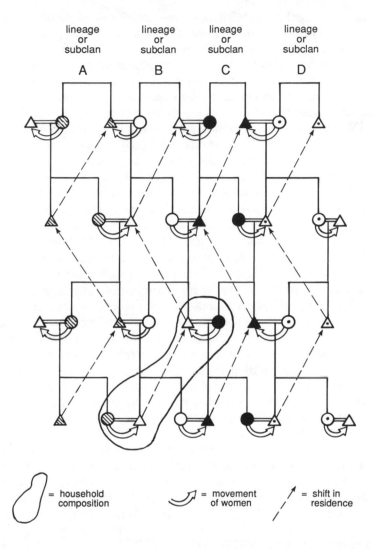

lineage or subclan	lineage or subclan	lineage or subclan	lineage or subclan
A	B	C	D

= household composition   = movement of women   = shift in residence

Fig. 1. Structure of FasiDa marriage

of the opposite moiety who provided funerary services for the deceased are recompensed, a totem pole is built in honor of the deceased, and a new house is built for his successor, the new chief. The three-sided structure is evident in the potlatch in the division of the opposite moiety into two groups, the affines of the deceased and the affines of the new chief.

In contrast, among the Haida, there are two basic types of potlatches, the Sik! or mortuary potlatch and the Walgal potlatch which takes place after the building of a new house for the chief. At the mortuary potlatch, the guests are from the opposite moiety but are affines of the deceased chief who have conducted his funeral and have carved and erected the mortuary pole and are being recompensed for these services. At the house-building potlatch sometime later, the guests are the affines of the new chief. The Sik! and Walgal potlatches combined are the equivalent of the Tlingit mortuary potlatch. The three-sided structure of Tlingit potlatch resolves itself into two separate events among the Haida. The triadic structure is the basic ordering structure of these two societies. This is apparent not only in a variety of cultural domains but it is most strikingly seen in the behavior at the large-scale ceremonial distributions of the potlatch.

The triadic structure of father's sister's daughter marriage is the basic ordering structure of Haida and Tlingit society. The continued presence of moieties is an obvious indication of the antecedent forms of these two societies. The continued presence of the possibility of marrying mother's brother's daughter, mentioned by the ethnographers, despite the preference for marriage to father's sister's daughter and the latter's structural concomitants, is another clue to the nature of the antecedent form of Tlingit and Haida and the probable presence of bilateral cross-cousin marriage in that antecedent form. The antecedent structure was therefore probably some form of dual organization, in which, on focal ceremonial occasions — funerals — one side, the guests, performed services for which the other side, the hosts, recompensed them with goods. Concomitant with this dual organization was an exchange of women between the two sides, and a rule of bilateral cross-cousin marriage.

Athapaskan societies, which are contiguous with the societies of the Northwest Coast, have preserved many of the characteristics of this antecedent form. Athapaskan societies vary in the degree of formalization of social structure, in amount of contact with the Northwest Coast, and in degree of complexity. On the basis of these variations, we have divided them into three groups for analytic purposes and selected several for more intensive examination (see Rubel and Rosman 1983 for fuller discussion).

The first group, which we labeled the inner ring, consisted of societies with direct contact with the Northwest Coast. Those examined were Eyak and Tahltan. The second ring of societies, not directly bordering on the Northwest Coast area, included Kutchin, Tanana, Tanaina, and Kaska. The third and outermost ring of Athapaskan societies consisted of those in the Mackenzie drainage area. They are geographically farthest removed from the Northwest Coast societies and show the greatest degree of difference.

The societies of the second ring conform most closely to the hypothesized antecedent structure for the Northwest Coast. These societies have matrilineal descent and formal moieties or groups that operate as opposite sides, even when a third group is present "in the middle." Large-scale ceremonial exchange took place between opposite sides in commemoration of the dead. It seems probable that bilateral cross-cousin marriage was present earlier but was obliterated as a result of missionary prohibition of marriage with first- and second-degree relatives. We will briefly describe the Tanana and the Tanaina to illustrate the nature of dual organization in second-ring societies.

Among the Upper Tanana or Nebesna of interior Alaska, studied by McKennan, there were five bands, and families could shift freely from one band to another. There were two exogamous matrilineal groups each containing a number of vaguely delineated clans. McKennan indicates, "Inasmuch as a third group seems to have once existed on a coordinate basis with the other two, I have chosen to use the term phratry when referring to these larger divisions even though what remains of the former organization now functions as a simple moiety system" (McKennan 1959: 123). We will use the term moiety rather than phratry in describing the system of the Upper Tanana. The two moieties are vaguely identified with Wolf and Crow or Raven. McKennan states that first cross-cousins are prohibited as mates, but marriage between more distant cross-relatives is desirable. After a period of bride service, the couple usually lives matrilocally until the birth of the first child, but may also live patrilocally or neolocally. Leadership is achieved and is based on hunting ability and the wealth hunting brings, which is used for potlatching. This is a typical Big Man structure in which allegiance of followers is based upon gifts from the Big Man, and prestige is not passed on to heirs.

The potlatch is basically a mortuary ritual. Funerary services are performed by members of the moiety opposite that of the deceased and they are the guests of honor at a potlatch hosted by the deceased's own moiety. Beyond its mortuary aspects, the potlatch is also the means by which the host gains prestige. A man must potlatch at least once and preferably three times before marriage, and only a man who has potlatched could attract the following necessary to lead a war party. Any distant clansman's death could be the occasion for the holding of a potlatch if the giver has accumulated enough goods.

Members of the opposite moiety perform services at birth as well as at death. The midwife of the opposite moiety attends at the birth and buries the placenta. Hunting partners with whom one shares meat are also of the opposite moiety.

Tanaina are southwest of the Tanana, in the area surrounding Cook

Inlet in Alaska. The basic social structure of the Tanaina is that of dual organization. Exogamous matrilineal moieties are subdivided into named clans, but the moieties themselves are not named and have no distinguishing crests. They use a form of deictic referent — "us" and "them." According to Osgood, "settlements are made up preponderantly of members of one or the other moiety" (1937:156). Distinctions of wealth are important, but there are no rank differences. People of wealth, ability, and influence achieve positions of leadership. Family heads are referred to as *q'asq'a*. Osgood notes, "The position of *q'asq'a*, insofar as it may be said to be inherited, merely follows the descent of property from uncle to sister's son"(133). Q'asq'a in opposite moieties and in different villages have a formal named partnership which is established through the exchange of valuable presents. They offer each other potlatches and can exchange wives. In this case a man would have sexual intercourse with a woman of his own moiety.

Men marry women in the opposite moiety. Osgood indicates that man cannot marry either a first or second cousin. Nevertheless, in a footnote he states, "Sheldon, however, says first cousins are commonly married. One immediately suspects from the conflicting data that the explanation may be that a man may marry his cross-cousin but not a parallel cousin"(164 n. 49).

The opposite moiety is not ceremonially involved in birth or puberty, though it is involved in death rituals, when members prepare the corpse and cremate it. The mortuary potlatch, or "Big Potlatch," is held when the ceremonial mourning period has ended. The potlatch at Tyonek, which Osgood considers to be the more traditional area, is given by the moiety of the deceased to the opposite moiety which performed the burial services. When the guests arrive they feast, dance, sing, and play potlatch games for several days. What is to be distributed is accumulated from the members of the deceased's moiety, with the host adding what he has accumulated to this. All of it is distributed to the opposite moiety. As is apparent in the descriptions of the Tanana and Tanaina, the dominant structure is that of dual organization, which is no longer so obviously present in marriage but which is clearly the underlying structure of mortuary rites.

Before European contact and the introduction of the fur trade, the societies in the inner ring, Eyak and Tahltan, probably resembled those of the second ring. However, with the onset of the fur trade, these societies had greater contact with the Northwest Coast. The greater wealth they gained as a result of the fur trade enabled their systems to become more complex in that the wealth was used to enhance the prestige of individuals to the point where a rank system of titles emerged.

The Athapaskan societies of the third ring, such as the Slave, seem to represent a divergence from the prototype in a different direction from those of the inner ring. Matrilineality is lost as the basis for descent groups and sometimes matrilocal postmarital residence as well. Dual organization is present in the categorization of kinsmen as cross and parallel relatives, and sometimes in the settlement patterns of villages. The movement in the direction of this simpler form of organization is due to the fact that these societies occupy a sparse environment with meager resources; it may represent a still earlier form which developed into formal dual organization.

In a recent publication, Borden has concluded, from the archaeological evidence, that the matrilineal Northwest Coast societies represent an elaboration of a northern tradition that occupied an inland area at an earlier period (1975).

The Common Structure of Haida, Tlingit, and Trobriand Societies

In our earlier work, we demonstrated that Haida and Tlingit differ in underlying structure from Tsimshian, Kwakiutl, Bella Coola, and Nootka. It should be apparent that the cognatic societies of the Northwest Coast, like Kwakiutl, Nootka, and Bella Coola, which we have chosen not to deal with in this essay, have developed from a different antecedent structure than the northern matrilineal societies. However, Haida and Tlingit share an identical structure with Trobriand society in Melanesia (Rubel and Rosman 1970). The same structure of patrilateral cross-cousin marriage can be demonstrated as operative among the Trobrianders who have a preferential rule of father's sister's daughter marriage. The same diagrammatic representation of the model is applicable (see fig. 1). Like the Haida and the Tlingit, the Trobrianders have Crow kinship terminology. The Trobrianders have large-scale ceremonial distributions of yams called *sagali*, which are structurally identical to Haida potlatches. The two most important occasions for sagali are death and pregnancy. Marriage is not celebrated by any large-scale ceremonial distribution. Chiefly subclans hold large mortuary sagali when a chief dies and when the sister of the chief, who bears members of the chiefly subclan, is pregnant. When a chief in subclan B dies, his son's subclan, subclan A, which is also that of his father and his wife, performs the necessary mortuary ritual and a sagali is made by the new chief, the son of the deceased chief's sister. The hosts are subclan B, and the guests are subclan A who have performed the mortuary rituals. When the young chief's sister is pregnant, a sagali is made by her subclan, subclan B, for her father's subclan, subclan C, the other side of the structure. This is in return for services performed by that subclan, particularly the father's sister, during her pregnancy. The pregnant woman must avoid contact with her own husband's subclan, subclan A, for fear of sorcery. Thus, the three-sided underlying structure of sagali in the Trobriands is identical to the three-sided structure of potlatch in Haida and Tlingit.

In her recent work on the Trobrianders, Weiner (1976) emphasizes the role of women in the distributions of the mortuary sagali. Though the ethnographic data that she presents support our model, she does not use it, or any other model, in the analysis of her data. She discusses father's sister's daughter marriage, but only in terms of its statistical frequency. As described by Weiner, the prominent role that the deceased's father's subclan plays at a mortuary sagali alongside the wife's subclan makes no sense when each is viewed independently, but only becomes intelligible when viewed in terms of the structural model that we have proposed (see fig. 1).

The Evolution of Dual Organization in Island Melanesia

Following the method which we have used in our examination of Northwest Coast societies, we look for clues about the antecedent structure of Trobriand society in the synchronic description provided by Malinowski. Two classic problems have confronted analysts of Trobriand social structure: why do the Trobrianders have chiefs, and why do they have four clans? In the course of our discussion, we hope to provide tentative answers to these questions.

Unlike the Haida and Tlingit, the Trobrianders do not have named moieties. Nor do they permit any bilateral cross-cousin marriage, since marriage with the mother's brother's daughter is explicitly prohibited. However, given father's sister's daughter marriage and four clans, it rapidly becomes apparent that each clan is allied in marriage with two others, but the fourth clan is necessary to make the system operate. Laying the four clans out in this fashion suggests the structural possibility of moieties. This hypothesis was confirmed when we examined Malinowski's field notes.[1] He says, "Lukwasisiga and Lubula are said to be one moiety. Memalasia (Malasi) and Lubulabuta the other. . . . In *sagali* the Lus (Lukwasisiga) and Ll (Lubula) may join together. The M (Malasi) and Llt (Lubulabuta) may again join to make a joint sagali. Some mythical reference: when Lus and

---

1. We examined the full corpus of Malinowski's field notes on the Trobriand Islands in 1982. Though many people have reinterpreted Malinowski's Trobriand material, few, if any, of these appear to have consulted his field notes. We firmly believe that ethnographers' field notes should also be examined, if possible, in doing comparative research. Field notes reveal variations in observed behavior that often are not included in the published ethnography. In addition, field notes also present alternative possible interpretations that the ethnographer considered, but that were omitted from the published version.

Ll came out they referred to each other saying: 'You come with me. So did M and Llt.'" (Malinowski, n.d., 1962–63). In his published work on the Trobriands, Malinowski never mentions moieties. However, mention of them in the field notes indicates that there were still traces of dual organization when Malinowski did his fieldwork. This suggests the likelihood of dual organization as the antecedent of Trobriand social structure. We would expect this dual organization to take the form of two sides exchanging women with some form of bilateral cross-cousin marriage. We would expect mortuary rites to be the focal ritual in this antecedent form. At these mortuary rituals as well as at other rites of passage, we would expect that the two sides exchange crucial services as well as food.

Dual organization, in fact, is found in many places in Melanesia. We selected several societies in this general area with good ethnographic descriptions for closer examination as ones that might resemble the antecedent form of Trobriand society. Our sample to date has included: Lesu, Tabar, Tanga, Tolai, Lakalai, Siua Nagovisi, and Buin. We examine four of these societies in this paper: Lesu, Tanga, Nagovisi, and Siuai, which have in common matrilineal descent, an underlying structure of dual organization in which women are exchanged between two sides, and mortuary rites as a focal ritual.

Lesu

In Lesu, on the north coast of New Ireland, we find matrilineal moieties, Eagle and Fish Hawk, and matrilineal clans, and uxorilocal postmarital residence that produces hamlets with cores of matrilineally related women. Leadership within the clan is in the hands of old men who have achieved their position by virtue of wealth and personality. There are also other specialists who possess magical knowledge and are paid for their services. Before pacification, there was a separate position of war chief.

The village owns agricultural land communally, though women usually plant on the garden land used by their mothers. Each clan possesses a small piece of land and sometimes, additionally, a part of the reef or a passage of water. On this piece of ground, owned communally by all in the clan, lives a totemic pig or snake who acts as a guardian spirit of the clan.

There is a prohibition against marrying within one's own moiety and in addition a prohibition against marrying one's cross-cousin. The preferred marriage is between a man and the daughter of his female cross-cousin. Given this marriage rule, two men of opposite moieties are forbidden to exchange their sisters. Rather, they exchange sister's daughters.

In Lesu, some ceremonial exchanges are predominantly in the hands of women, while others are predominantly in the hands of men; the latter are usually held on the ground of the matrilineage cemetery, from which women are excluded.

At a birth, which always takes place in the natal hamlet of the mother, women of the opposite moiety assist in the delivery and are later recompensed for their services. To commemorate the birth, women of both moieties exchange coconuts and women of both sides receive gifts of coconuts and taro from the infant's mother's brother. At a second birth feast, which is clearly labeled a "woman's feast" since women dance and present speeches, taro is exchanged by the women of opposite moieties. They all receive meat cooked by the men who stand to one side. In contrast, the naming feast is an all-male feast. When a girl is an infant, a feast may be held for her "possible mates" in the opposite moiety. At such a feast, described by Powdermaker (1933), in honor of two infant girls, one from each moiety, the women of the two moieties feed the men of the opposite moieties, and this symbolizes their position as future husbands of the infant girls. At a girl's first menstruation, women of opposite moieties exchange cooked taro, and the girl being honored receives a special bundle of taro from her father's sister.

The initial event of a wedding is an all-night dance, which is followed by promiscuous sexual intercourse, except between men and women of the same moiety. On the day of the wedding, men and women of both moieties dance in honor of the couple and the bridewealth is distributed to members of the bride's clan and moiety. A mock fight between the women of the two moieties then ensues, while the men prepare the raw and cooked food (brought by the two groups of women) which will subsequently be exchanged.

The corpse of a man is always brought back to his natal hamlet cemetery for burial. At a funeral, the opposite moiety prepares the body and carries the coffin. If the deceased is a woman, women of the opposite moiety enter the cemetery grounds only to deliver the body. The women receive uncooked pig and baked taro outside the cemetery in exchange for these mortuary services. The final mortuary rites for several individuals of a single clan take place as part of the *malanggan* ceremonial cycle, which also includes the initiation of boys and is the focal ceremony for Lesu. This is essentially a male rite, and women are excluded from the ceremonial.

Tanga

The people of Tanga, described by Bell, inhabit a group of four islands sixty miles off the east coast of New Ireland. Descent is matrilineal and postmarital residence is avunculocal. The minimal kinship unit is the settlement, which is made up of a core of matrilineally related men. Upon marriage, a man moves to live with his mother's brother, receives a new name, is given land to garden, and is formally recognized as an adult member of his kin group. Wives never live in the territories of their own clans but in childhood live with their fathers and after marriage with their husbands.

A number of settlements comprise a local residential unit which acts in concert in activities such as communal pig drives. The matrilineally related men who form the kinship core of this unit make up the *matambia*, or subclan, although their wives and children come from other clans. The matambia has its own territory with recognized boundaries within which families garden in a range of different locations, as well as its own dance ground and sacred burial grove. Only members of the matambia may be buried in that grove, with some exceptions.

A number of matambia comprise a clan, or *funmat*. All members of the same clan consider themselves to be descended matrilineally from a common ancestress. These clans are associated with totemic animals and are linked to their territories in several ways. Clan myths refer to specific geographic features of clan territory. Moreover, ancestral clan ghosts share the land with the living and guard clan members from the evil ghosts which lie outside clan territory.

The clans in Tanga are divided into two unnamed groupings, though there is no formal moiety division, and within each group are allies to one another that never marry. Alliances between clans are marked by an affirmation of blood brotherhood, the exchange of names, and the extension of sibling terms to the members of the allied clan (Bell 1937–38:403). The extension of sibling terms bars marriage between the clans. Between the clans of the two sides of the moiety division there is traditional enmity, with these traditional enemy clans occupying contiguous territories; but despite their enmity, they intermarry.

These features describe a dual organization, but the conclusive evidence for the structure of dual organization among the Tanga is the Tangan marriage rule—preference for bilateral cross-cousin. According to Bell, "Owing to the fact that the brother-sister exchange type of marriage often occurs in Tanga, it so happens that a man's wife is not only his father's sister's daughter but also his mother's brother's daughter. A cousin of this type is known as a cross-cousin and so marriage in Tanga is of that variety called cross-cousin marriage"(Bell 1937–38:404). Sister exchange and cross-cousin marriage are really two surface manifestations of dual organization. Bell indicates that classificatory cross-cousin rather than actual cross-cousin is usually married, since the Tanga believe that a man who marries his real cross-cousin becomes bald (Bell 1935–36:183).

In discussing cross-cousin marriage, Bell tends to discuss the father's sister's daughter version of it, emphasizing that in those unusual cases when a son is permitted by the members of his father's matambia to remain on their land after he marries, marriage with his father's sister's daughter locates his children on their own subclan land. The son of such a man does not move after marriage since he is already on his own subclan land. This is the explanation that Malinowski offers for the preference for father's sister's daughter marriage among the Trobrianders. In Tanga, this marriage seems to be a way in which a man may attempt to remain on his father's land. However, in both Tanga and the Trobriands, even though such marriages are made, the men may be asked to leave.

Political leadership seems to operate at two levels in the social structure. Every matambia has one male leader, the *kahltu dok*, who acts on its behalf. He is usually, but not always, the senior male of the group. One kahltu dok, recognized from among the leaders of the various matambia that make up the clan as the head of the entire clan, organizes and controls the ritual activity of the clan. An important clan or subclan leader, who is a cunning warrior, a born leader of men, a skilled organizer of feasts, and a person of great wealth, can further increase his prestige and achieve the position of *ka:ltu taufi*, one who has social prestige to an extraordinary degree, by erecting a special and elaborate house known as *bungbung*.

Bell discusses a series of interrelated characteristics of the most socially important of the men whom he labels "chieftains." Such men, declared *kaik ta:rawen*, "sacred children," at birth, are accorded respect that approaches the severity of an avoidance relationship. They pass through the special adolescent ceremony *dafal*, which will be discussed below, under the auspices of their parents. Leaders of subclans and clans also have the power to restrict for a time the use of certain resources. They can taboo the gathering of tree crops for a time, for instance, so that the fruit will become plentiful for use at a future feast. When a large amount of food is going to be required for a rite, such as a mortuary feast or naming ceremony, the leader of a clan or subclan will organize the communal gardening. The leader of a subclan is, in addition, responsible for the organization of the building of the largest and most valuable kind of canoe, the plank canoe used for overseas voyages, and when he becomes aged and can no longer successfully supervise large-scale feasts, he selects his favorite sister's son to succeed him and assume his authority. In Tanga, too, there are a number of specialists who perform particular services and who are recompensed with pigs and shell valuables.

Most rite of passage ceremonies involve some kind of feasting or distribution. Bell indicates that there is a distinction between children of what he calls socially important subclans and children of ordinary clans (1935–36:190). The former usually become what are known as "sacred children." Bell mentions that a man's mother's brother is continually called upon to make payments of shell valuables in connection with sister's son's birth feast and naming feast, as well as his initiation into the secret society.

He notes that only the sisters' daughters of wealthy chiefs go through dafal, a puberty rite (Bell 1957:138). However, the rite is not limited to females. If the sister's daughter of a chief has been betrothed at infancy, which is a frequent practice, then the boy as well as the girl go through dafal together, and after the initiation they are regarded as virtually man and wife. Bell says that when this happens it is inevitably a cross-cousin marriage (1936–37b:87). He further states that "a family chieftain (*kahltu dok*), having decided to make *dafal* for his sister's daughter, interviews his wife's brother with regard to his own daughter, who is, of course, his wife's brother's sister's daughter [sic]. The two men, both leaders of different subsections (*matambia*) of different clans, place the matter before their respective families and it is generally arranged that both girls shall pass through the ceremony together" (1936–37b:86). It is clear from the description of the kinship relations of the two leaders that they are on opposite sides of the dual organization. These two chiefs are brothers-in-law. The details of this ceremony play out the underlying structure of dual organization. Two girls from two clans on the opposite sides of the dual organization go through the dafal ceremony and each side performs ritual service for the other and is recompensed. When the girls going through dafal are nubile, the ceremony may immediately be followed by the marriage of those girls. In such cases a special marriage feast is held.

There is no ritual or ceremony associated with marriage. Although there is infant betrothal and the two parties refer to each other as husband and wife rather than cross-cousin, the betrothal may be broken unless the boy and girl have gone through the dafal ceremony together. The latter is considered a legally binding betrothal (Bell 1937–38:406).

Death, the final rite of passage, is the most important one, providing many occasions for ceremonial distributions. Bell notes, "With these people, death is the *leitmotif* of their culture and their mortuary rites, which last for years and have endless social repercussions, are undoubtedly the most culturally satisfying and sustaining elements in the native life" (1933–34:291).

About five weeks after the initial burial, the corpse is exhumed and the skull, jaw, and limb bones removed by the deceased's heir and cleaned and placed in a basket which is hung in the rafters of the men's house. While specially prepared gardens are maturing, a funeral house is erected, and along with it a guest house for visitors from other islands. Members of the deceased's clan assume responsibility for furnishing the elaborately carved posts for the funeral house, as well as baskets of food and pigs for the funerary feasts. These individuals are the chief mourners.

The most important event of the funeral cycle of ceremonies symbolically marks the departure of the spirit of the deceased person. The skull, arm and leg bones, and spear of the deceased are removed from the men's house where they had been stored by his sister's son. He mounts the roof of the funeral house with them and remains there while a group of relatives chants, referring to the heir by the name of his dead mother's brother. He now assumes that name. He descends from the roof and places the bone relics back into the rafters of the men's house. According to Bell, this is followed by "a large amount of feasting and dancing, accompanied by many displays of clan rivalry" (1936–37a:328).

Every five to ten years a clan holds a series of rites to commemorate the clan members who have died during that time. All the clans in Tanga receive invitations, and relatives in Muliama on New Ireland and in Feni are also invited. The aim of the clan is not only to commemorate its dead, but also to impress all with its prestige. The event is arranged according to a dual organization. It should be recalled that the two sides are traditional enemies and also intermarried with one another. As Bell notes, "The whole rite was organized in accordance with this rivalry between the two groups of clans concerned" (1946:52). The chief of the clan holding the event to commemorate their dead is the focal point in the exchanges, and when the "opposite" side comes to present pigs to him, there is an exchange of mock hostile behavior. The ceremony involves direct reciprocal exchange in that men who come with pigs leave with pigs. Closely connected to the mortuary rites are the initiatory rituals of the graded Sokapana male secret society. Membership is not obligatory for all males.

It is clear from this description that the underlying structure of Tangan society is that of dual organization. Though there are no named moieties, dual organization is manifested in the exchange of women in marriage and in the exchange of goods and services at all the important ceremonial rituals.

Nagovisi

The Nagovisi live on the greater Buin plain of Bougainville Island in the Solomons. They have totemic matrilineal moieties, named Hornbill and Eagle, and matriclans subdivided into two additional levels of segmentation. The concomitant mode of residence is uxorilocal, though residence may have been more flexible in the past. The hamlet is formed around a core of matrilineally related females, with their in-marrying spouses coming from elsewhere. The "first born" of a lineage is always a woman. She controls shell valuables for the clan or lineage, is nominally in charge of its garden land, and plays the major role in clan ceremonies at rites of passage. Among the Nagovisi the term *momiako* is applied to the woman who is the leader of the matrilineage. Though she may not be the most senior (firstborn), she is the one who directs activities and controls its land and wealth. Men may also be referred to as momiakos, but their renown seems to be based on their role in the feast-giving of their wives' groups. There is no competitive feasting among Nagovisi.

The Nagovisi practice bilateral cross-cousin marriage. In precontact times, marriage with first bilateral cross-cousin seems to have been preferred, but now some feel that it is too close and second cross-cousin is more suitable.

A number of rites of passage are celebrated. There are "growing-up ceremonies," which may even begin at the fetal stage, and continue through birth, first washing, and so on. At these ceremonies, moiety ancestresses are evoked, as at a girl's first menstruation. These ceremonies are clan affairs, performed at the clan holy place. The individual is adorned with heirloom shell valuables of the clan, and the older women of the clan perform the rites over him or her. The guests are given cooked food, which they take home with them. Men are present at these occasions, but in the background. Weddings in the past involved a payment of shells from the mother of the bride to the mother of the groom, a type of "groom price" payment.

At present, these have been superseded by bride price payments (Nash 1978a). Funerals, which are the most important occasions today for feasting, are prepared by the women. They are the primary wailers and dancers at the funerals, and they determine the scale and importance of the funeral feast. Payments, called *nalina*, may be requested by the descent group of the deceased from the deceased's affines, if the deceased, during his or her lifetime, had acquired a great deal of shell money. According to Nash, this event is structured in terms of the two moieties. The mortuary feasts which follow for a year or so after the death involve the interaction of the deceased's clan and his affines (his wife and son), and also the exchanges of food and pigs.

Siuai

The Siuai live just south of the Nagovisi on the Buin plain of Bougainville, but closer to the coast, and are more isolated than the Nagovisi. The Siuai have totemic matrilineal clans, subclans, and matrilineages. Each clan has a mythological history which is a charter for possession of a tract

of land, a series of shrines associated with episodes involving clan ancestresses, and its own form of magic. Matrilineages are the effective units
in garden land ownership and also share totems, shrines, and their own
exclusive magic. There is no invariable rule of postmarital residence, though
Oliver indicates a preponderance of virilocality. A man may only continue
to reside in his father's hamlet after his father's death if he has made a
sizable mortuary payment to his father's lineage. If he chooses to, he may
decide to return to the land of his own matrilineage. Uxorilocality is another, less common alternative. The kinship cores of hamlets, therefore,
consist of various combinations of kinsmen.

The only explicit Siuai marriage prohibition is against marriage with
a member of one's own clan. The preferential marriage rule as stated by
Oliver is, "Siuai should and sometimes do marry an actual cross-cousin;
and marriage between distant classificatory cross-cousin is even more frequent"(1955:81). There are many communities, according to Oliver, in
which two numerically strong matrilineages have continued to intermarry
over many generations by means of cross-cousin marriages. In contrast,
certain other clans among the Siuai may not intermarry. Various reasons
such as sharing or being descended from the same totem are offered by
the Siuai as explanations, though Oliver himself notes that these features
may be manifestations of an underlying structure of dual organization
(Oliver 1949:51 n. 37; 1955:470).

There are two basic types of exchange ceremonies among the Siuai.
The first type of exchange ceremony commemorates rites of passage and
is considered "the affair of women." The second type is the competitive
feasting activity of the *mumi*, or Big Man, from which women are excluded.

Matrilineal leadership is associated with the first type of ceremony.
The leadership is said to be in the hands of the "firstborn" who controls
the shell money and the magic owned by the matrilineage. Oliver notes
that this person is frequently a woman (elsewhere he says "usually"). A
child is born in the natal home of its mother. Though the naming rite is
considered to be an affair of females, both men and women participate.
At the beginning of the ceremony, female guests perform women's songs
and dances. The father of the child provides the pigs and prepares the food.
The lineage "firstborn" performs the matrilineal magic over the child to
make the child grow. One of the pigs is ritually strangled by the child's
mother's brother, and the meat from this pig is distributed raw only to
matrilineal mates of the child. Other guests, including the child's father,
receive pieces of the other pigs. This same type of ceremony, involving
matrilineage-owned magic and the distribution of pigs, also takes place
to mark other milestones in the child's life, such as first visit to the

matrilineal shrine, first visit to the garden, and so forth. There are no formal puberty rites or boy's initiation rites.

Though the betrothal is arranged by the fathers of the bride and groom, the initial bridewealth payment at betrothal goes to the prospective bride herself. The main bridewealth payment is used by the father of the bride to buy pigs which are slaughtered and distributed at the wedding. Rites involving matrilineal magic of the bride's clan are performed by the old women of that lineage. This too is considered a "women's affair." Though pigs are distributed to all of the guests, a man cannot gain renown through such distributions.

Conversely, mortuary rituals involving the exchange of pigs do not employ matrilineal magic and seem to be the concern primarily of the males of the deceased's matrilineage and that of his wife and son. An important part of the mortuary ritual is the payment of numerous strings of shell money by the wife and sons of a deceased man. This *nori* payment is used by the matrilineage of the deceased man to buy pigs to be slaughtered for the mortuary feast. Making the nori payment gives the son continued rights to reside and garden on his father's matrilineal land. Through nori payments, tracts of land have passed from one matrilineage to another.

The second type of ceremonial exchange among the Siuai is competitive feasting of the mumi, which centers around the men's house. The following of a single mumi consists of men from several matrilineages. Since in the past the mumi was a war leader, the symbolism of the activities involved in the competitive feasting is the symbolism of warfare. Each mumi is associated with a *horomorun* spirit that dwells in the men's house. Though these spirits were historically linked with matriclans, they are presently associated only with mumis and not with kin groups. The spirit is antithetical to women, who are barred from any activity associated with the mumi; they cannot go near the men's house and may not eat pork from pigs slaughtered at the mumi's competitive feasts.

The Underlying Structure of Dual Organization in Melanesia

While it is apparent that these four societies of Melanesia all have an underlying structure of dual organization, there is also a degree of variation. We began our discussion of Melanesian societies by posing the question concerning the antecedent structure of Trobriand society. We hypothesized that this antecedent structure would have dual organization. We would suggest here that the process of transformation begins with a structure of dual organization like that in Lesu. This is transformed into a more complex form like that of Tanga. Tanga seems to most closely resemble the immediate antecedent of Trobriand society. However, the structure of Nagovisi, which in many respects is very similar to that of Lesu, develops into the structure of its neighbor, Siuai, going in a different direction.

We can best understand these transformations by looking at how these four societies vary. There are two significant dimensions of variation. One of them is political leadership. In Lesu, there is a rudimentary form of Big Man structure, since clan leadership is based on age and wealth. In Nagovisi, matrilineages are led by Big Women who control wealth and direct gardening activities. Men may gain renown, but it is by participation in the feast-giving activities of their wives' matrilineages and not in an arena of competition.

The Siuai are the classic example of Big Man structure, with followers recruited from various matrilineages. Matrilineal affairs in Siuai are controlled by the firstborn, usually a woman. Tanga has the most developed form of political organization. We find chiefly offices, with chiefs accorded deferential behavior and controlling resources. There are rules of succession in that a mother's brother will select his favorite sister's son to succeed him. These leadership characteristics make Tangan chiefs similar to those of the Trobriands.

The second major variable is that of postmarital residence. Both Lesu and Nagovisi have uxorilocal postmarital residence, with the core of the hamlet a group of matrilineally related women. The transformations from this basic form go in two different directions. One transformation is from the uxorilocal residence pattern of Lesu to the avunculocal pattern of Tanga. Avunculocal residence, with its core of matrilineally related men, is associated with matrilineal control of garden lands and a more complex leadership pattern. Matrilineal control over garden land is not found in Lesu, where the village communally owns the land. However, this pattern of avunculocal residence and matrilineal kin group control of horticultural land is found in Trobriands and, as in Tanga, is associated with chieftainship. The second transformation from Nagovisi to Siuai is somewhat different. In Nagovisi, uxorilocal residence is combined with matrilineal control of land, but this control is in the hands of the female leaders of the matrilineage. The transformation from Nagovisi to Siuai involves the shift from uxorilocal residence to a preponderance of virilocality. Matrilineal kin groups no longer have residential unity. This results in the mixed kind composition of residential units, since sons can continue to reside in the hamlets of their fathers by making the mortuary payments after the death of the father. This entitles them to use the matrilineal land of their fathers and is the way such land is passed from one matrilineage to another. The Big Man, or mumi, draws his followers from the mixed kin group population surrounding his men's house.

In all four societies, the mortuary ritual is the focal ceremonial. The *malanggan* rites in Lesu, the mortuary ritual for several members of a matrilineal clan, clearly illustrate dual organization. In Tanga, dual organization is still the underlying structure for the mortuary rites but, in addition, the rites have become the vehicle for succession to leadership position, as is also the case in the Trobriands. The mortuary rites of Nagovisi are like those of Lesu, with exchanges between moieties. In Siuai, the deceased's kin group and the kin group of his affines exchange, but this becomes the mechanism for the passing on of land from father to son.

In some ways, our discussion of Melanesian transformations is evocative of the ideas of Rivers ([1914]). Rivers noted the widespread occurrence of dual organization in this area and considered it to be the prototypic form of social organization. He recognized the differences between the Austronesian- and Papuan-speaking peoples and saw the moiety system as the result of conquest. He hypothesized that the culturally more advanced Austronesian-speaking population formed the other. In some of these Melanesian societies, native conceptualizations presented the opposite sides of the moiety division as physically and linguistically distinct. Rivers used this information to support the argument that the moieties arose through conquest. He interpreted oppositional behavior between moieties as the survival in symbolic form of the earlier conflict between conqueror and conquered.

Our discussion of Rivers raises the question of the historical relationship between Austronesian- and Papuan-speakers as well as the general topic of the relationship between race, language, and social structure. In this essay, we have confined ourselves to a discussion of social structure transformations. Linguists and archaeologists working on societies in Oceania are currently concerned with the reconstruction of culture history in this area. Pawley (1982), among others, has recently suggested that Proto-Oceanic, the reconstructed parental form of the Polynesian, Micronesian, and Austronesian languages of Melanesia, originated in the general area of the Bismark Archipelago where most of the Melanesian societies discussed in this essay are to be found.

In his reconstruction of the social structure of Proto-Oceanic speakers, Pawley presents two contrasting terms and their glosses: *galapa* meaning Great One or chief, and *gariki* meaning Little One and referring to the son or heir of the Great One. In the "daughter" Austronesian languages of western Melanesia, the cognates of the term *galapa sometimes mean chief and sometimes mean Big Man, as in Kwaio. The term *gariki has dropped out in all these languages except Arosi, where it means "the little one" and refers to the son of the chief. The opposite situation pertains in the Polynesian languages where *galapa disappeared and *gariki, which originally meant "the little one," son of the chief, now refers to the chief. On the basis of this evidence, Pawley concludes that the language community of Proto-Oceanic had a political organization with rank and chieftainship. This would seem to contrast with the view presented in this essay. There are several possible explanations for this. The first possibility, the one offered by Pawley, is that devolution rather than evolution occurred and that the Austronesian-speaking societies in Melanesia which, he hypothesizes, formerly had chiefs have Big Men today. A second possibility is that Papuan speakers who occupied the islands in eastern Melanesia prior to the arrival of Austronesian speakers maintained their simpler forms of social structure with Big Man leadership, but adopted Austronesian languages. The third possibility is that the social structure of Proto-Oceanic speakers was one with a Big Man structure, not chiefs and rank. In this interpretation, *galapa, the term found in Melanesia in contrast to *gariki, would be glossed as Big Man, not chief. Due to rather meager linguistic evidence from Melanesia, Pawley incorrectly assumes that the Polynesian forms of social structure with ranking and chieftainship characterized the entire Proto-Oceanic population.

In a recent article based upon linguistic evidence, Blust presents a reconstruction of Austronesian social organization, from which the social organization of Proto-Oceanic speakers is presumably derived (1980). Both dual divisions and ranking are attributed to the reconstructed Proto–Malayo-Polynesian social structure. While the presence of dual organization supports the argument of this paper, the feature of ranking again raises the possibility of devolution.

A Comparison of Transformations in the Northwest Coast and Island Melanesia

In comparing the series of transformations from the Northwest Coast–Athapaskan area and Island Melanesia, two widely differing parts of the world, it becomes apparent that the same kinds of transformations took place. We demonstrated earlier the identities of structure between Haida and Tlingit on one hand and Trobriand on the other. This common underlying structure relates kin groups to one another in a particular fashion and is manifested in a preferential rule of marriage with father's sister's daughter and a pattern of large-scale ceremonial exchange potlatch and sagali that links one group with two others. All three societies are ranked chieftainships with succession from mother's brother to sister's son.

As the complex societies in these two areas are identical, so too the simpler forms from which they arose are strikingly similar. There are general features that the two areas share in common. Matrilineal descent is widespread in both areas; likewise, mortuary rites are the focal point of ritual life. In both areas, the simpler societies tend toward uxorilocality, and as they become increasingly complex they become avunculocal, as in Tahltan and Tanga. Avunculocality seems to be connected with more evolved leadership patterns, with specified rules for inheritance of leadership positions, and expansion of the areas of control and political power. The simpler societies like Lesu and Tanana have rather rudimentary types of leadership with uxorilocal postmarital residence rules, while in Tahltan and Tanga we see incipient forms of chieftainship.

In both areas, in the simpler societies, there is some kind of direct exchange of women between two sides. This is sometimes expressed in terms of direct bilateral cross-cousin marriage or some more complicated form such as is found in Lesu, where a man marries his cross-cousin's daughter and two groups exchange nieces. So far we have found nothing on the Northwest Coast that parallels the sequence from Nagovisi to Siuai, that is, a matrilineal society with virilocal residence and a Big Man structure where followings cross-cut descent groups. This Big Man structure also undercuts the underlying structure of dual organization that is observable in Siuai primarily in the marriage rule.

Having laid out the possible sequences of development for the societies we have been considering, we would like to turn briefly to the mechanisms that may have led to these developments. Transformations from the Athapaskan prototype to the more complex structures of the northern matrilineal societies of the Northwest Coast probably came about in the following manner. The resource base of the northern Northwest Coast societies is characterized by greater abundance and variety than that of the Athapaskan societies, making possible much greater wealth accumulation. With this increase in wealth and goods, leadership positions that had been of the Big Man type among the Athapaskans become fixed and hereditary on the Northwest Coast. The mortuary feasts of the Athapaskans become the true mortuary potlatches of the northern Northwest Coast, at which the claim of the new chief to the position is validated by the acceptance of goods on the part of other chiefs who come as guests. There is continuity with the Athapaskan event in the return of goods to the affinally linked clan of the deceased for mortuary service. At the same time, there is a significant distinction in that potlatch is tied to the institutionalization of the position of chiefly leadership which was not present among the Athapaskan. The grandness of scale of these mortuary potlatches is in accord with the enlargement of the resource base.

Greater resource abundance also permits population to increase. Though seasonal migration in response to resource variability still takes place, permanent village settlements are larger than among the Athapaskans and are sometimes referred to as towns. Ownership of resources becomes clearly defined and is in the hands of social groupings like matrilineages. The chief of the matrilineage is in control of the exploitation of those resources. On the Northwest Coast, matrilineal descent remains the basis for social groups, though there are now matrilineages, matriclans, matrilineal phratries, and matrimoieties. While band membership in Athapaskan groups is subject to fluctuation, there is much less movement between groups among the northern Northwest Coast peoples, and residential units become more fixed in their composition.

Finally, an important change occurs with respect to control over manpower. In the Big Man political structure of Athapaskan groups, leaders must attract and hold onto their followers by being successful hunters and distributors of gifts. With the death of the leader, the group disperses. The matrilineage, which is the resource exploitation group among the northern Northwest Coast societies, has continuity over time and a more or less stable membership. It does not collapse upon the death of the chief. This permits more systematic exploitation of the larger resource base and is in contrast to the band organization of the Athapaskans. The contrast is in the continuity of social units and the chiefly position in the Northwest Coast versus the flexibility of the hunting group of the Athapaskans, which disintegrates when the leader loses his ability or dies.

The mechanism of transformation in Melanesia parallels that of the Athapaskan–Northwest Coast case. Those societies that have undergone the transformation to more complex forms are better located strategically and thus are involved in more intensive, larger scale interisland trade (see Friedman 1981). These societies, like Tanga and Trobriands, have more kinds of shell valuables and other forms of wealth. With this increase in wealth and valuables, flexible Big Man leadership becomes fixed chieftainship with a rule of succession. Chiefs control manpower and resources: they can taboo the harvesting of crops, organize manpower to build funerary houses and large plank canoes, and organize and control manpower for warfare which is larger in scale. As on the Northwest Coast, mortuary rites are grander in scale and are, at the same time, the means of public announcement of accession to chiefly position. Matrilineal descent remains the basis for kin group affiliation, but there are more levels of kin groupings.

There is, of course, one very significant difference between these two areas — the mode of production. The societies in Melanesia are based primarily on horticulture, while the Northwest Coast and Athapaskan societies depend on hunting, fishing, and foraging. Despite the totally different constraints of these two modes of production, the structural transformations seem to be the same. From this, we suggest that similarities in the forces of production are not what is important but rather similarities in relations of production. Meanwhile we have seen that dual organization as a basic structure for organizing societies is found among peoples as different as Melanesian horticulturalists and Athapaskan hunters and gatherers. Under certain conditions, as we have demonstrated, it is transformed into a different type of structure in both these areas.

REFERENCES

Bell, F. L. S. 1933–34. Report on field work in Tanga. *Oceania* 4:290–309.
———. 1935. Sokapana: A Melanesian secret society. *Journal of the Royal Anthropological Institute* 65:311–41.
———. 1935–36. The avoidance situation in Tanga. *Oceania* 6:174–98, 306–22.
———. 1936–37a. Death in Tanga. *Oceania* 7:316–39.
———. 1936–37b. Dafal. *Journal of the Polynesian Society* 45:83–98.
———. 1937–38. Courtship and marriage among the Tanga. *Oceania* 8:403–18.
———. 1946. The place of food in the social life of the Tanga. *Oceania* 18:36–60.
———. 1948–49. The place of food in the social life of the Tanga. *Oceania* 17:139–72, 310–27; 18:36–60, 233–48; 19:57–75.
———. 1957. Male and female in Tanga: Being a description of certain sexual aspects of the ritual life. *Mankind* 5:137–48.
Blust, Robert. 1980. Early Austronesian social organization: The evidence of language. *Current Anthropology* 21:205–48.
Borden, Charles E. 1975. *Origins and development of early Northwest Coast culture to about 3000 B.C.* Archaeological Survey of Canada, paper no. 45. Ottowa: National Museum of Man.
Durlach, Theresa M. 1928. *The relationship systems of the Tlingit, Haida and Tsimshian.* Publications of the American Ethnological Society, vol. 11. New York: G. E. Stechert and Co.
Friedman, Jonathan. 1981. Notes on structure and history in Oceania. *Folk* 23: 275–95.
Lévi-Strauss, Claude. [1949] 1969. *The elementary structures of kinship.* Rev. ed. Trans. J. H. Bell, J. R. von Sturner, and R. Needham. London: Eyre and Spottiswoode; Boston: Beacon Press.
Malinowski, Bronislaw. N.d. Field Notes. London School of Economics.
———. 1922. *Argonauts of the Western Pacific.* London: George Routledge and Sons.
———. 1929. *The sexual life of savages in Northwestern Melanesia.* London: George Routledge and Sons.
———. 1935. *Coral gardens and their magic.* London: Allen and Unwin; New York: American Book Co.
McKennan, Robert. 1959. *The Upper Tanana Indians.* New Haven: Yale University Publications in Anthropology, vol. 55.
Murdock, George Peter. 1934. Kinship and social behavior among the Haida. *American Anthropologist* 36:355–85.

Nash, J. 1974. Matriliny and modernization: The Nagovisi of south Bougainville. *New Guinea Research Bulletin* 55.

―――. 1978a. A note on groomprice. *American Anthropologist* 80:106–8.

―――. 1978b. Women and power in Nagovisi society. *Journal of the Society of Oceanists* 34:60, 119–26.

Oliver, Douglas. 1949. *Studies in the anthropology of Bougainville, Solomon Islands*. Papers of the Peabody Museum vol. 29, nos. 1–4. Cambridge: Harvard University.

―――. 1955. *A Solomon Island society: Kinship and leadership among the Siuai of Bougainville*. Boston: Beacon Press.

―――. 1973. Southern Bougainville. In *Politics in New Guinea*, ed. Ronald M. Berndt and Peter Lawrence, 276–97. Seattle: University of Washington Press.

Osgood, Cornelius. 1937. *The ethnography of the Tanaina*. New Haven: Yale University Publications in Anthropology, no. 16.

Pawley, Andrew. 1982. Rubbish-Man commoner, Big Man chief: Linguistic evidence for hereditary chieftainship in Proto-Oceanic society. *Transactions of the Finnish Anthropological Society* 11:33–52.

Powdermaker, Hortense. 1933. *Life in Lesu: The study of a Melanesian society in New Ireland*. London: Williams and Norgate.

Rivers, W. H. R. [1914] 1968. *The History of Melanesian society*. 2 vols. New York: Humanities Press.

Rosman, Abraham, and Paula G. Rubel. 1971. *Feasting with mine enemy: Rank and exchange among Northwest Coast societies*. New York: Columbia University Press.

Rubel, Paula, and Abraham Rosman. 1970. Potlatch and Sagali: The structure of exchange in Haida and Trobriand societies. *Transactions of New York Academy of Sciences,* 2d ser., no. 6: 732–42.

―――. 1983. The Evolution of exchange structures and ranking: Some Northwest Coast and Athapaskan examples. *Journal of Anthropological Research* 39:1–25.

Sahlins, Marshall. 1981. *Historical metaphors and mythical realities*. Ann Arbor: University of Michigan Press.

―――. 1983. Other times, other cultures: The anthropology of history. *American Anthropologist* 85:517–77.

Saussure, F. de. [1915] 1966. *Course in general linguistics*. Trans. Wade Baskin. New York: McGraw-Hill.

Swanton, J. 1905. *Contributions to the ethnology of the Haida*. Memoir of the American Museum of Natural History, vol. 8, pt. 1. Publication of the Jessup North Pacific Expedition, vol. 5, pt. 1.

Weiner, Annette B. 1976. *Women of value, men of renown*. Austin: University of Texas Press.

Chapter 10

Historical Dimensions of Dual Organization: The Generation-Class System of the Jie and the Turkana

John Lamphear

The Jie and Turkana belong to a subgroup of the Eastern Nilotic linguistic community of eastern Africa, sometimes referred to as the Ateker community.[1] Numbering approximately 33,000, the Jie, who inhabit a compact territory (1,300 square miles) in central Karamoja District, Uganda, are one of the smallest Ateker societies. The Turkana, occupying a much larger region (24,484 square miles) in northwestern Kenya, are perhaps the largest Ateker society, with an estimated population of over 200,000. Linguistically, the two peoples can be described as speaking slightly different dialects of the same language, and there is a broad correspondence between many aspects of their sociocultural systems as well.

Economically, they represent two distinct categories of subsistence within the range available to the Ateker community. The Jie area, with an annual average of twenty-seven inches of rainfall, and up to forty inches in some favored western areas, supports a mixed economy in which dry-grain agriculture and pastoralism are equally important. The country of the Turkana, located below the steep escarpment that forms the modern boundary between Uganda and Kenya, is much drier, receiving a scant six inches of rain annually in most plains areas, and about thirty inches in some upland areas. Their economy is mainly nomadic pastoralism, although their society traditionally has included a few pockets of cultivators, fishermen, and hunters.

Dualism occurs in both societies in a variety of ways, but an actual binary system of dual organization traditionally has been expressed mainly

---

1. The term Ateker replaces Central Paranilotes, and Katapa replaces Agricultural Paranilotes, which were used in some of my earlier writings.

through the generation-set system (*asapanu*). The Jie continue to follow a generation-set organization with strong binary implications, but in the Turkana system such implications are, at best, now dim and theoretical. I will attempt to show how such differences were developed by examining the historical traditions of these two societies.

The Jie "Paradox"

The generation-set system of the Jie, from which that of the Turkana initially was derived, appears in some ways to present a prime example of the "unwieldy, almost bizarre mode of social organization" (Baxter and Almagor 1978:2) that, it has been argued, such systems typify. The Jie system has been described by Gulliver (1953, 1955; Gulliver and Gulliver 1953) and myself (Lamphear 1976) and it is an important element in the broader analyses of Stewart (1977), Abrahams (1978), and Spencer (1978). These analyses perceptively describe the "paradox" of the Jie system by showing that it could not possibly function in the manner described by the Jie. The essential problem stems from the basic (and, according to the Jie, irrevocable) principle upon which the system rests: a man can be initiated only into the generation-set following his father's. The Jie system is a cyclical one, with two named alternations, Ngitome (Those of the Elephants) and Ngikoria (Those of the Ratels); the sons of Ngitome must be Ngikoria, and vice versa. To add to the complexities, a careful historical reconstruction strongly suggests that the successive generation-sets are inaugurated at approximately forty-year intervals, and the sets themselves are divided into parts or "age-sets," on the basis of coevality and biological age.[2]

The problem, then, is the inherent difficulty of reconciling generational and biological age, similar to the problem identified in investigations of the *gada* systems of various Oromo peoples (among others, see Legesse 1963, 1973; Baxter 1978). In the case of the polygynous Jie, many men produce children over a period of forty or more years, so there can be a wide range of ages among the potential initiates of a given generation-set. Indeed, Spencer (1978) has produced statistics based on his own investigations of the Samburu, which demonstrate that the range of ages increases significantly for succeeding generation-sets, rapidly leading to problems of "overaging" and "underaging" (Stewart 1977), which would

---

2. Spencer (1978) has suggested a span of fifty-five years and even provides a "revised" chronology based on this figure. But an approximate forty-year span is indicated by my own historical investigation and by the independent investigations of other oral historians working with neighboring communities (Lamphear 1976: chap. 2).

seem to deny entry into the system to a significant portion of adult Jie males. One is tempted to conclude that the Jie, like the Boran, must present an "intellectually tidy" representation of their system, with any "protuberances . . . tucked in or covered over" (Baxter 1978:165). Clearly, there must be some form of "slip mechanism" (Spencer 1978:136) or perhaps "structural amnesia" (Stewart 1977:220ff.) to accommodate those individuals who are out of step with their system and to preserve at least a facade of the system itself. Even so, Spencer concludes that the Jie system has begun to break down over the past century.

This suggested breakdown seems even more likely when one examines the generation-set system of the Turkana. The Turkana system does not appear to contain the same paradoxical elements as that of the Jie. Instead of trying to maintain the temporal succession of generation-sets, the Turkana are portrayed as having given up and shifted their emphasis from generation to age, so that all men are initiated at "the proper age" (at about twenty). This has led to a continuous overlapping of the two alternate generation-sets and concurrent initiation of their constituent age-sets (Gulliver 1958). This process has been described as a breakdown of the system the Turkana derived from the Jie, which has, indeed, "atrophied to a mere shadow" (Spencer 1978:11) of the original model. Thus the notion that unwieldiness and a propensity for deterioration are inherent in the Jie system is powerfully reinforced.[3]

Given this theoretical analysis, it is surprising that neither Gulliver nor myself were aware of the inherent problems in the system as well as of any symptoms of breakdown in the Jie system. The reason for our lack of awareness was simple: to all appearances, the Jie system functions almost exactly as described and betrays no hint of looming deterioration. Neither Gulliver nor I observed any significant number of men being out of step with the system. Rather, the great majority apparently were being initiated at the proper age, and inaugurations of new generation-sets were taking place at the proper time, that is, when the survivors of the "grandfathers" generation had dwindled to a few, mainly old men, at approximately forty-year intervals. The Jie clearly derive a deep sense of pride and satisfaction from their system, and one gains the impression that if serious inconsistencies exist, they themselves must be largely unaware of them. So, too, must be several other communities, who regard the Jie system as the fundamental example of how a generation-set system should be constructed and function.

---

3. A similar breakdown has been suggested for the system of the Labwor, which again clearly was inspired by that of the Jie (Abrahams 1978).

Systematizing the rule complexities of any class system based on time, although fascinating, is fraught with risk (Baxter and Almagor 1978:4). To paraphrase Baxter's observations of the Boran (Baxter 1978: 156), the Jie do not find their system puzzling or paradoxical. Rather, they "find their way through its maze of rules and of rituals, as they need to. . . . It is only foreigners who use other, and more naive, cognitive categories, who need a guide or notice dissonance." With such caveats firmly in mind, one is still obliged to consider briefly the irrefutable demographic problems revealed by the theoretical analyses. How *do* the Jie attempt to reconcile generation and age?

From all indications, the Jie do not seem to regard underaging as a very serious problem. One method they employ to deal with it is to permit an overlapping of generation-set initiations, similar to that of the Turkana, whereby adolescent potential members of the final age-sets of the "fathers" generation can be initiated concurrently with the initial age-sets of the "sons" generation.[4] And yet this overlap period cannot be allowed to go on indefinitely or the entire system would quickly get out of hand and deteriorate into one similar to that of the Turkana. Historically, the Jie appear to have tolerated no more of an overlap than two age-sets, a maximum time span of ten or twelve years. If the span between the inaugurations of generation-sets is taken to be about forty years, this gives a total of about fifty years for the recruitment of generations-set members.[5] That figure is intriguingly close to that derived by Spencer (1978) from his statistical model as being the span at which the Jie system would "run with minimum difficulties" (139), with the number of grossly overaged or underaged men reduced to a very small fraction of the total.

Nevertheless, there would still be *some* underaged men who could not be included even within an approximate fifty-year span, and their existence would magnify the problem of underaging in successive generations. Other Ateker societies, such as the Karimojong (Dyson-Hudson 1966), have solved the problem by allowing such individuals to slip a generation and be initiated, on the basis of age and coevality, with the

---

4. Although some of Gulliver's informants denied that this could happen and even stated that all the initiations of the "fathers" generation must be completed before those of the "sons" could begin, Jie oral tradition contains abundant indication that this was a common occurrence historically.

5. It is interesting to note that the Jie inflexible generational succession and approximate forty-year span between inaugurations are precisely the same criteria as those upon which the Boran *gada* system ideally is supposed to operate (Baxter 1978:158). In the case of the Jie, timing is at least partly derived from a family of hereditary first-initiates (Lamphear 1976: chap. 2).

set following their proper one, or two below that of their fathers. But the Jie are adamant that this cannot occur in their system. As Mabuc Loputuke, my Jie father, counseled me before my own initiation: "A son can be initiated only into the generation-set following his father's. We consider the second generation-set after the father's to be the *same* as the father's. Could a child be initiated, then, into the same generation-set as his own father. That is foolish. . . . How can a father and a son be the same?"

In all of their descriptions to me of their system, the Jie emphasized its cyclical nature and stressed the close identity of alternate generation-sets: "Grandsons enter the place of grandfathers." Each generation-set is given a distinguishing nickname (a great boon to an oral historian laboring to formulate a chronological reconstruction), but alternate sets share the common "real" name of either Ngitome or Ngikoria, together with common praise songs and a wide range of associated ornaments, decorations, and hair styles.

Having been told that a man could not slip a generation, as with the Karimojong, I never thought to ask (nor, as far as I know, did any other observer of an Ateker society) whether he could slip down *two* generations and so "enter the place of his grandfather" in that way.

According to all testimony and actual observation, the approximate forty-year interval between inaugurations of generation-sets is reflected in the procreation period of most Jie men: they begin producing children at about forty and end at about eighty. It is difficult for men much below the age of forty to accumulate enough bridewealth animals to conclude a marriage (Gulliver 1955). (In a single notable exception to the rule against slipping a generation, some informants stated that a man's illegitimate sons born before he marries are initiated into the *same* generation as the father.) In my investigations into Jie oral history, I talked with most of the men over seventy-five, and although I did not collect the data systematically, I can recall only one instance of a man in his eighties who was still producing children. His case was considered marvelous by the Jie, and he was renowned throughout the entire community for his "achievement."

Given these considerations, I suggest that a two-generation slippage easily would accommodate the problem of underaging, with no individual who had been born too late to be incorporated into his proper generation-set being more than about forty years old (overaged, but not grossly so) before another proper set (with the appropriate real name, praise, songs, ornaments, and association with alternate groups of ancestors) comes into existence. While serving to eliminate the problem of underaging, such a mechanism would not, in essence, violate the irrevocable principle of the Jie system; things are kept tidy, not only intellectually but practically as well.[6]

On the other hand, the Jie routinely acknowledge that overaging exists in their system, and they state that some men become middle-aged or old (a few even die) as they wait for the initiation of their proper generation-set. No attempt is made to "tuck in" this particular "protuberance." Such men typically form the initial age-set of a newly inaugurated generation-set, but according to all testimony and actual observation, these individuals constitute only a small minority of a set's membership. Nevertheless, this category of individuals is an important element in the whole formulation of the Jie system, as I shall show.

Historical Aspects of the Jie Generation-Set System

Even if the Jie system does incorporate a whole range of slip mechanisms, amnesias, or other elaborate devices to help neutralize its inconsistencies and inhibit its deterioration, we are still confronted by the more important and relevant question of why they should bother to preserve so unwieldy a system. Why should they not simply let the system atrophy, as the Turkana apparently have done?

A careful examination of Jie myths and historical traditions helps us understand why. Such an examination shows that the Jie system is deeply rooted in fundamental cosmological concerns. To paraphrase Baxter and Almagor's observation (1978:28) on the *gada* system of Oromo, it is "the organization of a belief system." The age-class systems of the Nilotic-speaking peoples all contain principles of both generation and age. In his examination of the Maa-speaking branch of the Eastern Nilotes, Spencer (1983) discerns a gradation, with the generational principle strongest in the north and decreasing in importance to the south. He attributes this gradation to the pioneering southward movement down the Great Rift Valley by younger men at the vanguard of the pastoral Maasai, thus enhancing their status and diluting the gerontocratic and generational preoccupations of northern groups such as the Samburu.

---

6. There may well be other mechanisms that work against underaging and overaging. Adoption, for instance (which appears to occur more frequently among the Jie than among the Turkana), might serve to get some individuals back in step. As neither Gulliver nor I explored any of these mechanisms in any systematic way, however, I refrain from investigating them further. There has been more than enough speculation on the rule complexities of the Jie system as it is!

Spencer's observations can be broadened considerably to encompass all the various Eastern and Southern Nilotic speakers. Thus one finds the strongest generational principles among the Ateker branch of the Eastern Nilotes, who, according to historical and linguistic evidence, were the last to leave the Nilotic cradle-land of the southern Sudan and join the migrational flow southward along the Great Rift. In comparison, the Southern Nilotes and the Maa-speaking branch of the Eastern Nilotes who preceded them, all stress the principles of age and coevality (usually entailing circumcision) in their systems. One is led to conclude that the Nilotic systems were originally based on generational principles, with biological age principles stressed by those societies whose dynamic processes of migration carried them farther and farther from the ancestral homeland.

An investigation of Ateker historical traditions reinforces this idea. The traditions of the eastern branch of that community depict a comparatively short migration distance from the southeastern corner of the Sudan southward to the dry grasslands of the Koten-Magos hills above the escarpment dividing present-day Uganda and Kenya. Having established themselves as a compact community in this region, probably around the middle of this millenium, the group developed an economic focus on cattle pastoralism, which soon generated significant ecological pressures and subsequent fragmentation. Many traditions associated with the dispersal of this Koten-Magos community contain as a central cliché—that is, "a highly compressed and deceptively simple statement of meaning that refers to a much more complex reality" (Miller 1980:20)—the image of young people taking livestock to dry-season camps and never returning, leaving the old people behind to fend for themselves. Two different versions of the tradition exist. One is perpetuated by the Karimojong (southern neighbors of the Jie), who present themselves as the "old men" from whom all the other eastern Ateker broke away in a series of secessions by the "young men." The other, the Jie version, depicts an initial separation of quarreling coevals, with the proto-Karimojong elements removing themselves a short distance from the proto-Jie elements and forming an independent community. Several further traditions depict a series of secessions by young men from the Jie, leading to the formation of the Toposa, Nyangatom, Jiye, and Turkana communities, as well as elements of Luo-speaking Langi and Labwor, and a separate secession of young men from the Karimojong, leading to the formation of the Dodos (Lamphear 1976: chap. 3).

As I have argued elsewhere (Lamphear 1983), these traditions can be interpreted from several different perspectives. In my view, the Karimojong tradition can be regarded as little more than a functionalist "political charter," giving etiological reinforcement to present-day associations and alliances. The Jie version, on the other hand, is demonstrably a more historical statement, containing a vast storehouse of detained information woven about the central cliché (Lamphear, forthcoming). Moreover, only the Karimojong accept the validity of their version, while all the other communities, including even the Dodos, accept the Jie version or a close variation of it.

From a structuralist perspective, the central cliché can be seen to embody important values and concerns of the Jie and most other Ateker communities. Given the harsh environments, the mobility of the pastoral economy, and the highly egalitarian (and often nearly acephalous) political systems, it must have been enormously difficult to foster a sense of group solidarity. The danger of secession by part of the community was an ever-present concern. The annual departure of young men with the herds for remote dry-season cattle camps is still viewed as a moment of potential crisis, when repressed fissiparous tendencies might surface. The Jie hold important *akiwodokin* ceremonies before "freeing" livestock to go to the camps. In these ceremonies, the elders admonish the young men to return with the animals at the proper time and threaten them with supernatural sanctions if they do not. The elders further underscore the importance of group solidarity by recounting the traditions, which graphically portray the undesirable consequences of secession: fragmentation of a once-unified Ateker community.

In human society, trust is a fragile quality (Eisenstadt, in this volume): it must be actively constructed and maintained (Almagor, in this volume). With the Jie, "sons" easily could gain the upper hand if they were allowed to compete with "fathers," simply by taking advantage of their departure to the camps to secede permanently, taking the community's livestock. Such competition cannot be tolerated, even if symbolically expressed as the incorporation of fathers and sons into the same generation-set. For this reason, the Jie cling tenaciously to the irrevocable principle upon which their system is based.

Another important aspect of the Jie system is derived from their subsequent historical experience. Following the breakup of the Koten-Magos community, probably toward the close of the seventeenth century, the Jie moved slightly to the west, establishing themselves in the area of central Karamoja they still inhabit. The traditions associated with this movement center on a light gray bull (*engiro*) found grazing with wild animals in the area. The bull provided the name for the major river course of the new region (Longiro) as well as the name the early Jie took for themselves,

Ngiro, "the people of Engiro." The name Jie (more properly Ngijie, "the fighting people") was not adopted until the second half of the nineteenth century. Engiro, Longiro, and Ngiro all refer back to Dongiro, the mythical ancestral homeland in the Sudan where the Ateker claim they, and many other Nilotic-speaking peoples, originated: "the place where human beings began."[7] Thus, from their historical traditions, the Jie derive a powerful sense of being at the center of their world, the descendants of elders who were left behind by the pioneering forays of restless young men. As noted above, this image is reinforced by the traditions of several other Ateker societies (as well as some that are now associated with the Luo linguistic community, such as the Langwi and Labwor), which consider important elements of their societies as historically derived from the Jie. Some of these societies claim that important mystical symbols of their new corporate identities originally were derived from the Jie as well.

Following the establishment of their community near the Longiro River, the Jie underwent a process of political evolution that was sharply distinct from those of the other Ateker communities. To begin with, their migration was the shortest of any, only a scant twenty or thirty miles from the Koten-Magos area. The migrations of most of the other Ateker carried them much farther; the Toposa, for example, went into the southern Sudan, and the Turkana, well into north-central Kenya. During their migrations, most of the other Ateker communities came into close and significant contact with other cultural linguistic communities, including the Maa-speaking branch of the Eastern Nilotes, the Southern Nilotes, and various Cushitic-speaking groups. As I will argue below, powerful social influences were derived from these contacts, and most of the expanding Ateker communities incorporated large numbers of aliens. Significantly, these various alien communities possessed age-class systems of their own, systems that stressed principles of age rather than generation.

In contrast, the Jie interacted only with groups to the west, with Luo-speaking communities and western Ateker groups that had been strongly influenced by the Luo. These societies, for the most part, had no strong age-class organization, and it is likely that in those few that did, generational preoccupations were strong. The main band of Luo-speaking outsiders whom the Jie encountered and absorbed became the largely separate Rengen major division. Historical evidence shows that while the Rengen exposed the Koten-Magos Jie to aspects of Luo kinship, they themselves

---

7. The Jie also claim to have invented the generation-set system originally subscribed to by all the Ateker, attributing it to their semimythical founder Orwakol. My admittedly more modest investigations of the traditions of several other Ateker groups revealed that none of them, including the Karimojong, made any similar claim.

incorporated the Jie generation-class organization. Economic influences flowed both ways. Until the closing years of the nineteenth century, the Jie engaged in little military activity, again in sharp contrast to most of the other, farther ranging groups (Lamphear 1976). Kinship organization was focused on "clan hamlets," closely interacting sets of full brothers (Gulliver 1955) whose settlements were clustered in specifically designated clan areas of permanently settled territorial divisions. The Jie, then, evolved as an extremely tight-knit community, spatially, socially, and politically.[8]

All of this, I suggest, had important implications for the evolution of the Jie generation-set system. The essential purpose of any age-class system has been perhaps best captured by Baxter and Almagor (1978:24): "Age-systems are a device to make the cruel descent through life to decay appear as if it were an ascent to a superior, because senior, condition." However, in practically all of the age-class systems on which data exist there is some provision for the "retirement" of elders as they attain the highest rungs of the gerontocratic ladder. To some degree this seems a cruel practical joke: when a man has finally attained the "superior, because senior, condition," the rug is abruptly yanked out from under his feeble limbs, and authority passes to younger, more vital men.

The Jie system seems virtually unique in that retirement of senior elders is unthinkable, and the attainment of rights by junior men does not depend on the seniors leaving the system. An elder is thought to continue to accrue wisdom and mystical powers until he dies, and he remains a vital force in the community. "Even if an elder becomes foolish and speaks like a child, still he is wise because he is old. He grows closer to God. The capacity of his blessing increases. Until he dies, an elder gains in power."[9]

As Abrahams perceptively has noted (1978:46), the spearing of oxen at initiations and on other ritual occasions among the Jie implies "a sort of sacrifice, analogous to tribute to a divine king . . . in which living and, in a sense, sacred persons . . . are among the main recipients." Indeed, this notion of sacrifice is reflected in the way the Jie themselves describe the purpose of their system: "The purpose of *asapanu* is to feed the elders. By feeding them, younger men show they respect them and obey them."

The Jie are deeply appalled by the systems of neighboring societies, such as the Karimojong, where the senior men do retire and where senile

---

8. In fact, historical evidence suggests that there may have been another Ateker community whose experience closely paralleled that of the Jie. There were the rather mysterious Magos, a group that was nearly exterminated in the nineteenth century, the survivors taking refuge with the Pian section of the Pian Karimojong.

9. This is apparently a deviation from the usual pattern suggested by Baxter and Almagor (1978:14) in which elders do not exercise power just because they are older or because their set has accumulated mystical powers.

elders are sometimes the brunt of derision and joking ridicule. Although the Jie system involves a promotion ceremony (*akitopolor*) in which the "fathers" generation is raised to elderhood by the surviving "grandfathers," the latter by no means relinquish their authority, and they continue to be considered true elders (Lamphear 1976: chap. 5).

Baxter and Almagor (1978:19) have warned that an overemphasis on the narrow political functions of age-systems has presented a major barrier to our understanding of these systems. That warning is well taken, but the authority of Jie senior elders, although unquestionably expressed within a strongly ritual context, still impinges strongly on vital judicial, military, and economic areas. I have suggested that the political authority of senior elders is rather stronger among the Jie than among many other societies with age-class systems (Lamphear 1976: chap. 5).[10] Historical traditions indicate that the Jie elders withstood important challenges to their authority in the nineteenth century. The first was from powerful families of hereditary Firemakers who, in the early years of the nineteenth century, usurped the office from the clans who previously held it and grafted to its aspects of Luo kingship, becoming in the process important symbols of Jie corporate identity. Although the new Firemakers took on some of the powers traditionally held by the elders, especially within the judicial realm, the elders retained ultimate control over the functionaries and over the generation-set system. The Firemakers were drawn from a fairly narrow range of kinsmen, but it was the elders who actually elected successors to that office; the elders also saw to it that the clan that had been replaced by the usurpers continued to provide the hereditary first-initiates from whom the whole system derived its timing. Similarly, the elders retained ultimate authority over military matters, even when a brilliant military leader emerged during a period of dire emergency at the very end of the century (Lamphear 1976: chaps. 6–7).[11]

Another important feature of the Jie generation-set system is its strongly corporate nature. Because the Jie permanent settlements occupy a very small area (barely twenty miles long and wide), it is possible for entire age-sets, and even generation-sets, to congregate for important observances. It is also possible for all the senior elders, even the most infirm and senile, to be present on such occasions, carried on the backs of young men or donkeys, if need be. This compactness also is reflected in the basic kinship organization, the clan hamlet, consisting of mutually cooperating

---

10. One is forced to return to the basic lesson in traditional African politics taught us by Fortes and Evans-Pritchard (1940:xxi) a generation ago: "In Africa it is often hardly possible to separate, even in thought, political office from ritual or religious office."

11. It should be noted at this point that in many respects the Jie Firemakers resembled more closely the Oromo *Kallu* than, for example, the *Laibon* of Maa-speaking societies.

siblings. Indeed, Abrahams (1978:57) has pointed out the apparent relationship between Jie kinship structures and their strong commitment to
generational principles, noting that "the sibling group can . . . be considered as the archetypal generation group."

Another difficult problem presents itself at this point, however. Spencer
(in this volume), taking his inspiration from a study of the Pathan, has argued that age-class systems, and indeed dual organization itself, can be seen
as a balance that offers incentives both to "winners" and to "losers." Among
the Jie, the senior elders, who embody a nearly sacred aspect, who wield certain political authority, and who are not forced into retirement in their de-
clining years, clearly must be regarded as winners. But what of the losers?

Given the nature of their system, with its suggested forty-year span
between inaugurations, the wide ranges in biological age of the members
of a given generation-set, and the implied problems of overaging discussed
above, relatively few men can ever hope to achieve the status of senior elders. Ironically, only those of the more junior age-sets of a generation are
likely to live long enough to enjoy this status, with men of the senior sets
(especially those of the most senior set of all, composed largely of the
overaged men who are out of step with their generation), dying long before they can gain generational seniority. Clearly, these must be the losers.

In fact, the condition of the losers is mitigated by several factors. In
the first place, the Jie system lacks the "role phase" identity that typifies
the systems of such peoples as the Maa speakers, where principles of
biological age are stronger. The life of a mature uninitiated man is in most
ways the same as that of the initiated: he can own livestock, take part in
raiding activities, marry, and father children. Initiation confers maturity
only in a ritual sense: only initiated men can be active participants in most
religious observances (Gulliver 1953).

In his examination of the Dassanetch, Almagor (in this volume) has
described a moiety system, with associated ritual activity, that parallels
the system of generation-set alternations. He has suggested that for the
Dassanetch, the alternations can be regarded as the structure, while the
moieties, existing outside of it, can be seen as the antistructure. Although
the Jie have no moiety system analogous to that of the Dassanetch, they
do have a whole range of ritual activity that stands outside of the alternation hierarchy, is largely independent of it, and, to a degree, provides an
antistructure to it.

Most of this ritual activity is carried on within the framework of territorial divisions, and much of it focuses on the hereditary Firemakers.
In this activity a hierarchy is derived from kinship groups. An acknowledged ranking of clans exists in every division; some clans provide hereditary officers ("the people of the axe" and other functionaries) who serve

as important ritual assistants to the Firemakers (Lamphear 1976: chaps. 2 and 6). Other important rituals are held by individual clans. In all of these ritual activities, kinship group affiliation takes precedence over generation-set identity, providing an opportunity for uninitiated men to participate to some extent in the religious life of their community.

It is possible, too, for any man to gain prestige and authority completely outside the generation-set system. Outstanding individuals can build wealth in livestock, practice the arts of healing, divination, and prophecy, and display superior military skills as battle leaders ("the bulls of the herd") irrespective of their incorporation into or status within the alternations. "When I was younger, I fought in many battles as an uninitiated man. I was grown by then and had married wives. I killed enemies. . . . Even at Kaabong [one of his first battles] I led a band of men, some of whom were [initiated men of the] Ngikosowa, [generation-set], all of whom I brought back to their homes safely" (historical interview with Lotiang Ekothowan, 15 January 1971).

During middle age, both initiated and uninitiated men shift their attention away from the generation-set system and become preoccupied with more mundane activities. From their mid to late thirties, and on to their late fifties or early sixties, they pursue the goals of marriage and establishment of their own households and herds. This activity takes place within the context of the clan hamlet, as aging fathers distribute more and more animals from the family herds to their maturing sons (Gulliver 1955); in the process, the fathers reduce their chances of taking additional wives late in life.[12] As Gulliver (1953:165) has noted, age organization serves the supernatural side of life, while kinship serves the secular side. Moreover, because seniority among the Jie is relative to a given set of circumstances, even in the highly improbable event that all the middle-aged siblings of a clan hamlet were uninitiated, there would still be a definitely perceived seniority, with the younger men being "even more uninitiated," if one may so phrase it, than their elder brothers.[13] Also, uninitiated men tend to associate with their "proper" age-set and, in a manner similar to that of the Boran (Baxter 1978:177), to act as though they were members of that set.

Despite such factors that mitigate the condition of uninitiated mature men, the Jie undeniably equate such men with the lowly status of children and women, who are likewise prohibited from any real participation in

---

12. This seems to parallel the situation in some *gada* systems (see, for example, Hinnant 1978), where elderly men all but withdraw from participation in economic activity as their own herds dwindle to only a few animals. Thus the Jie expression of the generation-set system, "to feed the elders," can be regarded as quite literally true.

13. In fact, Gulliver (1953:154) shows that the determination of seniority within a clan hamlet is a complex process, but the general point still holds.

many important ritual functions and are denied access to the structured hierarchy of seniority through the generation-set apparatus. Full ritual maturity can be gained only through initiation. When men finally gain entry to the system after a wait of forty years, or perhaps even more, how can the Jie system compensate those losers who had the misfortune to be born overaged, out-of-step misfits?

Here principles of coevality come into play, although they are distinctly subordinate to generational principles. Compared to most other age-class systems, especially those in which coevality is the dominant factor, that of the Jie is far less fraught with intergroup tensions and rivalries. In the case of the Maa speakers, for example, such tensions provide an important dynamic to the very functioning of the system itself, but in the process they make the retirement of senior men obligatory. Nevertheless, coeval principles do produce some tensions and rivalries in the Jie system. Most of these are expressed within the context of a single generation-set; the senior age-sets try to exert their control over junior age-sets by withholding (though eventually granting) permission to assume the decorations proper to their generation and by performing *ameto* ("group punishment") to keep the juniors in line (Lamphear 1976: chap. 5). In this way sibling rivalries are channeled into a symbolic, controlled framework, and the competition that cannot be allowed to occur between "fathers" and "sons" is channeled into rivalries between age-sets (see Hinnant 1978:222). Pressures of the sort found among the Maa speakers are largely absent, however, and are keenly felt only at the bottom of the structure, as overaged men press for the inauguration of their generation and as successive groups of young men of the proper age campaign for entry into the generation as constituent age-sets.

It will be recalled that the overaged men typically become the first initiates of a newly inaugurated generation. They form the first age-set of that generation, and, unlike all the age-sets that follow (composed mainly, if not entirely, of men of the proper age), the first is not given a distinguishing age-set name. Rather, they are known by the name of the generation-set as a whole. In effect, they are the embodiment, the personification of the generation-set: in an almost literal sense, they *are* the generation-set. As such, they are the ultimate dispensers of privileges and the ultimate source of control over their juniors. None can reasonably expect to live long enough to be included among the ranks of the surviving senior elders of the "grandfathers" generation, but neither will most of their immediate juniors, men of the proper age, in the next several succeeding age-sets. It appears then, that the Jie system provides admirably well for these out-of-step, overaged men. To classify them as losers in the overall system seems largely inappropriate.

Historical Aspects of the Turkana Age-Class System

The historical experience of the Turkana provides a study in contrast with that of the Jie. As noted above, the Turkana origin tradition is derived from that of the Jie and replicates it in many intricate details; in their central cliché, they describe themselves as seceding young men. They still refer to the land of the Jie as the land of the ancestors or fathers. The Jie concur with the image and frequently comment that "because they were only young men, they never learned the rituals connected with the generation-set system or with Firemakers properly" (Lamphear, forthcoming: chap. 1).

Within a short time of their break away from the Jie, the Turkana embarked on a period of far-ranging territorial expansion, more extensive than that of any other Ateker people, by which they gained control of the vast country they now inhabit. In the process, any semblance of the compact, highly corporate Jie sociopolitical community was lost. As they ranged farther and farther afield, it became manifestly impossible to assemble congregations of senior elders or individual age-sets. The Turkana's nomadic life transformed the kinship organization, with clan hamlets dissolving into a system of independent households focused on individuals rather than on sets of interacting brothers (Gulliver 1955; Abrahams 1978).

Even more important, they joined the flow of other East African pastoralists in the migrational descent down the Great Rift Valley and encountered the rear guard of those Maa-speaking, Southern Nilotic-speaking and Cushitic-speaking groups that had preceded them. They wrested control of resources and territory from these groups and in the process absorbed large numbers of them. In the same way that the Jie came to epitomize the center, the Turkana, to paraphrase Turton's observations (1979:197) on similar migratory processes of the Mursi, "were expansion," or to put it another way, the periphery.

As I have argued elsewhere (Lamphear 1988:27–39), it would be a mistake to regard this dramatic expansion of the Turkana strictly in military terms, although raiding activity certainly provided at least one important dynamic to the process. But as has often been acknowledged, generation-set systems do not lend themselves well to military organization and activity (see, for example, Baxter 1978:177). Turkana traditions reveal that during the initial phases of their expansion (until after the inauguration of the Ngiputiro generation-set sometime after 1800), military activity was organized as it was among the Jie, with overaged uninitiated men participating in raids: "In those days . . . anyone, even the uninitiated, could go and fight. The Turkana fought to get food [raid livestock]. What would the uninitiated eat if they just remained at home?" This even led to a proverb, still frequently heard among the Turkana: "Does the stomach distinguish between men?"

Following the inauguration of the Ngiputiro, however, the Turkana system was transformed into the one outlined at the beginning of this essay, with the age-sets of the two alternations, Ngimoru and Ngirisoi, initiated concurrently (Gulliver 1958; Lamphear 1988:37–38). Faced with much more military action than the Jie would encounter, at least until the very end of the nineteenth century, the Turkana required a more efficient system for mobilizing the young fighting men. Age-sets began to fulfill the role of military units, each with its specifically assigned place in tactical formations (Gulliver 1958; Lamphear 1988:37–38). Initiation became synonymous with participation in raids, the the Turkana system began to resemble in some important ways the systems of the alien communities they absorbed, where considerations of age were paramount (see Baxter and Almagor 1978:22).[14]

Earlier investigations of the Turkana have noted some of the factors in this transformation. Gulliver (1953, 1958), for instance, has identified both the military and the demographic aspects. Spencer (in this volume) has also discussed demographic aspects, suggesting that "the younger generation could not be contained" any longer by the older, because individual mobility was inherent in the expansion process.

But these and other earlier investigations (including my own) have not taken into proper consideration the cosmological factors rooted in the Jie perception of themselves "as the center" and the obverse perception by the Turkana of themselves "as expansion." Instead, we have tended to focus on the inherent instability of the Jie system with all of its "paradoxes," so it comes as no surprise that the Turkana system should seemingly break down or atrophy so quickly. I suggest, rather, that the changes in the Turkana system represent far less a process of breakdown than they do a conscious, even creative, adaptation to a whole range of new circumstances that demanded change. The Turkana, free from the cosmological constraints that bound the Jie, could effectively respond to that demand with the necessary innovations.

But this change created yet another problem. If the Turkana devised a system that was better equipped to deal with new military demands and economic circumstances (by providing, as Gulliver has noted [1958:917], an opportunity for men to be "drawn out of small circles of specific in-

---

14. Spencer (1978:145), in suggesting that military considerations caused the Jie to effect similar innovations at the turn of the twentieth century, largely misinterpreted my descriptions of the military system forged by the brilliant war leader Loriang (Lamphear 1976: chap.7). There is no historical evidence to support the "changes" suggested by Spencer in the Jie generation-set system at that time.

dividual relations into a wider sphere"), in the process the authority of the senior elders was seriously diluted (Gulliver 1958; Spencer 1978), leaving the Turkana without a definitely perceived focus of their corporate identity.

This brings us to another aspect of the Turkana historical experience, which, although of vital importance, has received insufficient attention: the nineteenth-century rise of the prophet-diviners (*emuron*, pl. *ngimurok*). These powerful functionaries arose more or less simultaneously with changes in the age-class organization and the concurrent decline in status of the senior elders. Whereas the Jie elders were able to withstand the challenges of emergent hereditary functionaries and to exert ultimate control over them, the reverse happened with the Turkana.

As with features of their transformed age-class system, the inspiration for the new Turkana prophet-diviners clearly was the model of very similar functionaries in the alien communities they encountered and assimilated during their territorial expansion. By the nineteenth century, many of the Kenyan Rift and highland communities (especially those subscribing to age-class systems based on age-sets) had such functionaries. Although their powers were expressed in a ritual context, many wielded decidedly political authority and had come to represent the focus of their community's corporate identity, even to the extent of representing "emergent centralizing figures" (Munro 1975:29).

With the Turkana the prophet-diviners came to replace the elders as directors of military organization and strategy and as the chief intermediaries with god (Gulliver 1958; Lamphear 1988:38), again in a direct reversal of the situation with the Jie. "The *ngimurok* were the ones who directed the army as to how it should raid. The elders merely prayed for [its] success. . . . Therefore, if an army disobeyed the instructions for the raid, it was the *emuron* they disobeyed rather than the elders" (Lamphear 1988). The prophet-diviners took over the task of "keeping the young men in their place" by asserting direct control over the age-sets. In the process, a system began to emerge somewhat like that of the Nguni, of age-regiments at the disposal of an emergent centralizing figure.

Thus, to a degree perhaps even greater than that found among Maa-speaking communities, the Turkana prophet-diviners began to control and to transcend the age-class system. A new, more monolithic hierarchical system based on their authority rapidly took over from the graded, complementary hierarchy of the generation-sets. As Fox (in this volume) has noted, "category without complement" can no longer be considered a binary system, so the system deviated, perhaps irrevocably, from the Jie model of dual organization. Tragically, the process had reached the point of irreversibility by the early decades of the twentieth century, when the

Turkana were deprived of their prophet-diviners by the relentless "pacification" efforts of the early colonial administration. The Turkana elders were
unable to reassert sufficient authority to control the activities of a semi-
professional military class of young men that had emerged under the leadership of the prophet-diviners (Gulliver 1958). Raiding activities by these
men escalated to a point where they even attacked the Jie, who represented
the "ancestral center." In the minds of Jie and Turkana elders alike, this
constituted an unparalleled sacrilege (Lamphear 1988).

There is insufficient space to treat any of the other Ateker communities
in any detail, but following the disintegration of the Koten-Magos community, their evolution more closely paralleled that of the Turkana than
that of the Jie. Almost without exception, these communities undertook
longer migrations, wider territorial expansion, and closer interaction with
alien communities than did the Jie. All of them evolved age-class systems
in which considerations of coevality challenged the Jie commitment to
genealogical succession. At least three groups, the Toposa, Dongiro, and
Jiye, still regarded the Jie as the center, and oral traditions describe delega-
tions from these communities making regular visits to the country of the
Jie "to learn the proper way of *asapanu.*" (One such delegation, said to
have appeared shortly before my arrival, was witnessed by all of my informants.) The Labwor, a society partly derived from Jie ancestors but
heavily influenced by the Luo and based on an essentially agricultural
economy, appear to have abandoned the generational principles of their
system very rapidly in the early twentieth century with the advent of the
colonial administration (Abrahams 1978), in a manner quite similar to
agricultural communities elsewhere in East Africa (Baxter and Almagor
1978:23).

    The Karimojong, while continuing to retain some image of their so-
ciety as "at the center," evolved a generation-set system quite distinct from
that of the Jie. Significantly, this system accentuated age principles to the
extent that men could slip down a generation and be initiated—from the
Jie perspective—into the set of their own fathers. The dynamics of the
system clearly rested on a tremendous degree of intergroup tension (Dyson-
Hudson 1966) and on the enforced retirement of senior elders. The Karimojong even deviated from the terminology of the other Ateker communities
by using the word *anyamet,* which to them means "age-set" (that is, a constituent part of the generation-set based on biological age), to refer to the
corporate unit the others call *asapanu,* or "generation-set."

    One important reason for this development was probably the close
interrelationship of the Karimojong with the Southern Nilotic Pokot and
with a now defunct society called the Iworopom, who were probably a

Maa-speaking community (Lamphear 1976: chap. 6). Earlier observers (for instance, Peristiany 1951) have noted the influences that the Karimojong clearly had on the age-class system of the Pokot, but it would be naive to suppose that influences did not flow both ways. The Karimojong, who embarked on a territorial expansion rather like that of the Turkana, were surely influenced to effect adaptations in their system.

In summary, then, the significant differences between the generation-set systems of the Jie and the Turkana can be seen more as a result of the particular historical circumstances outlined here than as the result of inherent factors of disintegration in the systems themselves. The Jie, with their profound historical sense of being at the center of their universe adhered and are committed to a system that appears to occupy a central place in their lives.

The Turkana age-class system, on the other hand, reflects such commitment to dualism far less strongly. After the expansive nineteenth-century migrations away from the center, these Turkana were very different from the Turkana of a century before. New circumstances and new ideas produced fundamental shifts in their belief system and transferred their focus to a new, more politically centralized, and therefore less dualistic, center.

Because of their specific historical experience, the Jie sought to preserve the generational oscillation of their system, which, although apparently so fraught with difficulty as to constitute a paradox, allowed them effectively to resolve the contrary forces vested in their dualistic perceptions and to derive a deep "recurrent refreshment" (Baxter 1978:176; Almagor 1983:641). As Abrahams (1978:62) has phrased it, their system implies even the transcendence of mortality; for all its difficulties, it is indeed the "well-nigh ideal . . . conception of a well-ordered progression of a society through time."

References

Abrahams, R. G. 1978. Aspects of Labwor age and generation grouping and related systems. In Baxter and Almagor, eds., 1978:37–67.

Almagor, U. 1983. Charisma fatigue in an East African generation-set system. *American Ethnologist* 10:635–49.

Baxter, P. T. W. 1978. Boran age-sets and generation-sets: *Gada,* a puzzle or a maze? In Baxter and Almagor, eds., 1978:151–82.

Baxter, P. T. W., and U. Almagor. 1978. Introduction. In Baxter and Almagor, eds., 1978:1–35.

Baxter, P. T. W., and U. Almagor, eds. 1978. *Age, generation and time.* London: C. Hurst.

Dyson-Hudson, N. 1966. *Karimojong politics.* Oxford: Clarendon Press.

Fortes, M., and E. E. Evans-Pritchard. 1940. *African political systems.* London: Oxford University Press.

Gulliver, P. H. 1953. The age organization of the Jie tribe. *Journal of the Royal Anthropological Institute* 83:147–68.

———. 1955. *The family herds.* London: Routledge and Kegan Paul.

———. 1958. The Turkana age organization. *American Anthropologist* 60:900–922.

Gulliver, Pamela, and Philip H. Gulliver. 1953. *The Central Nilo-Hamites.* London: International African Institute.

Hinnant, John. 1978. The Guji: *Gada* as a ritual system. In Baxter and Almagor, eds., 1978:207–43.

Lamphear, John. 1976. *The traditional history of the Jie of Uganda.* Oxford: Clarendon Press.

———. 1983. Some thoughts on the interpretation of oral traditions among the Central Paranilotes. In *Nilotic studies,* ed. R. Vossen and M. Bechhaus-Gerst, 111–26. Berlin: Dietrich Reimer Verlag.

———. 1988. The people of the gray bull: The origin and expansion of the Turkana. *Journal of African History* 29:27–39.

———. N.d. *The scattering time: Turkana responses to the imposition of colonial rule.* Forthcoming.

Legesse, A. 1963. Class systems based on time. *Journal of Ethiopian Studies* 1:1–29.

———. 1973. *Gada: Three approaches to the study of African society.* New York: Free Press.

Miller, Joseph, ed. 1980. *The African past speaks.* Hamden, Conn.: Folkestone.

Munro, J. F. 1975. *Colonial rule and the Kamba.* Oxford: Clarendon Press.

Peristiany, J. G. 1951. The age-set system of the pastoral Pokot. *Africa* 21:188–206, 279–302.

Spencer, P. 1978. The Jie generation paradox. In Baxter and Almagor, eds., 1978: 131–50.

Stewart, F. H. 1977. *Fundamentals of age-group systems.* London: Clarendon Press.

Turton, D. 1979. War, peace and Mursi identity. In *Warfare among East African herders,* ed. K. Fukui and D. Turton. Osaka: National Museum of Ethnology.

Chapter 11

The Moieties of Cuzco

R. Tom Zuidema

Dual divisions in villages, towns, and larger political entities were, and still are, a distinctive trait found in Andean forms of social organization. Spanish chronicles and administrative documents from after the conquest of the Inca empire in 1532 reported on them repeatedly. One of our early chroniclers, Polo de Ondegardo ([ca. 1571]: 49, 135) emphasized that every town or province was divided into two parts (*saya*), called *hanan* ("upper") and *hurin* ("lower"). Nevertheless, except for their importance in Inca administration, generally little more is said about dual divisions. Only in two cases do the chronicles provide us with particulars about their importance for other aspects of Andean culture such as kinship, calendrical rituals, and the ancestor cult. One is that of Cuzco, the capital of the Inca empire, located in present-day southern Peru, and the other an unspecified town or province near Lake Titicaca. In this essay I will concentrate on our earliest information from Cuzco and use that from Lake Titicaca for comparative purposes.

Recently a complete version of the first chronicle on Cuzco and the Inca empire, written by Juan de Betanzos [1551], has been found and published. Until this fortuitous discovery, only the first fourth of this chronicle was known. We now become more aware that Betanzos was the only author close enough to the time of the conquest of Cuzco (1533) to understand the role of dual divisions in both the political organization of the city itself and in the intermontane valley where it was located. Other chroniclers like Gutierrez de Santa Clara [1544–48], Polo de Ondegardo [1559], Sarmiento de Gamboa [1572], Molina [1574], Guaman Poma de

---

My thanks go to Colin McEwan for his critical interest in this essay and his stylistic suggestions.

255

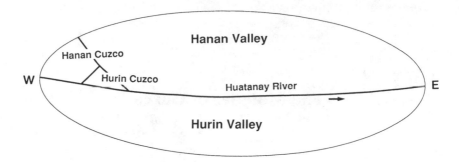

Fig. 1. The two kinds of moieties in Cuzco

Ayala [1615], and Cobo [1653] fill out the picture with useful details, but they were describing a kind of petrified, Spanish interpretation from which one can hardly reconstruct the pre-Spanish reality. Here, therefore, I will follow Betanzos's description, turning to later sources where appropriate for certain details.

The Problem

A central problem in the analysis of dual organization in Cuzco is to understand the ideas behind a system that had cosmological significance and that was used as an administrative tool and in the organization of the calendar and important rituals.

Administratively, there were two kinds of moieties in Cuzco. The city, built within the confluence of the headwaters of the river Huatanay, was divided into a higher part called Hanan Cuzco and a lower part called Hurin Cuzco. Its valley, some twenty kilometers in length and running from west to east, was again divided into a Hanan part, located north of the river Huatanay, and a Hurin part, south of the river. The city belonged to the higher western end of the Hanan valley, thus both Hanan Cuzco and Hurin Cuzco were located there (fig. 1). The question, then, is how did the Incas work out the relationship between the two types of dual division or moieties, that of the city and that of the valley? Betanzos casts his description in terms of the heroic deeds of an Inca prince, Inca Yupanqui, who defended Cuzco against the attacks of a rival people, the Chancas. He tells how Inca Yupanqui rebuilt Cuzco and reorganized the valley and how after his marriage and crowning as a king he was renamed Pachacuti Inca. His place in the Inca dynasty and the place of the earlier kings are completely ahistorical and, as Betanzos makes clear, can only be understood in terms of the ancestral cult, since this was used in the political organization of Cuzco and its valley. I will describe this organization first from Pachacuti Inca's point of view and then discuss his place in the dynasty. All the descendants of the mythical conqueror of the valley, Manco Capac, and his sister-wife were considered as "Incas" (in plural). Those who descended from marriages with non-Inca women had to live in Hurin Cuzco, Hanan Cuzco being reserved for descendants of marriages with Inca women. The residents of Hanan Cuzco referred to those in Hurin Cuzco as *huaccha* (poor) *concha* (sister's child) (Betanzos [1551]: 77–78). It was as if Inca women had married non-Inca men rather than the other way round.

Pachacuti Inca assigned lands to all the Incas (from both Hanan and Hurin Cuzco) throughout the whole valley. Here, however, they had to live together with two other groups of people: first, the descendants of the original inhabitants of the valley conquered by the Incas; and second, the people brought in from a limited area immediately beyond the valley who provided labor in the rebuilding of the city and for the canalization of the Huatanay river.[1] The latter came with their own food and built their own storehouses in the valley. We may assume, however, that all these non-Inca people were also allotted certain land-rights for purposes of living and subsistence while engaged in state projects in the valley.

We can best understand the relationships in the valley between Hanan Incas, Hurin Incas, pre-Incas, and non-Incas in terms of a further administrative division that the Incas applied here. The Hanan and the Hurin valleys were each divided into five sectors, all ten sectors having access to the river Huatanay (Zuidema 1986; Zuidema, *"Ceques* and *Chapas"* and "What Does the Equation . . . Mean?" n.d.).[2] Hanan Incas, Hurin Incas, pre-Incas, and non-Incas could reside in each sector. Thus, in contrast to their circumscribed location within the city, the Hanan and the Hurin Incas were distributed in a nonlocalized way throughout the valley. The valley moieties served primarily an administrative purpose.

Pachacuti Inca, as king, entered into marriage alliances with Incas, pre-Incas, and non-Incas. He gave Inca wives to the pre- and non-Inca lords who were represented with their people in the ten sectors of the valley, thereby establishing among them ruling families to be used in support of his own royal family. He also received ten daughters as wives from the nobles of the Hanan Incas and another ten from the Hurin nobles, thus

---

1. These people may well be classified together with others who later came from much farther away in the empire. This remains a problem to be addressed.

2. This tenfold division appears to be a local application of the Andean administrative practice of defining political units in terms of groups of one hundred, one thousand, and ten thousand families.

distinguishing ten families in each group (Betanzos [1551]:33, 57, 75, 99–100). We can infer that a correspondence existed between the two groups of ten families in the city and the ten sectors of the valley, an inference that finds support in an observation made by Gutierrez de Santa Clara ([1544–48]: 3:214). He tells us that Pachacuti Inca assigned five relatives from Hanan Cuzco as administrators of the five sectors in the Hanan valley and five other relatives from Hurin Cuzco in the Hurin valley. To this extent, then, the internal division of the city was reflected in that of the valley.[3]

The city moieties were embedded as localized entities within the valley organization and were recognized as two of the five sectors of the Hanan valley. This inclusion is reflected in the Inca calendar, where the year was divided into thirteen periods that I will call here the "Inca months" (Zuidema 1982a, 1982b, 1987).[4] The ten groups of Incas represented in the valley sectors, two groups of the pre-Inca population, and a single group of people representing the non-Incas as outsiders had to fulfill ritual obligations, each group in its designated month. Thus the pre-Incas were associated with the two months of planting (around September, before the coming of the rains) and of harvest (around April, after the rains). People from outside the valley were related to the month when they had to bring their harvest products to Cuzco (roughly May and the beginning of June). Then their lords brought presents to the Inca king and received other gifts in return. Within this system Hanan and Hurin Cuzco were in charge of the two months right before and after the December solstice. The Hurin sectors of the valley were associated with the half year beginning with the one month around the June solstice until the month before the December solstice (including the month of planting), and the Hanan sectors with the other half year (including the month of harvest). The month when foreigners came to Cuzco was not related to any valley moiety. Despite the tight relationship between the spatial and the temporal organization of the valley, we observe that on one hand the valley was divided into ten spatial units, while on the other it needed thirteen social groups for the functioning of its calendar. This is because the organization of the valley and the divisions of the calendar express different principles, both

---

3. There is a possible discrepancy between the data of Betanzos and of Gutierrez. If nobles from both Hanan and Hurin Cuzco lived in all parts of the valley, one would not expect that the lower ranked nobles from Hurin Cuzco administered the five Hurin sectors. Nonetheless, we will see that a calendrical role was assigned to the Hurin valley akin to that of the nobles of Hurin Cuzco.

4. The descriptions of the months are primarily based on the following sources: Betanzos [1551]:65–74; Cieza [1551] 1967: chap. 7; Polo [1559]:16–26; Molina [1574]:25–67; Guaman Poma de Ayala [1615]:235–60; and Cobo [1653] 2:207–22.

fundamental to the Inca. The organization of the valley expresses the dualism proper to Inca society. The calendar embeds this dualism in the wider scheme of things. Inca society contains Incas and pre-Incas (also significantly divided into two); the whole society is also contrasted with the outside world, whose role is recognized in the thirteenth month of the calendar and in the animal rituals that I discuss below.

The fact that each of these thirteen social units demanded temporal representation was recognized and codified in the context of a system of royal ancestors. Here the new information that Betanzos provides is revealing. As we have already seen, he initially states that it was the descendants of Manco Capac who were divided among Hanan and Hurin Cuzco. Later he makes clear that only the descendants of Pachacuti Inca himself by the ten wives of Hanan Cuzco and the ten of Hurin Cuzco lived there ([1551]:150). Those belonging to the high nobility and probably descending from his first wife in Hanan Cuzco were called *Capac ayllu*, "the royal descendants."[5] Their month, before the December solstice, was called *Capac raymi*, "the royal feast." All his descendants by the other wives had been obliged to take new surnames. Betanzos does not say which "surnames" they took — although he claims that the Spaniards researched this matter — but Sarmiento, Molina, and later chroniclers make clear that we are dealing here with the groups known as *panacas*. According to them, Capac ayllu was associated with Tupa Yupanqui (a son who succeeded Pachacuti Inca only after an older brother had ruled as crowned king during Pachacuti Inca's old age). All the people with different surnames, who were the other descendants of Pachacuti Inca, were called *Hatun ayllu Iñaca panaca*. Thus the distinction between the two names of Capac ayllu, as "sons," and of Hatun ayllu Iñaca panaca, as "sisters' sons," was carried on for a number of generations.

We remember that relatives of Pachacuti Inca in Hanan and Hurin Cuzco also obtained land rights in each of the other eight sectors of the valley and that from among them the administrators for these sectors were selected. The ranks of these administrators and of their subjects were symbolically represented by eight (probably nonhistorical) ancestors of the royal dynasty before Pachacuti Inca, a representation that could exist notwithstanding the fact that these same administrators (and other relatives)

---

5. The term *ayllu* was — and in many parts of the Andes still is (see for example, Isbell 1978) — used in two different contexts that should be kept separate (Zuidema 1977). First, it applies to the kindred of a person; second, it refers to any sociopolitical unit with certain rights on land that functions within a larger local or regional political whole. In the context of the name of Capac ayllu, ayllu clearly refers to "kindred." In the context of the valley administration, there were many ayllus, organized by the ten sectors, all or most of which were probably local units.

were subsumed under the double name of Hatun ayllu Iñaca panaca when they lived in Cuzco. We can distinguish the four administrators who, together with the king, ruled in the Hanan valley as *Hatun ayllu* and the five in the Hurin valley as *Iñaca panaca* (Zuidema, "Dynastic Structures," n.d.). It was the existence of the administrative concept of ten sectors that conditioned the ancestral concept of eight generations before Pachacuti Inca and of the two later generations of him and his son.[6]

Later, when Inca ideas about their past had become petrified within the context of Spanish historiography, Huayna Capac, as the last ruler before the Spanish conquest, was considered as an eleventh king.[7] He himself was not associated with any moiety or sector of the valley. As lord of the whole empire, he was the ancestral representative of the king in the month corresponding to May-June, when foreign lords came to Cuzco in order to pay their respect to the Inca king as their "lord of lords." Tupa Yupanqui (tenth king), Pachacuti Inca (ninth king), and the eight ancestors before them were the local representatives of Hanan and Hurin Cuzco and of the ten sectors of the valley. It is for this local reason of spatial organization that ten ancestors (beginning with Manco Capac) were recognized before Huayna Capac (Zuidema 1986).

I mentioned that the six Incaic months beginning with the month before the December solstice (and including the month of harvest) were assigned to the sectors of the Hanan valley. This relationship was also expressed ritually as an antagonism between both moieties that began in the first month, called *Capac raymi*, and ended in the sixth month immediately following harvest (around April). Betanzos gives us a detailed account of the rituals in Capac raymi, when boys were initiated into manhood, and of the second month, *Capac raymi Camay quilla*, when this newly acquired manhood found expression in a ritual battle between Hanan and Hurin Cuzco. The harvest rituals were described most perceptively by an eyewitness in Cuzco two years after the conquest. He refers to the moieties only in an indirect way. However, his description agrees well with two accounts of a harvest ritual from a town near Lake Titicaca where the role of the moieties is central. These accounts clarify the picture, since the rituals were probably similar in Cuzco.

---

6. The chronicler Garcilaso de la Vega el Inca ([1609]: bk.7 chap. 9) — the son of an Inca princess and a Spanish conqueror — was very much aware of the fact that the panacas did not descend from former kings and that the Spanish historiographers misunderstood the information given to them, placing the panacas, as they did, in the context of a supposedly historical dynasty and giving each king his own panaca (see Zuidema 1986).

7. It is clear from Betanzos ([1551]:126) and other chroniclers that more than one king was remembered between Huayna Capac (as the eleventh king) and Pachacuti Inca (as the ninth).

I will conclude my general remarks about the moieties of Cuzco with a consideration of the information on kinship as introduced here. Pachacuti Inca called his relatives in Hurin Cuzco *concha*, "sisters' sons," though they descended from Inca men and their non-Inca wives. The king had also given Inca wives to the non-Inca lords living around Cuzco. Apparently he entered into a direct and symmetric marriage exchange with each of them. In addition to these alliances, he received wives from ten families in Hanan Cuzco and from ten in Hurin Cuzco. We may assume that he entered into direct exchanges with each of these families too. As a consequence of this system of alliances, nine families had had to adopt new "surnames" and became associated with the nine sectors outside Hanan Cuzco. It is for this reason that these families bore after their own names the epithet panaca, "group descending from a man's sister (*pana*)," each being a group of concha.

Direct exchanges were carried out in the hierarchical framework of the king, located in the political center, and each of the ten local units of the valley (one being his own). Betanzos also mentions ([1551]:62) exogamic relationships between whole moieties, including those of Cuzco and of its valley. However, a later chronicler, Murúa ([1611–18] 1962 vol. 2:62–63), makes clear that such marriage relationships between moieties could only be maintained by the lords representing these. Murúa was probably right. Direct marriage exchange between two men or families was, and still is, well known in the Andes, but exogamic moieties have not been found anywhere. The only recognition of a direct alliance pattern in Inca kinship nomenclature is found in the hierarchical context of calling the son of an Inca by a secondary or non-Inca wife "sister's son." Direct exchange of women, be it of a hierarchical or a nonhierarchical kind, or be it on the personal level or on that of lords representing political units, was central to Andean political practice. The exchange of sisters by lords of moieties was part of that system, but fully functioning exogamic moieties apparently did not exist.

Dual Organization and the Calendar: The Months of Capac Raymi and Capac Raymi Camay Quilla

I have already mentioned the connection of Hanan and Hurin Cuzco to the months of Capac raymi and Capac raymi Camay quilla, respectively. This connection leads me now to consider the rituals carried out at these times that revolved around the initiation of the noble youths.

While the term *raymi*, "feast," in the name of both months refers to their solar character, the extra name of the second month includes the term *quilla,* "moon, month, lunar celebration." Thus, while the rituals of Capac raymi were celebrated during fixed dates in this month, the observation of the moon played a decisive role in determining the timing of the rituals of Capac raymi Camay quilla.[8] Within the royal (*capac*) context of both months there was a male-female and a solar-lunar opposition expressed. Capac raymi was the month of the high nobility (Capac ayllu), when the rituals opposed the initiated men to the noninitiated youths. But the association of Capac raymi Camay quilla with Hatun ayllu Iñaca panaca makes us aware of yet a second male-female opposition, of ayllu to iñaca, that was probably related to the division of moieties in the valley.

Capac Raymi

Only noble sons could participate in the initiation rituals of Capac raymi. The feast (for a particular boy)

> had to be given by the richest of his relatives. It was necessary that his relatives helped and favored him in that feast, (in that way) maintaining a brotherhood and confederacy. (Betanzos [1551]:66)

The rich relatives were known as *Huaccha cuyac,* "those who love (*cuyac*) orphans and the poor (*huaccha*)." Betanzos used this term earlier when talking specifically about the king and the queen in relation to those non-Inca peoples who had given the king the mothers of his sons called *huaccha concha,* "the poor sisters' sons." These sons lived in Hurin Cuzco and the term reveals that in Cuzco the position of the neophytes was compared to that of poor orphans and affines.[9]

In the preparatory rituals of the month before Capac raymi special attention was paid to women.[10] The female relatives of a boy wove a black

---

8. The month itself had a fixed position in the calendar, but its rituals were celebrated beginning with the first two days of the new moon after the December solstice, followed later by six days beginning with the full moon. The name of the month derives from *camay,* "to produce, to give fruit," or *camay,* "the task in the work" (Taylor 1976; Duviols 1978), and from *quilla,* "moon."

9. The term *huaccha cuyac* was also used in the context of initiation rituals elsewhere. A document from central Peru, defining the particular role of the mother's brother in initiation, claims that in the case of orphans the role was taken over by the rich nobles (Duviols 1974–76:280–81).

10. I should explain briefly the astronomical significance of the period beginning with the month before Capac raymi till the last possible date of the lunar rituals extending beyond Capac raymi Camay quilla. The period included the four Inca months that organized the time of 107 days when the sun at noon passes to the other, southern side of the sky from where it normally is. With the heavy rains, the earth returned to the greenness of primordial times with no seasons and moieties. The purpose of the initiation was to establish contact

shirt for him and brewed four vessels of maize beer for his feast. At the same time, the boy had to collect "straw," i. e., *ichu* grass, in the high *puna* grasslands. Not only did he prove his ability to survive in the wild without food or drink; he also honored the weavers with grass "to sit upon" (Betanzos [1551]:66; Molina [1574]:47). The rituals of Capac raymi progressed in three stages, each stage being related in turn to the visit and worship of three sacred mountains, Huanacauri, Anahuarque, and Yahuira, all lying on the southern horizon of the Hurin valley. Besides their roles in this month, each mountain also had its particular significance for another month. The first mountain, Huanacauri, to the southeast, was visited during the month of the June solstice that began the Hurin half of the year. Non-Inca people came with their harvest and with presents to pay homage to the king.[11] The second mountain, Anahuarque, closer to the south, was considered the ancestress of the pre-Inca people. Her worship was related to women, to the queen, and to the feast of planting in September. The last mountain, Yahuira, stood on the western outskirts of the city and its importance is only mentioned during Capac raymi. These rituals thus represent a progression from non-Inca to pre-Inca to Inca.

In the first ritual of Capac raymi, the boys went up to Huanacauri, making their own sandals of grass. They received a bundle of grass with some woolen strands dangling from it which they had to carry upside down during the following days. In the second ritual they raced down from Mount Anahuarque with lances, from each of which hung the same woolen strands, representing the hair of a trophy head (Cieza de León [1551] 1967: chap. 7) and Murúa [1611–18] 1962: vol 1:35). The race was in honor of the mountain who had risen with the waters of the flood and who therefore was considered to have been light and swift during the flood; this purpose was further emphasized by the fact that the boys were preceded in the race by girl-associates who served them with beer at the foot of the mountain. In the third and last ritual outside town, the boys received their earspools on Yahuira, these being attached to their unpierced ears with a woolen string. In the final days before the solstice, their parents presented them to their sponsors at the feast in the plaza. These men were dressed with a puma head and skin over their own heads and backs and played four large drums. The pumas had golden spools in their ears. The initiation for the boys ended in private, when their ears were pierced on a cultivated field near a spring of water.

with the ancestors, to separate the youths from the non-Inca people and their mothers' household, and to confront them with Inca society at large.

11. In the origin myth, Manco Capac, the first ancestor, came down from Huanacauri to take possession of the valley, carrying out the initiation rituals of his successor.

Each time the boys returned from the mountains, their fathers, mothers' brothers, and lords "civilized" them by whipping their legs and commemorating the ancestors (*huari*) in songs (also called *huari*). The three rituals show a progression from outside to inside. The grass and wool that first identified them with the puna as *purun*, "wild," was later hung as a trophy from their lances. The grass may have symbolized an act of service, as when the boys gave their female relatives (the weavers) grass to sit upon, or when a groom shoes his bride with sandals of grass (Cobo [1653]: 2: 248), or when a son-in-law brings grass to his father-in-law's house to cover its roof (Guaman Poma de Ayala [1615]:847). Upon their return from Anahuarque, the boys imitated the warriors who at the beginning of planting in September had driven out illnesses and evil to the borders of the territory of the non-Inca people serving Cuzco, thereby preparing the valley itself for peace, fertility, and domestic life (Molina [1574]; Cobo [1653]; Zuidema 1964:5–7).

Capac Raymi Camay Quilla

In contrast to Capac raymi, the accent in the next month, Capac raymi Camay quilla, was on society organized in moieties and panacas. Another contrast was in the role of women. In Capac raymi they had been absent, except for the girls serving the boys coming down from Anahuarque, and female participation was limited to the preparatory rituals of the month before. In Capac raymi Camay quilla they were represented equally with men, except for the very first ritual of transition between both months which still belonged to the boys.

One of the last acts in Capac raymi had been that the boys bathed, received new tunics, and were "stoned" (Betanzos [1551]:69) by their relatives with green *tunas* (cactus fruits). Each uncle gave his nephew a shield, a sling, and a club. Then, on the first day after the new moon in the month of Capac raymi Camay quilla, the boys divided themselves according to their moieties and battled each other with the green tunas.[12]

During the night of the next full moon, all the panaca nobles took up a long rope, the men on one side and the women on the other, and began to dance winding through all the streets of town (Molina [1574], Cobo [1653]). Just after sunrise they entered the plaza, spiraling around

---

12. Betanzos gives an interesting description ([1551]:145–48) of the funeral rituals of Pachacuti Inca that are similar to those of Capac raymi Camay quilla and that might have been carried out at the same time of the year. As part of those rituals, an army of Hanan Cuzco had to battle an army of Hurin Cuzco and had to win, just as Pachacuti Inca during his lifetime had also always won in war. If we can accept that Hanan Cuzco had to win also in the calendrical rituals, the reason was, of course, that then it was in charge of the rituals.

the king who sat on his throne, and then dropped the rope. Earlier on, people had brought old black llamas to the plaza and pierced their ears. During the dance, ten precious tunics, contributed by all the divisions ("parcialidades" in Spanish) of town, were burned in sacrifice. Two tunics were offered to the sun, two to the moon, two to the thunder god, two to the god Viracocha (the "Creator" god, according to the Spaniards, who at that time "resided in the Ocean") and two to the earth. After sunrise two young llamas were sacrificed "for the health of all people."

The ten tunics and the ordered sequence of their dedication to the gods identifies the divisions as panacas in their hierarchical relationships. Of the two tunics offered to each god, one was probably given by a Hanan panaca and the other by a Hurin panaca. The act of burning the textiles was sandwiched between the rituals involving the old llamas, who were not killed and who received earspools, and of the young llamas, who were killed. The old llamas were subsequently divided among the non-Inca people of the four *suyus*, the provinces outside Cuzco. The pair of young llamas finds its parallel in the pair of each kind of tunic, and the animals probably symbolized the position of the recently initiated men. Given that the ten panacas were in charge of the rituals of ten of the thirteen months, the young men were in a position similar to that of the pre-Inca inhabitants of the valley, charged with taking care of the months of planting and harvest. The old people, then, were classified with the people coming from the outside. While in Capac raymi the neophytes were compared to a general group of outsiders, in Capac raymi Camay quilla the young initiates were introduced into Cuzco society, later gaining prominence in either Hanan or Hurin. These rites therefore deal with a progression from the outside to the inside, from the non-Inca world to the Inca world, before focusing in their last stages on the dualistic complementarity of Inca society. The ritual during full moon of the month of Capac raymi Camay quilla laid primary stress on the five principal components of the Inca cosmological system. Further study of the Inca calendar would show how each of them also operated once during the Hanan half of the year and once during the Hurin half.

Kinship and Dual Organization in the Harvest Rituals of Cuzco and Lake Titicaca

Although the initiation rituals of Capac raymi entailed family relationships—with the female relatives, the parents, the mothers' brothers, the lords as adoptive parents, and the girl-associates all involved—this information does not enable us to study the particular relations between Inca kinship practices and dual organization. The rituals of Capac raymi Camay quilla placed emphasis on the role of the moieties but no explicit mention is made of kinship practices. On the other hand, two early descriptions of harvest rituals near Lake Titicaca combine the two elements. These are similar in various details and in their overall intent to a fascinating description of a harvest ritual witnessed in Cuzco by a Spaniard (Molina el Almagrista [1552]:82), two years after the conquest of the city. Even if the author does not refer explicitly to moieties or kinship, it is probable that they did play an important role here and I will use the Lake Titicaca accounts to argue for their existence in Cuzco.

Harvest in Cuzco

The harvest rituals of Cuzco were the last occasion when the recently initiated boys played an important role. They were the first to carry the maize from the valley in procession into Cuzco. A broad avenue was formed with tents, sheltering the mummies of the panaca ancestors with their attendants (Molina el Almagrista [1552], Cobo [1653]). The material from Titicaca enables us to suggest that the panacas of Hanan were on one side of the avenue and those of Hurin on the other and, moreover, that they were ranked in a descending order as observed from the position of the king, who was seated where the procession started. Later the boys hunted "dwarf llamas" and distributed the meat in small portions among all the participants.

Harvest Rituals in the Region of Lake Titicaca

In the first account, included in the Aymara dictionary of Bertonio, ([1612]), the author describes how during the harvest ritual, called *sucullu*, all the mothers who had given birth in the preceding year came to the plaza with their babies. Young men returned from hunting vicuñas (a species of small, wild llamas), whose blood they collected in the stomachs of the animals themselves. We are not given a kin connection between hunters and mothers but most probably they were affinal relatives, or young men defined as such.[13] Each uncle of a child, called *lari* (mother's brother, wife's father),

---

13. I conclude this from our information on the term *lari*. While this word alone means MB or any male relative on mother's side, and while *quimsacallco lari* ("eight lari") means "all the male relatives of the wife as called by her husband and her sons," the duplicated version of the word, *lari lari*, refers to "people of the puna, who do not recognize a cacique." The synonym *choquela* adds the detail that they subsist by hunting, while another synonym *lari uru* compares them to the dirty, uncivilized *Uru* fishermen of Lake Titicaca.

made a blood-line over the face of the child (as was done in Cuzco in similar rites of passage), and its mother was given the meat of the animal to eat. An aunt on the father's side (*ipa*), who could be replaced in this by the wife of the lari, took the child out of its cradle.[14] Three different kin groups were involved in the ritual: the adolescent affines, the mothers, and the aunts and uncles. While the only people mentioned were women or those connected through women, the fathers were conspicuously absent. Their role, however, was central in the political rituals that I shall deal with now.

The other account, probably from the same area, places the custom of *sucullu* in a setting where moiety rituals are explained better than anywhere else.[15] Some two to four thousand men (probably heads of family) came together in the town plaza of the *hatun curaca* (overlord). In front of him, the lords of one moiety, called the "herders," were seated on the right of a long avenue and those of the other moiety, the "fishermen," on the left. The highest ranked lords sat closest to the hatun curaca.[16] Next to each lord of the first moiety stood his successor with a staff. In the second moiety each lord was accompanied by his wife; the most important wives played large drums. First the fishermen danced in a line advancing toward the herders, then withdrawing. The sons of the herders reciprocated with offerings of coca, first to all the lords (perhaps including those of the other moiety) and then to all the blind, the poor, and the buffoons. Then came the familiar ritual, described by Bertonio, of bringing out the mothers with their babies and another ritual where all the widows were honored. Births and deaths among the population were recorded on *quipus* (knotted cords).

We detect in Herrera's description an apparent dominance of the herders over the fishermen in terms of a male-female opposition. The herder moiety stressed the connection between a lord and his successor

---

14. Similar rituals occurred in Huarochiri, central Peru (Urioste 1983, apps. 1 and 2, 247–65). They dealt with the birth of twins and of children born with a double crown in the hair. They express in a pronounced form those executed for all children. While the parents of the twins carried out an onerous penitance, relatives prepared the following celebrations. Five young men, defined as son- or brother-in-law (dH, ZH) collected coca and hunted a very small kind of deer, *lluychu*. Later they carried the lluychu around and offered people the meat to eat. Being born with two crowns announced the birth of twins and here the description concentrates on the ritual of first haircutting. The MB of the boy or the FZ of the girl cut a first lock of the hair and then were followed in this act by the other people.

15. The description is found in Herrera y Tordesillas ([1601–15]: decada 5, bk. 4, chap. 6), a late historian who was never in America. He probably took it from an early source; internal evidence points to Lake Titicaca.

16. Matienzo ([1567]:20) describes similar rank orders in what is now Bolivia. Rivière (1983) discusses a striking modern parallel.

(probably his son). The latter acted as a *huaccha cuyac*, "he who loves the poor," the same role as that held in Cuzco by the king and the queen and by the rich men (*Capac ayllu*; *Capac churi*) who organized the initiation feast of a noble boy. The fisherman moiety stressed the husband-wife connection. The two moieties expressed a relationship parallel to that found in Cuzco between Hanan and Hurin, both moieties as viewed from the position of the king.

Conclusions

The Comparison of Cuzco and Titicaca

I have described for Cuzco two types of dual organization. In the first, the king gave sisters to lords from outside Cuzco and obtained children that he called huaccha concha. The equation of a man's secondary children (obtained by women from non-Inca wifegivers) to "sister's children" (where the "sisters" were married to wifetakers) can be seen as a symmetric alliance between unequal partners. In the second, the huaccha concha, who were the outcome of those exogamic relationships, received in Cuzco and in its valley a territorial recognition as lower moiety, Hurin, equal to that of the upper moiety of Hanan. While the king and high nobility were called huaccha cuyac in relation to the non-Incas as huaccha and Hurin Cuzco as huaccha concha, in Titicaca the role of huaccha cuyac was given to the successors of lords in the moiety of the herders, giving us to assume that the moiety of the fishermen was cast in the role of the huaccha concha.

While I compared the harvest rituals of Cuzco with those of Titicaca, another parallel exists in the attention that both societies payed to the role of moieties in life cycle rituals. I mentioned how in Cuzco, in the month of Capac raymi Camay quilla, the old, middle-aged, and young people were represented. Near Lake Titicaca there was an administrative interest during the harvest rituals in counting the recently widowed people and the newborn children.

Moieties and Political Organization

Moieties are still frequently found in the Andes. They have a tendency toward endogamy, and no example of exogamy has ever been found. How do we combine this preference with the notion of symmetric alliances? Betanzos mentioned marriage alliances between moieties as a general feature of southern Andean society, but Murúa, more correctly, formulated such an interest in the context of an ever more encompassing system of dual organizations, defined by a political hierarchy. Exogamic relationships between moieties were not maintained by the marriages of their constituent families but by those of their curacas. These lords established their alliances on successively higher levels and over longer "political distances." A growing distance was combined with an inverse genealogical interest, so that men of each higher rank were allowed to marry more endogamically. This culminated in the king's marriage to his own full sister, symbolizing an alliance between Hanan (upper) and Hurin (lower) at the level of the state and the cosmos. In the case of Pachacuti Inca's marriage — which in Betanzos's and later descriptions was the paradigm for any royal marriage — he was the son of the sun, while his sister was named after the ancestress, Mama Anahuarque (Sarmiento de Gamboa [1572]), of all pre- and non-Inca people representing the goddess of the earth Pacha Mama.[17]

Turning now to Andean kinship practices, we note that direct exchange of sisters between two men or two families was an ideal in Andean society shortly after the Spanish conquest and remains so today. The practice is taken as a metaphor for the ceremonial relationships between moieties, just as, for instance, in the case of the town of Huanca Sancos, department of Ayacucho, the two ayllus of each moiety call each other "brother" and the two moieties call themselves "brother-in-law," even if no association to real marriage between them is intended (Zuidema, field notes). In an early myth from central Peru a god calls the people of one province "sons" and those of a nearby province he calls "sister's sons," as if they were in dual relationship to each other.[18] The situation near Lake Titicaca suggests a combination of the two practices. The father-son relationship in one moiety and the husband-wife relationship in the other may have implied links to the overlord that were described as male in the first moiety and as female in the second. But the moieties also came together to carry out, in the space in between them, the rites of passage of a child. While the practice itself was real enough, it may have been used to symbolize an alliance between the moieties. I suggest that in Cuzco, too, a combination existed of the moiety distinction of "sons" and "sister's sons" of the king with a symbolic representation of direct, symmetric alliance between the moieties themselves. While near Lake Titicaca the dual distinction

17. The indigenous chronicler Joan de Santacruz Pachacuti Yamqui also establishes a state-cosmos interest in the marriage of Manco Capac's parents. His father was called "Lord House" and his mother "Mother Earth Diviner." His father's father represented the Hanan province of Cuzco and his mother's father the Hurin province (Santacruz Pachacuti [1613]; Zuidema 1977, 1986).

18. The myth occurs in the same document where the practice was also reported of a rich noble person being the sponsor of the initiation of an orphan. Moreover, one of the two provinces mentioned was that of Huanuco (Duviols 1974–76:277–78), where the practice of sister exchange, or of a sister against a female servant, was known (Zuidema 1977).

probably had an ethnic origin, opposing the Aymara people as herders to the Uru people (and perhaps the Puquina people) as fishermen, in Cuzco it received two other and different interpretations. First, there was the distinction of Hanan and Hurin Cuzco that was the result of a relationship based on the conquest by the Incas of the pre- and non-Inca peoples. Second, there was a largely administrative distinction applied to the moieties of the valley. In the three cases (of Cuzco, Titicaca, and central Peru), however, the dual distinction was interpreted from the point of view of a king, lord, or god as one between sons and sisters' sons.

Moieties and the Calendar

One question remains: Why were the two Cuzco valley moieties represented in mirror symmetry? Why was such a diametric opposition necessary? The calendrical organization of the panacas points us to a plausible answer. The Hurin panacas were of almost equal rank to those of Hanan. The opposition was not a static one of female-male, outside-inside, wet season – dry season, but one of a *movement* from the outside to the inside and from dry season to wet season, balanced by a counter-movement from the inside to the outside and from wet season to dry season. Both moieties received equal time in the year, equal ritual attention, and equal spatial recognition. Such a temporal point of view helps us to see the roles of the months of Capac raymi (related to Capac ayllu) and of Capac raymi Camay quilla (related to Hatun ayllu Iñaca panaca) not so much in terms of a hierarchical, concentric opposition, but as a diametric, cyclical one. Both months marked the beginning of Hanan-time. The rituals of the boys to be initiated in Capac raymi, however, reflected a movement from outside to inside as was true for Hurin-time. They were preceded by rituals where women played a dominant role. The neophytes strove towards the position of Capac and the month itself was named after the Capac churi (royal sons). The general purpose of Hurin-time was to attract outside female fertility towards the center. In Capac raymi Camay quilla, however, the purpose was not to recapitulate past events (as the rituals of the neophytes had done), but to predict the outcome of the crops. People were concerned with the return of the dry season and with the arrival of harvest, when the king could once again enter into exchange with foreign lords (Zuidema, "At the King's Table," n.d.). Leading up to this event the role of the recent initiates in harvest had been important as hunters, imitating the role of affines. They were the product of affinal relationships and now became integrated into the moieties of Hatun ayllu and Iñaca panaca within town.

Marriages were concluded in the dry season. Bertonio describes how recently married couples would not have sexual relationships from planting to harvest.[19] Their fields were cultivated by relatives, and only after obtaining the seeds of the harvest could they themselves plant.[20] They would then become owners of land in their own right, as heads of family, each being identified with a panaca and a moiety. Capac ayllu, belonging to Hanan Cuzco, represented the goal of the Hurin half of the year, and Hatun ayllu Iñaca panaca, belonging to Hurin Cuzco, initiated the rituals of the Hanan half of the year. The two city moieties were, in a sense, the inverse of the valley moieties. Chroniclers mention the three most important feasts in Cuzco as being those of planting, of Capac raymi (spread over the two months around the December solstice), and of harvest. In the month of planting, concern focused on the outside of Cuzco, driving out evil and illnesses into the four directions and attracting female fertility in order to revive the earth. In the last of the three feasts, harvest was brought in through the avenue formed by the moieties. Capac raymi integrated the descendants of the outsiders into the moiety organization of Cuzco.

The Application of the Distinction Made between the City and the Valley Moieties

To conclude I wish to comment on the use made of the moieties in political decision making for those living in Cuzco and its valley. It seems clear that when the nobles represented themselves in Cuzco itself, they were assigned places to live according to genealogical principles, either in Hanan or Hurin Cuzco. At the same time, they also had interests in the countryside. Two examples illustrate how the mythological and legendary histories of the Incas may have handled such a double interest.

In one example we are dealing with a case where a single name Capac Yupanqui (royal Yupanqui) was used, not only for a brother of Pachacuti Inca whose mother came from the Hurin part of the valley and who is mentioned as a general highest in rank after his brother, but also for the royal ancestor of the first panaca in the Hurin part of the valley. It is possible that we are dealing here with one and the same person (Zuidema 1964:129–33).

---

19. Bertonio [1612], s.v. "Qhuiñi apatha," "Satathapitatha," "Collithapiratha," and "Collijastha."

20. Probably, the recently married couples themselves fulfilled functions as guardians of the fields and at the borders of the town, as is still done today (Condori Mamani 1977:38–39).

The use of the valley moieties is particularly revealing in the case of Huascar and Atahuallpa, the sons of Huayna Capac who were involved in a civil war at the time of the Spanish conquest.[21] Huascar started off as the king in Cuzco and Atahuallpa as the rebel in Ecuador. Some chroniclers say that Huascar became disgusted with the nobles of Hanan and that he switched to the Hurin side. Betanzos ([1551]: 194), who probably knew best, says, however, that Huascar was *born* in Hurin and that Atahuallpa *belonged* to the panaca of Pachacuti Inca. Notwithstanding the hierarchical difference between the two brothers, even the king could belong to Hurin! Possibly, Huascar and Atahuallpa were Hanan and Hurin in their hierarchical distinction and Hurin and Hanan in the geographic one, respectively. I see it as quite possible, therefore, that one and the same person could occupy different positions in terms of Hanan and Hurin in Cuzco and in the valley. A person was attached to land in either the Hanan or the Hurin part of the valley and at the same time could be either a *churi* (son) or a *concha* (sister's son), or be either a person of pre-Inca origin in the valley or of non-Inca origin from outside. Having accepted, however, a location in the valley, he would participate in the ritual roles assigned to his panaca and moiety there.

In this essay I have analyzed dual organization in Cuzco during Inca times. By establishing a historical baseline for ethnohistorical and ethnographic studies, it is now possible to select critically for comparative purposes from information elsewhere and give more life to our body of data on Cuzco. Lévi-Strauss (1958) first analyzed dual organizations as these occur in the Gê and Bororo societies from central Brazil. Later ethnographic research sharpened our theoretical understanding of the forms of social organization involved (Maybury-Lewis 1979; Turner 1984:335–70; Maybury-Lewis, in this volume). Parallels between moieties here and in the Andes include symbolic oppositions between heaven and earth, male and female, (movement toward) inside and (movement toward) outside, and of the half-years related either to growing and ripening of the crops or to dry and wet seasons. Another comparative problem concerns exogamy. While in the Andes symmetric alliances were and are favored on the family level, they never led to the formation of exogamic moieties. Andean moieties strongly reflect differences based on conquest (e.g., in order to obtain extra female fertility) and economic specialization (e.g., the distinctions between herders and farmers and between herders and

---

21. Although I have analyzed this example before (Zuidema 1983), the new version of Betanzos now adds significant new details.

fishermen). Marriages were and are shunned between such groups. It may have been the political alliances of their lords, combined with an ideal of symmetry, that gave Andean moieties their peculiar and distinctive character, using the concept of marriage alliance as a metaphor while not applying it in reality.

REFERENCES

Bertonio, Ludovico. [1612] 1984. *Vocabulario de la lengua Aymara.* Cochabamba: Centro de Estudios de la Realidad Económica y Social, Instituto Francés de Estudios Andinos, Museo Nacional de Ethnografía y Folklore.

Betanzos, Juan de. [1551] 1987. *Suma y narración de los Incas.* Madrid: Atlas.

Cieza de León, P. de. [1551] 1967. *El señorío de los Incas.* Lima: Instituto de Estudios Peruanos.

Cobo, Bernabe. [1653] 1956. *Historia del nuevo mundo.* Madrid: Biblioteca de Autores Españoles, vol. 82.

Condori Mamani, Gregorio. 1977. *Autobiografía.* Cuzco: Centro "Bartolomé de las Casas."

Duviols, Pierre. 1974–76. Une petite chronique retrouvée: Errores, ritos, supersticiones y ceremonias de los Yndios de la provincia de Chinchaycocha y otras del Piru. *Journal de la Société des Américanistes* 63:257–97.

———. 1978. Camaquen Upani. In *Amerikanistische Studien*, ed. R. Hartmann and U. Oberem, 132–44. St. Augustin: Anthropos-Institut.

Garcilaso de la Vega, el Inca. [1609] 1960. *Comentarios Reales de los Incas.* Madrid: Biblioteca de Autores Españoles, vols. 133–35.

Guaman Poma de Ayala, Felipe [1615] 1987. *Nueva crónica y buen gobierno.* Madrid: Historia 16.

Gutierrez de Santa Clara, Pedro. [1544–48] 1963. Quinquenarios o historia de las guerras civiles del Peru. Madrid: Biblioteca de Autores Españoles, vols. 165–66.

Herrera y Tordesillas, Antonio de. [1601–15] 1944–47. *Historia general de los Hechos de los Castellanos en las islas i terra firme del mar oceano.* Asunción del Paraguay: Editorial Guaranía.

Isbell, Billie Jean. 1978. *To defend ourselves: Ecology and ritual in an Andean village.* Austin: University of Texas Press.

Lévi-Strauss, Claude. 1958. *Anthropologie Structurale.* Paris: Plon.

Matienzo, Juan de. [1567] 1967. *Gobierno del Peru*, ed. G. Lohmann Villena. Lima: Institut Français d'Etudes Andines.

Maybury-Lewis, David, ed. 1979. *Dialectical studies.* Cambridge: Harvard University Press.

Molina, Cristóbal de. [1574] 1943. *Fábulas y ritos de los Incas.* Lima: Miranda.

Molina el Almagrista, Cristóbal. [1552] 1967. Relación de muchas cosas acaescidas en el Peru, atribuidas a Cristobal de Molina el Almagrista. Madrid, Biblioteca de Autores Españoles, vol. 209.

Murúa, Martin de. [1613] 1962. *Historia general del Peru, origen y decendencia de los Incas.* Ed. M. Ballesteros Gaibrois. Madrid.

Platt, Tristan. 1986. Mirrors and maize: The concept of *yanantin* among the Macha of Bolivia (1978). In *Anthropological history of Andean polities*, ed. John V. Murra, Nathan Wachtel, and Jacques Revel, 228–59. Cambridge: Cambridge University Press.

Polo de Ondegardo, Juan. [1559] 1916. Los errores y supersticiones de los indios. In Colección de libros y documentos referentes a la historia del Peru, (CLDRHP), ser. 1, vol. 3:1–43. Ed. H. H. Urteaga and C. Romero. Lima.

———. [ca. 1571] 1916. Relación de los fundamentos. In CLDRHP, 3:45–188. Urteaga and Romero.

Rivière, Gilles. 1983. Quadripartition et idéologie dans les communautés Aymaras de Carangas. *Bulletin de l'institut français des études Andines* 12 (3–4): 41–62.

Santacruz Pachacuti Yanqui, Juan de [1613] 1950. Relacion de antigüedades deste reyno del Peru. In *Tres relaciones de antigüedades peruanas*, ed. M. Jiménez de la Espada, 207–81. Asunción del Paraguay: Editorial Guaranía.

Sarmiento de Gamboa, Pedro. [1572] 1943. *Historia de los Incas.* Buenos Aires: Emecé.

Taylor, Gerald. 1976. Camay, camac et camasca dans le manuscrit Quechua de Huarochiri. *Journal de la société des américanistes* 63:231–44.

Turner, Terence. 1984. Dual opposition, hierarchy, and value. In *Différences, valeurs hiérarchie*, ed. J.-Cl. Galey, 335–70. Paris: Ecole des Hautes Etudes, Sciences Sociales.

Urioste, George L. 1983. *Hijos de Pariya Oaqa: La tradición oral de Waru Chiri (mitología, ritual y costumbres).* Syracuse, N.Y.: Maxwell School of Citizenship and Public Affairs.

Zuidema, R. Tom. 1964. *The Ceque system of Cuzco: The social organization of the capital of the Inca.* Leiden: Brill.

———. 1977. The Inca kinship system: A new theoretical view. In *Andean kinship and marriage*, ed. R. Bolton and E. Mayer, 240–81. Special Publication no. 7. Washington, D.C.: American Anthropological Association.

———. 1982a. *Catachillay*: The role of the Pleiades and of the Southern Cross and A and B Centauri in the calendar of the Incas. In *Ethnoastronomy and Archaeoastronomy in the American Tropics*, ed. A. F. Aveni and G. Urton, 203–29. Annals of the New York Academy of Sciences, vol. 385.

———1982b. The sidereal lunar calendar of the Incas. In *Archaeoastronomy in the New World*, ed. A. F. Aveni, 59–107. Cambridge: Cambridge University Press.

———. 1983. Hierarchy and space in Incaic social organization. *Ethnohistory* 30 (2): 49–75.

———. 1986. *La civilisation Inca au Cuzco.* Paris: Collège de France and Presses universitaires de France.

———. 1987. South American calendars. In *Encyclopedia of Religion*, ed. Mircea Eliade et al., 3:16–21. New York: Macmillan.

————. N.d. *Ceques* and *chapas*: An Andean pattern of land partition in the modern valley of Cuzco. Forthcoming.

————. N.d. What does the equation "mother's brother = wife's father" mean in Inca social organization? Forthcoming.

————. N.d. At the king's table. *History and Anthropology,* forthcoming.

————. N.d. Dynastic structures in Andean culture. In *The northern dynasties: Kingship and statecraft in Chimor*, ed. M. E. Moseley. Washington, D.C.: Dumbarton Oaks. In press.

Chapter 12

The Organization of Action, Identity, and Experience in Arapesh Dualism

Donald Tuzin

Dual organization is a prominent feature of societies in several regions of Papua New Guinea, most notably the coasts and lowland hinterlands of the Papuan Gulf (Maher 1967; cf. Hau'ofa 1971), the Trans-Fly (Williams 1936), the East and West Sepik (Thurnwald 1916; Bateson 1936; Kaberry 1941; Mead 1947; Gell 1975; Tuzin 1976), and certain of the islands lying off the northeastern mainland (Powdermaker 1933; Epstein 1969; Hogbin 1970). Such forms also occur in the highlands and south coast of West Irian (Serpenti 1956; Van Baal 1966; O'Brien 1969). Although a systematic comparative study of these systems does not yet exist, one can discern a gross distinction between what might be called "elementary" and "complex" dual organizations, based on the respective presence or absence of *exogamous* moieties (cf. Lévi-Strauss 1949). When the dual organization is primarily embedded in exogamous moieties, as is the case in insular Papua New Guinea and in the highlands of West Irian, its social centrality is guaranteed by the radiations of human and material exchange that integrate kinship, marriage, and descent matrices in this part of the world (see Rubel and Rosman, in this volume). The resulting social edifice, while it may have complicated features, represents the qualitatively simple ramification of basic exogamic requirements. Interestingly, this simplicity evokes the question of whether, in these systems, dualism exists as an independent operating principle or is merely a sedimentation of reciprocal actions that are "dualistic" only in a notional sense. Some, perhaps many, of the dual organizations found on the Papua New Guinea mainland are divorced from (or have never been wedded to) marriage institutions and are based instead on nonexogamous moieties. In these "complex" systems the dualistic principle is not in serious ontological doubt even though it may not be fully cognized by the actors. For one thing, speaking of the par-

277

ticular system to be described here, its workings exhibit both virtuosity and semiotic productivity in the direct structuring of social domains as diverse as ritual and ceremonial action, subsistence, settlement choice, conventional political rivalry, economic exchange, and supratotemic configurations; it also invades the psychocultural provinces of myth and personal identity. More definitively, this principle shows its autonomy by working upon itself: propelled by its own logic, the dual organization may undergo involutional refinements in which moieties are created within moieties. This is centrality of a different kind, one borne not by the dual organization's narrow investment in marriage exchange, but by the freewheeling, seemingly inexhaustible tendency of its governing principle to transfigure nearly everything it touches in sociocultural life.

This essay deals with certain social and cognitive aspects of a complex dual organization found in the East Sepik region of Papua New Guinea. In view of my purpose, which is to examine the overdetermined character of this system, it is worth noting how my interest in the subject came about, for I did not originally intend to study a dual organization system. Although societies in the area were known to possess these social forms, I assumed in advance that this aspect of the setting would not directly affect my main research question, which was how a particular Plains Arapesh village — Ilahita — had managed to achieve and maintain a population size which, at 1,500 persons, was extraordinarily large by Papua New Guinea standards.[1] Various suggestions had been offered as to why settlements in this general area typically failed to grow beyond about 300 inhabitants, the favored one being that the informalities of the so-called Big Man complex were incapable of integrating polities of more than a few hundred persons. Accordingly, I predicted that Ilahita's phenomenal size rested on unusual development of political institutions, perhaps along the lines of an incipient chieftainship or of some other centralizing tendency.

To my surprise and initial consternation, political leadership in Ilahita proved to be, if anything, radically diffuse; power relations appeared bewilderingly haphazard, albeit considerable authority was concentrated among the ritual elders of the men's cult, the Tambaran. Closer study, however, showed that this diffuseness was intricately patterned by the

1. Fieldwork in Ilahita village was conducted in three visits totaling twenty-one months during the period 1969–72. Major funding was provided by the Research School of Pacific Studies and the Australian National University, with a supplementary grant-in-aid from the Wenner-Gren Foundation for Anthropological Research. The author is grateful for their generous support. For their wisdom and unfailing collegiality, greatest thanks go to Professors David Maybury-Lewis, Uri Almagor, and the other members of the Jerusalem conference on which this volume is based. The diagrammatic materials included in this essay first appeared in the author's volume *The Ilahita Arapesh: Dimensions of Unity* (1976) and are reproduced here with the permission of the University of California Press.

village's dual organization, the involutions of which rival in complexity anything known in the ethnographic literature on this subject. On one hand, this organization defines the ritual classes operative in the men's cult, thus giving form to an institution that by virtue of its instrumental, expressive, and doctrinal features is fiercely supportive of village solidarity. On the other hand, the dual organization is the principal framework for intravillage competition and dispute. Just as the village's component descent and residence groups comprise the natural segmentary units, and therefore describe in their arrangement the cleavages along which the community is most vulnerable, the cross-cutting of these units by an elaborate system of dualistic oppositions and alliances deprives them of their autonomy and welds them into a structured, higher-order unity which is the village itself. Tensions that might escalate into serious disaffections or violence are, so to speak, co-opted by the dual organization and are enlisted into the *conventional* rivalries prescribed within the organization. Thus domesticated, these energies reaffirm and strengthen that which, in their wild state, they would tear apart. The key, then, to Ilahita's phenomenal growth and internal adaptation is to be found in the dynamics of the dual organization.

These eufunctional effects of the Ilahita dual organization, however convincingly they might be demonstrated, give only partial insight into the meanings and motivations that comprise its efficient causes. Beyond being a physical entity, the village is, to be sure, a reified concept, and its continued solidarity is valued for both practical and mystical reasons. And yet it is unlikely that any Arapesh could even describe the entire dual organization, let alone credit it as the genius of village integration. This leads to the major problem of this essay, which is to understand how the dual principle of classification regularly conjoins with moments of social action to *re*create, in a manner not calculated by the actors, the dual organization, the village, and, in a sense, the villagers themselves. My argument is that the Arapesh are more than hapless heirs to their form of social organization, they are also motivated by a sense of moral and aesthetic appropriateness to apply a dualistic construction to their affairs. Whether or not this motivational element fully explains the almost obsessional zeal with which the Arapesh bifurcate their social universe, I feel safe in saying that it must not be ignored in any adequate account of complex dual organization, social action, and cultural meaning among these people.

I shall begin by sketching the structures of the Ilahita dual organization and their implications for social action. Much of the information is abridged or excerpted from lengthier accounts published elsewhere (Tuzin 1976, 1980), but this repetition is necessary as a groundwork for the rather different sort of question I am asking of the material in the present context.

The Ilahita Dual Organization

The Ilahita Arapesh are a dialect group of approximately 5,000 speakers who inhabit seven large, sedentary villages, of which Ilahita itself is by far the most populous. Subsistence is based on varieties of yam, taro, and other garden products, supplemented by sago and, to a much lesser extent, wild plants and animals. Local endogamy is favored—in Ilahita itself, over 93 percent of extant marriages were contracted within the village—and sister exchange is the preferred (and, until recently, exclusive) arrangement, with deferral options and liberal adoption practices helping to make this possible on a regular basis. Although the dual organization does not govern marriage selection, there is considerable internal and comparative evidence that this was a functional saliency at some former time and that the relatively late shift from a dispersed to a nucleated settlement pattern, and the novel integrative needs that arose therefrom, was accompanied by a shift from an elementary to a more complex marriage pattern. Specifically, the forerunner of today's nonsystematic sister-exchange preference was, according to my reconstruction, a system of prescribed bilateral cross-cousin marriage, with or without formally constituted, exogamous moieties (Tuzin 1976). Since bilateral cross-cousin marriage is nothing more than a lineally projected repetition of sister-exchange transactions, such a shift could have been accomplished by the imposition of a simple, though structurally far-reaching rule prohibiting marriage between the descendants of a sister-exchange union. This prohibition is extant and supposedly remains in effect for six descending generations, which, in fact, places its expiration time well beyond the depth of normal genealogical reckoning among the Arapesh.[2]

---

2. In an interesting parallel case involving the Marind-anim of southwestern New Guinea, Van Baal (1966:38) writes, "Among the coastal communities absence of moiety-exogamy detracts from the importance of moiety dualism, although the moieties still have a function in religious thought and ritual." A comparison with the inland communities, in which the dual organization operates in marriage exchange, leads the author to conclude that the coastal forms have decayed in response to acculturative influences. Without disputing Van Baal's reading of the Marind-anim evidence, my interpretation of similar changes among the Ilahita Arapesh yields the opposite conclusion, namely, that the shedding of marriage-control functions represents a fully indigenous, evolutionary response by the dual organizations to the integrative demands of a radically expanding village population. Far from weakening the dual organization this change, so to speak, liberated the dual principle of classification, thereby fostering its expansion into many different areas of sociocultural life. What appears certain in the Arapesh case, is that the shift from exogamous to agamous moieties followed as a structural entailment of the shift from "elementary" to "complex" marriage forms; hence my use of Lévi-Strauss's vocabulary (1949) to designate the types of dual organization that are potentially associated and harmonic with these respective marriage arrangements.

For present purposes, then, we are justified in regarding the *village* as the social universe in which the dual organization flourishes. Seen from the air, Ilahita is a spider-like array of eighty-three residential hamlets strung out along the flattened tops of a series of converging ridges. Each hamlet is named and consists of the dwelling and yam-storage houses of one or two patrilines. These hamlets are in turn grouped into a number of named, residentially discrete and socially integrated wards, which are the largest subunits of village settlement structure. Minimally, a village contains two such wards, in which case they are isomorphic in name and membership with the village moieties. In addition to this residential basis, moieties are seen to comprise discrete sets of totemic patriclans; indeed, the moieties are themselves (supra)totemic, at least to the extent that each is identified with a particular bird emblem.

Originally, Ilahita possessed four wards, grouped two by two as the Laongol and Bandangel moieties. During the last eighty to one hundred years, however, war refugees from elsewhere in the region added two new wards to the village: Ilifalemb ward was populated en masse by an entire refugee village which, because it was socially and ritually self-sufficient, was permitted to retain semiautonomy from the host village; Nangup ward began as a sort of refugee camp sheltering small bands from various shattered settlements. Their assimilation to the main village involved a bit of social engineering that illustrates the reflexive workings of the dual organization. In conjunction with the establishment of the ward, descent-group fragments were pieced together into newly proclaimed patriclans. But rather than add the new ward to one or other of the village moieties, it was split into two sociologically constituted halves — one recruited to the Laongol moiety, the other to the Bandangel moiety. This solution was adopted, first, to preserve the symmetry of the preexisting dual organization, and, second, to effect what was correctly foreseen to be the most rapid and thorough integration of the newcomers into the social affairs of the host village. Consequently — and leaving aside the semiautonomous ward of Ilifalemb — the moieties of Ilahita each comprise two and one-half wards.

The moieties described are mutually integrated in complex ways by the structures and activities associated with two lower-level, mutually cross-cutting dual divisions, and parties to which I have termed "submoieties" and "initiation classes," respectively. Each ward is divided into two sub-moieties, with resident patriclans belonging to one or the other, ideally in equal numbers, but sometimes temporarily imbalanced owing to the vicissitudes of clan segmentation and extinction. Although residentially segregated, the submoieties converge on the jointly owned, central ceremonial plaza, which is the scene of nearly all collective activities involving the ward. The submoiety fulfills an important ritual function — providing wild pork for cult feasts — through controlling its own heirloom pig magic and a forest hunting reserve in which "its" pigs abide in purported readiness to be netted when needed. In other ritual contexts, the submoieties are characterized as "male" and "female," respectively. Finally, each submoiety is individually named, often adopting the name of its most important clan, in addition to which *all* submoieties of the village subscribe to a generic, dualistic terminology that is indicative of their relative precedence in cult activities. Thus, all submoieties are either Afa'afa'w ("those who go first") or Ondondof ("those who come behind"). Because of this generic, cross-cutting feature, the village submoieties are as inclusive as the moieties within which they nestle.

Initiation classes are more finely localized within the patriclans. All clans are divided, always and only, into two subclans. As hereditary initiation partners, subclans and their agnatically related members, both collectively and individually, trade back and forth the ritual patrimony they share. Subclans are also the exogamous units of this society, and there is highly suggestive evidence that in former times they bilaterally exchanged women as well as cultic favors. Be this as it may, complementary subclans are termed Sahopwas ("line of the older brothers") and Owapas ("line of the younger brothers"). The implied genealogical hierarchy is not to be taken literally; rather, it is a metaphor signifying that the group called Sahopwas currently holds senior place in the cycle of cult initiations (Tuzin 1980). At the next turn in the cycle, marked by the entry of Owapwas novices into the penultimate grade of the cult, the names and associated prerogatives reverse themselves between partner subclans. The form of reciprocity, then, is that of an alternating asymmetry, which in the minds of the actors amounts to a dynamic, creative equilibrium; that is to say, in contrast with the structural staleness of symmetrical dualism, the asymmetry of these initiation classes achieves conceptual equilibrium while always keeping the Maussian gift prominently at issue. This gift, around which so many social activities revolve, consists of the multitude of ritul, economic, and political debts that are incurred and repaid at each turn in the initiation cycle.

Just as the dualism of submoieties operates at both ward and village levels, so the dualism inherent in subclan relations is projected onto the village level. This occurs because, both in a formal ritual sense and in the way ritual prerogatives carry over into everyday social action, *all* Sahopwas see themselves as united in important ways against *all* Owapwas, and vice versa. And yet, from the standpoint of village integration, this opposition is benignly comprised: first, by the solidarity enjoined upon complementary subclans by virtue of their corporate estate; second, by the

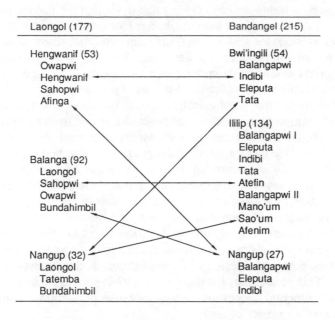

Fig. 1. Scheme of Ilahita dual organization

competing commitments resulting from membership in a submoiety; and third, by the pulls of neighborliness and common cause — not to mention extensive kinship obligations — which are the main vectors of social life within the ward.

In sum, the Ilahita dual organization is predicated on three perfectly cross-cutting dual divisions, localized at village, ward, and clan levels, respectively (see fig. 1). With an integrative genius worthy of Cleisthenes, the system virtually insures that no major social unit (moiety, ward, submoiety, or clan) can be so united in all (or even very many) matters as to become estranged from the village. Add to this the fact that this system developed under conditions of chronic and intense regional warfare, and we can begin to appreciate how important the dual organization was and is to Ilahita's durability as a large village.

Before turning to some specific instances of the dual organization's involvement in social action, I should mention that the principle of dual classification by no means exhausts itself in the three divisions just described. Finer discriminations in cult standing are signified by each initiation class being divided into "Junior" and "Senior" subclasses roughly corresponding to adjacent adult generations. Subclasses are in turn subdivided into age-sets—Balangaisi and Owangufwisi—which refer to the older and younger halves in a line of (real) siblings. Moreover, both of these dual divisions (subclasses and age-sets) are generically represented at the village level, in the manner just described. Finally, at the structural and metaphorical ground of the entire system we have the kin-type dyad Sahaloman and Owaloman, "older brother" and "younger brother."

With impressive mechanical precision, the dual organization computes the unique place of each male over the age of five (when he enters the lowest grade of the cult) in the social universe of the village.[3] The system's six-tiered calibration virtually guarantees that no two individuals will share an identical constellation of social ties and obligations. For this reason we may say that the dual organization is the principal instrument in the creation of Arapesh personhood. But however elegantly this system serves the needs of social and cognitive integration, however attractive would be a purely functionalist explanation of its existence, I will later suggest that its persistence also bespeaks the actors' aesthetic, emotional, and indeed moral fascination with the workings of the dualistic principle, as such. This means that the dual organization should be analyzed both as an instrumental agency and as an expressive projection—a subject of Person and an object of Self.

Dual Organization and Social Action

As described, the dual organization is a systematic, idiomatic rendition of all descent, residence, and ritual relations in the village. Since these relations also constitute the prime differentiae of everyday life in Ilahita, it follows that any understanding of the organic character of the dual organization requires, as flesh to bones, attention to social action. Indeed, so attuned is the dual organization to the precise points of social cleavage, one is moved to regard it as a mechanism of internal adaptation by means of which the village social system counteracted its own divisive tendencies. At any rate, the subject of Ilahita dual organization and social action is immense (Tuzin 1976, 1980) and the best that I can achieve here is to characterize it by means of illustrative vignettes. The first involves a case of political advancement and succession.

1. To maintain honor and self-esteem a man must regularly fulfill his exchange obligations and contribute his fair share to the massive feasts held under the auspices of the dual organization. This requires an ability to produce gardening and hunting surpluses over and above his domestic

---

3. See Tuzin (1980:177–80) for a striking instance of this computation involving the placement of spirit portraits inside the men's cult house.

needs. Most men pursue their careers in stride, and if occasionally a bit of bad luck forces them to seek help from agnates, no one particularly notices. Chronic underperformance, however, causes a man to be despised and to lose his voice in the formal debates and harangues that highlight the great feast events. Other men are ambitious and diligent (and usually polygynous) enough to excel in the production of food surpluses. They are the ones to whom needy agnates and other kin turn for assistance; they are also the Big Men of the village, the ones whose voices prevail in discussions of public interest.

The opportunity for extraordinary renown arises when an untimely death creates a vacancy in the system of initiation-class exchange. Although close agnates of the deceased usually come forward to assume his immediate and future partnership obligations, if they are unable or unwilling to do so the way opens for someone else to claim the rights and duties of the dead man's ritual estate. Little incentive exists for nonagnatic members of his own initiation class to do this, since the ritual welfare of the deceased's exchange partner(s) is of minor concern to them. Rather, it is an ambitious someone from the opposite initiation class (but from a clan other than that of the deceased and his partner) who steps forward to assume the highly prestigious, but highly onerous, "middle position." Thenceforward, or for as long as he is able to sustain the burden of having to produce double surpluses, he operates the exchange system in both directions at once. In addition to doubling his political weight and leverage, he doubles the amount of ritual and feast goods he *receives,* thus enabling him to stage lavish giveaways and thereby to extend the range of persons who are beholden to him. Few men are able to sustain this pace for more than a few years, and at the time of fieldwork only six held the enviable middle position.

What, then, is the legacy that these men bequeath to their sons? The Arapesh regard it as proverbial that ambitious men sire ambitious sons, and they attribute this to the direct inheritance of the father's blood, which is the alleged repository of the personality. More likely, the proverb's factuality lies in the positive example, the specific advice and coaching, and the various tangible and intangible resources that such a father gives to his sons. The Arapesh also recognize that fraternal rivalry—a common problem in this society—is most acute among the offspring of men who stand "in the middle." This is where the dual organization, as it were, comes to its own rescue, and also to the rescue of an elemental situation fraught with socially mischievous potential. Stated simply, the father invokes the principle of primogeniture in conferring his hereditary ritual estate on his older son, while passing the one he acquired on to his younger son.

Note the effects of this maneuver. First, by arranging for its transmission, the father has secured his claim to the acquired estate. Second, the rivalrous brothers have been removed from direct competition over the patrimonial estate and have been placed in opposite initiation classes. Should any tension persist from, say, deeply rooted psychological sources, this is fully sublimated through the general rivalry that is conventional between initiation classes. Third, because the sons become active in the management of these estates as soon as they reach adulthood, the father's economic burden relaxes while he is still politically active enough to enjoy the fruits of his act. Ideally, in fact, a man moves to acquire a second estate when his sons are entering late adolescence, so as to minimize the length of time during which he must single-handedly discharge the added obligations. Finally, the act amounts to a legal usurping of a ritual estate of another clan, especially if — and this is usually the case — the clan is in political or numerical decline. This great coup easily justifies the minor risk that the younger son (or his lineal issue) will become assimilated to the other clan.

The preceding is only one example of how the dual organization structures and rationalizes political action. The convention of taking the middle position is a mechanism of political advancement, a means by which a man may provide a worthy and ambitious younger son with an estate and political base of his own, and a device for neutralizing elementary tensions, which if left unattended could have inordinately large and adverse effects on village harmony and integration. And yet, from another point of view, all these are merely incidental to the process by which the dual organization repairs itself.

2. The second example illustrates how an individual is able, thanks to the structures of the dual organization, surreptitiously to humiliate a foe in the opposite submoiety, thereby achieving his purpose without being indicted as a troublemaker within the ward. Two background comments are required. First, among the Ilahita Arapesh the institution par excellence for resolving interpersonal conflicts without recourse to physical violence is yam competition (Tuzin 1972). Such contests may occur between groups in the village — moieties, wards, and submoieties — but for now I wish to discuss only competition between individuals. Second, the gross opposition between village moieties is modulated by the fact that *like* submoieties in opposite moieties regard each other as aggressive competitors, whereas *opposite* submoieties in opposite moieties regard each other as allies.

Consider, then, the protracted chain of events shown in figure 2. The diagram shows the relevant parties according to their membership in moiety, submoiety, and initiation-class divisions. The transaction occurs in

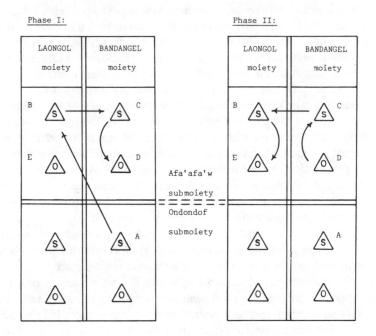

Fig. 2. Yam attack using semimoiety structures

two phases, the offering and the return. In each phase are shown two wards, directly opposed in opposite moieties (Laongol and Bandangel) separated by a vertical double line. The horizontal double line divides both wards into their two submoieties, Afa'afa'w and Ondondof. Within each box formed by the coordinates is contained the initiation-class partnership; that is, the box represents a totemic clan. These are represented as individuals in partnership, with an inscribed "S" and "O" for Sahopwas and Owapwas, respectively.

Suppose that A has a grievance against D who belongs to the opposite submoiety of A's own ward. A waits until he has a fine long yam ready for harvest. He conceals its existence from all save a few close confidants. When it is harvested, A carries it secretly to man B, who is the particular rival of man C. This transfer would have been prearranged between A and B, on the basis of what they recognize as the ritual alliance noted above.

The day after B receives the yam from A, he presents it to C—ostensibly because they are ritual competitors who intermittently exchange long yams. It is presented as though B himself had harvested it, and C has no reason to query this claim. Moreover, C in turn presents the yam to his initiation-class partner D, the man for whom the yam was intended in the first place. Neither C nor D realizes that it is A who is behind it all.

It should be explained that A's strategy depends on his understanding of the particular relationship between C and D. If their relations are currently at an ebb, D may well refuse to accept the yam from C, for he is not obliged to take it. C would then face the difficulty of having to find another Owapwas man who is willing to accept the yam, for it would be extremely humiliating for him (or any other Sahopwas) to eat it himself. My example assumes that the relations are cordial and that D accepts the yam. If the relations were known to be strained, A would have arranged for E to be the middleman, by which means D would receive the yam directly. In this case D, because he was not on good terms with C, would face the possibility of having to eat the yam himself.

The return is made to the Laongol middleman at such time as either C or D produces a comparably sized yam. (It was one of the conditions of D in accepting the yam to eat that he would not be solely responsible for making the return.) This yam is given to B who passes it on to E for consumption. Note that the return yam does not proceed all the way back to A. This is, in effect, out of recognition by B that A provided the means for his scoring a public victory over his ritual enemy at no cost to himself. A's reward is that of enjoying the discomfiture of his personal enemy, savoring the private satisfaction that he was the cause of it.

I could pursue this example further, but enough has been said to illustrate how individuals use the higher levels of the dual organization to attack enemies closer to home. In the process aggressive impulses that would otherwise disturb the peace of the ward, and would for this reason rebound to the instigator's political disadvantage, are directed along lines of *conventional* competition and alliance, thus serving the greater good of village integration without prejudice to ward solidarity. In the process, also, the dual organization prospers and is reaffirmed.

3. Asked why other villages have not expanded the way theirs has, Ilahita men typically emphasize the disruptive effects of sorcery attacks and accusations. Ilahita certainly has its share of sorcery activity, insofar as it subscribes to the idea that all deaths save those of the very young and very old are the handiwork of sorcerers. Indeed, because of its size and correspondingly large number of deaths, Ilahita has a potential sorcery problem of unusual magnitude. But Ilahita also possesses a means — to my knowledge not found elsewhere in the area — whereby sorcery beliefs are mitigated in their antisocial effects. As in my previous examples, this device operates through the dual organization.

The senior spirits of the men's cults, known individually and collectively as Nggwal, supposedly feast on the mystical essences of yams, pigs, and, most delectably, humans. Traditionally the steady stream of enemy dead flowing from battles and human sacrifices satisfied their cannibal appetites. In the early 1950s warfare and human sacrifice were effectively banned by the Australian administration, whereupon, it is said, Nggwal began feeding in earnest on his own people. Thus, today, when an untimely death occurs, especially that of a prominent individual, divination procedures often reveal that Nggwal was implicated in the sorcery deed, either by instigation or by passive approval. The deceased's past actions are reviewed until a religious delict, committed by himself or a family member, is recalled to be the presumptive reason for present misfortune. The actual sorcerer is assumed to be someone in the opposite initiation class, perhaps the deceased's own initiation partner, since it is their duty to monitor and enforce proper ritual conduct among their partners. Because of Nggwal's divined involvement, however, which renders the deed an act of ritually sanctioned punishment, no specific identification is sought, nor is any reprisal allowed. In the end, therefore, the power of sorcery is confirmed and yet palliated in its antisocial effects, the morality and ethics of the men's cult are upheld, the community is warned that religious transgressions will eventually be punished by death, and, withal, the dualistic initiation-class structure is revalidated as a framework for social action.

Many other examples could have been cited to illustrate that the perfection of fit between social action and the dual organization, far from being accidental, indicates that each is an adaptation to the other — two sides of a coin which, it is important to add, is culturally minted. To be sure, the dual organization is a social heritage; Arapesh individuals are socialized to the knowledge of how one lives within and through it. But if this were the full extent of it, then our depiction would be woefully mechanistic, as static as the coin in my jejune metaphor. In my view, each instance of conjunction between the dual organization and social action is also an act of cultural casuistry or, if you prefer, signification; it is the creative application of a codified, yet inexplicit, principle to the problem at hand. And because this principle is deeply implicated in the Arapesh sense of themselves, of their moral and aesthetic intuitions concerning the acts of others in absolute and relative perspective, each successful conjunction is, in addition to all I have said, a satisfying instance of fulfilled identity. If the question of meaning is separable from that of function, as I believe it must be, then this reification of a cultural principle, induced in the context of social action, is where the meaning of the Ilahita dual organization lies.

Identity and the Dual Organization

In contrast with many other societies possessing systems of dual organization, the Ilahita Arapesh have exercised their enthusiasm almost entirely in terms of social rather than cosmological classification. True, they will tell you that the moon is a "man" and the sun is a "woman," but this thought does not go very far beyond its simple statement. The dualistic opposition between (supernatural) "water" and (mortal) "dry land" is symbolically productive (Tuzin 1977), but only in the sense that it helps to integrate a cultural subsystem containing other equally important, non-dualistic ideas. The Arapesh dual organization is therefore not the social embodiment of the cosmos. Rather, as if mocking its own assumptions, the dual organization embodies two psychocultural vectors: *as structure,* it mirrors a cognitive schema that demands the presentation of opposites; *as process,* it satisfies the corresponding emotional demand to have these self-imposed oppositions resolved or transcended. Because, as shown above, the dual organization is quintessentially both structure and process, it simultaneously signifies, acts upon, and reconciles the existential disjunction between living wholes and the mundane, inanimate parts of which they are composed. Again, I am limited by space and time to only a few illustrations of how this principle of mergence or unification independently manifests itself.

1. A crucial predicate of the entire kinship, descent, and naming system is that bones are inherited from one's father, flesh from one's mother. These elements are for naught, however, without the provision of blood, which, as mentioned earlier, is the repository of personality. Flesh and bones are clearly important as spiritual links to one's forebears; they are essential organic constituents. But without the blood-bearing personality, one does not exist as a moral human being. This is shown by the fact that whereas flesh and bone persist for a time after death, blood and personality are transformed almost instantaneously. The immediate corruption of blood corrupts the personality, turning it into a maniacal, homicidal, cannibalistic ghost eager to prey on the very persons who loved it in life.

In sum, while the bones-flesh opposition naturally concords with the fact-of-life observation that males and females interact to make babies, and with the native recognition that the structure of male groups is converted into a process through the agency of wives and mothers, neither of these would obtain without the created, creating individual. Likewise, it is only the workings of blood cum personality that proves this heap of bones and flesh is *alive*—an independent sentient being, a moral self.

2. The men's cult devises a staggering array of illusions designed in various ways to enhance the mystery of its secret knowledge and activities, while conveying to women and uninitiated males a sense of the awesome powers of the senior cult spirits, who supposedly take on material form and interact with the men during their ritual seclusions (Tuzin 1980). Unearthly spirit "voices" produced by secret sound-making devices are the most effective devices, for they directly transmit to naive listeners the mystery they are designed to signify (Tuzin 1984). Flutes, trumpets, panpipes, and whistles impersonate the voices of lesser spirits and their avian companions. The voice of the senior spirit(s), Nggwal, however, is radically different in character and significance. It is produced by an operator who sings mightily into a hollow, open bamboo tube about four meters long and seven centimeters in diameter, the opposite end of which rests in a large hourglass drum. The resulting sound is a remarkable enhancement and distortion of the human voice. When twenty or thirty of these pipes are used in chorus, the collective effect, especially when heard from a distance over the night air, is stunning. I would liken it to a pipe-organ, but this would not do it justice; for combined with the organlike majesty of the sound, there is the subliminally felt presence of a chillingly immense, almost human, voice. According to cult members, this is no impersonation— it literally *is* the voice of Nggwal. And it is magical.

Nggwal's song renews the creative process of all species. This enactment is the central secret of the cult, while the drums and pipes that make it possible are its most closely concealed sacra. And yet, taken separately, these pipes and drums are viewed as simply mundane, everyday objects that no one would bother to hide. Their sacredness, mystery, and creative power emerge from their miraculous *conjunction* of dualistic opposites— dualistic because, as the men themselves remark, the penetration of drum by pipe is an image of coitus. In their merging a higher unity is created, a sentient being which is Nggwal. But as ritual midwives in this blessed event, the men know very well that the metaphysics of Nggwal is a projection of the metaphysics of their own selves: when pressed to declare the truth behind the layered illusions of Nggwal, one sophisticated informant replied with a smile, "Nggwal is what men do."

3. My final example is taken from the realm of submoiety flute music, which embodies a minor version of the creational theme just described. The music is performed by an ensemble of four flutes called, in order of increasing length, *balanga, mbol uwali, mbol ahili,* and *mamana. Balanga*

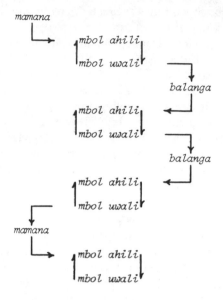

Fig. 3. The structure of submoiety flute music

has the meaning "head" or, in this context, "leader" or "starter"; non-musically, this term refers to the father of a family. The *mbol* ("pig") flutes are paired and are of slightly different lengths. The adjectives *uwali* and *ahili* are difficult to translate, but together they generally convey the sense of "this and that." The meaning and etymology of *mamana* are not known precisely, but informants speculate that it is related to the term for "mother," *mama'wen.* As shown in figure 3, a low rumbling trill from the mamana signals that the song is about to begin. Then enter the paired mbol, who exchange the song rapidly back and forth between them, establishing the refrain. The song actually begins when the balanga flute breaks into the refrain and carries the tune alone. As the flutist tires, the refrain reenters until the balanga takes command again with renewed vigor. This continues through several sequences until the mamana reappears to signal the approaching conclusion, which is carried by the mbol pair.

    The structure of the music consists of alternating paired phrases of opposed pitch and intensity. The soft background quality of the mamana contrasts with the stridently assertive balanga, and between them is the high-low, back-and-forth exchange of the refrain couplet. The effect on hearing is of complementary opposition repeatedly transcended at a higher, more insistent level. In the light of the general sexual symbolism of the proprietor submoieties, and of the familistic flute names, it appears that we are once again dealing with a symbolic enactment of the creative process. The fruit of balanga-mamana interaction is the paired flutes of the refrain, suggesting, with their different pitches, children of opposite sexes.[4] As the Arapesh put it, these are "our children of the forest"—the pigs upon which ritual action (and therefore, as they understand it, cultural existence) depends, the pigs whose welfare and abundance are the responsibility of the submoieties.

The preceding examples illustrate an important theme in Arapesh metaphysics, namely, that the successful conjunction of complementary opposites is a creational event, the magic of which brings forth a unity that is not reducible to its parts considered separately. The event is equally aesthetic in nature, for it is the objectification of feeling (Langer 1953); specifically, it is the virtual and inherently satisfying resolution of division. Whether or not the divisions of mind and society are prior and inevitable—a difficult philosophical problem—it seems beyond reasonable doubt that the *habits* of mind and society are such as to contrive divisions in order to achieve their preconceived transcendence (cf. Seeger 1979:392). Just as the composer contrives tuneful contrasts in order to pursue his preconceived, symphonic object, so the Arapesh contrive dual divisions in order to pursue their preconceived ideal of harmony within and between self and society. Insofar as the destinies of self and society are mutual, resolutions occurring in the one evoke sympathetic response in the other. At the risk of becoming baroque, I propose that the Arapesh scheme posits a *double* dual organization: an elementary one constitutive of the Self, and a complex one constitutive of Society, the two of which are finally united by the operating principle they share.

This returns us to the elementary-complex distinction postulated at the beginning of this essay. It is no mere coincidence that the dualisms embodied in corporeality, ritual, and music are centered on the image of sexual congress. The conjunction of sexual opposites is, after all, the prototypic creational act, involving what is perhaps the only dual division that is fully natural and uncontrived. As a form both elementary and elemental, it is the model of and for all created unities. Moreover, this generalization applies without modification to the *complex* dual organization of Arapesh society; for, despite the absence of moiety exogamy and

---

4. The theme of alternately sexed siblings appears at important junctures in myths that recount the origins of culture and of humanity itself; see, for example, Tuzin (1980:1–8, 206–7, 332–34). The narrative contribution of this theme is to establish the conditions for brother-sister incest, an image of intensely creational significance for the Arapesh, and one that is symbolically implicated in the institution of sister-exchange marriage.

its direct embodiment of sexual complementarity, the dynamics of Arapesh social organization prospers from the power of the elementary image, not by drawing on the latter's substance, but by adopting its organizing principle.

Conclusion

The Ilahita dual organization is an adaptation of truly excellent integrative power and finesse. Comparing it with the simpler versions found in smaller Arapesh villages, one can discern rather clearly the involutional character of its historical development. As the population expanded beyond the limits of a workable kinship network, the primordial moieties swelled and spawned internal dual divisions to which were delegated certain specific social functions previously discharged by the moieties. Further growth generated further subdivisions, progressively removing the moieties from the domain of social action, until today they exist almost purely as a meta-organization, the sole purpose of which seems to be that of holding the working parts of the system together. As I have tried to show, the workings of these internal structures are virtually identical to the structures and processes of social action.

Although Ilahita's success as a large and stable village must be credited to its dual organization, it would require an excess of structuralist-functionalist zeal to conclude that this integrative office is where the meaning of the system resides, if by "meaning" we refer not merely to the logical properties of the system, but rather to the significance that the dual organization holds for the cultural actors who live it. As a complex *structure,* the dual organization has no emic significance whatever, for the Arapesh are not aware of its existence. They recognize *parts,* its dualistic subdivisions, because these are directly implicated in social action; but they do not trouble to conceive that the parts fit together as a total system.

To identify meaning, then, we must examine the workings of the system in and through social action, which is the locus of recognition, understanding, and manipulation on the part of the actors themselves. Thus, the finely geared nature of the dual organization serves to rationalize nearly any conflict as an instance of a standard dual opposition, thereby implying equally standard procedures for its resolution. To the actors the satisfaction gained is that of seeing this structured opposition deployed and transcended for the sake of achieving a new or renewed social harmony. But harmony is merely unity in a dynamic form, and it would be truer to Arapesh perceptions of the matter to say that the workings of the dual organization create and recreate an image of the unified self raised to a social power. At the same time, these workings confer satisfactions of a deeper, psychocultural order. These appeal to a moral and aesthetic predisposition to view the world, including the separable parts of one's body, as a presentation of contrarieties—oppositions which, through a benign alchemy known only to humans, can be merged to create a transcendant unity, a dynamic harmony, an identified self. By its workings the dual organization aligns social reality with inner experience. This is why and where it holds meaning for the Arapesh.

REFERENCES

Bateson, Gregory. 1936. *Naven: The culture of the Iatmul people of New Guinea as revealed through a study of the "naven" ceremonial.* London: Cambridge University Press.

Epstein, A. L. 1969. *Matupit: Land, politics, and change among the Tolai of New Britain.* Canberra: Australian National University Press.

Gell, Alfred. 1975. *Metamorphosis of the cassowaries: Umeda society, language and ritual.* London: Athlone Press.

Hau'ofa, Epeli. 1971. Mekeo chieftainship. *Journal of the Polynesian Society* 80 (2): 152–69.

Hogbin, Ian. 1970. *The island of menstruating men: Religion in Wogeo, New Guinea.* Scranton, Pa.: Chandler.

Kaberry, Phyllis M. 1941. The Abelam tribe, Sepik District, New Guinea: A preliminary report. *Oceania* 11 (3): 233–58, (4): 345–67.

Langer, Susanne K. 1953. *Feeling and form.* New York: Scribner's.

Lévi-Strauss, Claude. 1949. *Les structures élémentaires de la parenté.* Paris: Presses universitaires de France.

Maher, R. F. 1967. From cannibal raid to Copra Kompani. *Ethnology* 6:309–31.

Mead, Margaret. 1947. The Mountain Arapesh: Socio-economic life. American Museum of Natural History: *Anthropological Papers* 40 (3): 163–232.

O'Brien, Denise. 1969. Marriage among the Konda Valley Dani. In *Pigs, pearlshells, and women: Marriage in the New Guinea highlands,* ed. R. M. Glass and M. J. Meggitt, 198–234. Englewood Cliffs, N.J.: Prentice-Hall.

Powdermaker, Hortense. 1933. *Life in Lesu: The study of a Melanesian society in New Ireland.* London: Williams and Norgate.

Seeger, Anthony. 1979. What can we learn when they sing? Vocal genres of the Suyá Indians of central Brazil. *Ethnomusicology* 23:373–94.

Serpenti, L. M. 1956. *Cultivators in the swamps.* Assen: Van Gorcum.

Thurnwald, Richard. 1916. Banaro society: Social organization and kinship system of a tribe in the interior of New Guinea. *Memoirs of the American Anthropological Association* 3:253–391.

Tuzin, Donald F. 1972. Yam symbolism in the Sepik: An interpretative account. *Southwestern Journal of Anthropology* 28:230–54.

———. 1976. *The Ilahita Arapesh: Dimensions of unity.* Berkeley and Los Angeles: University of California Press.

————. 1977. Reflections of being in Arapesh water symbolism. *Ethos* 5:195–223.

————. 1980. *The voice of the Tambaran: Truth and illusion in Ilahita Arapesh religion.* Berkeley and Los Angeles: University of California Press.

————. 1984. Miraculous voices: The auditory experience of numinous objects. *Current Anthropology* 25:579–89.

Van Baal, Jan. 1966. *Dema: Description and analysis of Marind-anim culture (south New Guinea).* The Hague: Martinus Nijhoff.

Williams, F. E. 1936. *Papuans of the Trans-Fly.* Oxford: Clarendon Press.

Chapter 13

The Maasai Double Helix
and the Theory of Dilemmas

Paul Spencer

Among those anthropologists who have invoked the theory of games, Fredrik Barth went further than most in his analysis of dual organization among the Pathan.[1] His concern was with constant-sum or "zero-sum" games, and he clearly implied that if dual organization among the Pathan is grounded in the calculated transactions of political life, then this may be true of dual organization elsewhere. The present essay is concerned with a more recent elaboration of the theory of games such that the gains of the winners do not necessarily tally with the losses of the losers. In fact, the theory of variable-sum, or "nonzero-sum" games is not really about any·popular analogy between politics and games. It looks beyond the jostle for power and touches on the inherent contradictions and paradoxes of social life noted by such writers as Machiavelli, Hobbes, Marx, and Durkheim. It is really a rather basic, even stark, theory of dilemmas. Dual age organization among the Maasai provides an opportunity to explore this theory in an ethnographic setting.

Two Models of Maasai Age Organization

Among the Maasai-speaking peoples of East Africa, there are two models of age organization, each concerned with a different type of dualism. The first, proposed by Gulliver (1963) in his study of the Arusha, is more applicable to the southern Maasai and concerns an opposition between two broadly equivalent halves. The second, elaborated in my own study of the Samburu, relates to the most northern group of Maasai and concerns the

---

1. See Barth 1959; Bailey 1969: chap. 8; Southwold 1969:28–29; Bateson 1949, 1960; Goffman 1961, 1969; and Lévi-Strauss 1963:297–98.

opposition between an older half and a younger half. Following an earlier reappraisal of these two models (Spencer 1976), my fieldwork among the Maasai proper has revealed a totally unexpected but logical gradation from south to north in these two types of dualism.[2]

In Gulliver's analysis of the Arusha, each age-set of men spans about fifteen years. As the men mature, they are in effect jostling their forerunners for power and are jostled in turn by their successors, in much the way the first form in a school chivvies the second form, and so on. This rivalry between adjacent age-sets encourages an alliance between alternates: age-sets A and C are both potential rivals of age-set B and hence are natural allies, just as B is a natural ally of D. This is expressed as a firestick alliance, in which the members of the senior age-set of each pair are patrons, who initially kindle a fire to bring the junior age-set to life: A kindled a fire for C and is his firestick patron, as B is for D, and so on. These firestick alliances are linked together to form two opposed age moieties, (A + C + E + ...) versus (B + D + F + ...), which progress in perpetuity.

Over time, there is a natural oscillation of moral advantage between the two age moieties. When members of age-set A are in their fifties, they combine experience with the capacity to assert themselves politically. They can claim to be the ruling elders, coupling this with their role as firestick patrons and allies of the age-set C men, who are in the prime of their twenties and can claim to occupy the traditional role of warriors or ruling "moran." In due course both groups will be outclassed by their younger rivals. The moral advantage will then shift to the other age moiety, with age-set B emerging as the ruling age-set of elders and age-set D as the ruling moran. This leads to an aperiodic cycle of about thirty years (two times fifteen) during which political advantage shifts from one age moiety to the other and back again, with no more than two age-sets active in either moiety at any time.

Superimposed on this natural swing of advantage is a degree of opportunism, especially at those points in the cycle when there is a fine balance between the two age moieties; for a time, astuteness can tip the balance either way. Inevitably elders of age-set A men lose their vitality, but if they can cope with the attempts of age-set B to discredit them prematurely, then B for a time will be denied some of the prestige they might otherwise claim, and A will have scored a moral victory. The ideal for A is to stave off retirement and then bow to the inevitability of aging at a time of their own choosing and not under duress. This is linked to a corresponding struggle between age-sets C and D as rivals in moran-

---

2. My fieldwork among the Samburu was undertaken in 1957–60 (Spencer 1965), and among the Maasai in 1976–77 with support from the Social Science Research Council and the School of Oriental and African Studies, London.

hood, in which there is a stronger element of physical coercion, but a similar process. Inevitably, age-set C steps down as ruling moran at some point, but then returns to the arena fifteen years (half a cycle) later and contends for the most prominent position in elderhood. In Gulliver's model, ceremonies marking each promotion merely celebrate what has already taken place in the political arena.

It is useful to look beyond the Arusha to their powerful neighbors, the Kisonko Maasai, for it is they who are the true originators of the Arusha system; they not only give the ceremonial cue for each promotion, but they also pursue the system more rigorously. In Kisonko, as age-sets succeed one another, the procession of ceremonies in the two age moieties must keep in step. Hence it is not just that ceremonies validate the status quo, as Gulliver suggests, but that they also preempt the next political reality and have a wider significance. Figure 1 is an approximation of Gulliver's model of the Arusha age moiety system, but it is deliberately slanted toward Kisonko practice. It may be viewed in two ways. First, one can follow around the spiral from boyhood to old age, which shows at a glance why the age-sets are spaced about fifteen years apart: three age-sets, covering forty-five years, are the active span of a man's life, typically from about the age of twenty to sixty-five years. Each male is in the ruling age moiety for two-thirds of this time, first in the prime of his youth and then in the prime of his elderhood. In between he is in a period of latent elderhood, adjusting to the transition as he builds up his family and herd.

The second approach is to view the diagram synchronically along the broken line. This indicates the position of the age-sets within the two moieties at a single point in time, with preeminence among both moran and elders wholly weighted in favor of one age moiety. The situation will be exactly reversed fifteen years later, when the diameter has rotated clockwise through 180 degrees.

The Samburu, or northern, model is also contained within this diagram, but here the binary opposition lies within the ruling age moiety: between the moran and their firestick patrons. Instead of being natural allies of the moran, as in the Arusha-Kisonko model, these elders are their patrons in an altogether more forbidding sense, on behalf of society at large; the moran are regarded as ungovernable juniors. This is not an aberration, but the product of their pastoral economy, which favors a much higher degree of polygyny than exists among the agricultural Arusha. Young men typically remain bachelors until the age of thirty, while power, in terms of possession of wives, cattle, and ultimate authority, lies wholly with the elders. This regime is administered by their firestick patrons, diverting potential strain from the family: generally relations are cordial between close agnates and tense between the moran and their patrons. The

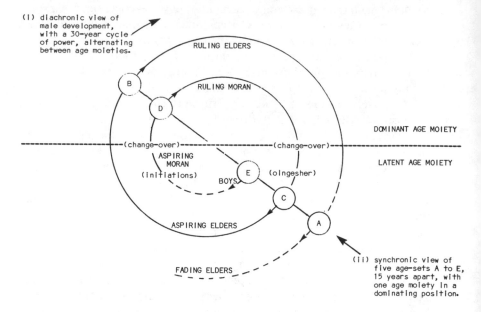

Fig. 1. The Arusha-Kisonko model of alternating power between age moieties

moran undergo a prolonged adolescence; they are suspended between childhood and fully recognized adulthood throughout their twenties. They are relegated to the fringe of Samburu society and associated symbolically with the bush, where they still cling to the glamorous niche that was at one time held by warriors on whom the survival of the group depended, and sport certain flamboyant privileges associated with their status. In this vacuous situation, each successive age-set of moran develops into a delinquent cult, engaging in stock theft, adultery with the wives of elders, and a kind of gang warfare among themselves. The elders have the formal attributes of power, but in truth there is a slight power vacuum lower down the age scale. A degree of delinquency, which has its own popular appeal, is the price the elders pay for maintaining their polygynous regime. Indeed, it is also their pretext, for they can point to the delinquencies of the moran as proof that they are childish and lacking in respect and must be kept in their place. The longer the moran can be kept in this state, the higher the level of polygyny among the elders. And the longer the moran must wait, the greater is their stake in a system that will increasingly favor them as they grow older. In this sense, their prolonged bachelorhood is an investment in elderhood: it is the price they have to pay.

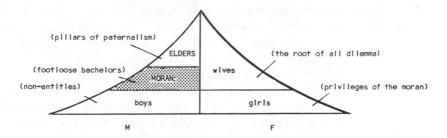

Fig. 2. The samburu model of elders versus moran

This opposition corresponds to two complementary ideologies. To be an elder is to avoid the attributes of moranhood, and to be a moran is to avoid those of elderhood. Each role is defined in opposition to the other. The elders, backed by religious sanction, avoid all physical violence, while the moran tend to get involved in affrays arising from their secular notions of prestige and prowess. The elders are in control of all ceremonial activity, while the moran are ceremonially controlled. The elders are domesticated and respected for their wisdom and authority, while the moran are notorious for their unpredictability. The elders are plain, their heads are shaved, they wear long, indistinctive cloths or blankets wrapped loosely over their shoulders, and they avoid the color red. The moran are colorful, with an elaborate braided hair style that glistens with red ochre, and they wear short, clean cloths — often red — tied tightly around their chests. The elders are married, are self-effacing, and do not dance, while the moran ostensibly avoid married women, are flamboyant, and their dancing is a central feature of ceremonial display. Although the elders are in authority, everyone, even among the elders, dotes on the youthful ideals of moranhood. The oppositions between these sectors of Samburu society are summarized in figure 2.

Clearly, the Samburu and the Arusha-Kisonko models entail quite different types of dual organization. Viewed over time, the binary opposition in the Arusha-Kisonko model is between structurally equivalent moieties composed of age-sets. In the Samburu model, the binary opposition is not between age-sets as such but between age grades associated with the roles and ideologies of youth and age, respectively. In the course of settling down, each age-set of moran transfers to the side of the elders. The two models correspond broadly to Lévi-Strauss's diametric (or better, symmetric) and concentric types of dual organization (1963: 135); as he notes, the two types may correspond, not to different forms of organization, but to different ways of describing one organization. The Arusha-Kisonko age moieties are concentric by turns, for instance, and can only be regarded as symmetrical over a longer period. Conversely, the Samburu moran are not wholly subservient; through their delinquencies, they are in a sense sparring with their patrons and shifting the central arena in their direction, thus providing the elements of a more symmetrical game. This distillation of a more complex reality into basic components lends itself readily to analysis based on the theory of games. But let me stress one point: whether or not the types of dual organization discussed by Lévi-Strauss — or, for that matter, the theories of games — are illusory, dual organization is firmly established in the Maasai age system. These two models form the basis of further discussion.

Asymmetrical Competition and the Cat-and-Mouse Dilemma

Gulliver's analysis of the Arusha system presents a transactional model in which the two age moieties are contending for primacy, especially at a time of changeover. His presentation resembles Barth's earlier analysis of dual organization among the Pathan, and is similarly inspired by pithy principles of political realism. Resorting to the theory of games, Barth (1959) argued that as power shifts from one moiety to the other, there is a dynamic equilibrium brought about by transfers of allegiance by men holding the balance of power. This balance is what game theorists call a saddle point, where the maximum the losers are prepared to concede is also the minimum the winners are prepared to demand or, by analogy, the highest point across a saddle is also the lowest point along its length. Dual organization is thereby explained as a balance that offers greatest incentive to both winners and losers. Each moiety can exercise power for an equal share of the time over the thirty-year cycle, and both would oppose any bandwagon surge of support in either direction that would ultimately eliminate the losers — and the game itself. In the Arusha-Kisonko model, too, the elders are engaged in a game with its own dynamic interplay. There is no transfer of allegiance, because membership is fixed, but moral victories are earned by manipulating the interpretation of any dispute to give one moiety or the other the political initiative. Basically, each age moiety can claim power for about one half of the time, which in Barth's model is an acceptable compromise for both sides. Yet for the aspiring Arusha-Kisonko man it is even better than that, for half of the cycle claimed by his own moiety covers two thirds of his active life span — the prime of youth and the prime of elderhood. Before this period he is fit only to aspire, and afterward he rises above politics. Statistically, by normal gaming standards, the Arusha-Kisonko do rather well.

Beyond this, there are two reservations concerning Barth's approach. The first is that among the Maasai, dual age organization is embedded in rules that antecede any competition; at most, therefore, this organization is only sustained by competition. The second reservation is that Gulliver's examples indicate quite clearly that among the Arusha the principal competition for advantage is between patrilineages over agricultural land; this lies outside the age organization, which in contrast is typified by a reluctance to get involved in confrontation. At most, the competition appears to be a rhetorical one that reflects a concern about power but does not contend for it, except, arguably, at the point of changeover every fifteen years or so (Spencer 1976:160–64). However, it is precisely this period of changeover that I am concerned with here, especially among the Kisonko Maasai, who are not agriculturalists and are not reluctant to defend the interests of their own age moiety.

At the time of changeover both age moieties of the Kisonko, but especially the moran, face a dilemma that well illustrates a particular type of asymmetrical game. To wrest control from their predecessors, a newly initiated age-set must assume for themselves the flamboyant privileges of moranhood; they cannot beg to be given these privileges, for they would be refused. They are still young and few in number, and they are challenging experienced moran, who will beat them if they catch them usurping privileges. No one doubts that the seniors have physical strength, and their supreme privilege is to be the vigilant defenders of their territory. If the aspiring junior moran can outmaneuver them and display their superior vigilance by sporting other forbidden privileges and avoiding a beating, then popular attention switches to their side. The ruling moran are humiliated, and any further defense of their privilege becomes hollow: next time it could be a real enemy on a stock raid that flouts them. In effect, the mouse has come out to play; the cat has botched it.

With this example in mind, we may return to a theoretical framework in which the essentials of each scenario are reduced to a basic dilemma facing the two players or sides. There are four possible outcomes, depending on the combination of their choices. Perhaps this is a travesty of sociological analysis, but let me repeat that this theory, like Lévi-Strauss's treatment of dual organization, seeks to reduce society to some very basic dualist principles, and it is appropriate to consider its possible relevance in this work.

In the game of Cat and Mouse, the four outcomes are ranked 1 to 4, according to preference for each side separately, as shown in figure 3. In their rivalry over the privileges, the most desirable outcome for the older moran (as Cat) is the least desirable outcome for the younger moran (as Mouse). In other words, if their rankings are regarded as penalty points

a

RULING MORAN (cat)	ASPIRING MORAN (mouse)	OUTCOME	PENALTY POINTS (= rank preferences)	
C	M		C	M
maintain vigilance	bid for privileges (unsuccessfully)	C prove strength & humiliate M	1 -	4
relax vigilance	bide their time	M display weakness: moral victory for C	2 -	3
maintain vigilance	bide their time	C seen to be jittery: moral victory for M	3 -	2
relax vigilance	bid for privileges (successfully)	M prove their mettle & humiliate C	4 -	1

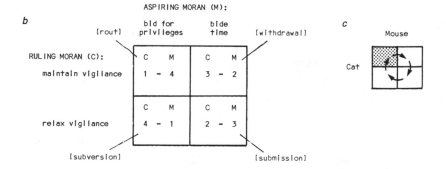

b

ASPIRING MORAN (M):

	[rout]	bid for privileges	bide time	[withdrawal]

RULING MORAN (C):

maintain vigilance

C M	C M
1 - 4	3 - 2

relax vigilance

C M	C M
4 - 1	2 - 3

[subversion]   [submission]

c

Mouse

Cat

Fig. 3. The Cat-and-Mouse dilemma facing ruling and aspiring moran

  a. The choices and their outcomes

  b. Structure of the Cat-and-Mouse dilemma

  c. The Cat-and-Mouse sequence as a tail-chasing exercise with no saddle point

(which amounts to the same thing), the total number of penalty points in each outcome adds up to 5. Expressed in this way, Mouse's gain is Cat's loss, and this is still a constant-sum game.

It may be noted that in this dilemma there is no saddle point, as every income tax inspector must know. If both sides *knew* the choice of their opponents, one of them would choose differently. If the ruling moran knew that the aspiring moran were about to make a bid for the privileges, they would be more vigilant, reducing their penalty from 4 to 1 ($4 \rightarrow 1$); if the aspiring moran knew that the ruling moran were vigilant, they would not make a bid ($4 \rightarrow 2$), and so on. One can trace round figure 3b with a succession of "ifs" in an endless clockwise cycle (fig. 3c).

In real life not all dilemmas are quite as neat, and even this example does not account for every outcome or nuance. But formal games theory is concerned to identify the basic hidden dilemmas that underlie complex situations, and in this instance, at least it is not too bad a fit. The Maasai themselves tend to see the dilemma of the moran in these clear-cut terms, and it is not too dissimilar from the dilemma of the Arusha elders in their attempts to discredit one another in debate, as portrayed by Gulliver. The aspiring elders (junior patrons) are poised to raise the stakes in debate if the ruling elders (senior patrons) have dropped their guard by failing to attend in sufficient numbers $(3 \rightarrow 1)$, and so on.

The limitations of figure 3 become evident when one turns to an equivalent dilemma associated with the Samburu model. In this instance the delinquencies of the moran are pitched against the vigilance of the elders, and to reduce this to a constant-sum game stretches the point. Face to face, the elders must be respected, but when their backs are turned, the moran may be tempted to switch their attention to the wives and cattle of the elders, who find it impossible to maintain a watch on every wife and every cow all the time. The moran will be severely punished if they are caught, but if they are not, they will have cocked a snook at their seniors in addition to indulging their appetites. However, unlike the battle over privileges, the game is covert and has a different meaning for each side. If the moran commit adultery and get away with it, then in their terms (and in their private gossip) they have scored points against the regime imposed on them; but if the elders never even know or suspect, then in *their* terms they have not ostensibly lost. If the moran are caught, then in different senses both sides are losers: a cuckold can never really win. The moran feel that they get away with enough to give the game some spice, while the elders suspect that the moran get away with too much, but they cannot prove it. In other words, the ranking of preferences in figure 3b no longer reflects the scale of penalties for both sides, and thus one is in the realm of variable-sum games, where the gains of one side do not exactly tally with the losses of the other, which is inevitable whenever mice try to gamble with cats. Yet the structure of the dilemma expressed in figure 3c, with no saddle point, remains, and the precise values adopted in figure 3b only add color. The present argument is concerned only with the heuristic structure of these dilemmas and not with absolute values or penalties, which remain for the most part incalculable. The method of ranking shown in figure 3 is retained in later examples purely to illustrate the variations of this structure.

A variable-sum game is sometimes described as a constant-sum game with Providence at a higher level, which affects the nature of competition at a lower level. This is well illustrated in Davenport's study (1960) of

the strategies of Jamaican fishermen, in which he invoked the theory of
games. At the lower level the fishermen were competing with one another
for a better haul and a greater share of the market, but at a higher level
they were in a sense competing with the weather and uncertain ocean cur-
rents, which determined the scale of their profit or loss. In fishing close
to the shore for a safer small catch, or out at sea for a risky larger catch,
they were playing Cat and Mouse with the elements, as it were. One may
object that the elements have no strategies and make no conscious choices.
But from a fisherman's point of view (as a decision-making Mouse) this
makes no difference, and the elements conceal their hand as effectively as
any Cat. In this sort of situation elsewhere, the figure of Providence may
be personified as a kind of Cat: in European folklore, the cowled figure
of Death lurking among the living; or Machiavelli's cruel goddess Fortuna
poised against the wits of men; or, in Africa, the specter of witchcraft.

In the case of the Samburu moran, their frolics are a Cat-and-Mouse
game with Providence rather than with the elders. Or more precisely, in
the elders' definition of the cosmos they identify themselves as the agents
of Providence in determining the destiny of the moran; they swing in their
own favor the penalties of a game that otherwise on the whole favors the
moran. In this Cat-and-Mouse view of Providence, every person has a
guardian spirit who protects him in normal times but who will abandon
him if he is justifiably cursed by someone he should respect. The senior
person's power is that his own guardian spirit responds to his blessing by
extending protection to the junior (who is then doubly protected), or responds to his curse — if he uses it frugally — by bringing disaster. If a moran's
respect for his firestick patron, say, has lapsed, then he is abandoned by
his own spirit and, on being cursed, he is castigated by the patron's spirit.
He is then prone to sudden misfortune, perhaps being struck by lightning
or walking into a rhinoceros. He must make reparations as quickly as possible to obtain a blessing. Figure 4 shows the Samburu perception of the
outcomes in terms of the automatic responses of the two spirits to the ini-
tiatives of their dependents. It can also be viewed in terms of two half
cycles leading from the initial provocation to the subsequent process of
placation (Spencer 1959; 1965:186–87, 272; 1973:113).

The Hobbesian Dilemma and the Game of Chicken

In the previous situation the players are in complementary roles, and the
Cat's dilemma is different from the Mouse's. In further games to be considered here, the players have strictly equivalent roles and face identical
dilemmas with symmetrical outcomes. This lends itself to an extension of
the menagerie of complementary species, but these refer to the nature of

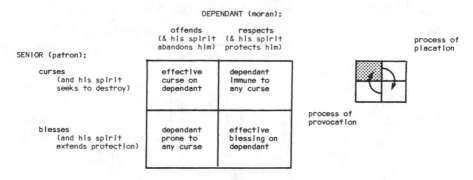

Fig. 4. Providence and the Cat-and-Mouse dilemma in Samburu cosmology

choice within each scenario rather than to the roles themselves. One has Hawks and Doves in situations of confrontation, Bears and Bulls in the stock market, and Foxes and Lions in Pareto's cycle of elites. In interpreting the relevance of the theory of variable-sum games, or dilemmas, I rely on Anatol Rapoport's simplified presentation (Rapoport 1960, 1969; Rapoport and Chammah 1965, 1969), avoiding the more complex mathematical treatment of Luce and Raiffa (1957), which goes well beyond the scope of the present paper. Rapoport considers a wide variety of variable-sum scenarios, but among these are two which, like Cat and Mouse, are strikingly pure examples: the Game of Chicken and the Prisoner's Dilemma. In fact, one is led to infer that within the limitations of this approach, all dilemmas ultimately may be reduced to combinations of these three. They appear to establish the basic dimensions of relevant possibilities (see fig. 9).[3] And as will become evident, because these dilemmas reflect facets of reality, any particular ethnographic encounter may entail more than one game.

The Game of Chicken is a matter of naked confrontation in which at the higher level both contenders are playing Mouse to Providence as Cat. It is the dilemma of two hell-bent motorists confronting one another on the crown of the road. If the nerves of one or the other or both crack at the last moment, then it is simply a constant-sum game: one wins, one

---

3. Altogether thirty-six scenarios of this form are conceivable. However, the Game of Chicken and the Prisoner's Dilemma are the only symmetrical possibilities that pose genuine dilemmas. Other nontrivial possibilities can be viewed as a combination of one of these two (with two saddle points or with one ambivalent point, respectively) and the game of Cat and Mouse (asymmetrical and with no saddle point). Beyond this, an infinite variety of penalties may be considered, which color the scenarios but do not affect the three basic structures.

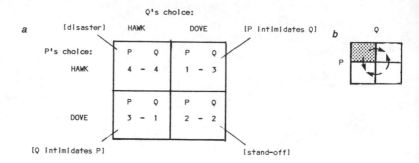

Fig. 5. The Game of Chicken
  a. The structure of the dilemma (DOVE = Chicken)
  b. The sequence of Chicken with two saddle points. Intimidation either by P
or Q tends toward domination.

loses, or they both draw. This again is shown as a simple matrix in figure
5, with the rankings (or penalties) of these benign outcomes adding up
to the constant sum of 4 (1 + 3, 2 + 2, 3 + 1). But if neither swerves,
then Providence claims its due from the mangled heap. This is a paradigm
of the dilemma facing Hawks and Doves, and it is the horrendous possibility of a double miscalculation that gives the game its character. Providence's deathly grin looms over the striving of the players. In the fourth
outcome the penalty for *both* sides is maximum: 4 + 4 = 8. And in the
event of a true disaster the penalty would of course be of a different order,
even assuming that one can assess the value the players place on their own
lives.

    If recovery from disaster is possible, then the game may be viewed
as a sequence of rounds with further encounters. It could build up to a
runaway feud until one side cracks. Once that occurs, intimidation by one
side over the other is a saddle point in the game: if in one round P in-
timidates Q (fig. 5, top right), then in the next round P has no incentive
to become a Dove (1→2), and knowing this, Q has no incentive to become
a Hawk, which would lead to disaster (3→4). Thus the relationship stabilizes
on this outcome, with P dominating Q. Instead of the stable situation of
near equality suggested by Barth, one has a stable situation of inequality.

    Reverting again to the period of changeover in the Arusha-Kisonko
model, the Game of Chicken summarizes another aspect of the competition between ruling and aspiring moran. It acknowledges the possibility
that in this competition more may be at stake than a constant-sum tussle
for the possession of the privileges of moranhood, and that as time wears

on and the aspiring moran grow in strength, the probability of a vicious clash increases. Popular accounts of infighting among the Maasai (and especially the Kisonko) concern precisely this brittle situation. Here the elders act in unison to prevent direct confrontation, regardless of their own age moiety loyalties. In effect the vulnerable extremity of the Arusha-Kisonko model is contained by switching to the Samburu model in which the elders assert their gerontocratic power. As I noted earlier, in different contexts both models apply to the Maasai, just as a variety of games apply to these models.

So long as the ruling moran are clearly superior to the aspiring moran, they play a mild game of Cat and Mouse. Aspiring moran sport the privileges in secret and run away at the approach of any ruling moran. The more cocky they become, the more vigilant their seniors, and the more vigilant their seniors, the more wary the juniors. The elders seek to intervene before the game takes a sinister turn as the juniors gain in strength and confidence. The firestick patrons of the ruling moran in particular point out to them that this may be their last opportunity to retire with grace and in full command. Once a feud builds up with their rivals, the immediate outcome for the seniors may be victory, but ultimately as they age there can only be defeat: "These are privileges of 'children'" they point out, "and they are not worth a single human life," which is simply another way of pointing out, as they become equal in strength, that the relatively benign game of Cat and Mouse can build up to a vicious game of Chicken. The scenario switches to the Samburu model, and the ruling moran save face by bowing to pressure from their firestick patrons.

Because moran are obliged to respect elders, the Samburu model does not readily lend itself to this dilemma between contending equals. In any confrontation, the elders always intimidate the moran. However, the dilemma does have its niche in their ideology. The firestick patrons' power to intimidate resides in their curse. And faced with this threat, the moran should always show respect and placate their patrons in whatever way is demanded in return for their blessing. In practice, there is always an ultimate display of respect, and a blessing is never withheld. In theory, there is always the ultimate threat: to break a firestick. If the patrons were to do this in a fit of pique, it is maintained that the whole age-set of moran would die out. Even worse, a vital link in the chain of alternate age-sets would be severed, and the age moiety itself would die out permanently. When the patrons explain this awesome possibility to their firestick wards, they suggest that in exasperation they might invoke the ultimate response to a total breakdown of respect from the moran, matching Hawk with Hawk and facing the prospect of annihilation. It is held up as a possibility so shocking as to be unimaginable, and yet clearly it has its place in the collective imagination, coloring the intimidation imposed by the elders.

The Game of Chicken is none other than the Hobbesian dilemma of the passions that drive men to a war of all against all. By contrast, Barth's scenario, by equally logical steps, reduces conflict to just two balanced coalitions. Turning from the constant-sum model to a variable-sum model leads to the possibility of a runaway situation and the elimination of either side, or both. In elaborating Barth's argument, Bailey (1969:29) dismissed this possibility abruptly, arguing that "no political structure can permit destruction to be carried beyond fairly narrow limits." Yet as Hobbes noted, order (and hence well-intentioned political structures) cannot be taken for granted. Bailey's principle did not save the powerful Laikipiak or Logolala from annihilation in their civil wars with the Maasai, and the ethnographic literature is replete with instances of conflict in which whole regions have been torn apart and devastated by feuds, leaving a state of chaos (for example, Bateson 1936:192; Haimendorf 1967:67). This leads one to look beyond the context of the game itself to the mechanism maintaining the rules, rather as Hobbes tried to do, in order to appreciate the existence of order and the limits of gaming, beyond which society is no longer a mere game.

Confidence and the Prisoner's Dilemma

The Prisoner's Dilemma entails a significant modification of the basic rules of the Game of Chicken, shifting the worst outcome for either player to domination by the other; the rankings in figure 5 are then modified as shown in figure 6. This leads to a radical transformation of the dilemma.

In this scenario, P and Q are prisoners who have been separated for questioning on complicity in some crime. For convenience the penalties (ranking) of each outcome may be expressed as years of imprisonment. In isolation, each prisoner has to consider how far he can trust the other, which partly hinges on how far he can assume that he is himself trusted. If P and Q trust one another and reject their inquisitor's advice to confess, then they have a reasonable chance of a shorter sentence on some lesser charge (say, two years each). But if P can trust Q to remain loyal, then he may be tempted by the promise of leniency to confess, forcing Q to serve the maximum sentence (say, four years against his own remission to just one year). But if Q suspects that P will be tempted in this way, then his best course is to confess also, to obtain at least a nominal remission of one year: they will both then serve three years. It is evident from figure 6 that the best joint outcome is achieved only by both parties having total trust in one another and rejecting personal advantage (2 + 2). The worst joint outcome is when they share a self-seeking mistrust of one another

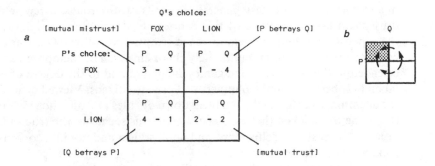

Fig. 6. The Prisoner's Dilemma
  a. The structure of the dilemma
  b. The sequence of the Prisoner's Dilemma with one saddle point. Betrayal either by P or Q precipitates mutual mistrust.

(3 + 3). The remaining two outcomes spell the best outcome for one player and the worst for the other (1 + 4). Here one may borrow from Pareto the characteristics of Lions, those who are prepared to show trust and to abide by the rules, and Foxes, those who have no trust and exploit the loyalty of Lions for their own ends.

If the essence of the Game of Chicken is raw nerve, then in the Prisoner's Dilemma it is trust. Each has to ask himself: "What would I do if I were him asking myself: 'What will he do?'" Or more simply, "How far do we trust one another?" The inquisitor plays the role of Providence, bent on sowing mistrust and securing the maximum penalty. The dilemma is raised above the psychological reasoning of transaction analysis. It is a paradigm of the robustness of social institutions: those who belong to them either trust in the readiness of others to subscribe to the rules, or they lack this trust.

As with the Game of Chicken, one can modify the nuance of the dilemma by varying the punishments associated with each outcome or by playing a sequence of experimental games in succession to explore the process whereby trust between players can be built up or destroyed (Rapaport and Chammah 1965). Confidence hinges on each one's perception of the other, and between them they build up or destroy the spirit of an alliance. So long as trust prevails, individuals sacrifice their immediate interest to the greater good (2 + 2), but if one sector is self-seeking at the expense of others, then general mistrust and discord become rife, there is no incentive for the individual to rebuild trust, and mistrust prevails (3 + 3). Reverting to the Chicken metaphor of the use and abuse of the highway code in a society where courtesy generally prevails on the roads, a few selfish drivers can take advantage of this courtesy to dominate the highway at the expense of others. Others are then tempted to follow. The spirit of courtesy breaks down, and ultimately chaos ensues. The metaphor can be extended to the spirit in which games are played and to the degree of collaboration between public planners and private citizens. Viewed cynically, the dilemma leads logically to a breakdown of rules and an ethos in which the Game of Chicken thrives. According to this scenario, the true saddle point lies in mistrust, selfishness, and hooliganism and not in a consensus to keep conventions intact.

In this respect, the Prisoner's Dilemma is also the games theorists' dilemma, Hobbes's dilemma, and the bane of all planners. It seems to lead inevitably toward anarchy. The Hegelian-Marxist resolution of the dilemma is that the self-destruction of one social formation (game) bears the seeds of its successor with a new set of dilemmas in a dialectic process of social evolution. Here, Pareto's less radical insight (1963:1515–16), which assumed revolutions without evolution, is easier to handle. In his analysis of cycles of elites in European history, the end point of the dilemma was not a melee of Foxes. As he saw it, when the Foxes subverted society beyond a certain point, the Lions would rouse themselves and reestablish confidence in the basic institutions of society. At first sight this may be regarded simply as the Lions playing Cat to the Foxes' Mouse in a continuous cycle, as in figure 3c: when the Lions were vigilant, the Foxes bided their time; then when the Lions dropped their guard, the Foxes usurped power, provoking the Lions to reemerge, vigilant once more. However, this would misconstrue the dilemma, just as it would miss the charm of a Tom and Jerry cartoon. The Prisoner's Dilemma is not between a party of Foxes and a party of Lions, but between the choice for each player of being a Fox or being a Lion. Similarly, the Pareto cycle does not concern an alternation of moieties, but the development of an ethos that shifts support from one form of government to another. Lions and Foxes are strategies and not players. The emergence of the Foxes in this cycle indicates an inherent institutional weakness, and the reemergence of the Lions suggests a hidden strength. This is more than Bailey's "political" structures that oppose destruction beyond narrow limits. Political intrigue leads down the slippery slope toward mistrust, whereas the flight back to mutual trust has to be seen more as a religious act of faith. The scenario of the prisoners in figure 6, with much to lose and little to gain, leads to an interpretation that slides from trust to mistrust. For the reverse process one needs a different scenario where the players have nothing to lose and everything to gain by showing trust. The matrix in figure 7a, for instance, could apply to a rebel faced with the possibility of joining an uprising that seeks to upgrade social existence from gloom and despair to hope in a new future, if only a widespread confidence in this change can be generated. The rebel has to place his destiny where his ideals lie. Instead of an act of betrayal ($2 \rightarrow 1$), an act of faith is required ($3 \rightarrow 4$) in the hope that others will respond ($1 \rightarrow 2$). In other words, the dilemma has to be approached from the opposite end. Whether the saddle point is mistrust or trust depends entirely on the ideological premise of the player (or the analyst): both premises can be self-fulfilling. Seen from one angle, this is the Prisoner's Dilemma; seen from another, it is also the Rebel's Dilemma. The whole cycle, as Leach (1964:xi) noted, has two opposed and alternating ideologies, rather as the cycle in figure 4 has two complementary halves.

This argument has a direct relevance for Barth's analysis of Pathan dual organization, where opportunism hardly generates trust. His model leads step by step and quite logically to a precarious balance between two volatile coalitions of opposed factions (Barth 1959:17–18). And yet, he notes, the balance is surprisingly stable and peaceful. This leads him to acknowledge the dilemmas and constraints in which a succcessful leader finds himself obliged to make major concessions to his principal rivals in order to retain their compliance in the status quo (trust). What he assumes to be a constant-sum analysis becomes more powerful by inadvertently straying into variable-sum theory. At this point, the volatile balance between factions becomes a dual organization.

The dual organization of the Arusha-Kisonko model provides its own symbolic imagery of Foxes and Lions in relation to age loyalties. The very high expectations that express the warm and selfless fellowship within an age-set reflect the Paretovian Lion. Between adjacent age-sets (of opposite moieties), on the other hand, there is a Foxlike mistrust. Indeed, the sorcerer is the Maasai image of a Fox: nefarious, incomprehensible, antisocial, and the antithesis of all that is desirable in an elder and especially in a member of one's own age-set. Moran have a clean image in this respect: they resort openly to the spear and not to an invidious spell. The archetype of the sorcerer is a perverted elder of the other age moiety. When members of either age moiety—moran and patrons—perform one of their rituals, the details of the performance are kept secret, and members of the other age moiety are firmly excluded from the village. The possibility that one of their number is a sorcerer lurking somewhere in the bush colors the ritual drama. This mistrust comes to a head at the time of changeover (which is clearly all things to all games); in Kisonko, especially, the ruling and the aspiring elders suspect one another of sorcery at this time and may even move to separate villages and avoid taking food together. Only when the younger men are clearly masters of the situation and the older men have lost the will to persist can the changeover be said

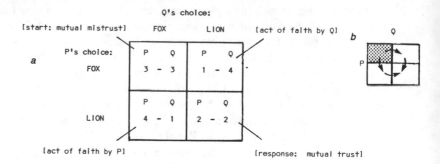

Fig. 7. The Rebel's Dilemma
  a. The structure of the dilemma
  b. The sequence of the Rebel's Dilemma with an alternative saddle point and
a longer-term payoff.

to have taken place, and then a measure of accommodation between age
moieties is possible. The younger men claim the attributes of power, and
the older men tend to become less involved in community affairs.

The process in the Samburu model of separating boys from their
families at circumcision and reincorporating them fifteen years later
as elders is an extended rite of passage that can also be viewed as a
Pareto cycle. Initially, at circumcision, the adjustment of the age system is overdue, and there is general good will toward the new moran,
whose reputation is still untarnished. This does not last, however, for
as they feel their strength and their new freedom, they aspire to the
prestige of warriorhood, daring one another and indulging in Games
of Chicken among themselves and of Cat and Mouse with the elders.
In this way, a reputation for irresponsibility builds up on one side and
a tally of grievances on the other, as the elders lose control. The moran
in their vacuous situation have litte incentive to mend their ways, and
the elders have a pretext to delay the promotion of the moran, under-
pinning their gerontocratic regime and prolonging the mistrust between
them. If the elders as Cats are vigilant and as Hawks are showing their
talons, then as Foxes they are playing for time. Playing for time is playing for wives and ensuring a higher degree of polygyny. Delay is of the
essence.

The return of the moran and the elders to a state of trust is achieved
through a steady process of accommodation. Inevitably, the moran have
to be accepted as elders, just as they have to accept the inevitability of
their own elderhood. In their first flush of moranhood, they had neither

reputation nor a real stake in the system. With the passing of years, they acquire both, and having consummated their moranhood, they have nothing further to look forward to except elderhood. The game that led them along the path toward mistrust loses it impetus, especially when a new age-set of moran is initiated and captures popular appeal. To emphasize their own superiority, the senior moran have little alternative other than to behave with a new maturity. The first to marry and become an elder should be their ritual leader, who is regarded with awe and associated with the destiny of his age-set and the danger of misfortune. It is a vivid expression of the Rebel's Dilemma facing the moran at this time. The first Lion to be exposed in a world of Foxes is supremely at risk. Following his lead, other senior moran cultivate the trust of older men, marry, and cross over to elderhood.

Age Cycles and Catastrophe Theory

The theory of variable-sum games takes the argument a stage beyond constant-sum games by examining some more fundamental dilemmas, but it too has its limitations. It assumes that the nature and ultimate outcome of each game are shaped by its context, overlooking the extent to which critical outcomes in turn can modify the context and resolve the dilemma by changing the game, a point discussed by Bailey (1969:186ff.). Logically, the next step is some model that incorporates this further dimension; this is provided by catastrophe theory (Isnard and Zeeman 1976). While this theory lies beyond the scope of the present exercise, it is at least possible to indicate how the Pareto cycle can be replicated as a "single-cusp catastrophe." In figure 8 the folded surface represents the shifting equilibrium (the saddle point) in a three-dimensional model, with the fold representing ambiguity. As the cycle progresses, there are in theory two (saddle) points of equilibrium—the upper and the lower surface. At the edge of the fold, ambiguity ceases, with a "catastrophic" switch to the other surface. In figure 8a, the cycle for the Arusha-Kisonko model starts from the arrowhead in the unfolded area, where the situation is relatively unambiguous and the moran and elders of the latent moiety are still too inexperienced to challenge their seniors: there is no discrepancy between status and age. However, the increasing discrepancy in age, as the seniors mellow and their rivals mature, builds up pressure for change and increases their mutual mistrust (shown vertically in the diagram). One then enters the ambiguity of the folded area and a phase of mounting crisis when the Foxes are trapped in a situation that increasingly favors Lions. This is resolved at the fold in a catastrophic switch of power to the other age moiety. With the changeover, the strains of the age system are eased,

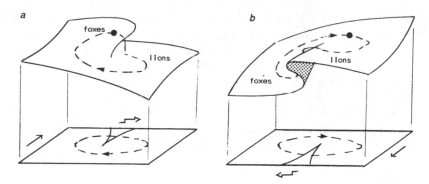

Fig. 8. The Pareto cycle as a "catastrophic loop" (after Zeeman 1974). Each folded "equilibrium surface" is shown projected onto a base to indicate the cyclical process that builds up to maximum ambiguity at each fold: *straight arrow* = increasing discrepancy between social and physical age; *bent arrow* = increasing pressure for change; *black circle* = point of changeover in age-set cycle.
   a. The Arusha-Kisonko model as a Pareto cycle
   b. The Samburu model as an inverted Pareto cycle

ambiguity is removed, and increasingly the new ruling moiety assumes its new role. For the remainder of the cycle, with the ambiguity removed, a sense of order prevails.

Figure 8b entails a transformation of the cycle to portray the Samburu model, with a refolded equilibrium surface. Some time after a new age-set of moran has established itself, there is a catastrophic lapse into mistrust. Or perhaps it would be more accurate to show this as a cascade of lapses (a series of smaller folds) as relations between elders and moran plunge toward a Fox-ridden impasse following each deviation by the moran and heavy response from their patrons. Matters remain thus until the age discrepancy of boys and moran builds up pressures toward new initiations. From this point the older moran are trapped in a Rebel's Dilemma, and the stage is now set for a slow buildup of trust, from Foxes to Lions.

Conclusion: Complementary Models and the North-South Dualism

Any attempt to apply theory to ethnographic data is necessarily reductionist and the victim of its own limitations. And a theory that attempts to reduce society and its processes to the games people play can be tantalizing (see Barth 1959; Rapaport 1960; Bailey 1969), or daunting (see Neumann and Morgenstern 1947; Luce and Raiffa 1957), or merely trite (modesty forbids). There are clear parallels of rules, strategies, and so on, matching the variety of social life with the variety of scenarios suggested by different types of games. The relevance of such a theory for the present work is that dual organizations, like games, reduce social life to two complementary sides; but because there is choice, the stability of each side cannot be taken for granted, especially when there is competition between the two.

The present essay has taken up the argument in relation to an elaboration of the theory that is concerned with dilemmas at a higher level and the problem of stability. At this level the players are together in the same collapsible boat contending with Providence, and their problem is founded in the basic dilemmas of social existence. The logic of the theory reduces the dilemmas of interacting pairs to three (or four) basic forms, each associated with a vivid and extreme scenario in which the players have roles that are larger than life. These are brought into a composite framework in figure 9. In Weberian terms, they are ideal types, removed from empirical reality; and yet, like some ritual dramas, they reflect the uncompromising essence of that reality in the face of Providence. Indeed, in the examples considered here, the stereotypes of the players and even the specter of Providence are symbolic figures in Maasai ritual dramas that play on the inescapable dilemmas of certain transitions in social life.

This essay has considered two different types of dual age organization. The Arusha-Kisonko model in the south is concerned with a cyclical process in which opposed groups alternate between the central arena and the periphery as their members mature. The Samburu model in the north is concerned with the dialectics of the opposition between elders and moran, who have contrasting life styles. In the Maasai-speaking area there is a gradation of these models from north to south that survived the transition to modern times. To account for this stability, one is led to search for some interplay between the two models. At first sight they are incompatible: for in the southern model, moiety rivalries bring moran and their patron elders into close alliance, while in the northern Samburu model, the problems of gerontocratic control bring them into indirect confrontation. Thus where one model is applicable, the other, almost by definition, is not. However, they are complementary in that the most critical points of each model occur at quite different phases of the age cycle. The rivalry between age moieties becomes most acute at times of changeover, while the strain within the ruling moiety becomes most acute during the long delay between changeovers. Or to express this slightly differently, both models apply to all Maasai, but at different periods of their lives: mistrust switches from a general concern over the problems of moranhood during the peak of their reign to relations between the age moieties during the period of

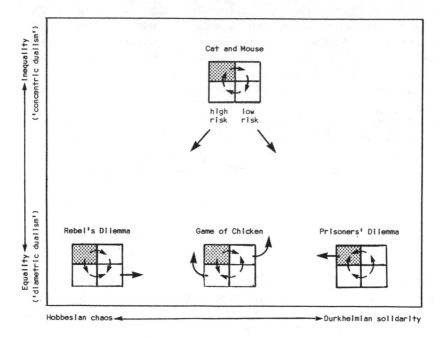

Fig 9. The four dilemmas in an eternal triangle

changeover. The solution to the Hobbesian dilemma, therefore, appears to be that the game itself switches between arenas. What might appear to be an impasse of mistrust at one stage is transformed as the scenario changes. Because the two models cut across one another, when one model is bedeviled by the Prisoner's Dilemma and the buildup of mistrust, the stage is set in the other for a renewed spirit of compromise, resolving any Rebel's Dilemmas as trust is reconstituted.

More than this, these complementary aspects of the system are themselves organized as a duality that unites the Maasai as a people, as the ceremonial focus associated with each model switches between north and south. Among the Kisonko in the south, the changeover ceremony, *olngesher*, is the principal festival on behalf of all Maasai, heralding the changeover of power between age moieties. In the north the cue for other Maasai occurs when a new age-set of future moran is brought to life by the firestick patrons in Keekonyukie kindling their first ceremonial fire. This reveals a dialectic process between the two models and between north and south, switching from one arena to the other in a Paretovian double helix. Maasai of other tribal sections are keenly aware that these events take place at opposite ends of their region and at different phases of the age cycle. These are the only two events that orient all Maasai in time and space, making them keenly aware that they are a single people and synchronizing their local age systems. The prescribed sequence of the elaborate ceremonial cycle provides a vivid collective representation of the Maasai age system. At any one time popular gossip reflects an awareness of the current position for all Maasai and of each next step locally. Insofar as the analogy of an evolving game has some validity, it is this collective awareness that acts as umpire — almost providence itself — serving as a commentary on the state of play and dwarfing the manipulations of individuals and even of age-sets in their prime.

For the individual players there is no repetitive cycle, but a series of transient games. As a Maasai matures, he experiences each of the roles associated with these games and emerges in old age on the side of Providence. By the time his age-set loses the will to battle on, his wisdom is that he has seen it as a participant from every angle. He can reflect on the games younger men play and on the relevance to these games of the ceremonies that middle-aged men control, and he can reflect on the changing configuration of their age organization. Once he reaches old age, he does not get any older.

REFERENCES

Bailey, F. G. 1969. *Strategems and spoils: A social anthropology of politics.* Oxford: Blackwell.

Barth, F. 1959. Segmentary opposition and the theory of games. *Journal of the Royal Anthropological Institute* 89:5–21.

Bateson, G. 1936. *Naven.* Cambridge: Cambridge University Press.

———. 1949. Bali: The value system of a steady state. In Bateson 1973:80–100.

———. 1960. The group dynamics of schizophrenia. In Bateson 1973:199–214.

———. 1973. *Steps to an ecology of mind.* St. Alban's: Paladin.

Buchler, I. R., and H. G. Nutini:, eds. 1969. *Game theory in the behavioral sciences.* Pittsburgh: Pittsburgh University Press.

Davenport, W. 1960. Jamaican fishing: A game theory analysis. In *Papers on Caribbean anthropology*, 3–11. New Haven: Yale University Publications in Anthropology, no. 59.

Goffman, E. 1961. *Encounters: Two studies in the sociology of interaction.* Indianapolis, Ind.: Bobbs-Merrill.

———. 1969. *Strategic interaction.* Philadelphia, Pa.: University of Pennsylvania Press.

Gulliver, P. H. 1963. *Social control in an African society: A study of the Arusha agricultural Maasai of northern Tanganyika.* London: Routledge and Kegan Paul.

Haimendorf, C. von F. 1967. *Morals and merit*. London: Weidenfeld and Nicolson.

Isnard, C. A., and E. C. Zeeman. 1976. Some models from catastrophe theory in the social sciences. In *The use of models in the social sciences,* ed. L. Collins, 44–100. London: Tavistock.

Leach, E. R. 1964. *Political systems of Highland Burma: A study of Kachin social structure.* Reprint. London: Athlone.

Lévi-Strauss, C. 1963. *Structural anthropology.* New York: Basic Books.

Luce, R. D., and H. Raiffa. 1957. *Games and decisions.* New York: Wiley.

Neumann, J. von, and O. Morgenstern. 1944. *Theory of games and economic behavior.* Princeton: Princeton University Press.

Pareto, V. 1963. *The mind and society.* Ed. A. Livingston. New York: Dover.

Rapoport, A. 1960. *Fights, games, and debates.* Ann Arbor: University of Michigan Press.

———. 1969. Games as tools of psychological research. In Buchler and Nutini 1969:127–50.

Rapoport, A., and A. M. Chammah. 1965. *Prisoner's Dilemma: A study in conflict and cooperation.* Ann Arbor: University of Michigan Press.

———. 1969. The Game of Chicken. In Buchler and Nutini 1969:151–77.

Southwold, M. 1969. A games model of African tribal politics. In Buchler and Nutini 1969:23–43.

Spencer, P. 1959. Dynamics of Samburu religion. Paper presented at the East African Institute of Social Research, Makerere.

———. 1965. *The Samburu: A study of gerontocracy in a nomadic tribe.* London: Routledge and Kegan Paul.

———. 1973. *Nomads in alliance: Symbiosis and growth among the Rendille and Samburu of Kenya.* London: Oxford University Press.

———. 1976. Opposing streams and the gerontocratic ladder: Two models of age organization in East Africa. *Man,* n.s. 11:153–75.

Zeeman, E. C. 1974. On the unstable behavior of stock exchanges. *Journal of Mathematical Economy* 1:39–49.

Chapter 14

Obligations to the Source: Complementarity and Hierarchy in an Eastern Indonesian Society

Elizabeth G. Traube

This essay is about the social construction and preservation of the past in an eastern Indonesian society. It is intended both as an ethnographic analysis of an ideology of exchange and as a contribution to the sociology of knowledge. Linking these two concerns is the question of how dual categories may be socially realized as hierarchical relationships.

The Mambai of East Timor conceive of their society in narrative terms, as a transformation of an earlier state of unity and wholeness. Ritual exchange obligations project the narrativized past onto the present in the form of a primordial whole that both opposes and includes its parts. The past lives on in the present as a hierarchical relationship between the protagonists in exchange relationships.

Mambai epistemology is also based on a distinction between whole and part. Knowledge that refers only to existing conditions is defined as partial and incomplete and is opposed to an encompassing form of knowledge that comprehends the present as the outcome of temporal processes. The Mambai express this distinction in a botanic idiom. Full knowledge of becoming is represented as the union between a tree's fixed trunk and its branching tip, whereas knowledge confined to present states of being is rootless and unanchored, a mere tip or part of a greater totality. Process appears in this idiom as the condition of intelligibility of structure, which is itself conceived of as the processual unfolding of a unified scheme.

Nor is it only society that is defined in narrative terms. An uncompromising insistence on narrative coherence is an essential feature of Mambai discourse, and the coming into being of society is subsumed under a single, encompassing world-plot that has its trunk in cosmogonic processes. Hence the primordial events of cosmic creation are the ultimate

321

condition of intelligibility of society, the source of an authoritative form
of knowledge, uniquely empowered to interpret ongoing social life.

Cosmogonic knowledge is sacralized, in the Durkheimian sense of
the term. It is protected by interdicts that regulate its acquisition and
transmission and set it apart from profane or partial understandings of
the world. Collectively regarded as the distinctive possession of a certain
category of persons, the trunk story of creation is radically restricted in
its circulation. It is withdrawn not only from everyday discourse, but from
ritual discourse as well, yet it intervenes ubiquitously and forcefully in
Mambai life, in the form of an absent presence or untold remainder, as
a perpetually deferred promise of plentitude. The sacralization of knowledge poses an intriguing problem in the analysis of myth, which I take
up in the second half of this essay. The analytical task is not simply to
account for the production of a structured narrative, but also, and more
importantly, to elucidate the discursive processes that give rise to a culturally meaningful absence.[1]

The Whole in the Part: Dualism, Exchange, and Hierarchy

Since van Wouden's pioneering study [1935], eastern Indonesian peoples
have been associated in the anthropological literature with a pervasive or
ubiquitous principle of complementary dualism. The Mambai are no exception. Their collective representations attest to an abiding cultural concern with complementarity. Whether at the level of society or of the encompassing cosmos, order is insistently defined as the product of a balance
of opposites, and a scheme of interrelated dual categories (such as male-
female, inside-outside, trunk-tip, above-below) is brought to bear in con-
stituting meaningful relationships. Yet Mambai society bears as little re-
semblance to classic models of dual organization as do other societies in
this area (see Fox, in this volume). There is no one all-embracing institution such as a moiety system, but rather a proliferation of particular dual
structures that regulate diverse realms of social life.

The basic social unit in Mambai society is a descent group known
as a "house" (*fada*). Houses unite and interact with one another in a variety of ritual contexts, and dual categories are used to define these ritual-
ized relationships. Each individual house group is responsible for the life
cycle rites of its members and is represented on such occasions as a divided
and balanced world, modeled on the ideal complementarity of male and

---

1. I have borrowed the phrase "meaningful absence" from Michael Silverstein's essay
(1984) on the linguistic bases of avoidance behavior.

female. Certain houses claim relations to one another through their male founders and cooperate in the performance of the annual agricultural cult. These ritually enacted interhouse ties are expressed by a set of interconnected dual categories, including trunk and tip, elder and younger, inside and outside. Houses also maintain enduring affinal alliances which, while requiring a minimum of three lines (an ego-group, its wife-givers, and its wife-takers), are conceived of in dual terms. Oppositions between male and female, brother and sister, parent and child, and trunk and tip are employed in particular alliance contexts to represent the relations of wife-givers to wife-takers. Finally, houses are also the ideal units of larger communities, conceptually modeled on the concentric opposition between center and periphery.[2]

Moreover, while complementarity is an integral cultural feature of all these dual structures, another is categorical asymmetry. Apprehended in their social contexts of use, one element within any given pair of dual categories is marked as superior to its complement, and the differential ranking of complementary categories expresses hierarchical relationships. The principle of asymmetry operates with such regularity that the system is best characterized as one of dual inequality, a dualism of mutually, but asymmetrically, dependent parts.

As the asymmetry of dual categories is context specific, it could be argued that the categories themselves are logically unstable, maintaining inconsistent internal relations with one another. This is, admittedly, one way of comprehending certain observable classificatory phenomena. Consider, for example, the categories of male and female, which are used in the context of affinal exchange relations to differentiate wife-givers and wife-takers. Wife-givers are symbolically male, and they are explicitly superior to their "female" wife-takers. But the gender categories also correspond to the spatial categories of inside and outside, which are used in other social contexts to structure socially inhabited space. Mambai communities, for instance, are conceived of in terms of a fixed and immobile ritual center that is superior to an active periphery. The respective inhabitants of the asymmetrically opposed realms are attributed female and male characteristics, producing a reversal in the value of these categories with respect to the marital alliance context.[3]

The problem with this approach is that it overlooks the temporal character of the dual categories and consequently fails to account for an

2. See Traube 1986 for a full discussion of the house system.

3. In an analysis of similar classificatory schemes amongst the Atoni of western Timor, Schulte Nordholt comments on the discrepancy between diarchic and marital categories. His (in my view unsatisfactory) conclusion is that "a different set of principles must apply in each case" (1971:205).

essential feature of the classificatory scheme. Superiority and inferiority in status are not a function of the content of synchronic relations of categorical opposition and correspondence (male:female::outside:inside . . .), but rather of the diachronic relations that symbolic categories express.[4] Thus the superiority of wife-givers, I would argue, reflects neither their symbolic attribute of maleness nor any combination of homologous categories (male = front = east . . .). It is rather that maleness, in the alliance context, stands for the status of wife-givers as the *original sources* of women.[5] From this temporal perspective, which is that of the Mambai themselves, wife-givers are the encompassing social category that includes both male and female. Similarly, as we shall see in more detail, the inside-female ritual authorities are regarded as the original sources of masculine power-tokens, now possessed by rulers associated with the outside. Inasmuch as there is a contextual permutation of values, its nature may be more precisely defined: in the alliance context, the category of male represents the original whole, whereas in the context of the community, the idea of wholeness can be expressed by the category of female.[6]

The constant operative principle in the two contexts empowers one term in an opposition to represent both that part of a totality that remains after subtractions (defined as male in the case of wife-givers and as female in the case of ritual authorities), and also the original totality that precedes the act of division. Valeri (in this volume) has isolated similar part-whole structures in Moluccan classifications and has emphasized their temporal bases. Through a symbolism that requires careful consideration, the past lives on in the present in the form of an encompassing part that stands for an original whole.[7]

---

4. See Valeri (1982) for an analysis of synchronic and diachronic relationships in the Hawaiian temple system; see also Sahlins (1985). In Polynesia, as in eastern Indonesia, the totality to which structure refers is not a synchronic system of oppositions and correspondences, but is rather the changing relations between cultural categories.

5. The Atoni, like the Mambai, represent wife-givers as the generative sources of life. Schulte Nordholt provides ample documentation of this point. For instance, while the term *atoni amaf*, which refers to wife-givers, has the literal meaning "masculine father," wife-givers are also classed as *bab hanif*, which Schulte Nordholt glosses as "life-giving, life-generating affine" (1971:107).

6. This "inconsistency," if that is the proper term, is effectively muted by the Mambai, who de-emphasize the "maleness" of wife-givers and the "femaleness" of ritual authorities, and represent both categories of persons as "old mothers and old fathers." As Sahlins (1985) remarks of apparent inconsistencies in Polynesian classifications, "if there is a recurrent ambiguity, there must be a consistent, non-contradictory way of stating this. The structure itself is not contradictory, though it repeatedly reproduces such empirical effects."

7. The basic concept of hierarchical encompassment derives, of course, from Dumont (1970) who, however, takes a purely synchronic view of hierarchy. Valeri argues, in contrast, that the inclusion of a contrary, on which hierarchical encompassment is based, demands a diachronic perspective (personal communication).

These differential relations of parts to the conceptual whole reflect a critical feature of dual structures in Mambai society. Dual social structures are not conceived of as primordial divisions, inherent in the nature of things. They are rather conceived of in narrative terms, as the products of actions that shatter earlier states of plenitude, breaking up primordial totalities into complementary but unequal parts. The overall shift from unity to duality is objectified in narrative representations as a process of subtraction and partition. More concretely, narratives tell of ancestral acts of giving and taking that separate persons or objects from their original sources and give rise to lasting obligations between the sundered parts of the whole.

Dual categories bring these processes to bear on ongoing social exchange relations. Opposed as encompassing whole to encompassed part, the protagonists in formal exchange transactions are linked by the past acts that created division, and they come together to commemorate an earlier state of unity. Totality before division, the conceptual basis for the asymmetry of exchange obligations, is socially expressed in reciprocal but unequal transactions between groups ranked as primordial donors and receivers. In social exchange the temporally structured opposition of a whole to its parts is realized as a hierarchical relationship.

Dual classification, exchange, and hierarchy are thus the analytically distinguishable features of socially lived experience. Schemes of dual categories express the temporal character of exchange obligations that unite and hierarchically differentiate social groups, and it is the total social phenomenon that needs comprehension. The analysis that follows takes for its focus a particular pair of categories, one which serves as a cultural paradigm of the opposition between whole and part. Moreover, whereas other categories take on temporal significance in particular contexts, these are intrinsically temporalizing categories. They are used in exchange contexts to project the past onto the present and also to mark off the past as the restricted source of sacred knowledge.

Temporalized Space: The Past in the Present

In both formal and informal speech, the Mambai make extensive use of the botanical categories of *fu* and *lau*. *Fu* is a cognate of a single Austronesian term meaning "trunk," "base," "origin," or "source." It can be used with the sense of "beginning" or "cause." *Lau* signifies "tip," "peak," "crown," or "extremity." It is used in reference to the uppermost or outermost limit of objects that stand fixed in place, and also to represent the culmination of temporal processes, with the sense of "end," "outcome," or "result."

I shall gloss these terms more or less consistently as "trunk" and "tip," thereby preserving a characteristic Mambai emphasis on botanical referents. For Mambai, the relations between fu and lau are exemplified in a tree, which can be conceived of both as a product and as a process of growth. The idea of process is essential, and it would be misleading to treat the temporal senses of the categories as metaphorical extensions of a spatial relationship. Trunks come before the branching tips they support, and the multiple usages of *fu* and *lau* work simultaneously to temporalize space and to spatialize time.

The Mambai use these categories to represent a variety of objects that stand fixed in place, balanced between below and above. In cosmological discourse the vertical axis is associated with Mother Earth and Father Heaven, the primordial beings whose interaction generates and sustains the cosmos. Complementary cosmic dualism is ritually expressed through the image of the world tree, an *axis mundi* located at the center of space, which unites cosmic levels. Rooted firmly in the earth, where the terrestrial female "steadies the trunk," the tree rises straight up to the sky, where the celestial male "secures the tip."

Emphasis is placed in these representations on the upright and erect form of a structure that centers the cosmos at the point where below and above meet. Ritually, this centering and mediating function is assigned to an assortment of sacred objects, including mountains, houses, altars, and posts, all of which are formally addressed in dual terms, as the union between their fixed trunks and erect tips. As center points, where opposed spheres come together, such objects are channels for the concentration and diffusion of cosmic energy, and the Mambai also oppose trunk and tip along a concentric axis that runs from center to periphery. This axis is also embodied in the image of a tree paradigmatically, an immense banyan tree, fixed and erect at its center, and extending outward in all directions. In the full ritual invocation to which I alluded above, Mother Earth and Father Heaven jointly balance the world tree, "so that its tip may stand upright / so that its branches may spread outward."

Whereas the fixed and erect tree, secured at its two extremes by the deities, provides an icon of a static complementary order, the concentric imagery of ramifying branches supported upon a central trunk signifies a dynamic process of differentiation that unfolds over time. This temporally structured relationship between trunk and tip is the basis for multiple, overlapping metaphors of social hierarchy. A trunk, in these metaphors, is the encompassing part that stands for an original whole, and the unity *in* division of groups opposed as trunk to tip evokes the hierarchical ideal of unity *before* division.

Perhaps the most vivid and compelling notions of lost unity are conveyed in the Mambai conception of *fada,* the "house." The term designates both a group and a dwelling, but the socially significant dwelling is not an everyday domicile. The unity of a group is materially embodied in its "cult house" (*fad-lisa*), a named place of worship where ancestral sacra are kept and where house members reunite for ritual purposes. What I shall call the cosmology of the house attributes a single source to the multitude of house-groups into which the Mambai are presently divided. The unity of the source contrasts with the multiplicity of its products, or, as Mambai are prone to say, "the bits of the tip are many, but there is only one trunk."[8]

The cosmological trunk of the house system is composed by what the Mambai call the "Lone House" (*Fad Mesa*), the primordial abode of human-kind, which was built by Father Heaven and Mother Earth to shelter the human offspring of their primordial union. The Lone House is mythically located upon the mountain of origins, at the ultimate center of the cosmos, where the deities first come together. Cosmological narrative describes how the world is both composed and peopled from its center, through a process of concentration and dispersal that begins with the land itself. A "narrow and confined earth," condensed within the mountain, spreads outward toward the four quarters, pressing back the encircling waters of creation to become "wide and broad." A structurally identical narrative transformation organizes accounts of human history. Thus in the beginning there is the Lone House full and intact, closed in upon itself. History is a process of opening up the original house and scattering its contents. The activities of human beings, from the time of origins down to the present, make up a lengthy, winding journey that begins with the dispersal of the first ancestors from the mountain and results in the proliferating houses of the present social order.

If the Lone House stands for the ideal unity of all houses, the concept of an encompassing source is socially realized in local clusters of hierar-chically ordered houses. The constituent houses of such a cluster conceive of themselves as bound by a common past, some part of which is pre-served by each individual house group in narrative accounts of the wander-ings of its male ancestors. As a teller reaches backward in time to narrate the activities of his own house's founder, his tale rejoins those of other houses and becomes a part of a larger story of past unity and the origins of division. The act that creates division in house narratives is the parti-tion of a patrimony between elder and younger brothers. Elder brothers invariably remain inside the ancestral origin house, while younger brothers

---

8. With respect to marital alliance, for instance, an egocentric distinction is drawn between a group's ultimate wife-giving "trunk" or apical wife-givers and a theoretically infi-nite array of "leaf and tip daughters," made up of wife-takers, the wife-takers of wife-takers, and so on.

take up their share of a patrimonial sacra and "go off to the outside" to found new houses. Repeated over generations, the centrifugal movements of younger brothers divide and subdivide houses into what the Mambai represent as a perpetually ramifying array of junior "tip houses," centered around the senior "trunk houses" of common mythical ancestors.

Ancestral narratives provide charters for ritually enacted interhouse relationships. In the ideology of the house system, junior tip houses are ritually dependent upon their acknowledged trunks for fertility and well-being. During the rainy season, the cosmological time of birth, tip houses are expected to bring gifts of agricultural produce and participate in the annual rites held by their trunk houses. The legitimacy of a house's claim to seniority or trunk status is validated in practice by its ability to attract other houses to its seasonal rituals as junior tips. Although I cannot discuss the matter here, the system leaves open the possibility of a tip house converting itself into a trunk by putting itself forward as a ritual center in its own right.[9]

The periodicity of ritual life realizes the mythical sequence of condensation and dispersal as a perpetual alternation. Each year, the house cult of the rainy season reverses the outward flow of men and wealth objects, and brings together what has been separated at the place of origins. The reversal of spatial orientations is equivalent in ritual practices to the acts of filling and closing a container, and periodically restores an abandoned trunk house to its original fullness. Yet it would be inaccurate to interpret this ritually recreated unity as a mythic return to the time of origins. Hierarchical encompassment is not a dissolution or merging of parts into a whole, but is rather a representation of a whole *by* a part, and the encompassing Mambai trunk house stands for a wholeness that remains lost. Processes of change are registered in the very structure of the house rites. Divided in the act that unites them, the hierarchically ranked trunk and tip houses commemorate their original unity, while simultaneously marking the origins of their separation.

Mambai ritual life also unfolds at a higher level of organization, in designated cult sites which lend their names to the communities that unite them. The ideal structure of these communities is founded on relations among houses, and is expressed in a model of peripheral units oriented around a center. The center of each community is constituted by a pair of related origin villages, which stage rites that involve the community as a whole. In structure, then, the community resembles the concentric grouping of tip houses around a trunk, but whereas houses are ranked within

---

9. Viewed from the center, any given house may constitute a tip, whereas the same house viewed from *its* periphery may appear to others as a center.

the local cult in terms of their collateral relations to common ancestors, their status within the wider communal cult reflects the roles attributed to their ancestors in the first establishment of the community.

Like the cosmos and house system, the community is thought to have been composed from its center. Ancestors of the ritual centers are collectively regarded as the original sources of the power of rule, who established their dominion over outlying house groups in the mythical past. Their power, embodied in regalia of office, is said to have been given away to newcomers from outside of the community. Henceforth, according to narrative tradition, the old lords confined themselves to a ritual function. They "sat down to watch over rock and tree," Mambai say, while the outsiders assumed responsibility for the administration of the community.

The mythical act of renunciation thus creates a diarchic division between passive ritual authorities, who retain control over the cosmos, and active executive rulers, who exercise power over human affairs. Moreover, the diarchic relation is expressed in terms that call attention to its temporal, and hence hierarchical structure, for the narrative pattern is condensed in an opposition between the sacred "trunk of rule," retained by ritual authorities, and the worldly "tip of rule," given away to executive rulers. This image of sovereignty divided into a trunk and a tip expresses the differential relations of parts to the whole that make possible the absolute ranking of complementary statuses. As a term in a temporalized structure, ritual authority takes on a double significance of the part that both opposes and includes its complement. It is at once the absence of power, that part of sovereignty which remains after subtractions, and also the encompassing source of power, the totality prior to division.

The formula "absence signifies original presence" elucidates the narrative discourse that is carried on by ritual leaders. In the communal cult centers that I frequented, powerlessness was a ubiquitous theme. From the ongoing flow of discourse there emerged a particular figure, one that I have since encountered in Francillon's account of the Tetum kingdom of Wehali (1980:264).[10] It is the figure of an empty house, a diminished center-source, stripped of the powers that were once accumulated there. "All that

---

10. Wehali was long the sacred center of a realm in central Timor. Its sacral leader, known by the title Nai Bot or Great Lord, dwelt in a village called Laran (Center). Yet a visit to the Great Lord's abode turned up little in the way of sacred regalia of office. Perhaps, Francillon remarks, the lack of interest shown by Dutch administrators in this figure was understandable. Still, the death of the last Great Lord was mourned for over ten years by people from all over the island. And so Francillon continues: "If the man was nothing himself, if his house was merely a flimsy, undecorated, uninhabited structure with nothing inside, then to whom was this homage paid? The nothingness of the Great Lord, the emptiness of the sacred house, the impoverished condition of Laran were sufficient to represent the whole Timorese system, to which the people felt obliged to adhere."

remains here," say the guardians of the centers, "is a rock and a tree." To account for this condition was to explain how it came about. In this respect, speakers would refer to the activities˙of the mythical ancestors as masters of the regalia, collectors and donors of tokens, who alternately accumulated and distributed the signs of sovereign power.

The stressed emptiness of the center is itself a condensed narrative image of the old order's transformation, and thus embodies a claim to the hierarchical status of a source. Ritual centers, like local trunk houses, bring the past into the present by evoking the state of unity before division. Once again, however, this past that lives on in the present bears the traces of history, a history of subtraction and fragmentation, of renunciation and loss. Emptiness evokes a fullness that once was, but is no longer, and, as in the house cult, the past that is commemorated in community-wide rituals is also kept at a distance. On ritual occasions the regalia must be formally presented to their source, "to show respect for rock and tree." They are not, however, handed over to their original masters, but rather are carried throughout the performance by their present possessors. Between the time of origins and the time of outcomes lies an irreversible process of division, and if the dual categories that organize ritual action unite in dividing, so too do they divide in uniting.

My intent in this all too brief and schematic presentation has been to convey something of the sheer repetitiveness and force with which notions of lost plenitude intervene in Mambai social life. The Mambai view their institutions, their society, and the overarching cosmic order, in terms of a protracted process of becoming, and it is this cultural sense of history that needs to be accounted for in any study of Mambai dual organization. As apprehended by participants, the synchronic dualism of social life expresses diachronic relationships, and present social divisions take on hierarchical significance from the imagined unity that antecedes them.

Unlike an abstract past that is merely prior, the past conceived of as a source of origin is never over. Rather, as we have seen, it persists in the present as a dimension of space, embodied in the form of parts that represent original wholes. Nevertheless, this spatialized past-as-source is also past. The pastness of the past is affirmed in the oppositional structure of ritual action and in condensed narrative images of empty centers. Indeed, it would seem that where hierarchy rests upon exchange, as is the case in Mambai society, the pastness of the past is as essential as its ongoing presence. The social significance of the past derives from ancestral acts of giving and taking, prior transactions which initiate asymmetric exchange obligations. Founded on the perpetual character of obligations incurred in the past, social hierarchy requires the periodic reawakening in a collectivity of an idea that something (women, men, tokens) was once irreversibly separated from its source.

Yet hierarchical status is never solely a matter of exchange. In any society it also involves the keeping and accumulating of material or spiritual goods that differentiate their possessors from all others. In Mambai society the essential, hoarded good is a uniquely authoritative form of knowledge that takes the cosmogonic past as its source and referent. My concern in the remainder of this essay is with the past conceived of as a hidden treasure of unspoken words and converted into hierarchical status.

Spatialized Time: The Past as Value

The past that inscribes itself in Mambai social life is narrativized past. That is to say, it is not an assemblage of disconnected prior events, but a stage in the unfolding of a unified plot. The fiction or plot structure that gives narrative coherence to Mambai social life realizes the general narrative scheme of situation-transformation-situation as a movement away from totality.[11] We have already had occasion to remark on the weighting of Mambai thought toward initial situations of unity. Origins resume outcomes, since all the oppositional relations of the present are held to be included within the past. To submit to the socially authoritative plot structure is to experience a particular form of narrative coherence in which the significant relation is between the lived moment and a remote past.

Epistemological consequences also follow. For a consciousness dominated by the idea of origins, knowing consists of telling how what is came to be. Constructed as the culminating permutation of a plot, the present can only be fully understood in the context of what antecedes it. In an important sense, moreover, the Mambai assume temporal processes of becoming to be inscribed in synchronic structures, which bear the marks of their own origins. In any ordered array of co-existing entities, the Mambai see the promise of an untold narrative, one that only awaits a qualified teller to bring it into speech, or, as the Mambai would say, "to relate the walk" of the phenomenon in question.

What I have been calling origin narratives are described by the Mambai as "walks," and the expression is essential. The idea of a journey com-

---

11. In this regard, it is interesting to compare Mambai plot structures with those of the Rotinese (Fox 1980), or with Polynesian schemes analyzed by Sahlins (1981b) and Valeri (1982). Rotinese, Fijian, and Hawaiian myths of kingship seem to follow a supplementary logic of additions and totalization. They unfold not from an original plenitude, but from a primordial lack, which is resolved by an outside ruler who incorporates insiders and passes to the symbolic center of the realm.

prehends both the sequence of past events that is presented in a narrative account of origins and also the very activity of telling. Narrative discourse, as much as the events it relates, is thought of as a trip or journey across space and over time. Tellers endeavor to "follow a path" or "track an ancestor," that is, to retrace verbally the movements of the tale's protagonists.

In speech events that have the transfer of knowledge as their explicit purpose, the Mambai ideal is a perfect temporal correspondence between the two journeys. Events are to be related in precisely the order in which they occurred, without interpolations or anachronies. Mambai are notably intolerant of any perceived temporal disparities between the sequentiality of events and of the telling, or to use the narratological terms, between story and discourse or plot (Chatman 1978). What Mambai call for, with concern and not a little anxiety, is a discourse that is transparent upon the events it relates, a perfect temporal icon of its object. This ideal is invoked at two levels, that of the part and that of the whole.

At the level of the part, a well-formed walk or origin tale must be constructed around the opposition between a departure place and an arrival place. The teller must name the places where the subject of the tale first originated and eventually came to rest, and he must list all the places visited in between the two ends of the journey. Of such a teller, one who perfectly replicates the order of events in the order of the telling, Mambai say that "he speaks directly, from trunk to tip."

Individual origin narratives or walks, however, are not thought of as a collection of disconnected episodes. They are rather regarded as the mutually significant elements of a unified whole, the "walk of all things," and narrative performances are also evaluated in terms of the position of the story events narrated within this encompassing plot. What is at issue here is a teller's command of the relative sequencing of different walks, his ability to distinguish between earlier and later episodes, and to integrate them at the higher level of the whole story. At this level, Mambai concern for the represented sequentiality of events is compellingly expressed. Performances are retrospectively measured with respect to the ideal of an encompassing world-plot which, like its component episodes, progresses "from trunk to tip."

These by now familiar categories divide time itself, the story time of events, into two opposed stages: an earlier trunk-time of ultimate origins, and a later tip-time of outcomes, which endures down to the present. The division is approximately between the primordial events of cosmic creation and subsequent, more mundane occurrences that relate to the organization of human society. Cosmogonic events make up the "walk of the earth," the unique trunk of the world's story. But like the many ancestral paths that branch out from a single origin house, a multiplicity of walks succeed the original cosmogonic sequence. These later events have to do with the busy comings and goings of ancestors, which compose the countless "pieces of the tip" of a unified narrative. Time, literally shaped by events, submits to the pervasive tension between the one and the many.

The events of cosmic creation are the same in principle as those of house formation, following a similar pattern of condensation and dispersal, plenitude and lapse.[12] What seems most to concern the Mambai, however, is not that the same events recur in new versions, but that these events have unequal values within the spatialized model of time. The differential value of past events reflects their place within an order of occurrences, and is expressed in terms of relative distance from a central trunk. Hence the insistence on a narrative that registers events in the exact chronological order of their occurrence, for it is *in this spatiotemporal order* that their significance resides. Pattern or plot is apprehended as an intrinsic property of story sequence. It is neither added to events by discourse, nor is it hidden by the outward appearances of events; rather, it resides *in* their sequential order of unfolding.

This mythical time is not atemporal, but neither is it reducible to mere chronological succession. Rather, it represents a distinctive form of temporality in which the chronological relations of an abstract, linear time, before and after, earlier and later, are themselves apprehended as signifiers of hierarchical relationships. Chronological sequence or succession is modeled on structure, and expresses structure as process.[13]

Earlier time supports and centers later time, and the discourse that faithfully represents the fullness of time has the same asymmetric shape as its object. Telling the past becomes a form of anchored, centered, oriented speech. Narrative discourse that wanders backward and forward (or inward and outward) in time is said to "have no trunk" and it is therefore condemned to roam unanchored across the tip of the story. Hence, Mambai say, unless a teller first "seizes hold of the trunk," and roots his discourse in the original cosmic events of the walk of the earth, he easily becomes lost amid the twisting, tangled branches of the story's tip. To realize the ideal of a single, unified narrative that resumes the past and the present, a teller is obliged to start at the trunk, or as Mambai also say, "his words must make contact with the trunk." Such centered, anchored discourse is contrasted to that which "only makes contact with the tip" as whole story to partial performance.

---

12. Similarly, in Maori narrative tradition, the temporal structure of cosmogonic narrative is reproduced on a narrower scale as the local history of particular groups (Sahlins 1981a:14).

13. See also Vernant's analysis of temporality and structure in Hesiod's myth of the races (1983).

Whole and parts, moreover, are constituted by the contrast, and this is essential. Each time that Mambai loftily dismiss a narrative performance as a partial tip, they recreate the possibility of the deferred whole. Conversely, it is the stated absence of the whole, rather than any intrinsic properties of performances themselves that marks them as incomplete. Constituted as partial substitutes for an inclusive whole, narrative performances create a lack or deficiency; they demand to be supplemented with the missing remainder of the story. Hence the partial, open, unfinished character attributed to narrative performances and the idea of the whole narrative mutually condition each other. Or, in slightly different terms, the incompleteness of discourse is a price paid for preserving a promise of plenitude. The full knowledge to which the Mambai seem so attached intervenes in their life in the form of an absent presence, as a meaningful absence that depends on a dialectical relationship between partial performances and a deferred remainder.

All of this is more than a lofty metaphysics of narrative discourse. The tense, dynamic interactions of parts and whole are fundamental to the politics of narrative discourse in Mambai society. For if, on one hand, Mambai criticize among speakers of the past those whose discourse "has no trunk," they also recognize those who possess the trunk, but choose to withhold it. For persons in this latter category, the idea of a deferred, unsaid remainder is an instrument for the construction of hierarchical status.

The Social Distribution of Sacred Knowledge

Full knowledge of the past has a collectively recognized locus in Mambai society. It is said to reside in the ritual centers of communities, having been passed down over generations from the ancestors to their descendants. These ancestors, we may recall, are represented as the original founders of the community, who gave away the power of rule to others. Their descendants, left by this act "with only rock and tree," are regarded as the preservers, or better, conservers of the past. For in both their own self-images and in the perceptions of others, they do precisely that — they keep their knowledge to themselves. The destiny of trunk-knowledge is to be accumulated and hoarded as treasure, locked away from view and safely kept, as the Mambai like to say, "inside the stomachs of those who know."

Previously, I called attention to the temporally structured emptiness of ritual centers, which evokes a prior fullness and signifies the hierarchical status of a generous donor. But the centers are represented as full and closed in this one respect, as the repositories of sacred knowledge handed down from the deities to the ancestors, and from the ancestors to their decendants.

The Mambai identify sacred "words inside the stomach" as "trunk words" and contrast them to "tip words" that "go out from the mouth." This opposition between internalized, unspoken trunk words and externalized, spoken tip words distinguishes a hidden fullness of knowledge from the artful, oblique, and partial enunciations that both conceal and reveal it. The distinction plays a critical role in ritual communication. A detailed account of ritual communication requires a lengthy study (see Traube 1986). Here I merely note certain of its distinctive features and examine their social consequences.

What I find most striking about Mambai discourse in ritual contexts is its relatively non-narrative character. There are no full and coherent performances of origin myths on public, ritual occasions, and this applies especially to the creation story, the trunk walk of the earth. Ritual speech and actions are suffused with cosmic imagery and cumulatively represent the renewal of the cosmos as the fundamental concern of all performances. Yet no performer openly narrates a full account of the origins of the cosmos. Cosmogonic narrative in ritual contexts is not manifested as a textual essence, but in an activity of speaking and keeping silent, in what the Mambai view as partial performances, and pair with an unsaid trunk which *could* be disclosed by those with words inside the stomach. The narrative intervenes, in short, as an absent presence, in the form of an essential remainder from which everything in the rites is held somehow to derive. The burden of ritual performances is both to unleash a hermeneutic code and to defer resolution of its enigmas.

Ritual is apprehended by all participants as an experience charged with hermeneutic potential, to which individuals bring unequal interpretive abilities. Skilled interpreters, such as the two men with whom I became closely associated, can incorporate every detail of a performance, words, acts, objects, into a coherent narrative account of creation. The degree of coherence achieved by my two associates was impressive, and was no doubt partly a product of my inquiries. But the narrative style of interpretation that they selected reflects a deep-seated cultural disposition. To interpret, for them, was to "disclose the trunk" of the rites, by linking poetic speech and dramatic acts to an underlying story of world origins. Dense, interwoven metaphors; spare, truncated sequences of events; the withdrawals into silence that occur at key moments in ritual speech (as when the recitation of a series of place names leads to the mountain of origins) — all were interpreted by my instructors as indirect references to the creation of the cosmos by Father Heaven and Mother Earth.

But my point is not simply that rituals are seen as obscure, opaque texts that require interpretation. It is rather that the Mambai speak of rites as deliberately enigmatic forms, designed to exclude people from their full meaning. Interpretive competence presupposes sacred knowledge which, by convention, is differentially distributed within the community, and the enigmatic character of ritual performance is said to preserve the social division of knowledge. Only the ritual leaders, secure in their trunk knowledge, are formally expected to understand the full meaning of the rites. The "many men and many women" of the community who lack "words inside the stomach" are said to "grasp only the tip" of ritual events.

In these representations a hierarchical distinction between full and partial knowledge creates and maintains a boundary between insiders and outsiders. The distinction is both a condition and a consequence of ritual action, formally presupposed by participants and internalized anew over the course of a performance. For if the moral authority of ritual leaders rests on their claims to possess an encompassing form of knowledge, ritual action is the essential means of legitimizing such claims.

A central tenet of the diarchic ideology is that ritual authority works by attraction or influence, and not by coercive power. Jural sanctions to compel obedience are mythically represented as what the ancestors renounced; ritual leaders do not lay claim to sanctions of a mystical sort. Little emphasis is placed on an idea of mystical harm that might befall individuals who fail to attend a communal ceremony. The ideal is rather that the community will voluntarily comply with ritual summonses "out of respect for rock and tree."

In theory, if people come to the cult centers, it is because they recognize the authority of the guardians, which is visibly embodied in the fixed and silent rocks and trees. In practice, ritual leaders bring social pressures to bear during the preparations for a ceremony. They publicly invoke their unswerving dedication to the well-being of the community and of the cosmos, oratorically representing themselves as the steadfast preservers of tradition, embodiments of the unity of the group, who alone understand the true purpose of communal action. They use their authoritative knowledge to assert their hold over their immediate subordinates, who are in turn obliged to gather together the members of their own houses. If people submit and respond in great number, large attendance is itself an index of influence and legitimizes claims to status.[14] But status is not simply indicated by the volume of participation. It is also the product of an intersubjective relationship between leaders and followers that is created in and through the rites themselves.

If rock and tree are the visible marks of ritual status, the source of that status is the sacred knowledge that ritual leaders claim to possess.

---

14. See Errington 1983, which deals at length with the leader-follower relationship in southeast Asian polities, and specifically, with the importance of collective rituals as both "tests and demonstrations" of status.

The paradox that must be resolved anew in each performance is generated by the tension between public recognition of the claim and withdrawal of the knowledge. Ritual performance must serve a double function of concealing and revealing; it must mask the content of sacred knowledge, while simultaneously disclosing the fact of its possession. Structurally, hidden knowledge is analogous to hidden passion in the obsessive discourse of a lover. In both cases, as Barthes remarks of the lover's paradoxical situation, "the hiding must be seen" (1982:42).

In the formal logic of hierarchy the moral authority of one who knows is defined by the ignorance of others. But the practice of hierarchy entails mutual recognition of the asymmetric distribution of knowledge. The hiding must indeed be seen, and this is achieved in and through a ritual process. The pairing of opaque, enigmatic ritual expressions of knowledge with images of an unsaid narrative trunk instantiates the distinction between partial and full knowledge on which the authority of ritual leaders is founded. By simultaneously excluding outsiders from a hidden narrative, while marking insiders as its possessors, Mambai rituals reproduce the hierarchical relations they presuppose.

Mambai ritual leaders, I suspect, would feel an affinity with Mark's Jesus, who speaks in parables to exclude outsiders from his message. In Kermode's interpretation of Mark (1979:23–47), Jesus's narratives are deliberately obscure, "so that they may indeed see but not perceive, and may indeed hear but not understand," which could be rendered in Mambai as "so that they may see only the leaf, and may grasp only the tip." While the underlying principle of construction in both cases is parallelism, the two propositions have subtly different semantic values. The Greek distinction, which is preserved in English, is between seeing and perceiving. This cannot be exactly conveyed in Mambai, where the sensory relation to experience expresses the conceptual; the analogous distinction would be between seeing-perceiving a part as opposed to a whole. These related but nonidentical senses imply an important difference in referential extensions.

In the case of Mark's Jesus, reference is to a situation in which those excluded from knowledge fail to recognize the authority of the enigmatic speaker. Thus a community of knowing insiders defines itself in opposition to ignorant and indifferent outsiders, whereas Mambai enigmatic discourse aims at different social consequences. The rites must not appear trivial or senseless, as do Jesus's parables to those whom they exclude. Confusion, but not indifference, is the aim in Mambai ritual, for the social efficacy of enigmatic discourse depends on involving participants in a hermeneutic code to the point where they perceive that there *is* a hidden meaning which, although obscure to them, is nevertheless clear to others. Here outsiders are not turned away by the apparent meaninglessness of a discourse. Instead, they are drawn into a hierarchical relationship by a discourse that gives the impression of a meaningful absence.

There is an additional and, to me, significant difference between the two uses of enigma. Whereas Jesus uses obscure narratives to veil a message, Mambai think of that which speaks darkly as the relatively non-narrative ritual discourse that conceals and reveals narrative truths. Defined as the goal of interpretive activity, the trunk story of creation is clear and lucid, transparent upon the events it narrates. In itself, the story has no secrets. It is rather *kept* secret and converted into the unique base of knowledge that only a few possess.

This brings me to the last question that I want to pose, although my answer will be intentionally imprecise. The question is: In what sense does anyone know the trunk story that supports full knowledge? We have seen that the Mambai have ideal standards for measuring narrative competence and also conventions for attributing differential competence to hierarchically ranked categories of persons. But what do these ideals and conventions tell us about the nature and distribution of sacred knowledge of the past?

It is difficult for me to say whether or not Mambai ever realize among themselves the ideal of a full narrative account of ultimate origins. Those few who claimed to possess trunk words represented them to me as a gift received from a prior owner, usually a close relative, who was often said to have handed them over immediately prior to his or her death. By these accounts the transmission of trunk words is the culminating event in an individual life history, and I heard many tales of fathers who would accuse their sons of seeking to kill them by extracting their words-inside-the-stomach.

I do not know how closely accounts of full transmission correspond to actual narrative transactions. But I suspect that images of such scenes are projected onto a more diffuse, protracted process of seeking knowledge and used to narrativize personal histories. The same persons who represented their trunk knowledge as a gift received all in one sitting also told me of long evenings spent listening from the sidelines to the talk of their elders and of years of puzzling over the fragmented, enigmatic speech that they overheard.

This suggests to me that individual tellings of the creation myth are not best understood in terms of a text and its variants, as in narratological models of the twice-told tale. For if, as I suspect, individuals do not necessarily receive their cosmogonic knowledge in the objectified form of a full and coherent story, one cannot treat their textual products as modified retellings or patterned permutations of a prior text. Perhaps more to the point, even leaving aside the empirical obstacles to elicitation, the kind of insight that would be produced by comparing different variants of the creation myth to determine an underlying structure would not come to grips with the cultural significance of a narrative that is valued more in its absence than its presence and that plays the role of a signified rather than a signifier.

The story of world creation is the elusive product of ongoing interpretive activities, activities engaged in to different degrees by individuals as they attempt to make sense out of their own cultural representations and practices. That the product of such activities can be objectified in narrative form is not surprising. There is, as I have argued at some length, a pronounced cultural emphasis on narrative structuring, and other realms of social existence are not placed under the same restrictions that apply to cosmogony. Story-telling permeates Mambai life, and the basic plot structure of totality and division is an internalized master pattern. The temporality of structure is an essential premise of Mambai social thought, and processual schemes of oppositions and correspondences are available for interpreting the cosmos.

My point, then, is not that Mambai cannot tell the full story of the cosmos. I know from experience that some people can, and that they can tell it, moreover, with tremendous force and conviction. I am arguing that they *do* so only in strictly circumscribed situations, and that *what* they are doing is not so much retelling a prior text, as objectifying implicit knowledge in the culturally valued form of a full and coherent narrative sequence. Such narration is an interpretive act by which individuals at once give meaning to their own socially lived experience and construct their own identities in relation to their audiences.

There still remains the question of the social distribution of sacred knowledge. I am skeptical as to how closely the actual situation reflects the conventionalized attribution of full and partial knowledge to ritual leaders and followers respectively.

On one hand, my impression (and it is precisely that, a subjective, largely intuitive view, shaped by the particular conditions of my interactions with the Mambai) is that many ritual specialists are in fact indifferent tellers of the past, victims, in a sense, of their own strict criteria for well-formedness. With me, such persons regularly fell far short of the culturally valued narrative coherence and closure. Our meetings would open in an atmosphere of harmony, with agreement that our mutual concern was "to make contact with the trunk." But as the communicative event unfolded, the tellers seemed to grow increasingly vague and uncertain. They spoke in ever more halting tones, pausing often to look at me unhappily, perhaps warily. They would pursue some one narrative walk only to abandon it unfinished, and either move on to some other walk, or else fall silent. Perhaps their uneasiness derived solely from my presence, but other people of the ritual centers who attended such events did not seem to think so. In the aftermath of the telling, these onlookers would heatedly criticize the teller, protesting that they themselves had always doubted that person's claim to knowledge.

On the other hand, there may well be classificatory outsiders whose potential to tell the past is greater than they let on, but I had no access to their knowledge. I could never elicit more than the stereotyped response, "It is the old ones who know," which is premised on the assumption that sacred knowledge has designated owners and that a seeker must look for it in the proper places. But even in such places, inside the ritual centers, most people turned my questions aside by a similar strategy of deferral. Although ritual centers present a unified face to the outside world, they are divided when viewed from within by their members, and the hierarchical distinction between full and partial knowledge reappears inside the center itself. There, those who claimed to know only the tip drew on an idiom of tying or binding to reaffirm the wholeness of knowledge. Their own words, they would say, were "tied together with the words" of some other person, and they would advise me to seek out this other whose full knowledge encompassed that of the self.

To me, the major challenge for an analysis of Mambai origin narratives is not to determine precisely who knows what about what. It is rather to understand how the *idea* of a whole story that *someone* knows operates as a force in Mambai social life. My attention throughout has been focused on the imagination of a past out of which everything in the present derives. Most Mambai, I would argue, are less concerned with the precise content of the past than with preserving the certainty that someone knows it. They do not necessarily strive to order parts into a whole, and so to understand how everything hangs together, but rather content themselves with a faith that things do indeed cohere, and that the source of this coherence lies in the past. The ideal fullness of the imagined past intervenes most forcefully in Mambai life in the form of an absent presence, as an essential, untold remainder, in the meaningfulness of an absence.

There was only one person of whom I can say with certainty that the desire for full knowledge became a ruling concern, and that was myself. For I became caught up in the hermeneutic code of parts and whole. As I let myself be guided by Mambai instructions to "search for the trunk," my fieldwork gradually assumed the form of a quest for a full narrative. That quest necessarily led me to the ritual centers, and there I remained for much of my stay among the Mambai. That I did so may well have facilitated their appropriation of my presence into the story of the past. In my movements, Mambai seem to have read a return to the origin place of one who, knowing only the tip of the story, had recognized them as the keepers of the trunk.

Conclusions

Complementary dualism has long been regarded as a hallmark of eastern Indonesian societies and is sometimes invoked, in almost totemic fashion, to differentiate them from the hierarchical societies of western Indonesia and mainland Southeast Asia. While there is something to this contrast between a dualistic east and a hierarchical west, it should not be overdrawn. If dualism and hierarchy are logically distinct principles, the one based on opposition, the other on inclusion, then in eastern Indonesia the two have become inextricably intertwined.

It is a well-known and doubtless universal feature of binary logics that they unite what they divide, and divide what they unite. But the complementary principle of unity in division is not sufficient for hierarchy. Logically, a divided whole can be conceptualized as a union between two equal parts, which is more or less the point that Lévi-Strauss made in his classic, if ethnographically muddled and theoretically perplexing paper on dual organization (1956). The classificatory system that I have been examining is based on the idea of unity in division, but it is also a system that ranks what it opposes, and opposes what it ranks. Putting unity and rank together, as the Mambai do, we may say that theirs is a system wherein the idea of unity provides the principle for ranking complementary opposites. Categorical asymmetry rests on the capacity of certain terms to both include and oppose their complements, a phenomenon analogous to markedness in language. But in eastern Indonesian cultural systems, the coexistence of inclusion with opposition requires a manipulation of time.

Thus we have seen that the Mambai project an idea of inclusive unity onto the past and project that past onto the present in the form of a hierarchical relationship between encompassing whole and encompassed part. So long as their binary schemes are represented as synchronic systems of oppositions and correspondences, the logic of hierarchy remains obscure. Consistency, I have argued, is not to be found at the level of synchronic schemes of intersignifying oppositions, but rather in the unfolding relations between wholes and parts that are objectified in narrative models. Structural analysis has excelled at abstracting paradigms from narrative sequences, and some would identify these paradigms as the "mythical structures." But for those who actually operate the classificatory systems, analysis works the other way round to reinscribe paradigms into narrative sequences. As I hope I have established, there is much to be gained from adopting the indigenous perspective.

In conclusion, a few remarks with a comparative focus. If hierarchy is inseparable from dualism in eastern Indonesia, it is also true that the cultural emphasis on complementarity is pronounced. Consider the indigenous diarchies, where a "spiritually" superior leader is "temporally" inferior, whereas his "temporally" superior counterpart is "spiritually" inferior. At first sight, it would appear that context here is all-important. But on closer scrutiny there appears to be a tendency toward the absolute ranking of complementary functions. What varies is the precise configuration, and its temporal patterning. Thus on Roti, for example, it is an active, conquering, masculine outsider who mythically passes to the center of political space and personifies the unity of the domain. Dutch influence played a role in the hierarchical development of the executive function on Roti (Fox 1980), yet one need only look toward Polynesia to see that Rotinese rulers exploited potentialities inherent in diarchic structures.

By contrast, on Timor, at least among the Mambai, the Atoni, and the central Tetum, passive ritual figures stand for the wholeness of their realms. Although radically dissimilar on the surface to the sacral rulers of the classical Southeast Asian polities, the Timorese figures are the structural analogues of their grander neighbors. The impression of dissimilarity comes in part, I think, from differing inflections of the symbolic categories that relate sacred centers to peripheries. Rulers in the classical politics were the accumulators of power. Surrounded by a supposedly inexhaustible wealth of regalia, they could, in theory, give without being depleted, thereby demonstrating and expanding the extent of their realms. Such rules sought to embody an ideal fullness of power, power as presence, condensed at the center.[15] Sacral rulers on Timor are preeminently the distributors of power, who renounce all claim to the regalia of office and convert themselves into images of power's absence. Hovering over their empty cult centers, with only their rocks and trees, they embody the past as it lives on in the present, that is, in obligations to the source.

Formerly, the status of sacral centers on Timor was expressed in the annual presentation of harvest tribute by the realms. With the abolition of the tribute systems by colonial administrators, the exchange relations binding peripheries to their centers were weakened, although not dissolved. Cult life goes on, but not, according to the participants, with the same intensity or regularity that it once had. It may well be that the almost obsessive concern that Mambai ritual leaders show for the hoarding of sacred knowledge is connected to historically conditioned apprehensions of disunity and weakness at the center. That, however, is another essay.

---

15. On the classical insular and mainland polities see Anderson 1972, Tambiah 1976, Siegel 1979, Geertz 1980, and Errington 1983.

ACKNOWLEDGMENTS

The research on which this paper is based was conducted in East (formerly Portuguese) Timor between October 1972 and November 1974. It was funded by the National Science Foundation and the National Institute of Mental Health. I wish to express my appreciation to both.

An earlier draft of this essay was presented to the University of Chicago Anthropology Department and at the Conference on Dual Organization at the Hebrew University in Jerusalem. Comments and discussion in both these contexts were of immeasurable help in revising the essay. Most particularly, I want to thank David Maybury-Lewis and Uri Almagor, the co-organizers of the Dual Organization Conference.

For their comments, criticisms, and encouragement, I am especially thankful to James J. Fox, Gail Kligman, Marshall Sahlins, Michael Silverstein, Terence Turner, and Valerio Valeri. Finally, I am grateful to the University of Chicago students who participated in my seminars on the study of myth, narrative theory, and eastern Indonesian diarchies.

REFERENCES

Anderson, Benedict R. O'G. 1972. The idea of power in Javanese culture. In *Culture and politics in Indonesia*, ed. Claire Holt, 1–69. Ithaca: Cornell University Press.

Barthes, Roland. 1982. *A lover's discourse*. New York: Hill and Wang.

Chatman, Seymour. 1978. *Story and discourse*. Ithaca: Cornell University Press.

Dumont, Louis. 1970. *Homo hierarchicus*. Trans. Mark Sainsbury. Chicago: University of Chicago Press.

Errington, Shelly. 1983. The Place of Regalia in Luwu. In *Centers, Symbols, and Hierarchies: Essays on the classical states of Southeast Asia,* ed. Lorraine Gesick, 194–241. New Haven: Yale University Press.

Fox, James J. 1980. Obligation and alliance: State structure and moiety organization in Thie, Roti. In *The flow of life: Essays on eastern Indonesia*, ed. James J. Fox. Cambridge: Harvard University Press.

Francillon, Gérard. 1980. Incursions upon Wehali: A modern history of an ancient empire. In *The flow of life: Essays on eastern Indonesia*, ed. James J. Fox. Cambridge: Harvard University Press.

Geertz, Clifford. 1980. *Negara*. Princeton: Princeton University Press.

Kermode, Frank. 1968. *The sense of an ending*. New York: Oxford University Press.

———. 1979. *The genesis of secrecy*. Cambridge: Harvard University Press.

Lévi-Strauss, Claude. 1956. Les organisations dualistes, existent-elles? *Bijdragen tot de Taal-, Land- en Volkenkunde* 112:99–128.

Sahlins, Marshall. 1981a. *Historical metaphors and mythical realities*. Ann Arbor: University of Michigan Press.

————. 1981b. The stranger king. *Journal of Pacific History* 10 (3): 107–32.

————. (1985.) *Islands of history.* Chicago: University of Chicago Press.

Schulte Nordholt, H. G. 1971. The political system of the Atoni of Timor. *Verandelingen van het Koninklijk Instituut voor Taal-, Land- en Volkenkunde*, no. 60. The Hague: Martinus Nijhoff.

Siegel, James. 1979. *Shadow and sound.* Chicago: University of Chicago Press.

Silverstein, Michael. 1984. Unspeakable acts, undoable words. Typescript.

Tambiah, S. J. 1976. *World conqueror and world renouncer.* Cambridge: Cambridge University Press.

Traube, Elizabeth G. 1986. *Cosmology and social life: Ritual exchange among the Mambai of East Timor.* Chicago: University of Chicago Press.

Valeri, Valerio. 1982. The transformation of a transformation: A structural essay on an aspect of Hawaiian history. *Social Analysis* 10:3–41.

Vernant, Jean-Pierre. 1983. *Myth and thought among the Greeks.* Boston: Routledge and Kegan Paul.

Wouden, F. A. E. van. [1935] 1968. *Types of social structure in eastern Indonesia.* Trans. Rodney Needham. Koninklijk Instituut voor Taal-, Land- en Volkenkunde Translation Series, vol. 2. The Hague: Martinus Nijhoff.

Epilogue

Dual Organizations and Sociological Theory

Shmuel N. Eisenstadt

I was honored to be invited by David Maybury-Lewis and Uri Almagor to write an epilogue to this volume and express my views on the issues raised by the very rich harvest of materials on dual organization contained in it. Rather than summarizing the essays or referring to particular points in one essay or another, I shall pursue a macrosociological point of view and address myself to the more general points, as I understand them, which this volume as a whole brings to the fore.

The questions posed by the many varied aspects of dual organization, presented by anthropologists working in different parts of the world and pursuing their own theoretical perspectives are, first, how to make sense of such diversity and, second, and perhaps more important, is it legitimate to bring such a great diversity of phenomena under one canopy?

To approach this problem, it might be worthwhile to look back to the origins of anthropologists' concern with dual organization. The origin, nature, and function of dual organization puzzled anthropologists for more than a century (see the Introduction to this volume), but it was only Lévi-Strauss who gave this concept a theoretical articulation, which constituted a central part of his structuralist research program in the 1950s. This program emerged, as is well known, in part as a reaction against the functional school of social anthropology developed by Radcliffe-Brown and the first generation of his and Malinowski's students in England and the United States. It included such scholars as E. E. Evans-Pritchard and, especially, M. Fortes, R. Firth, Max Gluckman, Fred Eggan, and others.

The main emphasis of this school, an emphasis shared by the structural-functional school in the United States, was on the "organizational" or "systemic" qualities of societies, on the functional interdependence of their parts. Each part, even of rituals, festivals, and their symbolic contents, was analyzed in terms of its "functional" contribution to the working of the group or social system.

Against this school, Lévi-Strauss's structuralism emphasized five points. The first was that there exists within any society or culture a more real "hidden structure" that permeates the overt social organization and patterns of behavior. Second, the rules that govern this structure are not concrete rules of organization and are not derived from organizational or institutional needs or problems but are encoded in the human mind. Third, these rules constitute the deeper ordering principles of the social and cultural realms. Fourth, the most important of these rules, according to Lévi-Strauss and his followers, are those of binary opposition, which are inherent in all of the mind's perceptions of the world. They are the rules of transformation that govern the resolution of the contradictions. Fifth, these principles constitute the models by which society is structured, but they are not necessarily identical with the conscious models in the minds of its participants or symbolized in various concrete situations.

Lévi-Strauss's analysis constituted a crucial illustration of such "deep structure"; the principles of dual organization were seen not simply as principles of concrete social organization but rather as deep, sometimes hidden, unconscious principles permeating and structuring concrete organizations. The controversy that developed around his work, and in particular around his thesis of dual organization, is fully documented in some of the essays in this volume, especially in that of Maybury-Lewis. The various essays highlight most of the central analytical problems that were at least touched upon in this controversy. Above all they indicate how some of these problems are related to central concerns of sociological and anthropological theory, and they point to many still unsolved problems closely connected with the question mentioned at the beginning of these remarks: is it legitimate to bring this great variety under one canopy? And can we identify some general characteristics of the societies in which dual organization develops as well as their variations?

Certain major themes seem to be stressed in most of the essays on the different aspects of dual organization. The first such theme is that of exchange—exchange of goods or women, and also what may be called ritual exchange and the different types of game behavior and of the rules of game behavior involved in such exchange. The second theme is the crucial importance of the control of such exchange by different social actors and the struggle to maintain that control. The third, closely related theme is that of trust: of the impossibility of having continuous social interaction without trust and of the fragility of such trust; hence it is necessary to assure trust through special social mechanisms, one of the most important of which is the construction and control of the boundaries of collectivities.

Fourth, and closely related to the last, is the construction of symbols of collective and personal identity.

The fifth theme is the symbolization of basic conceptions of the cosmic and social orders, and the articulation and presentation of this symbolization in the society's central rituals. Sixth is the close relationship between the construction of trust and of boundaries of collectivities and symbolization, as well as between these two and the control of exchange; hence hierarchy and equality are important in symbolization. The seventh major theme is that of duality as an organizing principle of the cognitive, semantic maps in the societies discussed here.

The emphasis on these themes in the essays in this volume, even if in different degrees in each essay, indicates that the various dimensions of dual organization touch upon some basic problems of sociological and anthropological theory.

These themes are closely related to some of the basic assumptions of the sociological (and to some degree also of the anthropological) tradition as it has crystalized in the work of the founding fathers of sociology (above all, Marx, Durkheim, and Weber) and has continued since then. This tradition rejected the assumption, implicit in utilitarian ethics and classical economics, that the mechanisms of social division of labor in general, and in particular the market, were sufficient to regulate the social order. This tradition never denied the importance of the market and other such mechanisms, but it stressed that the very organization of social division of labor, of social exchange in general, and of the market in particular generates several problems that make the working of any social division of labor problematic.

The founding fathers of sociology stressed three aspects of the social order that cannot be explained by an analysis of organizational mechanisms of social division of labor. These are, first, the construction of trust and solidarity, stressed above all by Durkheim and to some degree by Tönnies; second, the regulation of power and the overcoming of attendant feelings of exploitation, stressed above all by Marx and Weber; and third, the provision of meaning and legitimization to social activities, stressed by all of them, but especially by Weber.

They all emphasized that the social division of labor generates uncertainties with respect to solidarity or trust, regulation of power, and construction of meaning; because of this, no concrete social division of labor can be maintained without taking care of these uncertainties. They emphasized the great tension between the organization of division of labor on one hand, and the regulation of power and the construction of trust and meaning on the other hand; the emphasis on this tension has been one of the most important heritages of the classical period of sociology.

The sense of this tension was to some degree lost in many of these works during the earlier phases of the functional school in anthropology; the symbolic realm was often seen as reflecting the social division of labor and ritual events, as a mechanism of social integration.

Since the late 1950s, and especially in the 1960s, this emphasis on the tension between the organization of social division of labor, construction of trust, and provision of meaning has come back into sociological and anthropological controversies. The original discussion of dual organization was to no small degree part of this controversy.

One central aspect of such tension, closely related to the study of kinship, and hence to the analysis of dual organization, is of special interest and can be identified on close reading of the various essays in this volume. This is the tension between the conditions that generate the construction of trust and the conditions that assure the availability of resources for the formation of institutional complexes and for complex division of labor. The construction and extension of trust in relation to kinship is analyzed and further developed in Eisenstadt, Sofer, and Adar, "Kinship, social structure, and social change" (typescript, Jerusalem, 1983) and the following observation is based on that analysis.

The continuous maintenance of trust in society rests on the predictability of activities and of mutual obligations. Depending on other factors, such as the extent of coercion employed, trust is most easily maintained through criteria of ascription—in particular, primordial particularistic ascription. These criteria specify first membership in solidary communities, which assures certain unconditional relations among its members and clear criteria of mutual obligation among them.

Thus, almost by definition, the conditions that make for maintenance of trust are best assured, even if in a very fragile way, in a relatively limited range of "social" activities or interaction. Such a limited range, however, may not be enough to assure maintenance of such trust in wider societal settings. At the same time, the conditions that assure some basic continuity of trust are inimical to the development of the resources and activities needed for the construction of differentiated institutions in wider societal settings.

Indeed, the very conditions that generate resources for a more complex division of labor and power relations tend also to undermine the simple or "primitive" settings of potential trust which may prevail unless counteracted by other forces in the more restricted types of social relations. In the most general terms, these conditions necessarily generate the problem of how to organize resources in some stable long-range patterns beyond those embedded in relatively narrow units, ascriptive and primordial.

The ability to do this depends above all on effectively extending the range of symbolism of trust, extending the boundaries of collectivities beyond the narrow scope of primordial units and connecting the extended trust with the broader scope of activities and the resources thus generated.

The tensions among the exigencies of organization of social division of labor, regulation of power, and construction of trust and of meaning are reinforced by the fact that these dimensions of social order are each articulated by different social actors — different carriers or elites.

The first of the major elites are the political elites, who deal most directly with the regulation of power in society. Second are the articulators of cultural models, whose activities are oriented to the construction of meaning. Third are the articulators of solidarity of the major groups, who address themselves to the construction of trust. All these elites act in conjunction, but also in tension, with one another as well as with the representatives of different aspects of the social division of labor and the interests it generates, and the concrete connections among trust, regulation of power, provision of meaning, and division of labor is constructed by these elites.

Coalitions of elites control the allocation and exchange of basic resources in the society primarily by controlling access to the major institutional markets (economic, political, prestige, cultural, and information), by controlling the production and distribution of that information which is central in structuring the cognitive maps of the members of a society or sector thereof. Between the various elites there necessarily develop potential conflicts and tensions about the control of resources; such tensions constitute an inherent component of the social order.

These problems bear on the possibility of the breaking up, through generation, of resources and of power, of basic yet limited trust; of extending trust beyond the minimal range of small ascriptive settings; and of connecting it with differentiated activities. All these problems are evident already in the family and kinship settings and in the structuring of the different patterns of interaction and "coalitions" that develop within such settings.

In almost all family and kinship settings the initial "coalition," from the point of view of the individual's life cycle, is that between mother and child. This coalition is usually based on a high degree (although varying in different settings) of unconditional trust, in which other, more conditional elements are at most secondary. But the totality of this initial interaction is broken as patterns of interaction extend beyond it and as the growing child begins to separate from the mother.

This process entails, first of all, the growing autonomy of the instrumental and power dimensions of social interaction and construction of meaning. Second, it entails the growing diversification of such activities and their organization in different constellations of coalitions. Third, it entails the breaking down of the balance among trust, meaning, instrumental activities, and power and the attempt to recrystalize them into new patterns.

The processes of breaking up and reorganizing trust are often repeated several times within the family and in kinship settings as well as in the structuring of family relations with the broader institutional setting. In all such situations the problem of extending trust and of recombining it with complex instrumental or power relations and broader meanings becomes very sharply articulated, mostly through the activities of different influentials or elites and the tensions and conflicts among them. The tensions are "solved" or coped with, in different ways in each society or sector, through coalitions among the elites that control the flow of resources between different sectors of the society. The concrete ways in which such control is affected or structured vary greatly between societies.

Here we come back to the problem of dual organization. Earlier discussions indicate very clearly that the term signifies some mechanism of control. But the essays presented here indicate, much more clearly than earlier discussions, that the term *dual organization* refers to several different types of mechanisms.

The first meaning of the term is that of concrete social organization, especially in terms of moieties, parts of villages, of generational classes or age groups, and the like. In all such cases, dual organization designates a social division of labor combined with the exercise of power and the construction of trust (see the essays by Almagor, Maddock, and Spencer). This entails different modes of control — of exchange and of conflicts — and struggles about control.

Of special interest here is the fact that the mechanisms of control are related not only to the "material" power aspect of social order but also to symbolic control, to the control of the cognitive maps of the society, of the basic social ideology prevalent or predominant within it.

This brings us to the second major connotation of dual organization, the fact that in some societies, the principles of dual organization are basic to conceptions of man and the cosmos (see the essays by Hinnant, Traube, and Yengoyan) and of the relations between man and nature (see the essays by Seeger and Werbner) and between man and society (see Tuzin, Valeri, and Zuidema). Principles of dual organization may constitute the central symbols of the world view of these societies (see Fox and Hinnant).

Insofar as this is the case, the symbols are most fully portrayed in the rituals of these societies. Such rituals constitute a central mechanism of cognitive or symbolic control in these societies (see Almagor, Rubel and Rosman, and Spencer). They usually entail also the legitimization of control over the exchange of resources (Rosman and Rubel), over the construction of boundaries, of collectivities (Lamphear), and over the regulation of power in terms of a broader meaning (Maybury-Lewis). Hence in such rituals are played out the basic themes and ambiguities inherent in the social order and attempts to overcome such ambiguities are made. The two major axes of the search for meta-meanings are the cosmological axis and the social axis.

The cosmological axis focuses on several issues, including the definition of relations between the mundane and transmundane worlds, their respective attributes, the distinction between them, and the different modes of bridging the distinction between them or resolving the tension between them. To use a Weberian term, we may call this the soteriological problem of the relationship of the resolution of tension to the main dimensions of human existence. Another such issue is that of defining the relations between culture and nature and defining the place of human beings and their personality and identity in relation to all these problems.

The social axis focuses on the tensions inherent in the symbolic structuring of social relations and of human interaction. In the most general terms these are the tensions among the social division of labor, the regulation of power, and the construction of trust and meaning. These in turn give rise to tensions between hierarchy and equality; between pursuing instrumental and adaptive goals and maintaining some order and meaning; between competition, authority, and power, on one hand, and solidarity, community, and participation in social-cultural orders, on the other; between individual and community, conflict and harmony; between power and relatively just distribution of resources and positions; between trust and search for broader meaning and autonomy of the human personality and the restrictiveness of any culturally prescribed social organization.

The distinctive characteristic of the rituals analyzed in some of the essays presented here (see Almagor, Hinnant, Traube, and Tuzin) is that the presentation, or playing out, of these meta-meanings is to a very high degree structured by certain types of principles.

Here we come to the third major connotation of dual organization — closely related to the second yet analytically distinct — that dualistic conceptions may also, as in the case of some of the Eastern Indonesian and aboriginal societies (Yengoyan), constitute the basic semantic map of a society. The organizing principles of the semantic map may be conscious or unconscious, and they may also crystallize into the basic ideologies of a society. Here, of course, we must remember that dual organizing principles of the semantic ways of a society have been identified also in more complex civilizations as has been demonstrated in Granet's classical work on China.

The essays in this volume point out that the term dual organization denotes different mechanisms of social and cultural control that are closely linked to the construction of social order and to the tensions inherent in that construction, problems that are of great importance for sociological and anthropological analysis. They indicate also several additional facets that are of great interest from the point of view of such analysis.

First, they indicate that these aspects of dual organization do not always come together or are even very closely interwoven; indeed, it is only in rare cases that they do come together. Second, the various essays in this book show that the location of these connotations of dual organization — that is, whether moieties or generational groups constitute the basic units and which aspect of the cognitive map of society is structured by dual principles — varies greatly from society to society.

Third, in many societies it is possible to identify the existence of some "dual" principles; they need not be central to the society's social or symbolic organization or to the organization of their semantic maps. Fourth, these essays indicate that between these different connotations of dual organization there may develop in any given society quite significant tensions or contradictions.

Explaining the ways in which different connotations of dual organization come together and are concretely organized constitutes one of the major challenges of the analysis of such societies — and one of great importance for sociological analysis.

In the most general terms this variety can be explained by the fact — recognized in general sociological and anthropological works, if not in the literature on dual organization — that each dimension of dual organization is related to different aspects of the construction of social order. Each dimension is probably articulated by different carriers and in different social situations, which do not always come together and which may be in opposition to one another.

Here we come to one of the lacunae of the research in this field, one which calls for further systematic study, namely the identification of such different social carriers. Different leaders or elites can be seen as the carriers or articulators of the various dimensions of dual organization and of the mechanisms and situations of control through which they regulate the cognitive maps, the systematic expressions, and the exchange of resources in their societies. The analysis of the exchange and control of resources has indeed identified the actors in the game, but that is not the case with respect to other connotations of dual organization. To my mind, it is here that some of the major directions of future research lie; the great richness of the materials presented in this book indicates both the possibility and the importance of such analysis.

Such research may throw some light on the types of societies and of cultural systems within which these different aspects of dual organization tend to develop. It seems that full-fledged dual organization is found mainly, or perhaps only, in societies with relatively low levels of technology and of social and economic differentiation. Full-fledged dual social organization seems to develop where principles of hierarchy either are relatively weak or are embedded in existing primordial ascriptive (mainly kinship or territorial) units—in other words, in societies in which no distinct state formation develops.

In most of the societies analyzed in this book, the principles of hierarchy, although they certainly exist and often are very important, do not give rise to distinct states with positions, ranks, or ascriptive primordial groups.

Even among the Maya, where hierarchical distinctions are obviously important, state formation is coterminous with wide kinship-territorial groups and there is no distinct autonomous state. Moreover, here dual organization seems to me to exist implicitly in the social division of labor rather than as an explicit organizing principle.

It is not yet clear, however, what kinds of societies with relatively low levels of technology and structural differentiation and lacking an autonomous state develop principles of dual organization, as against principles of corporate lineality for instance. Here again, it may be important to take a closer look at the structure of power ("political") and cultural elites and the models of social and cosmic order they articulate.

Parallel, perhaps more positive, indications can be proposed with respect to the symbolic and semantic dimensions of dual organization. The crucial elements are, first, the prevalence of basic primordial—biological and territorial—components in the symbols of personal and collective identity, a strong correlation between personal and collective identity, and the conflation of past and "end time," of Uhrzeit and Endzeit. Second is the prevalence in these societies of a strong parallelism or homology in the perception of mundane and "other worldly" reality, with little emphasis on a chasm between the transcendental and the mundane order. Indeed, as other conceptions develop and become institutionalized, as in the Axial Age civilizations, the principles of dual organization become much weaker. They may still be of some importance, as in China, in the structuring of the society's semantic maps, but no longer as the major organizing principles of symbolic reality. Third is the tendency for the symbolic boundaries of the major collectivities and subcollectivities to be quite close to the symbols of personal identity as related to such collectivities.

As the principles of organization of symbols and the semantic maps of societies tend to become looser, the importance of dual organization within them seems to become weaker. But here again we face the question of the specific conditions under which these different types of symbolic conceptions and semantic codes develop. This question is very closely related to the more general problem of developing a much more differentiated approach to the study of so-called "preliterate" or "pagan" societies and their cosmologies.

It seems to me that it is in the framework of these two poles—the structural pole and the symbolic and semantic pole—that the various combinations of connotations of dual organization tend to develop. The systematic analysis of these conditions, of the mechanisms through which these combinations become institutionalized, is still very much before us. But the very fact that these problems have been formulated, their relation to the central concerns of sociological and anthropological theory made more explicit, and possible directions of further research indicated, attests to the innovativeness of the research presented in this book.

Contributors

URI ALMAGOR is associate professor of social anthropology at the Hebrew University of Jerusalem. He has conducted field research among the Dassanetch of Southwest Ethiopia and the Herero of Northwest Botswana, and published articles on pastoral societies, age systems, the symbolism of the life cycle, and the phenomenology of scents. He is the author of *Pastoral Partners* (1978) and coeditor of *Age, Generation and Time* (1978) and *Comparative Dynamics* (1985).

SHMUEL N. EISENSTADT is professor of sociology at the Hebrew University of Jerusalem, where he has been a faculty member since 1946. His publications include *From Generation to Generation* (1963); *Revolutions and the Transformation of Societies* (1978); and, as coeditor, *Patrons, Clients and Friends* (1984); *Patterns of Modernity, Volumes I and II* (1987); *The Early State in African Perspective: Culture, Power and Division of Labor* (1988); and *Knowledge and Society: Studies in the Sociological Culture, Past and Present* (1988).

JAMES J. FOX is professorial fellow in the Research School of Pacific Studies at the Australian National University. He has conducted research in Indonesia, particularly eastern Indonesia, since 1965. His publications include *Harvest of the Palm* (1977), *Indonesia: The Making of a Culture* (1980), *The Flow of Life* and, as editor, *To Speak in Pairs* (1988).

JOHN HINNANT is associate professor of anthropology and African studies at Michigan State University. He has done fieldwork among the Guji Oromo of southern Ethiopia and has published on research methodology in the study of ritual and aging. Since 1984, he has conducted research on food-related issues among the famine-affected Oromo of eastern Ethiopia. Among his publications are "The Guji: Gada as a ritual system" in *Age, Generation and Time* (1977), "Revery and Normal Divination" with Dan F. Baurer in *Explorations in African System of Thought* (1980), and "The Position of Women in Guji Oromo Society" in *Proceedings of the Eighth International Conference on Ethopian Studies* (1988).

JOHN LAMPHEAR is an associate professor of history at the University of Texas at Austin. He specializes in the history of East African pastoralists and is especially

355

interested in the methodology of oral history and military history. He is the author of *The Traditional History of the Jie of Uganda* (1976).

KENNETH MADDOCK is associate professor of anthropology at Macquarie University. His main field research has been with aborigines in the Northern Territory of Australia, among whom he concentrated on religion, law, and social organization. His publications include *The Australian Aborigines: A Portrait of Their Society* (1972; 2d ed., 1982); *Anthropology, Law and the Definition of Australian Aboriginal Rights to Land* (1980); and *Your Land Is Our Land: Aboriginal Land Rights* (1983). His most recent book is *War: Australia and Vietnam,* coedited with Barry Wright, a Vietnam veteran.

DAVID MAYBURY-LEWIS is professor of anthropology at Harvard University. He has done fieldwork in Central Brazil, to which he has been returning for twenty years. He is currently working on a comparative study of the Indian question in the Americas. His publications include *Akwe-Shavante Society* (1967); *The Indian Peoples of Paraguay* (1979) with James Howe; and, as editor, *Dialectical Societies: The Ge and Bororo of Central Brazil* (1979) and *The Prospects for Plural Societies* (1984).

ABRAHAM ROSMAN is professor of anthropology at Barnard College, Columbia University. He has done fieldwork with the Kanuri of Northern Nigeria, in Iran, Afghanistan, New Guinea, and, most recently, in New Ireland. He is the coauthor, with Paula G. Rubel, of *Feasting With Mine Enemy* (1971), *The Tapestry of Culture* (1985), and *Your Own Pigs You May Not Eat* (1978).

PAULA G. RUBEL is professor of anthropology at Barnard College and Columbia University. She has done fieldwork with the Kalmyk Mongols in the United States, in Iran, Afghanistan, New Guinea, and, most recently, New Ireland. She is author of *The Kalmyk Mongols: A Study in Continuity and Change* (1967) and coauthor, with Abraham Rosman, of *Feasting With Mine Enemy* (1971), *The Tapestry of Culture* (1985), and *Your Own Pigs You May Not Eat* (1978).

ANTHONY SEEGER has done research among the Suya Indians in central Brazil and has published on their social organization, cosmology, and music. Among his books on these subjects are *Nature and Society in Central Brazil* (1981) and *Why Suya Sing* (1987). He is curator of the Folkways Collection and director of Folkways Records at the Smithsonian Institution.

PAUL SPENCER is primarily interested in the analysis of age systems and the cultural construction of aging. Since his appointment at the School of Oriental and African Studies he has supplemented his earlier anthropological research among the Samburu of Kenya with more recent fieldwork among the Maasai. His publications include *Samburu: A Study of Gerontocracy in a Nomadic Tribe* (1965) and *Maasai of Matapato: A Study of Rituals of Rebellion* (1988).

ELIZABETH G. TRAUBE is associate professor and chair of anthropology at Wesleyan University. She has done field research in East (formerly Portuguese) Timor. She is the author of *Cosmology and Social Life* (1986), a study of ritual and exchange in Mambai society, and is currently working on the interpretation of American mass culture.

DONALD TUZIN is professor of anthropology at the University of California, San Diego. His research interests include social anthropology, psychological anthropology, symbolism, and Melanesia. His publications include *The Ilahita Arapesh: Dimensions of Unity* (1976); *The Voice of the Tambaran: Truth and Illusion in Ilahita Arapesh Religion* (1980); and, with Paula Brown, the edited volume *The Ethnology of Cannibalism* (1983).

VALERIO VALERI is professor of anthropology at the University of Chicago. Since 1971, he has made repeated field trips to Seram and has published on ritual, symbolism, exchange, and power in Indonesia and Oceania. His book *Kingship and Sacrifice: Ritual and Society in Ancient Hawaii* was published in 1985.

ARAM A. YENGOYAN is professor of anthropology at the University of Michigan and the University of California, Davis. He has been making field trips to the Pitjantjatjara since 1966 and has published on various aspects of Pitjantjatjara culture. His publications include *The Imagination of Reality: Essays in Southeast Asian Coherence Systems* edited with W. A. L. Becker (1979) and "Theory in Anthropology: On the Demise of the Concept of Culture" in *Comparative Studies in Sociology and History* (1986).

R. TOM ZUIDEMA is professor of anthropology at the University of Illinois, Urbana. The focus of his research is on Inca culture and society at the time of the Spanish conquest, with a general interest in Andean culture in the context of Amerindian cultures of South America. His publications include *The Ceque System of Cuzco: The Social Organization of the Capital of the Inca* (1964), *Meaning in Mazca Art: American Social Systems and Their Mutual Similarity* (1965), *The Lion in the City* (1985), and *La Civilisation Inca au Cuzco* (1986).

Index